PUEBLO
BONITO

PUEBLO BONITO

George H. Pepper

Preface by David E. Stuart

UNIVERSITY OF NEW MEXICO PRESS
ALBUQUERQUE

Library of Congress Cataloging-in-Publication Data

Pepper, George H. (George Hubbard), 1873–1924
    Pueblo Bonito / George H. Pepper; preface by David E. Stuart.
    p. cm.
Originally published: New York:
American Museum of Natural History, 1920.

ISBN 0–8263–1735–9 (cl). — ISBN 0–8263–1736–7 (pa)
1. Pueblo Bonito Site (N.M.)
2. Pueblo Indians—Antiquities.
3. Pueblo Indians—Material culture.
4. Excavations (Archaeology)—New Mexico—
    Chaco Canyon National Historical Park.
5. Chaco Canyon National Historical Park (N.M.)—Antiquities
    I. Title

E99.P9P413 1996
978.9'82—DC20 96–29440 CIP

PREFACE

David E. Stuart

Just 100 years ago, in June of 1896, George Pepper, a twenty-three-year-old student of F. W. Putnam, began excavation at Pueblo Bonito in the Canyon of the Chaco, as it was then called. Twenty-four years later, in 1920, he published this account of his excavations through the American Museum of Natural History which (through Putnam) had been the academic sponsor for the brothers Hyde who funded the initial excavation. Because of their patronage, this project was known as the "Hyde Exploring Expedition," successor to an earlier Hyde expedition organized by Richard Wetherill at Grand Gulch, Utah.

In the seventy-six years since the original publication of this report, it has become a comparatively scarce document. In recent years, most students of southwestern archaeology cite this work from secondary sources, and a number of archaeologists trained in the 1970s, 1980s, and 1990s have never seen an original copy. Therefore this volume's republication will be cause for celebration among southwestern archaeologists.

In order to prepare these comments, I too, have read an original copy in its entirety for the first time in my career. In several senses, this is an amazing document. In the first place it meticulously records the details of material culture at one of the first great pueblo ruins to be extensively excavated in the American Southwest. In the second place, it remains amazing for the sheer richness of the artifact assemblage and the high level of preservation in portions of Pueblo Bonito as excavated during the summer seasons of 1896 through 1900. The photographic plates of intact roof portions of rooms 112 (fig.137:331) and Kiva roof details (fig 147:343) are eye-popping when compared to the archaeology that most of us see a century later. Finally, it is surprising for the kinds of anthropological questions it does *not* raise. Let me expand on these themes.

In 1896, only the sketchiest of details about the sequence of events in southwestern archaeology had been pieced together. When George Pepper and his labor crews, overseen by the Wetherills, began their excavation in the summer of 1896, it was still to be another thirty-one years before A. V. Kidder convened the first Pecos conference with the explicit task of organizing and summarizing what was then known about southwestern archaeology. In that sense, Pepper and colleagues such as N. C. Nelson (whose additions to this volume are valuable) were operating in an intellectual environment that was pregnant with information but largely barren of questions. Basic pottery sequences in the Southwest had not been worked out, and most of the formal types of pottery styles that contemporary archaeologists work with every day had not yet been named.

Moreover, Chacoan Society as a regional system had not yet even been conceptualized. The focus in this volume is clearly on Chaco Canyon itself and the dozen or so large ruins in it. Only secondary interest is expressed in some of the smaller ruins on the south side of the canyon. At the time of these excavations, no one had conceived of a "Chaco Phenomenon." In fact our contemporary, though evolving, conceptions of the Chaco Anasazi did not emerge until the 1970s. In 1896, roadways had not been identified. Certainly neither Pepper nor his crews imagined a system spread over 20,000–30,000 square miles—a regional complex comprising about 100 great outliers, as many as 10,000 small farmsteads, and a core not just focused on Chaco Canyon but interconnected by 400 or more miles of elaborately constructed roadways!

No, that is not what Pepper knew and saw. He and his crews were trying to get at the very heart of this ruin called Pueblo Bonito and retrieve its artifacts in order to create museum displays and determine the relative place of Pueblo Bonito in the larger context of what they then knew of archaeology in Mesoamerica and the greater Southwest. It was the possible relationships between Pueblo Bonito and the high cultures of ancient Mexico that most fascinated scholars at that time. The uncritical citations of Native American informants (pp. 25–26) seem unusual today because the ideas of a Montezuma (the Aztec Emperor) constructing Pueblo Bonito on his way South to Mexico, or of Chacoans hauling roofbeams in wheeled carts seem so patently impossible given current knowledge. For these reasons (and possibly due to influence from foreword author Clark Wissler) this monograph focuses primarily on a detailed description of artifacts (anticipating later trail-list methodology) and an organized presentation of recovered materials, room by room. Where artifactual analogs are sought in this text they are, often as not, being made with the Yucatecan Maya or the Río Panuco region in Vera Cruz. *Neither* an "Anasazi" nor a coherent "Southwestern Culture Area" had yet been born as working constructs.

In this sense it is reasonable to argue that we have come a very long way in southwestern archaeology in one century. We now ask questions based on a wealth of data from hundreds of excavated or tested archeological sites, and on lesser amounts of data from thousands of surveyed sites throughout the San Juan basin. In 1996, we have a much better conception of the overall nature of the Chaco Anasazi world and its workings than did Pepper and his colleagues. In contrast, however, most archaeologists of this generation will *never* excavate, or see excavated, a pueblo like Bonito—one both so well preserved and (most argue) so central to the workings of a well-integrated regional system.

It is necessary for contemporary students of archaeology to have access to this volume and read it with care. Pepper's *Pueblo Bonito* and Neil Judd's *Material Culture of Pueblo Bonito* (Judd 1954) are *the* best pair of books that archaeologists could have in their own libraries as primary records of details of construction and technique, possible levels of preservation in yet unexcavated sites, and photographs and drawings of a wider variety of artifacts than are usually seen either by the public or by professional archaeologists. One could do "ordinary" archaeological survey and test excavations for twenty seasons here in the Southwest under current constraints of time, money, and government/tribal regulations and never see half the variety of intact artifacts detailed here.

Having written, with Rory Gauthier, *Prehistoric New Mexico* some years ago (Stuart and Gauthier 1981), I probably ought to imply to my colleagues and current students that reviewing this manuscript to prepare a brief foreword was merely a pleasant exercise in recall. In fact, I learned from this volume. As I went through lists and kinds of artifact, I was even surprised. I was awed once again at the treasure trove of highly sophisticated artifacts—but also impressed by the presence of large quantities of "everyday" goods: buckskin, sandals, prayer sticks, unpainted pottery, pipes, bowls, points, arrows, cordage, baskets, ordinary manos/metates, and the like. Have we gone too far in emphasizing the public architecture of Bonito (Frazier 1986, Judge 1984, Judge et al. 1981), and played down its residential uses? Perhaps.

On the other hand this volume inevitably focuses on the many spectacular artifactual "specimens" removed for museum displays. That was the context of the times, and this expedition had as its explicit goal to produce exhibits on the Southwest for the American Museum of Natural History. While one might complain about the obsession with artifacts and a lesser focus on the fine points of excavation technique, it is fair to argue that in 1896, without both patrons and public interest in the display of these artifacts, funds for such an expedition/excavation would probably never have been obtained. One simply cannot get through this volume without being stunned at the collection of cylinder jars from room 28 (pp. 112–26); the remarkable collection of ceremonial sticks from room 32 (figures 53–64); the fourteen macaw skeletons found in room 38 (pp. 194–95); or the exquisite pottery and turquoise inlaid cylinder found in room 33 (figure 71:p.

169) along with many other artifacts and burials. The painted stone mortar in room 80 (figures 109 & 110: pp. 265–66), and the cache of round-bottomed pitchers in room 99 (figure 131:p. 312) are also impressive. In 1896 the obsession with artifacts *was* consuming. Pepper's own words illustrate this definitively: "Minor excavations were made in a number of rooms ranging from rooms 116 to 190. Nothing of special interest was developed in these excavations aside from the specimens shown in Figs 138 to 154 (Pepper 1920:339)." Thus dismissed are excavations in seventy-four rooms! Times, interest, and styles of research have changed dramatically.

Even though Pepper left us no meticulous record of excavation technique, no measurements of artifacts plotted in three-dimensional space, nor adequate notations of the kinds of soil and sand deposits in each room, this volume does focus on Bonito as the premier site in the region. That assumption has not changed in 100 years. This volume also set the stage for continued, more refined, Chacoan research in other ways. An enormous number of "high-status" artifacts were collected from about 100 rooms of the hundreds at Bonito. Pueblo Bonito, as a focus of elites, also remains a theme a century later (Vivian 1990; Cordell 1984; Lekson 1984). Nearly 70,000 items were shipped to the American Museum of Natural History—they remain the largest single, coherent, "provenienced" collection of Anasazi artifacts available for research.

Controversy (and envy?) surrounding the Hyde brothers' and the Wetherills' (McNitt 1957) "Indian trading" activities and the gratuitous dismantlement of portions of the site for their own uses (Lister and Lister 1981:48–61) led, in part, to a suspension of the Hyde excavations in 1900–1902 and passage of the Antiquities Act of 1906. These events preserved hundreds of other rooms for the far more careful excavations undertaken by Neil Judd (1920–27), which were sponsored by the National Geographic Society and published later (Judd 1954). By then tree-ring samples were being taken, and true stratigraphic control was the norm.

However, most of the kinds of laboratory techniques we now consider commonplace had not yet been developed during the time of either of these two great excavation campaigns (of 1896–1900 and 1920–27). There simply were no Carbon 14, no archaeomagnetic samples, no trace element analysis, no thermoluminescence, no obsidian-hydration dates done at the time of either excavation.

In short, as a scientific document the reissue of Pepper's field notes is not particularly important. What is important about this book is that it is the first and best primary record of Pueblo Bonito and a large assemblage of its retrieved artifacts at a formative stage in American archaeology. This is where excavations of such scale were first established as possible in the Southwest. Moreover, the distinctly cautious, scientific nature of American archaeology itself was forcefully shaped by both the promise and the subsequent controversy surrounding the Hyde excavations (Cordell and Stuart 1986). Both promise and controversy continue to be the grist of Southwestern archaeology today. We still grapple, albeit more knowledgeably, with the meaning of Pueblo Bonito and the role of Chaco Canyon in the Anasazi world (Stuart 1985; Crown and Judge 1991). So, partly because of Pueblo Bonito, we are still reluctant to excavate everything in sight, preserving portions of large ruins for future research techniques. American archaeology did learn indelible lessons from this project—lessons worth passing on to yet another generation.

University of New Mexico
May 1996

REFERENCES CITED

Cordell, Linda S.
1984 *Prehistory of the Southwest.* Academic Press, San Diego.
Cordell, Linda S. and David E. Stuart
1986 "Archeology and Anthropology, Part I: New Mexico In the Development of American Archeology." In *From Sundaggers to Space Exploration,* special issue of *New Mexico Journal of Science* 26 (1).
Crown, Patricia L. and W. James Judge (editors)
1991 *Chaco and Hohokam, Prehistoric Regional Systems in the American Southwest.* School of American Research Press, Santa Fe.
Frazier, Kendrick
1986 *People of Chaco: A Canyon and its Culture.* W. W. Norton & Co., New York.
Judd, Neil M.
1954 "The Material Culture of Pueblo Bonito." In *Smithsonian Institution Collections* 124, Washington, D.C.
Judge, W. James
1984 "New Light on Chaco Canyon." In *New Light on Chaco Canyon,* ed. David Grant Noble. School of American Research Press, Santa Fe.
Judge, W. James, W. B. Gillespie, Stephen H. Lekson and H. W. Toll
1981 "Tenth Century Developments in Chaco Canyon." *Archaeological Society of New Mexico Anthropological Papers* 6. Santa Fe.
Lekson, Stephen H.
1984 *Great Pueblo Architecture of Chaco Canyon, New Mexico.* University of New Mexico Press, Albuquerque.
Lister, Robert H. and Florence C. Lister
1981 *Chaco Canyon: Archaeology and Archaeologists.* University of New Mexico Press, Albuquerque.
Stuart, David E.
1985 "The Chaco-Anasazi Era." In *Glimpses of the Ancient Southwest,* Ancient City Press, Santa Fe.
Stuart, David E. and Rory P. Gauthier
1981 Prehistoric New Mexico. Reprinted 1996 by the University of New Mexico Press, Albuquerque.
Vivian, R. Gwinn
1990 *The Chacoan Prehistory of the San Juan Basin.* Academic Press, San Diego.

SUGGESTED READINGS

This volume does not really yield an overview of Pueblo Bonito or Chaco Canyon in the larger context of Anasazi archeology. Edgar Hewett first raised that complaint just before 1900! So, at the risk of omitting many worthy references, I am suggesting the readings below:

History of Chaco Research

1. Lister and Lister, *Earl Morris and Southwestern Archeology,* University of New Mexico Press, Albuquerque, 1968 (A slender but highly informative work on the early years).
2. Lister and Lister, *Chaco Canyon: Archaeology and Archaeologists,* University of New Mexico Press, Albuquerque, 1981 (*Definitive* for who did what and when pre-1981.)
3. Frazier, *People of Chaco: A Canyon and its Culture,* W. W. Norton & Co., New York, 1986 (A more recent and popular account by an outstanding science writer).

Material Culture and Architecture

1. This volume
2. Judd, *Material Culture of Pueblo Bonito, Smithsonian Institution Collections* 124, Washington, D.C., 1954 (The successor project to Pepper—a real classic).
3. Judd, *The Architecture of Pueblo Bonito, Smithsonian Miscellaneous Collections* 147, Washington, D.C., 1964 (Companion to above).
4. Lekson, *Great Pueblo Architecture of Chaco Canyon, New Mexico,* University of New Mexico Press, Albuquerque, 1984 (I consider this the definitive work on Bonito architectural technique, construction stages, and labor requirements. It is a superb and thoughtful book by a superb and thoughtful archaeologist.).

Overview of the Chaco Phenomenon and Anasazi Prehistory—in ascending order of geographic scope

1. Marshall, Stein, Loose, and Novotny, *Anasazi Communities of the San Juan Basin,* Public Service Company of New Mexico, Albuquerque, 1979 (This important, but scarce, volume reports the first regional surveys designed to discover and/or revisit the major Chacoan outliers. It laid the groundwork for widespread acceptance of a regional "Chaco Phenomenon.").

2. Vivian, *The Chacoan Prehistory of the San Juan Basin,* Academic Press, San Diego, 1990 (Magisterial!).
3. Stuart and Gauthier, *Prehistoric New Mexico,* University of New Mexico Press, Albuquerque, 1981 (A standard reference on New Mexico archaeology.).
4. Cordell, *Prehistory of the Southwest,* Academic Press, San Diego, 1984 (An excellent, advanced university text which engages both the data and competing Chaco theories.).

The Latest

1. Noble (ed.), *New Light on Chaco Canyon,* School of American Research Press, Santa Fe, 1984 (Many of these are papers of the National Park Service Chaco Center team, proof that your tax dollars are sometimes well spent!).
2. Crown and Judge (eds.), *Chaco & Hohokam: Prehistoric Regional Systems in the American Southwest,* School of American Research Press, Santa Fe, 1991 (An outstanding collection of papers.).
3. Morrow and Price (eds.), *Anasazi Architecture and American Design,* University of New Mexico Press, Albuquerque, in press (A series of intriguingly thoughtful and iconoclastic papers. See especially those by Stein and Marshall.).
4. Anything produced by the National Park Service Chaco Center.

THE CHACO ANASAZI ERA[1]

Whirlwind House . . . . Muddy Water . . . . Bee Burrow Ruin . . . . Coyote Sings Here. These names are more than poetry, they are part of the most remarkable array of archaeological ruins in all of North America. In prehistoric times, a great network of roadways radiated outward from Chaco Canyon National Monument. These once connected impressive sandstone citadels and large pueblo villages into a political and economic network worthy of the grandest feudal baron. Archaeologists refer to this as the "Chaco Phenomenon," and it has received lavish publicity. For all that, few people realize just how vibrant, how brief, and how fragile was the world created by Chaco Anasazi farming peoples a millennium ago.

The Chaco Anasazi once inhabited the northwestern quarter of New Mexico and adjacent areas of Arizona, Utah, and Colorado. Their territory included nearly 40,000 square miles, an area larger than Scotland. It has taken archaeologists fifty years of tedious survey on foot to locate more than ten thousand Anasazi ruins. These were created in the nine hundred years between A. D. 400 and 1300. But a stunning forty-three percent, or 5,000 of these ruins were built in only 150 years, between A. D. 950 and 1100! This powerful surge in village construction marks the heyday of the Chaco Anasazi. Everyone agrees that the roadworks were developed at some time during this period.

Most of the Anasazi ruins are small, scattered masonry-based pueblos of six to twenty rooms. Average ones have a floor area of from several hundred to several thousand square feet. These dot the basinlands and mesas of San Juan, McKinley, and Cibola counties. Areas of especially good soil and dependable water eventually drew more impressive concentrations of farmsteads. A number of these, like the settlement known as Kin Ya'a, grew into extensive farming centers, with dozens of free-standing pueblos, or roomblocks, scattered over a square mile or so.

Archaeologists have never been surprised to find large, distinctive masonry buildings erected at many of the farming enters. These "Great Houses," often multistoried, vary in size, but most are massive sandstone strongholds enclosing circular ceremonial chambers, or kivas. The number of kivas may be few or many, but two are commonly found enclosed in rectangular, monolithic cells of outsized rooms. These rooms are often without cooking hearths and artifacts. Some appear to have been purposely kept free of debris and clutter. Archaeologists disagree whether these were used as granaries, barracks, or the private apartments of local elites in Chacoan society.

Other "Great Houses" were built in unlikely places—smack in the middle of nowhere. The farming centers that should have grown to require public facilities just were not there. One example, the huge rectangular citadel or Pueblo Pintado lies on Chaco's isolated eastern frontier, about twenty miles from the major towns in Chaco Canyon. It once stood at least three stories tall, and sixty immense ground floor rooms enclosed seven kivas. Yet tree-ring dates suggest it was constructed rapidly in A. D. 1060 or 1061.

We now know that a prehistoric roadway connected Pueblo Pintado to the large towns in Chaco Canyon. From the ground, no roadway can be seen today, only a faint line of sagebrush runs into the distance. But airplanes have a better view.

Like the road to Pintado, most of the several hundred miles of suspected prehistoric roadways were first located on aerial photographs. "Remote sensing" specialists in Albuquerque began to identify possible roads a few years ago. They quickly learned that when photographed in midday sun, the roads were usually invisible, while aerial photographs taken in the oblique rays of early morning sunlight made the ancient linear roadways stand out.

Several years ago a team of government archaeologists decided to find out which of the "roads" identified on aerial photographs were real and just how old they were. This immense job continues, but initial results have been exciting. Segments of suspected roadway were surveyed on foot, test-trenched, and analyzed geologically. Some "roads" turned out to be fence rows. Others were recent. The team's geologist showed that the pressure of wagon and auto wheels on historic roadbeds compacted underlying mud into distinctive semi-circular soil plates. Though easily visible, no compression plates were found in trenches which crosscut roads connecting a number of ruined Anasazi towns. These were the real thing.

The Chaco roads were originally ten to thirty feet wide and had raised shoulders. Uniformity was important. Some sections were excavated, or graded, while others were built up. Their earthen surfaces were cleaned regularly and repaired when damaged by floods or erosion.

Today, in only a few places do the prehistoric roads still look like a road, so aerial photographs guided the archaeological survey crews. By following these, previously unknown ruins were found. Some were "Great Houses"; others were new and puzzling. Several dozen small, semi-circular stone walls were located on high vantage points along roads. Called "herraduras," or horseshoes, these often marked places where two roads diverged. They may have been windbreaks or stopping places.

Most Chacoan roads ran straight and did not curve with the terrain. Stone steps were cut into unavoidable cliff faces and detours often were marked by double grooves chiseled in bedrock. Some road segments were dual, like divided highways. In places these were also marked by stone grooves. To date, the great "North" and "South" roads from Chaco Canyon are best known. The former runs north fifty miles to Salmon Ruin near Bloomfield. The other runs south to the Chacoan towns between Grants and Gallup, passing through Kin Ya'a.

Archaeologists currently believe more than eighty Anasazi towns were connected to Chaco Canyon by roadways. One of the oldest farming districts was in the Red Mesa Valley between Grants and Gallup. Later, new towns were built and roadways were extended north to Colorado. In Chaco's final hour, sites like Aztec Ruin were built on the northern frontier. They generally date to the early A. D. 1100s.

It will take years to investigate the first road system in the United States and archaeologists may never master all the details necessary to completely explain the Chacoan period. We do not even know with certainty which languages were spoken nor how many tribal groups were involved in Chacoan development. But the basics of what actually happened are reasonably clear.

During the late A. D. 800s and early A. D. 900s population expanded rapidly. The number of villages and farmsteads increased dramatically. Economy shifted from mixed agriculture and upland hunting to increased dependence on the dry-farming of large-cobbed varieties of corn. Rainfall was not greater than today, but most came in late summer and was stable from year to year during much of the period. Efficient agricultural practices and extensive economic networks tapped the full potential of this climatologic consistency. There was a frenzy of building activity, art, politics, religion, and trade flourished.

The transition to the Chacoan period first took place in the lower, drier elevations of northwestern New Mexico. Early sites are characterized primarily by small roomblocks of above-ground masonry architecture, metates with more grinding surface, and the introduction of pottery types such as Red Mesa Black-on-white. The pre-Chaco style of pithouse village quickly faded from the scene.

During the Chacoan expansion there were several major shifts in settlement patterns. The first of these, about A. D. 900, involved a brief upstream move in village location. This relocation was dramatic in the Navajo Reservoir district and in the Chuska Valley north of Gallup. By about A. D.

950 this initial upstream/uphill movement terminated, and the essential settlement characteristic of the Chaco Anasazi emerged. At this time there was
a major downhill shift in village locations. Well-forested areas were abandoned, and there was increasing dispersal of small pueblos and farmsteads
throughout the western basins. This expansion eventually spilled out of the
San Juan Basin.

By about A. D. 1050, the dispersal of pueblo style farming villages was
near its maximum, reaching to the upper Pecos River valley. Continued settlement in forested, highland areas is notoriously hard to document during
the heyday of the Chaco Anasazi, yet many archaeologists have been slow to
accept this. In the Gallina highlands between Navajo Reservoir and Cuba
there was a general abandonment of upland villages between A. D. 950 and
1100. Population in the cool, forested Mesa Verde region was lowest during
the late Chacoan period, and the Zuni Mountains southwest of Grants were
largely vacated from roughly A. D. 1000 to A. D. 1200.

Economic patterns clearly illustrate the major shifts in settlement during
the Chacoan period. During the initial transition, trade in ceramic materials
and in exotic goods of many kinds increased dramatically over a wide geographic front. First, diverse ceramic styles developed rapidly in areas bor-
dering the upland perimeters of the San Juan Basin. This was followed by a
rapid extension of economic networks into the central basin. By A. D. 1000,
the middle of the Chacoan period, major adjustments in trading patterns had
begun to take place. The frequency of ceramics traded into Chaco Canyon
from the Red Mesa and Chuska Valleys changed over the course of time. By
A. D. 1100, late in the period, production centers for ceramics had again
changed, and economic activity focused on the Basin's northwestern margin
and the southern approaches to Mesa Verde.

Few people realize that only a moderate percentage of the ceramics used
at Chaco Canyon between A. D. 900 and 1150 were made there. Throughout,
imports came from production centers at the periphery of the San Juan
Basin. However, there was virtually no trade along the northeastern frontier,
a "no man's land" which separated Chaco country from the Gallinas highlands in the area of present day Highway 44.

The food economy of the Chaco Anasazi period strongly depended on
harvesting relatively large-cobbed corn and hunting very small animals.
This latter pattern is striking. Most meat consisted of cottontail, jackrabbit,
rodents, and small bird species. Domesticated turkey and wild vegetal foods
supplemented garden crops. While some large game animals were taken,
this use of small species is a hallmark of most Chacoan period diets.

There was substantial contact between the Chaco Anasazi of the San Juan Basin and villagers of the Quemado and Reserve districts to the south. Field research now in progress indicates that Chacoan roadways and villages may have penetrated as far south as Highway 60. The Gallup and Zuni areas seem to have been both important economic nodes and continuous sources of interchange from at least sometime in the A. D. 800s onward.

By about A. D. 1100, there had already been substantial Anasazi village expansion into the Galisteo Basin southeast of Santa Fe and eastward from the east slope of the Sangre de Cristos to the Las Vegas area. Here, there were no roadways and Chacoan influence was more tenuous. On the eastern periphery of the Anasazi homeland, villages were generally smaller, jewelry and trade goods fewer, and harvests more modest. Settled village life only lasted several centuries in the hinterlands east of the Pecos River valley and was never re-established there until recent times.

By A. D. 1100 an enormous, complex, and extremely fragile, regional Anasazi system was sustained as the Chacoan network assumed its final form. Although the economic and demographic network which underlay this development began to emerge at important agricultural localities as early as A. D. 900, many of the "Great Houses" and public facilities were constructed between A. D. 1080 and 1120, at the very end of the Chacoan era. Perhaps this terminal complexity was in part induced by an already overstressed agricultural system. Excavation at late Chacoan sites has yielded ample evidence that infant mortality was shockingly high, malnutrition common, and early death the norm.

The Chacoan boom ended rapidly. In many districts, the abandonment of basin farmsteads began about A. D. 1100. By A. D. 1150, settlement and daily economy had shifted over nearly all of northwestern New Mexico. Although a few large Chacoan towns may have lingered on, isolated and in a depressed state, for another generation or two, most of the San Juan Basin was vacant. Some groups resettled near long abandoned villages in surrounding uplands, while others pioneered in forested districts north of Santa Fe. The Chaco Anasazi pattern of dry-farming large-cobbed corn and storing surplus for trade also ended. By the early A. D. 1300s, after more difficult times, irrigation agriculture replaced dry farming among Puebloan successors to the Chaco Anasazi.

Archaeologists do not agree on the causes of Chacoan decline. Rainfall did become unstable in the early A. D. 1100s. Yet few societies fail because only one thing goes wrong. Perhaps one day we will know just which factors drove so vital a society to the twilight of the ambiguous, half-remembered legends passed down to today's Pueblo peoples. But for a time, roadways, granaries, and district trading villages wove nearly 40,000 square miles of scrubby basinlands into prehistoric North America's most remarkable economic and cultural force.

[1] Copyright © 1985 by David E. Stuart. Reprinted from David E. Stuart, *Glimpses of the Ancient Southwest,* by permission of Ancient City Press.

ILLUSTRATION SECTION

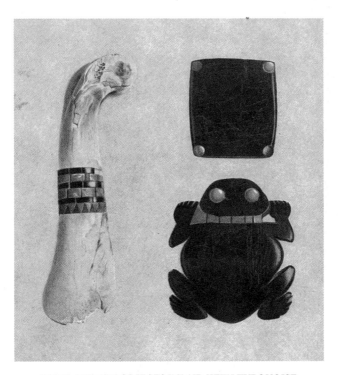

BONE AND JET OBJECTS INLAID WITH TURQUOISE

On a platform in Room 38 were found a number of objects among which were those shown in the accompanying plate. The bone scraper is of the usual shape but in this case is enriched by an inlay of turquoise and jet. The length of the scraper is 15.5 cm. The other objects are of jet, highly polished and inlaid with turquoise. For a detailed discussion of the objects found in Room 38 see pp. 184-195.
(H-5145, 10424, 10426).

A CYLINDRICAL JAR

A deposit of cylindrical vessels was uncovered in Room 28, a type of vessel not previously known in the area. The vessel shown here (H-3241) is 25.5 cm. high and 9.8 cm. in diameter.

A CYLINDRICAL JAR

Height, 23.2 cm.; diameter, 9.2 cm. (H-3236).

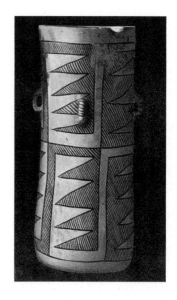

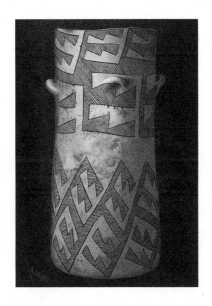

A CYLINDRICAL JAR

Height, 24 cm.; diameter, 9.9 (H-3262).

A CYLINDRICAL JAR (*Below left*)

Height, 18.5 cm.; diameter, 10 cm.
(H-3237).

A CYLINDRICAL JAR

Height, 25.3 cm.; diameter, 14.8 cm.
(H-3260).

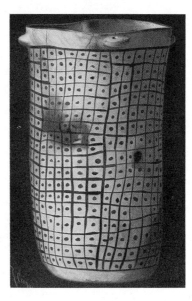

TWO PITCHERS FROM ROOM 28

Height of the larger 17.8 cm., diameter of the top
6.7 cm. (H-3277, H-3270).

A PAINTED BOARD

This board, found in Room 32, bears an elaborate design upon its
surfaces. The reverse side is shown in Fig. 65, p. 156. The face of
the board measures 16.5 cm. by 17.5 cm. and 1.7 cm. thick (H-4500).

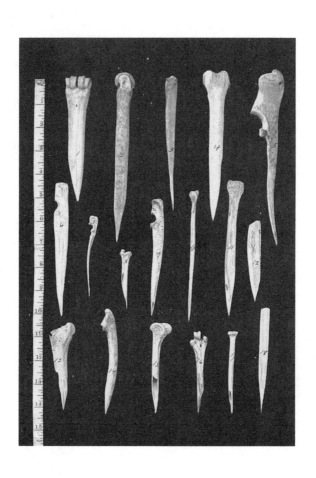

POINTED IMPLEMENTS OF ROUGH AND ORDINARY FINISH

Fig. 1 (H-10095). Awl or pointed implement made from distal end of metapodial of deer. From Room 162. Representative of ten specimens.

Fig. 2 (H-6146). Awl made from split half of distal end of metapodial of deer. From Room 67. Representative of thirty-nine specimens.

Fig. 3 (H-6143). Awl made from split quarter of proximal end of metapodial of deer. From Room 67. Representative of forty-two specimens.

Fig. 4 (12137). Awl made from hollow leg bone, possibly of the coyote. From Room 162. Representative of twenty-three specimens of the general type.

Fig. 5 (H-11756). Pointed implement improvised from the ulna or oleocranon bone of deer. Pueblo Penasco Blanco. Representative of ten specimens.

Fig. 6 (H-12136). Awl made from the ulna of a carnivor. From Room 162. Representative of four specimens, including Fig. 9.

Fig. 7 (H-11392). Pointed implement from ulna of small mammal. From débris outside the ruin. Representative of ten specimens.

Fig. 8 (H-2399). Finely pointed implement improvised from broken section of small mammal bone. Uncertain location. Representative of twenty specimens.

Fig. 9 (H-8632). Awl made from ulna of a carnivor. From Room 109.

Fig. 10 (H-8630). Pointed implement made from long slender fibula of an unidentified mammal. From Room 109. Representative of twelve specimens.

Fig. 11 (H-10686). Awl made from radius of coyote or fox. From Room 171.

Fig. 12 (H-2892). Awl improvised of splinter from mammal bone. From Room 26. Representative fo 135 more or less similar specimens.

Fig. 13 (H-10227). Awl improvised from fragment of large hollow bird bone, probably wild turkey. From Room 163.

Fig. 14 (H-9574). Awl made from curved and hollow wing bone. Uncertain location.

Fig. 15 (H-5984). Awl made from leg bone, probably wild turkey. From Room 64.

Fig. 16 (H-10103). Awl made from leg bone of a hawk. From Room 161.

Fig. 17 (H-11396). Awl made from slender hollow bird bone. From débris outside of ruin. Figs. 13–17 are representative of eighteen specimens.

Fig. 18 (H-10018). Awl made from split section of bird bone, delicately pointed. From Room 160. Representative of thirty-one specimens.

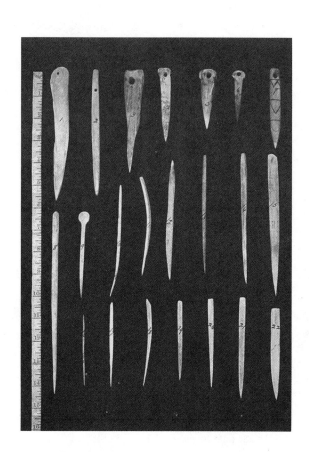

POINTED BONE IMPLEMENTS OF MORE OF LESS SPECIAL FORM AND FINISH

Fig. 1 (H-2720). Awl or bodkin of roughly split mammal bone, small perforation near butt. From Room 20.

Fig. 2 (H-8392). Bodkin of split mammal bone, original point missing. From Room 107.

Fig. 3 (H-8634). Bodkin made from split half of metapodial of deer, proximal end. Longitudinal perforation (not visible) through butt, above the visible transverse perforation. From Room 109.

Fig. 4 (H-8814). Bodkin made from split metapodial of some ungulate. From Room 60.

Fig. 5 (H-8237). Bodkin made from split half of metapodial of deer, distal end. From Room 105.

Fig. 6 (H-7383). Bodkin, rather small, made from split metapodial. From Room 86.

Fig. 7 (H-12835). Bodkin made from thick mammal bone, oval in cross-section, incised ornamentation. From Room 170.

Figs. 1–7 are representative of twelve speciments.

Fig. 8 (H-10799). Pointed implement of mammal bone; long, slender, roundish section. From Room 173. Representative of twenty-six specimens, including Figs. 13, 14, 19, and 20.

Fig. 9 (H-977). Pointed implement of pin of bone, slender, longitudinally curved, rectangular cross-section, expanded round butt. From Room 10. Representative of two specimens.

Fig. 10 (H-2547). Pointed bone implement, very slender, slightly curved point, round cross-section. From Room 12. Representative of two specimens, the other being Fig. 18.

Fig. 11 (H-5934). Pointed bone implement, slender, longitudinally curved, rectangular cross-section, squared butt. From Room 62. Representative of three specimens, including Fig. 17.

Fig. 12 (H-11244). Double-pointed bone implement, possibly an arrow foreshaft, though asymmetrical. Uncertain Chaco ruin. Representative of two specimens.

Fig. 13 (H-10011). Pointed bone implement, resembling a skewer; slender, nearly sym metrical, round cross-section. From Room 160.

Fig. 14 (H-6673). Pointed implement, of split mammal bone. From Room 78.

Fig. 15 (H-5641). Awl of split mammal bone, stout, well finished. From Room 54. Representative of fifty specimens, including Figs. 21 and 22.

Fig. 16 (H-10695). Double pointed bone implement, very slender and delicately pointed. From Room 171.

Fig. 17 (H-12834). Pointed implement of split bone, slender, longitudinally curved, rectangular cross-section. From Room 169.

Fig. 18 (H-10270). Pointed bone implement, slender, curved; possibly the point end of a longer specimen. From Room 163.

Fig. 19 (H-7686). Pointed bone implement, slightly curved, oval cross-section, rounded butt. From Room 92.

Fig. 20 (H-10459). Pointed bone implement, nearly straight, oval section, squared butt. From Room 169.

Fig. 21 (H-10458). Pointed bone implement, slightly curved, rectangular section, squared butt. From Room 169.

Fig. 22 (H-10166). Awl of split mammal bone, squared butt, ivory-like polish. From Room 161.

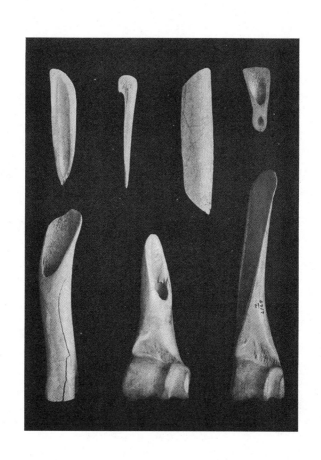

SCRAPERS AND CHISELS (*Left to right, from upper left*)

Fig. 1 (H-6169). Scraper or fleshing tool made from humerus of deer or elk. Apparently for use in the left hand. From Room 67. Representative of six specimens.

Fig. 2 (H-12106). Scraper or flesher of deer or elk humerus, apparently for the right hand. From Room 173. Representative of five specimens.

Fig. 3 (H-5116). Scraper or flesher of deer or elk humerus with condyle cut squarely off. From Room 38. Representative of two specimens. In addition there are eleven fragmentary specimens of the Figs. 1–3 type of implement.

Fig. 4 (H-2779). Scraper or chisel-pointed implement made from a phalangeal bone of deer. From a refuse heap. Representative of four specimens.

Fig. 5 (H-7517). Common scraper (both ends used) adapted from some angulate rib. From Room 85. Representative of five specimens.

Fig. 6 (H-7830). Fragmentary tool of the chisel-pointed variety. From Chaco Cañon. Representative of six or seven specimens.

Fig. 7 (H-7075). Combination awl and scraper split mammal bone. From Room 83. Representative of three specimens.

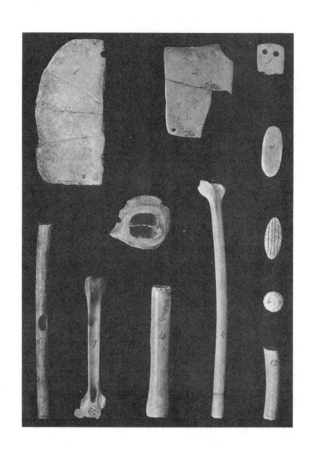

MISCELLANEOUS FORMS

Fig. 1 (H-6696). Fragmentary pendant of turtle shell, perforation in upper right hand corner. From Room 78.

Fig. 2 (H-10241). Fragmentary bracelet of thinly worked bone, perforated. From Room 163.

Fig. 3 (H-4173). Fragmentary bracelet of thinly worked bone. From Room 30.

Fig. 4 (H-8599). Thin oval disk of bone, purpose uncertain. From Room 109.

Fig. 5 (H-12814). Oval disk of bone, with simple incised decoration, purpose uncertain. From Room 171.

Fig. 6 (H-6193). Miniature circular disk or button of bone. From Room 71.

Fig. 7 (H-6838). Condyle portion of metapodial of deer, showing clean-cut scar by which it was removed. From Room 80. Representative of three specimens.

Fig. 8 (H-2783). Whistle of bird bone. From refuse heap.

Fig. 9 (H-12057). Scraper, or longitudinally worn femur of small mammal. From Room 168.

Fig. 10 (H-11286). Bead, or cut and semi-polished section of hollow bird bone. From Chaco Cañon.

Fig. 11 (H-6837). Bird bone with one condyle removed and a small bead in process of being cut off. From Room 80.

Fig. 12 (H-6188). Bead or cut section of bird bone. From Room 67.

Figs. 10–12 are representative of forty-three specimens.

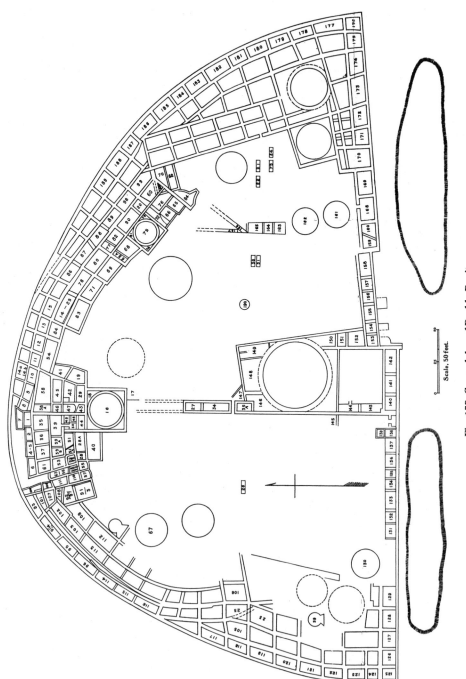

Fig. 155. Groundplan of Pueblo Bonito.

Scale, 50 feet.

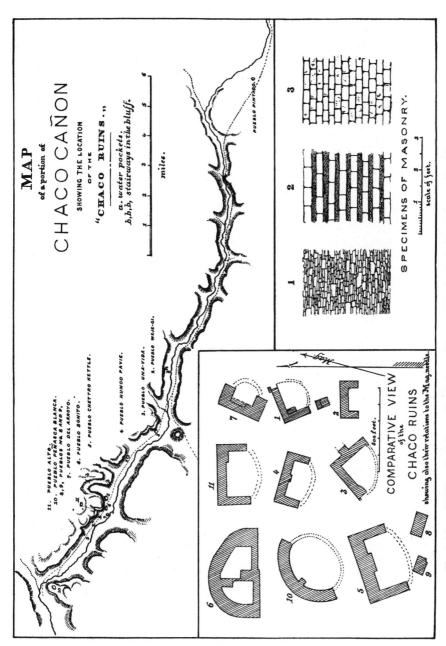

Fig. 1. Map of William H. Jackson, Tenth Annual Report, U.S. Geological and Geographical Survey, 1878.

ANTHROPOLOGICAL PAPERS

OF

THE AMERICAN MUSEUM
OF NATURAL HISTORY

Vol. XXVII

—

PUEBLO BONITO

BY

GEORGE H. PEPPER

NEW YORK

PUBLISHED BY ORDER OF THE TRUSTEES

1920

AMERICAN · MUSEUM · PRESS

PUEBLO BONITO

By George H. Pepper

FOREWORD

The following pages constitute the author's report upon certain archaeological excavations at the ruined Pueblo Bonito in Chaco Cañon, northwestern New Mexico. The work was begun in 1896 under the direction of Professor F. W. Putnam, then Curator of Anthropology at the American Museum of Natural History, and was a part of the Hyde Expedition for explorations in the Southwest. Mr. Richard Wetherill, noted for his many discoveries of Cliff and Pueblo remains, became particularly interested in the Bonito Ruin, which to him presented the greatest opportunities for investigation. Having previously formed the acquaintance of Messrs. B. Talbot B. Hyde and Frederick E. Hyde Jr., he presented his plans for the excavation of the ruin. These gentlemen were so impressed with the project that they resolved to finance the undertaking. They sought the council of Professor Putnam, who entered wholeheartedly into the enterprise as its scientific director. Mr. George H. Pepper was appointed field director. In the work of excavation he was assisted by Richard Wetherill and his four brothers. The excavations at Bonito occupied the summer seasons of 1896, 1897, 1898, and 1899.

In planning the work, care was taken to project a method that would record with precision all the observations made and particularly the positions of objects found in the rooms of the ruin. Not only were careful measurements of the position of each important specimen to be made as found, but all the more important were to be photographed *in situ*. This precision of detail was amply justified as the work proceeded, because some of the most significant points as to the uses of certain objects would otherwise not have been attained. For example, it was this painstaking technique that revealed the custom of placing small offerings in certain kiva posts.

A geological survey of the cañon was also a part of the plan. This was undertaken by Professor Richard E. Dodge of Columbia University, whose preliminary report will be found in the Introduction. It was hoped that such a geological survey would provide data to be ultimately correlated with cultural data obtained from the ruin and its contents. This correlation of geological data with the results of archaeological work is a much-neglected aspect of anthropological research in Southwestern United States and the fact that such geological coordination was planned as an integral part of this project stands as a tribute to the genius of Professor Putnam.

1

The author long delayed the preparation of this report in the hope that further work could be taken up at the ruin and that a more exhaustive study of the cultural problem of the Chaco could be prosecuted; but as neither of these desirable extensions of the work now seems possible, he decided to issue his notes in their present form as a record of what was done in this pioneer exploration of one of the most famous of the Chaco group. To this end he has given as full and detailed information upon each room as seems likely to be required by his more fortunate successors in this field.

Something less than half the rooms in the pueblo were excavated, 198 in all. Of these full technical descriptions have been given for all that were of special importance in characterizing the culture of the ancient inhabitants. These are taken up in serial order, their relative positions appearing on the groundplan, Fig. 155. It so happened that the various types of specimens were in the main segregated in individual rooms, thus making it possible to give a systematic treatment of these cultural characters as a part of the serial description of rooms.

During the long interval since the last Hyde Expedition the author published a few brief accounts of special rooms and features of the Pueblo as follows:—

Ceremonial Deposits found in an Ancient Pueblo Estufa in Northern New Mexico (Monumental Records, vol. 1, no. 1, pp. 1–6, July, 1899.)

Ceremonial Objects and Ornaments from Pueblo Bonito, New Mexico (American Anthropologist, N. S., vol. 7, no. 2, April–June, 1905.)

Human Effigy Vases from Chaco Cañon, New Mexico (Boas Anniversary Volume, pp. 320–334, New York, 1906.)

The Exploration of a Burial-Room in Pueblo Bonito, New Mexico (Putnam Anniversary Volume, pp. 196–252, New York, 1909.) These have not been repeated in the present publication.

Finally, in justice to the author it should be noted that what is here published are his field notes, supplemented by descriptive data for the most important specimens. The author is to be commended for his frankness in thus placing before us his field record in full so that future excavators in this ruin may have before them his first hand impressions and observations.

September, 1920.   CLARK WISSLER.

CONTENTS

3

LIST OF ILLUSTRATIONS.

INTRODUCTION.

The ruin known as Pueblo Bonito lies between the narrow walls of Chaco Cañon in northwestern New Mexico. Chaco Cañon's greatest claim for attention is due to the fact that Pueblo Indians built there a series of great walled-in towns at a time, which, from all obtainable information, was certainly a great many years before the Spanish Conquest The eastern limit of this great prehistoric waterway is in latitude 35° 56' 27" and longitude 107° 46'. From this point it stretches westward a distance of twenty miles. In the cañon bottom and on the cliffs that border it there are twelve large ruins and numerous smaller ones. In one stretch, hardly a mile in length, over forty small ruins and house sites have been counted.

The best general account of these ruins, including the one herein discussed, was published by William H. Jackson in 1878[1]. He gives a concise account of the group and its geographical setting together with large plans of the most important ruins. We have reproduced here (Fig. 1), his sketch map and condensed groundplans of the several buildings, to give an idea of the place of Pueblo Bonito in the group. As an introductory statement the following excerpt from Jackson's account can scarcely be improved upon:—

The great ruins in the Chaco Cañon, in Northern New Mexico, are preeminently the finest examples of the numerous and extensive remains of the works of unknown builders to be found north of the seat of the ancient Aztec Empire in Mexico, and of which there is comparatively little known even to this day. The first published account which ever appeared in regard to them is a short reference to the Pueblo Bonito by Gregg in 1844. His observations covered a period of eight years previous to 1840. In 1849 a military expedition under the command of Colonel Washington, then military governor of New Mexico, was sent against the Navajos, who were troublesome at that time, and their line of march traversed a portion of the cañon. The report of Lieutenant Simpson, of the United States Topographical Engineers, who accompanied the expedition, contained the first detailed and authentic account ever published of these wonderful ruins, and it has been up to this time the only source of information.

Prof. O. Loew visited the Pueblo Pintado in 1874, and a short description of it by him appears in the annual report of the Chief of Engineers for 1875.

My visit to the cañon of the Chaco in the spring of 1877 (May 7–15) was made with no idea of discovering anything new, but to see for myself and thus be able to compare more satisfactorily the highest development of ancient architectural skill as exhibited in these ruins with the extensive remains in the San Juan basin, and also with the pueblos of New Mexico and Arizona which are still occupied.[2]

---

[1] "Report on the Ancient Ruins Examined in 1875 and 1877" (*Tenth Annual Report of the United States Geological and Geographical Survey of the Territories embracing Colorado and Parts of Adjacent Territories, being a Report of Progress of the Exploration for the Year 1876. By F. V. Hayden*). Washington, 1878.
[2] Jackson, *ibid.*, 431.

The first to mention the Chaco ruins is Josiah Gregg, as just stated, but there may exist archive material not yet available to us, for Bandelier makes the following statement:—

In the middle of the last century a Spanish captain of engineers, Don Bernardo de Mier y Pacheco, went upon a scientific and political mission for the Crown in New Mexico. He explored the ruins of the country, and the numerous pueblos of the Cañon de Chaca (in the present home of the Navajos) excited his interest in the highest degree. When he began to concern himself about the situation of Quivira, it was supposed that he had plans and documentary evidences to assist him in finding the place. The measurements which he made in the ruins of the Chaca convinced the people that Quivira was there, and this conviction grew and spread rapidly. There was living at that time in Socorro on the Rio Grande an old Indian who was called "Tio Juan Largo." When he heard of the search of the Spanish officer, he protested at once against the idea that Quivira could be found in the northwest, and insisted that the ruins of the former mission of the Jumanos and Quiviras were east of Socorro, on the "Mesa Jumana."[1]

As de Mier y Pacheco's investigations were carried on in 1776, and Gregg wrote in 1844 this earlier account would certainly be most valuable in estimating the changes that had taken place in the ruin.

Lieutenant J. H. Simpson in his "Journal of a Military Reconnaissance from Santa Fe, New Mexico, to the Navajo Country" in August, 1849, found the ruins to be exactly as described by Gregg. Owing to the fact that Lieutenant Simpson's report on this great group was the first detailed description, it has been deemed advisable to quote that part which concerns Pueblo Bonito, *verbatim.*

Two or three hundred yards down the cañon, we met another old pueblo in ruins, called Pueblo Bonito.....................................This pueblo, though not so beautiful in the arrangement of the details of its masonry as *Pueblo Pintado*, is yet superior to it in point of preservation. The circuit of its walls is about thirteen hundred feet. Its present elevation shows that it has had at least four stories of apartments. The number of rooms on the ground floor at present discernible is one hundred and thirty-nine. In this enumeration, however, are not included the apartments which are not distinguishable in the east portion of the pueblo and which would probably swell the number to about two hundred. There, then, having been at least four stories of rooms, and supposing the horizontal depth of the edifice to have been uniform from bottom to top, or, in other words, not of a retreating terrace form on the court side, it is not unreasonable to infer that the original number of rooms was as many as eight hundred. But, as the latter supposition (as will be shown presently) is probably the most

---

[1]A. F. Bandelier, *The Gilded Man (El Dorado) and other pictures of the Spanish Occupancy of America.* New York, 1893. (p. 253.)
Bandelier stated later that he had been unable to find any documentary evidence concerning the present location of the plans made by this gentleman, but he felt quite sure that they were in a convent in Zacatecas in Old Mexico. If these plans could be found it would add most interesting data to our present knowledge of this great group of ruins, for with his measurements, he no doubt gave at least a general account of the condition of the ruins.

tenable, there must be a reduction from this number of one range of rooms for every story after the first; and this would lessen the number to six hundred and forty-one. The number of *estuffas* is four—the largest being sixty feet in diameter, showing two stories in height, and having a present depth of twelve feet. All these *estuffas* are, as in the case of the others I have seen, cylindrical in shape, and nicely walled up with thin tabular stone. Among the ruins are several rooms in a very good state of preservation—one of them (near the northwest corner of the north range) being walled up with alternate beds of large and small stones, the regularity of the combination producing a very pleasing effect. The ceiling of this room is also more tasteful than any we have seen—the transverse beams being smaller and more numerous, and the longitudinal pieces which rest upon them only about an inch in diameter, and beautifully regular. These latter have somewhat the appearance of barked willow. The room has a doorway at each end and one at the side, each of them leading into adjacent apartments. The light is let in by a window, two feet by eight inches, on the north side. There was among the ruins another room, which, on account of the lateness of the hour and the consequent despatch of our examination, escaped our scrutiny. This room having been represented by Assistant Surgeon J. H. Hammond and Mr. J. L. Collins (both of whom started from camp with us) as being more perfect in its detail than any of the others we had visited, and as indicating the use of *smooth plank* in the flooring, I requested the former to furnish me with a description of it.[1]

Surgeon Hammond's description of a room found among the ruins of the Pueblo Bonito is as follows:—

Sir: At your request, I send you a description of a room that I saw, in company with Mr. Collins, of Santa Fe, in the ruins of the Pueblo Bonito, in the Cañon of Chaco, on the 28th ult.

It was in the second of three ranges of rooms on the north side of the ruins. The door opened at the base of the wall, towards the interior of the building; it had never been more than two feet and a half high, and was filled two-thirds with rubbish. The lintels were of natural sticks of wood, one and a half to two and a half inches in diameter, deprived of the bark and placed at distances of two or three inches apart; yet their ends were attached to each other by withes of oak with its bark well preserved. The room was in the form of a parallelogram, about twelve feet in length, eight feet wide, and the walls, as they stood at the time of observation, seven feet high. The floor was of earth, and the surface irregular. The walls were about two feet thick, and plastered with a layer of red mud one fourth of an inch thick. The latter having fallen off in places showed the material of the wall to be sandstone. The stone was ground into pieces the size of our ordinary bricks, the angles not as perfectly formed, though nearly so, and put up in break-joints, having intervals between them, on every side, of about two inches. The intervals were filled with laminæ of a dense sandstone, about three lines in thickness, driven firmly in, and broken off even with the general plane of the wall—the whole resembling mosaic work. Niches, varying in size from two inches to two feet and a half square, and two inches to one and a half feet in horizontal depth, were scattered irregularly over the

---

[1]Simpson, James H. "Journal of a Military Reconnaissance from Santa Fe, New Mexico, to the Navajo country, made with the troops under the command of Brevet Lieutenant, Colonel John M. Washington, chief of the 9th military department, and governor of New Mexico, in 1849" (*Reports of the Secretary of War, 31st Congress, 1st Session, Senate Ex. Doc. No. 64*, Washington, 1850, 80–81.)

walls, at various heights above the floor. Near the place of the ceiling, the walls were penetrated horizontally by eight cylindrical beams, about seven inches in diameter; their ends were on a line with the interior planes of the walls they penetrated, and the surfaces of them perpendicular to the length of the beam. They had the appearance of having been sawed off originally, except that there were no marks of the saw left on them; time had slightly disintegrated the surfaces, rounding the edges somewhat here and there. Supporting the floor above were six cylindrical beams about seven inches in diameter, passing transversely of the room, and at distances of less than two feet apart—the branches of the trees having been hewn off by means of a blunt edged instrument. Above, and resting on these, running longitudinally with the room, were poles of various lengths, about two inches in diameter, irregularly straight, placed in contact with each other, covering all the top of the room, bound together at irregular and various distances, generally at their ends, by slips apparently of palm-leaf or marquez, and the same material converted into cords about one-fourth of an inch in diameter, formed of two strands, hung from the poles at several points. Above, and resting upon the poles, closing all above, passing transversely of the room, were planks about seven inches wide and three-fourths of an inch in thickness. The width of the plank was uniform, and so was the thickness. They were in contact, or nearly so, admitting but little more than the passage of a knife blade between them, by the edges, through the whole of their lengths. They were not jointed; all their surfaces were level, and as smooth as if planed, excepting the ends, the angles as regular and perfect as could be retained by such vegetable matter. They are probably of pine or cedar, exposed to the atmosphere for as long a time as it is probable these have been. The ends of the plank, several of which were in view, terminated in a line perpendicular to the length of the plank, and the plank appears to have been severed by a blunt instrument. The planks—I examined them minutely by the eye and the touch, for the marks of the saw and other instruments—were smooth, and colored brown by time or by smoke. Beyond the plank nothing was distinguishable from within. The room was redolent with the perfume of cedar. Externally, upon the top, was a heap of stone and mud, ruins that have fallen from above, immovable by the instruments that we had along.

The beams were probably severed by contusions from a dull instrument, and their surfaces ground plain and smooth by a slab of rock; and the plank, split or hewn from the trees, were, no doubt, rendered smooth by the same means.[1]

Jackson's later account is more precise and presents the ruin about as we found it in 1896:—

Five hundred yards below and also close under the perpendicular walls of the cañon are the ruins of the Pueblo Bonito, the largest and in some respects the most remarkable of all. Its length is 544 feet and its width 314 feet. By referring to the plan it will be seen that it only roughly approximates the usual rectangular shape. The two side wings are parallel with each other, and at right angles to the front wall, for a distance of 70 feet; the west wing then bends around until a little past a line drawn through the centre of the ruin transversely, when it bears off diagonally to join the east wing, thus resembling in its outline a semi-oval. Instead of a semi-circular wall, the court is enclosed by a perfectly straight row of small buildings run-

---

[1]Simpson, *ibid.*, 144–145.

ning almost due east and west, and is intersected by a line of *estufas*, which divide it (the court) into two nearly equal portions. A marked feature is the difference in the manner of construction, as shown in the character of the masonry and of the ground plan. It was not built with the unity of purpose so evident in the Pueblo of Chettro Kettle and some others, but large additions have been spliced in from time to time, producing a complexity in the arrangement of the rooms difficult to follow out. I spent several hours in endeavoring to unravel the intricacies of the foundations, and with better success than I imagined possible. The left-hand wing consists of three rows of rooms, eight in each row, 12 to 15 feet wide and from 12 to 20 feet in length. The outer walls are entirely demolished, but some of the interior walls reach to the top of the second story. In front of this wing and facing the court are the remains of what were probably three circular, partially subterranean rooms, probably *estufas*. The section adjoining this wing is in the shape of an almost perfect quarter-circle, and consists of five tiers of rooms, with nine rooms in each. The walls are standing quite generally as high as the second story. The outer tier of rooms of this section, which are only about 4 feet in width, seem to have been built on merely to assimilate this portion of the building with the rest, for they are evidently of different periods. The middle section is the most ruinous of all, but the great depth of the *débris* which covers several perfect rooms indicates that it originally possessed an equal height with the adjoining walls. The outer wall thus far is entirely ruined, hardly a stone remaining in place, but in the section that lies between the central line of *estufas* and the right-hand wing it rises up to the fourth story, and is in a remarkably well-preserved condition. Portions of it are evidently a quite late addition in the history of the ancient pueblo, some of the outer rows having been spliced or joined to the last wing in a manner which will be better understood by a reference to the plate than by any description. Several of the interior parallel and transverse walls are also standing fully 30 feet high. Many of the *vigas*, which are in excellent preservation, still retain their places and protect a number of rooms on the first floor. The outer wall of the east wing is in fair preservation, while the interior walls are in excellent order for at least two stories; the apartments in this and the adjoining section are of unusual size, and the walls of the ground floor are of a fine massiveness that has preserved them remarkably well. Within this wing are two *estufas*, one of which came up with and formed a portion of the second story. Across the front of the court there are two tiers of rooms about 25 feet in width, their fallen walls making a mound of *débris* 5 to 8 feet in depth, indicating that they were of considerable height. Every transverse wall could be easily distinguished. Interrupting this about midway is a solid parallelogram 65 by 115 feet in dimensions, in which are two *estufas* each 50 feet in diameter. A low mass of ruins connects these with two more somewhat similar *estufas* that adjoin the centre of the main building.

Having thus roughly sketched in the external forms of the ruin, I will devote some space to a description of some of its details.

The masonry, as exhibited in the construction of the walls, is quite dissimilar in the different portions, showing clearly that it was either built at different periods, or that it had been once partially demolished and then rebuilt. The three kinds of masonry shown in Plate LXII [Fig. 1], appear at various places throughout the building, and, in addition, there is considerable rough-laid plastered wall, like that which appears in many of the old ruins, and which is also characteristic of all the Moqui pueblos. In that part of the external wall which is now standing a different method of laying the stones is observed in each story. The first or lowest story is built in the manner of No. 2; the second as No. 1; while in the third story it is a repetition of the first. The straight row across the front of the court was built almost entirely like No. 2, and the buildings immediately adjoining partook of the same character. Most of the interior walls, especially in the east wing and the section adjoining it, were built in the manner of No. 1; but of larger stones. A large number of beams of wood were used to strengthen the walls; round sticks of three and four inches in diameter were built into the wall transversely, the ends trimmed off smooth and flush with the two outer surfaces, and larger timbers of from 10 to 15 feet in length and 6 to 8 in diameter were embedded longitudinally. We observed these in the outer wall only. The *estufas* in this ruin form an important feature, both from their number, size, and the excellent manner in which most of them were built. Referring to the plan (Fig. 2), the first that attract our attention are those in the centre, Nos. 1 and 2, which have been already referred to. Neither these, nor in fact any of the others, with the exception probably of some of the more indistinct ones, which are indicated by dotted lines, appear to have been subterranean. No. 3 is 40 feet in diameter and No. 4, 26 feet, both are considerably elevated above the general surface. The masonry in the circles of these four central *estufas* is yet perfect around their entire circumferences, and the only others in like condition are the two in the east wing, Nos. 5 and 6. Besides these six, there are at least fifteen others in various degrees of demolition. Nos. 7, 8, and 9 are unmistakably of the same character as the preceding, and also those numbered from 10 to 17, the last six especially, having considerable portions of their cylindrical walls remaining. The remaining ones have only great mounds of stones and earth to mark their sites. The interior of the court is very uneven, there being no level ground whatever. This, as in the case of the Pueblo Pintado, I think, indicates that it was occupied with many subterranean rooms. There are a number of rooms, the coverings of which have resisted the great weight of fallen walls, and are now in excellent preservation. These do not differ materially from those already mentioned, and, as Lieutenant Simpson and Dr. Hammond describe two that are in this ruin with considerable minuteness, I will say but little in regard to them. In one of these, a small room in the outer tier of the north side, which we entered by a small hole which had been broken through the exterior wall, we found the names of Lieutenant Simpson, Mr. R. H. Keen, and one or two others, with the date, August 27, 1849, scratched into the soft plastering which covered the walls, the impression appearing as plainly as if done but a few days previously. The pueblo was built within about 20 yards of the foot [of] the bluff, but a talus of broken rock occupies all of this space, excepting a narrow passage next to the northern wall, through which the trail passes. To the east of this are the ruins of several small buildings built upon a bench close under the rocks. The bench has been extended some distance by a wall of 6 or 8 feet height, built of alternating bands of large and small stones. A short distance beyond is a mass of ruins measuring 135 by 75 feet, in the centre of which are two circular rooms. From the east side of this a line of wall ran due south about 300 feet, meeting at a right angle another wall 180 feet in length, which was an extension of the south front of the pueblo.[1]

Jackson, *ibid.*, 440–442.

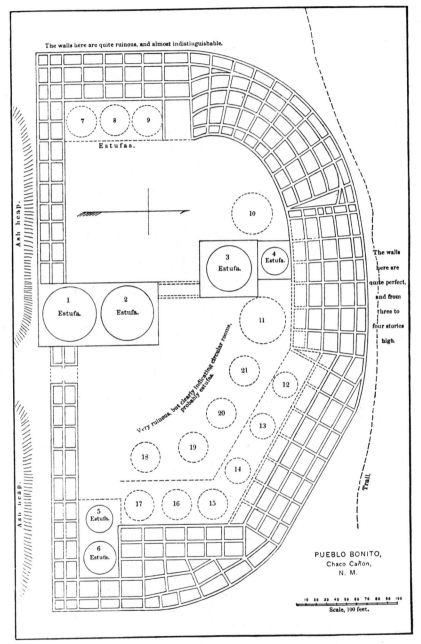

The walls here are quite ruinous, and almost indistinguishable.

Estufas.

7 8 9

10

3 Estufa.

4 Estufa.

1 Estufa.

2 Estufa.

11

Very ruinous, but clearly indicating circular rooms, probably estufa.

21

12

20

13

18

19

14

17

16

15

5 Estufa.

6 Estufa.

Ash heap.

Ash heap.

Trail.

The walls here are quite perfect, and from three to four stories high.

PUEBLO BONITO,
Chaco Cañon,
N. M.

10 20 30 40 50 60 70 80 90 100
Scale, 100 feet.

Fig. 2. Groundplan of Pueblo Bonito, William H. Jackson, 1878.

19

Fig. 3.   General View of Pueblo Bonito taken from the Mesa North of the Ruin.

20

Fig. 4.   Bonito from the Mesa, showing Excavated Rooms.

Fig. 5. North Wall of Bonito showing Joint of Old and New Walls.

22

The appearance of the ruin before excavations were begun is shown in Fig. 3. Professor Richard E. Dodge made a preliminary survey of the ruin as a basis for the construction of an accurate plan. Unfortunately, the writer was not able to return to the cañon to make the final survey necessary to such a compilation, but recently Assistant Curator Nelson of the American Museum of Natural History made an independent survey and drafted the general groundplan of the pueblo. Upon this plan as a basis, with my field notes and room plans, Mr. B. T. B. Hyde constructed the detailed outline in Fig. 155. The numbers on this plan show the rooms excavated and also refer to the corresponding text. Professor Richard E. Dodge made a preliminary study of the cañon from whose field reports the following excerpts are taken:—

I was occupied in work at the ruin from August 14 to September 9 (1900), inclusive. In outlining the problems presented, it seemed to me that there were three separate topics to be studied. First, the geographical conditions at the time of the Pueblo occupation, as compared with the present conditions; second, any evidence of climatic or geographical change; third, any evidences as to the lapse of time since the desertion of the pueblos by their ancient inhabitants.

My first thought was that the best solution of these problems might be found in a careful study of certain particular conditions to be seen in the walls of the arroyo. These evidences consisted of lenses of pottery, bones, beads, rolled adobe balls, etc., at a depth below the present plain surface, of from 14 to 17 feet. A careful study of an exposed section something more than thirty feet in vertical height in several places in the arroyo showed me, however, that the lenses of pottery, etc., could be interpreted in at least two different ways with equal truth. I therefore gave up further study in the arroyo for the time being, thinking it more advisable to study evidences about the ruin itself, hoping therefrom to get testimony that would aid the work in the arroyo.

My work at the ruin consisted, first, of a detailed study of the comparative weathering of the different rocks used in the pueblo walls, particularly at the top and the bottom of walls which are standing to a height of three stories; secondly, a study of the deposits about the ruin to a sufficient depth to reach pure sand; thirdly, a study of the deposits in the large dump heap to the south of the ruin; and fourthly, a study of any traces of the deposits to be found on the walls of the exposed rooms. I also made a careful lithological section from the foot of the cliff to the extreme top of the mesa, and collected specimens from the different layers so as to have material for studying the unweathered rocks similar to those used in the pueblo walls.

As a result of my reconnaissance I was convinced of the great length of time in which the ruins were occupied, as shown by the great depths of adobe and water and wind accumulated sand containing evidences of human occupation, to a depth of nearly twenty feet. It should be noted that the fragments of pottery found at the bottom of such sections were evidently of a similar type to those to be seen in great abundance over the surface.

A study of the exposed layers in several deep pits gave evidence of very striking changes in geographical conditions at a considerable period anterior to the desertion of the pueblos, particularly as shown by accumulations of gravels, clearly of water origin, at a depth of more than ten feet beneath an overlying accumulation of adobe and wind blown sand, in the top layers of which were evidences of several formerly occupied floors at different levels. Certain small remnants of water made gravels in the small recesses on the sides of some of the rooms on the south side of the ruin, and the very general stratification of the layers in the large dump heap also suggest extensive water action. These are some of the problems, the solution of which is at least suggested, but which must be determined by later, more extended, careful work.

The method of study of these deposits was purely geological, all measurements being made in reference to a chosen floor level, to tenths of a foot, and drawn in notebook to scale of tenth of an inch. Extensive collections were taken for office study. One of the difficulties in correlating the various water levels was due to the absence of an established base line, which is, I believe, contemplated for another year.

From the report on the second field trip:—

My attention was devoted to five lines of investigation as follows:—

a. Study of sections in excavations dug during previous winter at southeast corner of ruin and south of center of dump.

b. Study of section through eastern portion of dump and holes in eastern and western sections of dump, extending down to clean sand.

c. Mapping of dump and holes studied this year and last.

d. Study of rate and method of erosion of cliff face of northern mesa.

e. Careful mapping of surface wet weather streams draining into arroyo, and a rough study of arroyo deposits for one mile, for the purpose of locating deposits of human origin. I shall consider these several phases of work in turn.

Sections in Excavations. The sections of clean sand studied during the last two years number six in all, including the two mentioned as situated in dumps. The sections have been drawn to a scale of one-tenth of an inch to one-tenth of a foot, and have been plotted with care. As nearly as possible the datum plane is the same in each case, so that it will be possible to draw up a series of sections that will enable one to correlate the different layers found. Tentative correlation would seem to indicate an old water course running close to the front of the ruins at a depth of ten feet. Evidences of human remains occur to a depth much greater than this and reach more than twenty feet in one instance.

Sections in Dump. The western dump was sectioned horizontally last year and seemed to indicate widespread action of standing water during its formation. The longitudinal section in the eastern dump this year seems to corroborate the evidence, though it has not been possible to be sure as yet of the identity of the more evident water layers in the two sections. The height of the top water layers in the dump has been projected to and marked on a large rock on the south side of the Chaco Arroyo, but no time was available for search for water laid deposits on that side of the cañon. It is expected that careful leveling will enable us to correlate certain water laid deposits in the south tier of rooms in the ruin with the dump sections.

Location of Sections by Mapping. A careful plane table map was made showing location of several sections studied and of related ruins for the purpose of furnishing data available for working out grades of strata in office correlation of deposits. This mapping required a day's work, but seemed essential as giving the best available base for careful lateral measurements.

Cliff Profile. A study was made of the cliff profile on the northern side of the Chaco Cañon for the purpose of securing evidence as to the presence or absence of talus at different points in the cliff, and as to the relation of the ancient people to the talus deposits. The form of the cliff front is very peculiar near the ruin, but it has not been possible as yet to determine the reasons for the cliff profile, or to locate the fault in the Chaco Valley and the departure of the cliff front from the fault line. Evidence along this line should be very valuable in the future.

Mapping of Surface Streams. My studies of last year of the deposits shown in the arroyo walls above and below Pueblo del Arroyo suggested to me that the deposits were not formed, as has been suggested, during the aggrading period of the arroyo plain, but during the subsequent and present period of degradation. A study of the arroyo walls seemed to indicate that the human remains are restricted to a small stretch of the arroyo wall, as noted above. I therefore mapped the path of all the small streams entering the arroyo from above the eastern end of the Ruin down to the under cliff ruins at the western end of the fenced field, near "Joe's Hogan." This mapping showed that all the drainage of water from the vicinity of Bonito enters the arroyo somewhere within the section included between the side arroyo entering just upstream from the well marked lense of pottery, beads, etc., and the arroyo that enters just east of Joe's Hogan. This indicates that the present arrangement of drainage is such as would bring materials from Bonito to the particular places in which human remains are found in the arroyo walls. I consider this the most satisfactory single bit of testimony thus far secured.

These reports show clearly the value of geographical and geological studies in solving the problems arising from the excavations of such ruins and we hope that they may ultimately be carried to a definite conclusion.

Though of doubtful value some note may be taken of modern Indian traditions as to the history and fate of Bonito.

During the early part of the season of 1896 two Navajo Indians came into camp. One was an old man of about seventy, who knew no English, the other was a younger man who had been educated at Carlisle and who had traveled to some extent in the east. His name was Thomas Torlino and he was one of the interpreters used by Dr. Washington Matthews in his Navajo studies at Fort Defiance, Arizona. The older man gave considerable information concerning the old Pueblo people. He stated that his ancestors had been in touch with the old people of the Chaco region. At that time there was no arroyo in the center of the Chaco; it was a level plain and the Pueblo people cultivated all of the space between the cañon walls.

Simpson says:—

The soil in the *Cañon de Chaco*, though now very arid, seems to possess the elements of fertility; and, probably, when the ruined pueblos along it were instinct with life, it was cultivated.[1]

---

[1]Simpson, *ibid.*, 86.

Pueblo Alto, the ruin lying just north of Pueblo Bonito, on the cliff, was the "Chief's house." From its high position he could view the surrounding country for miles; then too, by going to the edge of the mesa almost all of the pueblos in the cañon could be seen. In this way he could keep an eye on his own people and his sentinels could note the approach of any hostile bands. He said that this was the richest "House" in the region and that his people, the Navajo were in the habit of exchanging game for corn and other produce with them. According to the statements of his fathers the old people left the region on account of the scarcity of water and that there were no records of the Navajo having fought with the Pueblo people who occupied this group of buildings. There were no irrigating ditches in the cañon, the people relying on the rain for their crops and for their drinking water. Regarding the big logs which were used in the houses he said that they came from large pine trees that formerly grew in the side cañons which branch from the Chaco and that they were hauled to the building on little wagons made of a small tree, having at either end a cross-section of a log for a wheel

Bandelier states:—

....When Mr. Simpson inquired of Nazlé, the well known Jemez Indian, about the ruins of the Chaca, he replied "that they were built by Montezuma and his people when on their way from the north to the region of the Rio Grande and to Old Mexico." When, a few weeks ago, I interrogated an Indian from Cochiti concerning the same ruins, he confirmed what I had been told years ago; namely, that Push-a-ya had built them, when on his way to the south. After inhabiting the Chaca villages for some time, Pushaya went to Zuñi, and thence into Sonora and Mexico.[1]

With this brief and inadequate introduction to the mysteries of Pueblo Bonito, we turn to the details of excavation. When the Hyde Expedition began work in the Chaco Cañon in 1896 camp was made near Pueblo Bonito, that ruin being the first objective. The refuse heap in front of the pueblo, that is to the south, was worked in an endeavor to determine whether burials had been made in it. There are two refuse heaps in front of the ruin. A large one, which was partly explored and a smaller one to the eastward of it. After the refuse heaps had been examined, attention was directed to the burial mounds near the base of the mesa on the southern side of the cañon. Two of these mounds were mapped and all of the burials in them photographed and the specimens removed. As this part of the work has no special bearing on the investigation of Pueblo Bonito it will be left for the final chapters of the report.

---

[1]Bandelier, A. F., "Final Report of Investigations among the Indians of Southwestern United States, Carried on Mainly in the Years from 1880 to 1885, Part II" (*Papers of the Archæological Institute of America. American Series*, IV, Cambridge, 1892), 304.

When the excavations in the mounds were finished the actual work in the pueblo was begun. In describing these investigations the arbitrary field numbering of the rooms will be adhered to. These numbers merely designate the sequence of rooms opened, but they will serve to locate their positions and show in what part of the ruin excavations were made.

Three of the rooms of the outer northern series were open. These places had been used by sheep herders and cowboys who happened to be in these parts, and some of them were used by Colonel Washington's troops when they were located in the Cañon during their Navajo campaign. One of these rooms was cleaned and used as a kitchen and storehouse for provisions, a second was fitted up as a darkroom for photographic work, and a third was used as a general storeroom. The cleaning of these rooms consisted in the removal of the accumulation of sand on the floors; no other changes were made in their appearance.

EXCAVATIONS IN THE PUEBLO.

The first series of rooms to be considered is one in the north central part of the pueblo. The rooms composing this series form a line extending east and west and are of the old style of architecture. They form a portion of the third row of rooms from the north and have been numbered 1, 2, 4, 5, 6, 7, 8, 9, and 10, as may be seen by the plan (Fig. 155). Room 3 is in another part of the ruin in a series of underground rooms which were partly open when discovered.

ROOM 1.

Room 1 was opened in order that the general type of architecture in this part of the ruin might be determined. The walls were composed of roughly quarried stones, loosely laid with a mortar of sand containing adobe. The masonry proved to be of very crude workmanship as compared with the adjacent outer walls, which represent the latest additions to the no doubt constantly changing pueblo.

Sand and fallen wall stones were removed to a depth of over four feet before anything of interest was found. In the débris removed, there was an occasional potsherd, but not until the floor was reached did the artifacts appear. Over the floor, which was made of carefully smoothed adobe, there was a deposit of closely matted material composed of the original contents of the room, left when it was abandoned, to which were no doubt added such objects as were suspended from the ceiling, and portions of decayed twigs that formed the retaining layer of the upper floor. To remove this layer, work was begun at the eastern end of the room.

The objects found were lying about in a state of disorder, none presenting the appearance of having been placed. They were well preserved and therefore can be studied in detail. The preservation of the destructible objects was in many respects equal to that of specimens obtained in the caves and cliff-dwellings.

Feather-Work. Feathers and quills were found in various parts of the floor area. There were four, the quills of which were practically perfect, and forty-five that were fragmentary. Ten quills have the proximal end prepared for the attachment of cords by means of which they could be attached to ceremonial paraphernalia, and of these, nine have the cords in place. All were from the wing feathers of the golden eagle. In preparing these feathers for suspension, the proximal end of the quill was flattened and then bent over upon itself, the flap measuring from half an inch to an inch in length. Around this double portion, and in some cases passing through the opening formed by the loop, was a two-strand cord of yucca fiber. There seems to be no definite form of procedure in applying this cord, as it differs in the number of knots as well as in the attachment of the last one, the cords from which were twisted and formed the two-strand attaching cord. Only one specimen retains this cord in its entirety (H-197). The manner of applying the knots to the feathers is similar to methods observed both in North and South America.[1] These feathers were evidently worn in clusters, suspended either from the hair, or from ceremonial garments or paraphernalia. The remains of two such clusters were found with the feathers. The best preserved has the remains of three quills and three sets of knots from which quills have fallen. The cord ends were tied in a loose knot, then the ends were brought together and tied in a flat knot. Tying the ends in this way left a loop about half an inch in diameter through which a cord could be passed in attaching it to another object.[2] A second specimen of the same nature was not as well preserved. The quills were missing, but from the five sets of knots which remained it would seem that the feathers employed had been much smaller than those used in the other one. They may have used the down feathers of the eagle in this group, as the two-strand yucca cord is much smaller than in the other specimen. A sixth cord was found in the bunch and, although devoid of the knots at the end, it seems quite probable that it once held a feather. If there were six in this set, it may be that this was the number usually employed in these feather pendants. Feathers grouped in this form have been found in other parts of the Southwest, especially in the caves and cliff-dwellings where such objects are better preserved than in the ruins of the open country.

Fragments of feather bands, such as are made and used in ceremonies by the Maidu[3] of California were found in this room. The largest section contains twenty quills. The quills used are those of the red-shafted flicker, *Colaptes cafer* (Linn.). The feathers of the same bird are used by the Maidu, but are arranged in a different manner. In the Pueblo Bonito specimen the quills alternate, whereas the Maidu start with three or more quills all the tips of which lie in one direction and then place a second layer composed of a smaller number of quills with the

[1]Mead, vol. 1, this series, 13; Kroeber, A. L., "The Arapaho" (*Bulletin, American Museum of Natural History*, vol. 18, 1907), 322.
[2]For a similar cluster in modern work see Kroeber, *ibid.*, 334—Ed.
[3]Dixon, Roland B. "The Northern Maidu" (*Bulletin, American Museum of Natural History*, vo 17, 1905), 149–154, 219.

tips reversed. The manner of fastening the quills seems to be the same in both regions. The quills are laid side by side and three cords are passed through them; one through the central portion, the other two being equidistant from it and within half an inch of the ends. In the Bonito specimen this cord is composed of human hair and has two strands. From the appearance of the individual quills it would seem that the greater part of the webbing had been detached before they were fastened together. From the appearance of one feather which was found with the other specimens, it is quite probable that the web on the tips of certain feathers was left for decorative effect.

Miscellaneous Objects. A number of pieces of rawhide and buckskin were found in the floor covering, but none of them had been shaped; if used at all, they must have been in their natural condition. The tail of a mountain rat, or some other mountain rodent had been carefully skinned and the hair removed, but there is no evidence that this had been used by the Indians.

Cords made of yucca fiber of various sizes and degrees of fineness were found. They were of the two-strand variety, and some of them retained the original knots.

Carefully smoothed twigs, 4 to 5 mm. in diameter, and 20 cms. in length were also found. There were three of these, one perfect, the other two broken. One of them (H-155) has a piece of yucca cord bound to its surface with sinew. These sticks were evidently used for some ceremonial purpose. A great many of them were found in Room 32 (p. 140).

Among the other objects found in this room was a natural pebble of dense hornblendic schist, measuring 9 by 11 cms., with a thickness of 3 cms. The naturally rounding sides have been worn until they are perfectly flat. In addition there were found two proximal ends of three reed arrows, in which the notching is well preserved, and on one of which there still remains an appearance of the feathering; fragments of pumpkin rinds, a small flat circular bead of light-colored stone, the claw of a mountain lion, fragments of two ceremonial sticks, a fragment of a sandal, and corncobs.

Architecture. In Fig. 6 the sides and a portion of the floor of the room are shown. The adobe forming the floor at the eastern end of the room had been broken into pieces by the falling of the walls and was therefore removed with the objects mixed in the débris. The floor beams, as here shown, are solid branches of pine, but compared with those found in other parts of the ruin, are very crude and do not show the usual care in selecting and trimming. The view in the accompanying photograph is toward the west. The rough irregular north and south walls are shown, the masonry being of a type denoting an intermediate period in the history of the pueblo. The blocks are made of cretaceous sandstone, the greater part of which was no doubt quarried on the mesa quite near the Pueblo on the north. In the western end of the room the character of the débris may be noted. It is composed of fallen wall stones, mixed with sand and adobe mortar, adobe from the floors, and portions of the almost decayed ceiling beams. The mass was chinked with sand which had blown from one part of the Cañon to another, whenever there was a heavy wind. Heavy rains and showers, which are quite prevalent in the fall, have aided in solidifying this mass. These several agencies have worked so successfully that the resulting composition is almost like concrete.

In Fig. 7 the northwestern end of this room is presented. The composition of the northern wall is shown to much better advantage than in Fig. 6. On the western wall, the plaster of sand and adobe is shown in a good state of preservation. In the angle of the floor formed by the north and west walls, an opening was found which connected this room with the one below it. It was five inches square, and had been covered with the flat stone, which lies beside it. When found it was in place.

In shape the room is rectangular. It is 11 feet 5 inches long, 5 feet 1 inch wide on the east end, and 5 feet 9 inches wide at the west end.

Room 2.

Room 2 lies directly west of Room 1 and is separated from it by a narrow wall. It is 10 feet, 3½ inches long, 5 feet, 4½ inches wide at the west end, and 5 feet 1½ inches at the east end. The walls were standing to a height of over six feet above the floor level at the time the room was explored. The room itself was similar to Room 1 in form and style of masonry. The series composed of Rooms 1, 2, 4, 5, 6, and 6a were divisions made with narrow walls between two parallel lines of soid masonry (Fig. 155). These division walls were carefully laid, abutting against the north and south walls, but never interlocking with them.

This room was filled with débris, the surface being on the same level as in Room 1. Nothing of interest was found in clearing the débris from this room, until a point about a foot and a half above the floor level was reached. The great depth of the deposit points to the fact that there had been a great many objects on the floor of the room directly

33

Fig. 6. Floor and Walls of Room 1.

Fig. 7.   Opening in Corner of Room 1.

Fig. 8.   Closed Doorway, Eastern Part of Bonito.

above this one. These fell with the floor and floor covering, when this part of the building was destroyed. Owing to the fact that the deposit was so thick, it was divided into two layers, one about a foot in thickness being removed before the one directly upon the floor was taken up. There were, of course, no definite areas that would differentiate the upper from the lower floor material, but the removal of the deposit in the way mentioned greatly facilitated the work. Among the two hundred and forty numbered specimens found in this room, a few directly upon the floor deposit may have been in the original positions in which they were placed by their owners, but the greater part of the material was scattered throughout the deposit by the falling of the beams and stones of the upper rooms. In describing this material only those specimens which seem to have retained their original positions will be mentioned as having been found at a particular point in the room. It will, therefore, be understood that all other specimens were found in the general deposit covering the floor.

Worked Wood. Among the first objects encountered were pieces of wood, cylindrical in form and with ends flattened. There were in all fifty-seven of these sticks, and seventeen of a similar form, but shorter. The longer sticks averaged 20 cms. in length, and 1.2 cm. in diameter. The ends are flattened and in most cases have been smoothed by grinding; some, however, remain practically as they appeared when finished with a stone knife. They are of almost uniform size, with their surfaces carefully denuded of bark and traces of branches. This suggests their use as gaming sticks, but the ends show no chamfering such as would be in evidence had they been used in a game similar to that of "sholowe" as played by the Zuñi. Then too the sticks are not marked in any way that would permit their use in such a game. On the surface of practically every stick there are incisions made with some sharp implement. These marks form spirals which, by their position, suggest that the sticks may have been used in cutting buckskin. To do this the strips of buckskin were wrapped around the stick and then revolved with the left hand while the right held the edge of a chalcedony or obsidian blade against it. The pressure of the blade on the buckskin and against the hard unyielding surface of the wooden cylinder would result in a cut much more accurate, it would seem, than in any other way. The smaller sticks are from 3 to 5 cms. in length and average about the same as the larger ones, with the exception perhaps of the diameter which is less than that of the larger specimens. There are no knife marks on the surface of these sticks and it would therefore seem that they had been used in playing some game. One of them is shaped like an hourglass, but most of them maintain the same diameter throughout their length.

Also a stick used by living Indians in what is known as a kicking game, was found; it is 10.5 cms. long and 2.7 cms. in width.

A slender ceremonial stick similar to those occurring in Room 33 was found here. The entire surface, from end to end, is marked with a spiral formed by holding the blade in the right hand and revolving the stick with the left. Finally, a number of fragments of worked sticks were found associated with other material.

A puzzling series of wooden objects, twenty-six in number, was found associated with the long and short sticks just described. They are flat on one surface with slightly rounding sides and a rounding top; they resemble the ends of bows. They range from 1.2 cms. to 7 cms. in length; the width and height varying, the greatest width and height being 1.7 cms. by 1.5 cms. One of these objects is decorated with a cross-hatch design, but none of the others show decorations of any sort. The Navajo Indians who were employed as workmen called these sticks *Tsin Takah*, and claimed that they were used with a basket tray in gambling. The Navajo name translated means wooden cards. The Navajo claim that the Pueblo people formerly used these objects in the same manner as the bone dice which are found in some of the rooms.

Matting made of reeds was found, but it had decayed to such an extent that only fragments could be preserved. Fragments of yucca leaf sandals were also found. A torch made from a bundle of cedarbark came from this room; one end was burnt showing that it had been used.

Basketry. Basketry was represented in the fragment of what was no doubt a meal or gambling tray. It is of the two rod coil type and has a herring bone edge on the angle of the rim. The tray must have been over 1½ feet in diameter. Another basket was found on the floor; it is 5 cms. in diameter and 1.3 cms. high. It had no doubt been filled with material when it was left, as the remains of the former contents reach almost to the rim at the present time.

Arrows. Evidently there had been a number of arrows in this room, and some of them remained in such a state of preservation that they could be removed. Among these there are six tang ends and other fragments of reeds, which have formed parts of arrowshafts. There is one specimen which still retains the end of the wooden foreshaft. Those that still retain fragments of feathers show that three were used; this was no doubt the usual complement for the regular arrows used in this pueblo. Some of the shafts show that they have been painted at the point where the feathering was adjusted. One especially, (H-319), has been covered between the points where the feathers are attached with what seems to be a sort of lacquer. This was applied either in the form of bands or else there has been a wrapping of fine cord which has caused ridges to appear in its surface. There are two wooden foreshafts of arrows, both in a fragmentary condition. The stone arrow points found in this room were of the narrow tapering form. There were seventeen of these and one small chalcedony knife; six of the arrow points were of black obsidian, the others being of chalcedony.

Miscellaneous Objects. In working out the material a great number of quids of corn-silk were found; at the time it seemed that they had been used as tobacco might be used by white men, but Mr. F. H. Cushing thought that the corn-silk had been chewed to obtain certain juices, as by the modern Pueblo Indians in dyeing arrows.

In one corner of the room a mass of over seven hundred pieces of chalcedony and other stones were found; they were chips such as are used in making stone implements. Many of them were quite small but there were no flakings to indicate that arrow points had been made in the room; neither were there flaking implements. The only objects of bone encountered, were a bone awl and what seems to be a fragment of a bodkin. The latter, however, might have been used as a flaker.

There were several small balls of piñon gum and one large piece of the same material; two galena crystals were also found. Small pebbles of azurite and malachite were scattered through the sand, and some of them had been used for paint-making. Yellow ocher was seen in various parts of the room and one ball of this material had retained its form, showing conclusively that it had been placed in a bag, probably buckskin, when it was in a pasty condition, as the marks of the bag may still be seen on the upper part where the crimping of the skin left deep impressions.

One of the few pieces of native copper found in the ruin came from this room; it is a nugget of irregular form and the sides show that it has been pounded to some extent. At the point were the pounding has been most severe the specimen measures 7 mms. in thickness. Very little turquoise was found; there were in all two small circular beads, one pendant, and fourteen inlays, and fragments of a turquoise matrix. Few animal bones were found, those of the rabbit and deer being the only ones represented. Pumpkin seeds, corncobs and piñon nuts were in evidence, and one shell of the cañon walnut. The latter had evidently been gnawed by chipmunks or other rodents. In the débris on the floor were also found a yucca cord with end knotted for the attachment of a feather; a disk of squash-rind perforated in the center and possibly used as a spindle whorl; a semicircular stick bound at either end and at the central part with yucca cord, used probably in one of their games; a bundle of roots; a flattened ball of yucca fiber containing leaves; and two stems of a whip cactus.

Among the most interesting of the stone implements were five rasping stones made of a rough friable sandstone of light color. From their appearance they must have been used in fashioning wooden objects. Four of them were no doubt employed in working on cylindrical objects, such as game sticks; whereas the fifth had a perfectly flat surface, such as could be used in smoothing boards or tablets. There were also four irregularly shaped hammerstones, also a hammer made of a natural pebble. A very thin form of sandstone jar cover was found, the largest being 10.5 cms., and the smallest 6 cms. in diameter; the thickness ranging from 2 to 5 mms. There were six perfect ones and twelve fragments; most of them had been carefully smoothed and the edges either rounded or ground at right angles with the surface. A large jar cover measuring 23 cms. in diameter, and another having about the same measurement, but almost square, represent the general types. Both were of sandstone with the edges chipped. The latter, though having sides which were almost square, maintained a general rounded form.

Pottery. A number of pieces of pottery found in this room retained remains of their former contents. One, a bowl with a handle near the incurved rim, has a hard compact mass covering the entire bottom, but the nature of the material has not been determined. This bowl was found in an upright position in the center of the room, with one of the small jar covers near it. Another fragment of a bowl contains a sedimentary deposit which, from its nature, seems to have been yucca juice. There were fragments of five bowls, all of grayware. Of the more perfect specimens is a bowl 12 cms. in diameter at the top and 6.5 cms. deep ; it is decorated on the inside with a terrace line and wave designs in black. This bowl was found in the eastern part of the room near the east wall. There were three other bowls, two of grayware, decorated on the interior with black designs, and one of undecorated blackware. All of these were small and were restored from fragments. A fragmentary dipper having a bowl 9 cms. in width was decorated on the interior and on the upper part of the solid handle. A bowl which formerly had a handle over the opening was found on the floor near the north wall about

4 feet from the west wall. .It is of the incurved type and has four projections which were no doubt made to represent breasts. On each of these is a decoration composed of four concentric circles. The handle was evidently broken when the vessel was in use and the irregular surfaces have been smoothed by grinding.

Another vessel which was restored from fragments is of a form seldom found in the Chaco region; it is a bowl with a broad flaring rim, the bowl itself is 7 cms. in diameter and 4 cms. deep. The rim is slightly cupped from the top of the bowl itself to its outer edge. This flaring portion gives the top of the vessel a diameter of 13 cms. The only decoration shown is a band on the upper surface of the rim, another where the rim joins the bowl, and terrace decorations connected alternately with the two rim decorations just mentioned. The color of the design is black.

From the character of the material found in this room it appears that it may have been a workshop. It may also have been used as a storeroom for certain materials, such as the stone chips which were to be used in making arrow points and other stone implements. There were no evidences of the raw material that may have been used in the room, and in fact, in all of the work in Pueblo Bonito no room has been found in which there were enough flakes to justify one in thinking that stone implements had been made there. There is only one place near Pueblo Bonito where there is conclusive evidence that such work was carried on and that is on a level stretch south of Pueblo Alto, situated on the mesa directly north of Pueblo Bonito. The natural conclusion would be that the room in question had been used as a workshop by some member of a family who occupied a series of rooms in this part of the building.

Room 3.

Underground Rooms. While the work in Rooms 1 and 2 was in progress a number of Indians were set to work in an underground room in the northwestern part of the building, this room being known as Room 3. It was one of a series of open rooms, the roofs of which had withstood the weight of the débris from the fallen walls of the rooms above. It was reached through a series of open rooms, extending in a northeasterly direction.

When Room 3 was entered, it was found to be filled to a depth of from 2 to 3 feet with sand which had washed in from the surface. Embedded in the sand, and in some cases completely covered by it, were skeletons of rabbits, which had no doubt fallen into the room and, being unable to escape, had died there.

The ceiling was supported by four heavy beams which averaged 1 foot in diameter and extended from the east to the west wall. Crossing them from north to south were small poles from 2 to 4 inches in diameter. These were strapped together in a number of places with yucca strings. Above them was a layer of split cedar which acted as a support to the adobe floor of the upper room.

In the south wall there was a niche 3 feet 4 inches long and 1 foot 8 inches high, and extending into the wall, a distance of 2 feet. It was 1 foot 10 inches above the ceiling beam and 2 inches from the east wall. Its top was composed of boards and the sides were plastered. The side walls of this niche were 1 foot 2 inches thick. There is a rounding corner at the back of the opening and the plaster extended through and joined that of the wall of the next room.

The walls were not well preserved and from the thick smoke layer on the surface of the plaster, it seems possible that this room had been used a great deal. There were numerous layers of plaster on the walls; in some places the accumulation was 4 inches thick. The stone work was rough and the east wall was of the post variety, with stones between the posts. The stones had not only been placed between the posts and cross beams, but small ones had been fitted around the posts. This, with the cover of plaster, gave the wall the appearance of one of the usual type in which stone only was employed. Owing to the fact that some of the surface had fallen, the unusual character of this wall was revealed. Six inches from the south wall and 3 feet 6 inches from the east wall, a fireplace was found, as shown in Fig. 9. It was composed of flat stones, set on edge, and was 2 feet wide on its broader axis, and 1 foot 6 inches wide on the sides extending east and west. On a line with the fireplace and 1 foot to the east of it was an opening, 1 foot square, that had formerly been an entrance to a passageway. This passage extended eastward under the east wall and thence to the surface. Directly below the eastern edge of the opening, a number of upright sticks had been placed, but for what reason, it is impossible to say. As these passageways are found in most of the estufas in these ruins, as well as throughout the Pueblo and Cliff-Dweller area, it would seem that this room, although of an angular instead of circular form, had been used as an estufa or council room. Wherever these openings and passageways are found there is generally a wall directly in front of them. The wall, in this instance, had evidently been made of flat stones, one of which may be seen in place.

Fig. 9. Interior of Room 3—a Square Kiva.

41

Fig. 10. Walls of Rooms 4 and 5.

42

The doorway in the western end of the east wall was 6 feet 8 inches from the east wall, 2 feet from the ceiling, and was 3 feet high and 1 foot 6 inches wide. It had formerly extended almost to the ceiling, but had been built in with stones to the place indicated by the measurements. This door led into another room which was proportionately filled with sand and which will be described later. One foot north of the south wall and about the same distance from the east wall, was an opening in the ceiling by means of which this room could have been reached from the one above. It was 3 feet long and 2 feet wide, and, when found, was sealed with matting and bunches of cedarbark tied with yucca leaves. Upon this foundation a layer of large flat stones had been placed.

The dimensions of the room were as follows: 12 feet 6 inches long, north wall; 11 feet 5 inches long, south wall; 15 feet long, east wall; 15 feet 4 inches long, west wall. The distance from the ceiling poles to the fireplace was 8 feet 5 inches.

The only specimen found in position was a pottery bowl, which is shown in Fig. 9. This bowl has an incurved top and was found on the floor near the east wall, less than two feet from the entrance to the passageway.

The specimens in this room were in the material that had accumulated on the floor. There were five manos, and a fragment of a sixth. There were two pottery feet, one of an animal which from the bifurcation was evidently a part of a figure of one of the ungulates, the other was the foot and lower portion of the leg of a human figure. The leg in this instance was of solid pottery, while the first was hollow. Bones of the deer, rabbit, and turkey were found, some of which had been broken to extract the marrow. A fragment of a deer antler was also found. These objects with a number of corncobs and pieces of yucca cord complete the list. One of the yucca cords is worthy of mention, owing to the fact that it is bound to a piece of skin which from its thickness, and from the hair which still remains, is evidently that of a bear or some other large animal having dark brown hair.

Room 3a. The room directly east of and adjoining Room 3, which for convenience' sake will be known as Room 3a, was the second of the series mentioned in the description of Room 3. Owing to the fact that no work was carried on in this room, the description will be confined to its general appearance, at the time that the work was being carried on in Room 3. The north wall was 14 feet 4 inches long; the south wall, 12 feet 6 inches, the east wall, 10 feet; and the west wall, 10 feet 2 inches. Ten feet from the south wall and joining the east wall was a partition about 8 inches thick, which extended northward 4 feet 4 inches, reaching to the ceiling at all points except the extreme western end, which was 5 inches below the ceiling beams. This wall was composed of poles placed in a perpendicular position, to which cross beams were tied, the whole being covered with mortar. The east wall of the main room was of this type, but on a larger scale. This room was probably on the same level as Room 3, but water had partly filled it with sand and débris until the ceiling beams were only 3 to 4 feet above the sand. The beams extended from north to south, were from 2 to 4 inches thick, and supported a layer of poles and brush. There was a door in this room which had been covered with matting, part of which was still in place. The ceiling beams in the central part of the room had been broken by the accumulation of the débris above them. There was a doorway in the western wall which was 2 feet 6 inches wide, and 2 feet below the ceiling beams. There was a small post in each of the southwestern and southeastern corners. These posts averaged 3 inches in diameter and extended through the ceiling. There were supporting beams extending east and west, about 10 inches thick, built into the top of the north and south walls. In the northwest corner of this room 3 feet 7 inches below the ceiling beams, there was a door or passageway to the next room. Owing to the fact that it was directly in the corner, the western wall of the room formed one side of it. This doorway was really the entrance to a passage, which was 4 feet long. The opening in Room 3a was 1 foot 6 inches wide, but on the opposite, or north end of the passage, it was 6 inches wider. The room to which the passageway led will be known as Room 3b.

Room 3b. The second room of the underground series, north of Room 3, is Room 3b. This room was 10 feet long on the north side, 12 feet 1 inch on the south side, 6 feet on the east side, and 6 feet 4 inches on the west. There is a doorway in the south wall 5 feet 8 inches from the west wall which was 2 feet 6 inches in height. The ceiling of this room was composed of logs, ranging from 3 to 6 inches in diameter, which extended north and south. Above these was a layer of twigs. Two feet 4 inches from the south wall and at the west end of the room was a post 8 inches in diameter, which supported a beam running east and west. This room was partly filled with sand and was not worked.

Room 3c. This room is directly west of Room 3b and will be known as Room 3c. The entrance was through a hole which someone had broken in the west wall. This room measured 12 feet 4 inches on the north, 10 feet 5 inches on the south, 10 feet 9 inches on the east, and 10 feet 9 inches on the west. Five feet 5 inches east of the west wall was a doorway, 1 foot 5 inches wide, 1 foot 10 inches from the ceiling. One foot 10 inches from the west wall and 3 inches from the south wall there was a post 9 inches in diameter which supported the only beam running east and west. This beam entered the east wall but had been broken off one foot from the west wall. Owing to the fact that none of the other ceiling beams had been burnt, it seems quite possible that fire had been employed to sever the log before it was put into the room. The ceiling of this room was composed of beams 3 inches in diameter, running from north to south. There were three poles protruding from the north wall; these probably extended through the wall from the next room.

Room 3d. Directly above Room 3c was another room which has been named Room 3d. The north wall was 10 feet long, the south wall 10 feet 5 inches, the east wall 5 feet 8 inches, and the west wall 5 feet 11 inches. In the south wall, 3 feet west of the east wall there is a doorway which is 2 feet 8 inches wide and 4 feet 8 inches high. This wall is 1 foot 6 inches thick, measuring from the floor to the ceiling beams. The room was well plastered; as in most of the other rooms the corners were rounded. In the western end there is a platform of clay about 1 foot high, extending from north to south. This platform was 3 feet broad. The ceiling beams extended from north to south and were from 2 to 3 inches in diameter. Above them were a number of rushes, most of them very small, and above these was a 2 inch layer of grass. There were two long loops of yucca leaves pendent from the ceiling at the eastern end of the room. These loops had probably been used for the suspension of objects. The door in the south wall seemed to be an entrance to a passageway as it was worked on either side and there were large beams above it. There is a possibility that it may have been a small room or closet, but owing to the fact that it was full of stones and débris, it cannot be definitely determined since the work in the north series of rooms claimed our entire attention after the work in Room 3 had been finished.

Room 4.

Continuing westward with the work in the series of which Rooms 1 and 2 form a part, Room 4 claims attention. It is rectangular in shape, 11 feet 5 inches long on the north side, 10 feet 11 inches long on the south side, 5 feet 4 inches on the west, and 5 feet 5 inches on the east. The walls and general style of masonry are the same as in Rooms 1 and 2. The specimens from this room were scattered throughout the débris, as the floor of the room above it had been burned and thereby allowed the material to fall into the room below, causing the specimens to intermingle with the stones and portions of the burnt ceiling beams. The specimens of this room were of very little importance. They consisted of utilitarian objects, associated with a few ornaments. In the former class there were fragments of pottery bowls of grayware, a jar cover made of sandstone 10 cms. in diameter, five hammerstones most of which were natural pebbles, a fragment of a combination hammer and smoothing stone, the sides of which are worn to such an extent that the object must have been used for many years.

There is one specimen, made from a natural pebble, which has been drilled in an interesting way. It is 5 cms. long, 4.7 cms. wide and 1.3 cms. in thickness, and tapers from the central portions to the edges on either side. The edges are rounded and there are four holes, 1 mm. deep and 3 mm. in diameter, placed equidistant on the edge. These places were probably drilled for the reception of inlays which, judging from the materials used in this pueblo, were of turquoise. The stone which forms this ornament is of a hard granitic structure.

Fragments of chalcedony, obsidian, azurite, malachite, turquoise, and fossil shell were found, also two small fossil shells of the *spirifer* family. A potsherd had been ground to a rectangular shape and as one side of it was decorated it may have been intended for a pendant; if so, the hole for suspension had not been drilled. A small pendant of red stone and a pendant formed of a hinge of a bivalve shell, completes the smaller objects from this room. There were five pointed sticks, averaging about 1 cm. in diameter, the ends of all of them having been burnt. Sections of individual willows showing the cutting and grinding of the ends, were found with the above mentioned sticks.

Room 5.

When the lower part of Room 4 was reached it was found that there had been a severe fire here. When half of the material had been removed from the room, the mass being composed principally of burnt ceiling beams and the adobe from the floor above it, it was found that the room had contained a mass of corn in the ear. As the work advanced, quantities of burnt piñon nuts were also found. As nothing in the way of ornaments or implements came from this room, it is safe to assume it was used for storage.

The measurements of this room varied somewhat from those of the room above it. Measuring at the floor level the north wall was 10 feet 9 inches long, the south wall 10 feet 6 inches, the east wall 8 feet 3 inches, and the west wall 8 feet 2 inches. The height from the floor to the ceiling beams was over 8 feet and this, with the walls of the upper room, made a height of over 14½ feet. In Fig. 10 Rooms 4 and 5 may be seen. The character of the masonry is the same as in the other rooms of this series. The western wall, the lower part of which is plastered, shows the joints of these division walls to good advantage. In the southern wall at the left of the picture a doorway may be seen. It is of the rectangular type which is the ordinary form of doorway in this pueblo. In the lower part of the room the dark mass formed by the burnt corn and piñon nuts is shown.

The opening in the west wall, in which a boy may be seen, leads to Room 6 which is directly west of Rooms 4 and 5.

Room 6.

Room 6 was partly filled with sand that had drifted through the crevices in the walls. There was at least three feet of open space between the roof beams and the top of the drift. When the sand had been removed, the floor layer was reached and in it, a number of animal and bird bones were found. None of these were worked and they were evidently the remains of meals. There were also pebbles, fragments of stones, several pieces of bone, and one piece of calcined bone. There was also a small fragment of a basket, fragments of wooden implements, squash-rinds and piñon nuts. The remaining objects were evidently used for ceremonial or artistic purposes. In all parts of the floor area fossil shells were found. Most of these are small, being under 3 cms. in length. They have been cleared of matrix adhesions, and among over one hundred and thirty specimens there were twenty that had been covered with a red or yellow ocher, showing that these specimens had been used in ceremonies. One of the shells had been broken open, exposing the calcite crystals in its interior. Several crinoid stems were found with the fossil shells, two chalcedony concretions of fantastic forms and the end of a strombus shell trumpet. Among other shell objects was a bead made from an olivella shell, a fragment of a large shell bracelet, a circular shell bead, and two shell pendants. In the débris there were also thirteen small pieces of stone, one being turquoise. There was also a small piece of iridescent iron ore which had no doubt appealed to the Indians on account of its brilliant colors. Lying directly on the floor but in various parts of the room were ten cedar sticks which had evidently been used as torches; there were also seven pairs of sticks tied together. These pieces had been split from a larger piece of cedar, the edges remaining in a natural condition, but the ends of some of them had been cut and squared. When found, some of these pieces still retained evidences of yucca cord, which had formerly bound them together;. perhaps they were cut into lengths in order that they might be the more readily split for torches. Among these wooden pieces one of the long sticks such as were described from Room 2 was found; it had cuts on its surface similar to those from that room.

Room 6a. Room 6a which was directly over Room 6 contained a number of specimens but most of them were small. There were twenty-seven chalcedony concretions similar to those found in Room 6. Many of them are almost transparent and, owing to the beautiful forms and colors, it is little wonder that primitive man should employ them for religious purposes. There was one massive piece found in the débris, which may have been used in making ornaments. A mass of calcite crystals protruding from the main block so as to form a rosette would naturally appeal to a primitive people in the same way as did the concretions. Such a specimen was found in this room. There were also worked pieces of gypsum, pieces of galena, ten in all, pieces of azurite and malachite, two turquoise beads, pieces of turquoise prepared for inlays and several pieces of turquoise matrix. There was also a broken chalcedony arrow point, a triangular shell inlay, a pendant made of haliotis shell, and a fossil bivalve covered with red ocher.

The base of a firedrill set, found near the floor level, was similar in form to some of the pointed sticks that have been noted from the preceding rooms. It is cylindrical in form save at the pointed end, and in the opposite end there is a cup-shaped cavity which is blackened from use. Six of the gaming or cutting sticks similar in size and form to the large ones found in Room 2 were taken from the floor layer. Three of them have the cuts on the surface, one shows no cutting, and the other two are in such a poor state of preservation that it is almost impossible to tell whether they have been used or not. It appears, however, that there had been no such cuttings on them. There are two sticks of the smaller form and four other fragments of the same diameter all of which show the crude cutting on the ends to good advantage, but none of them are finished implements. There is a ceremonial stick from this room which has the end fashioned into the form of a bear claw. It is nearly 13 cms. in length, but it is similar in form to those which were found in Room 32 (Fig. 55), which will be described when that room is under consideration. Another pair of the thin ceremonial sticks such as was described from Room 1 comes from this room. These sticks are slender, carefully formed pieces of uniform length, having rounded ends and are generally found in pairs; comparative study will not be entered upon, however, until Room 32 is reached for, as already stated, they are found in this room associated with a great deposit of ceremonial sticks (Fig. 52). In the floor deposit of Room 6a there was also a heavy two-strand yucca cord; braided and twined cord made of human hair carbonized by fire; a mass of seeds similar to those of the wild sunflower; pieces of squash rind and eagle feather quills; and a pottery foot, evidently of an animal figure. The figure itself must have been a very large one as the foot measures over 5 cms. in length, and 3 cms. in width with a correspondingly heavy leg; the wooden end of a baby board and a ceremonial object made from the skin of a small rodent completes the list of objects of general interest. There is, however, one specimen worthy of special

Fig. 11 (2865). Stick wrapped with Buckskin, Room 6.

attention. This object (Fig. 11) is 25.5 cms. long and the wooden part is evidently made of one piece. On the distal end the stick broadens and assumes a form similar to that of a deer foot. Directly below this foot there is a wrapping of sinew. In the central portion of the stick there is a wrapping of buckskin, which seems to be superimposed upon other layers of the same material. The end has been bound with sinew, and then carried upward toward the hoof end of the stick. It encloses a number of buckskin strips in the ends of which knots have been tied.

Room 7.

Room 7 lies directly north of Room 1. Because of additions to the pueblo at this point, the rooms here are irregular in form and taper to a point. The north wall is 14 feet 11 inches long, the south wall 12 feet 7 inches, the east wall which is convex on the side of Room 7, is 5 feet 6 inches long, and the western wall 3 feet 4 inches. The south wall, as seen in Fig. 6 showing Room 1, is irregular and laid up with roughly quarried stone. The north wall is built in a far more compact way, as is also the west wall. If the investigations had been carried westward from the line of the west wall, a heavy piece of masonry would no doubt have been encountered; for, owing to the fact that the space was only three feet in width, it does not seem probable that an open space would have been left at this point. The eastern wall is rather peculiar in that it forms not only the eastern wall of Room 7, but the northeastern part of Room 1, which is built with rough-edged stones, such as were used in the series running from Room 1 westward.

In Room 7 nothing of interest was found. There were five fragments of large smooth stones such as are used for work tables, a complete stone that had evidently been used as a door sill, and two arrow points. These specimens were found scattered through the débris, and are only worthy of mention as having been found in this particular room.

ROOM 8.

Room 8, lying directly east of Rooms 1 and 7 is irregular in form. The west wall is concave and measures 7 feet from the point of juncture with the north and south walls. The east wall is composed of stakes which had been plastered with mortar, making a serviceable, though not very strong, division wall. This wall is 6 feet 8 inches long, the distance from its center to the opposite wall being 7 feet. These measurements show that the room was almost square. The specimens found in this room are a bone knife, made from the leg bone of a deer, two distal ends of reed arrows which contain fragments of wooden foreshafts, and a piece of adobe from the cross wall showing the imprint of small willow sticks which were used over the heavier poles.

ROOM 9.

Room 9 curves in a southeasterly direction from Room 8. Owing to the changes made in this part of the building, this room is somewhat irregular in form. It measures 13 feet 7 inches on the north side, 14 feet 8 inches on the south side; it is 7 feet wide at the western end and increases in width to 8 feet along the eastern wall. The masonry was similar to that of the rooms just described, but of slightly better work-manship. The room was filled with the usual débris, composed of stones from the fallen walls mixed with sand and adobe plaster.

Pipes. A number of very interesting objects were found in the upper layers, showing that they had formerly been in one of the upper rooms. Nothing of special interest was found until the depth of 2 feet had been reached in the southwestern corner, where within the radius of a very few feet, five pipe fragments were found. One of these, as shown in Fig. 12b, is made of steatite. The stem and a small portion of the bowl were the only parts found; the stem is 5 cms. long and tapers from 1 cm. at the mouth end to 1.3 cm. where the stem joins the bowl. The material is a coarse green steatite; the surface has been smoothed to such an extent that it retains a high polish. The stem of this pipe had been broken while it was in use, and had been mended in a rather ingenious way. The two pieces were put together and a groove 1 cm. deep and 1.5 cm. long cut on the upper side, half of which was in either fragment. A similar groove was then cut on the under side. These grooves were perfectly straight, following the median line of the stem. From other objects of a similar nature found in this pueblo, it is safe to affirm that pieces of bone or wood were placed in these grooves and the stem wrapped with cord. There is a discoloration at the point of binding showing that the wrapped area was 2 cms. long. Steatite pipes from the Chaco area are rather uncommon. The bowl of this one formed an obtuse angle at its juncture with the stem, as may be seen in the illustration.

The stem of a heavy stone pipe was also found in the southwestern part of the room with the one just described. The fragment as found measures 5 cms. in length and 2.6 cms. in diameter. The greater part of the bowl was found in Room 10 (p. 54). Another fragment found with the above is the major portion of the stem and bowl of a pottery pipe. The fragment is a little over 5 cms. in length; the clay is of the usual gray color, covered with a white slip.

The stem and a portion of the bowl of a very short-stemmed pipe completes the list of the pipe fragments from the southwestern part of the room. The specimen in its entirety is 4 cms. long. The stem from the opening in the bowl to the mouthpiece is only 3 cms. in length. The general form and character of the pipe may be seen in Fig. 12c. The surface has been ornamented with black designs. The pipe itself is of the same kind of clay as the one just described and has the white slip upon which the design is painted.

Cloisonné Work. In the same part of the room in which the pipes were found and at about the same depth was a cloisonné object; the base for the design work is composed of sandstone. It is 6 cms. long and the fragment shows a rounding edge. From the contour it appears that the shape had been similar to that of the jar covers. This specimen may have been an ornate form of jar cover that was used in ceremonial observances. A similar specimen was found in another part of the ruin which seems to justify this identification. The work as shown is dissimilar to any known technique of the prehistoric Pueblo Indians. The nearest approach to this style of work is in the Panuco region of the

State of Vera Cruz, Mexico; it has also been found, in both cases on pottery vessels, in the State of Jalisco, Mexico. The designs on the specimen from Room 9 are in black, red, yellow, and white; the colors used to a great extent by the ancient Tarascan Indians of Jalisco. The basic color seems to have been black. This layer was probably allowed

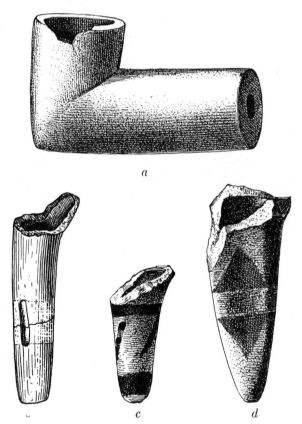

Fig. 12.   Pipes from Rooms 9 and 10.   *a* (773), sandstone;   *b* (769), steatite;   *c* (772), pottery;   *d* (935), pottery.

to dry, after which the designs were formed by cutting out such portions of the black pigment as were to be filled with other colors. The design covers the entire face of the specimen. The rim portion of the design extends over a centimeter on the under part of the object. This specimen is shown in Fig. 13; the shaded portions show the areas occupied by the different colors.

Miscellaneous Objects.   Among the other objects found in the débris from the upper rooms were two pieces of fossil shell and a section of an arm or leg of a pottery figure, probably a human form.   This section is 3 cms. long and of solid construction; it is of grayware and has four black bands spanning a part of its circumference.   An object of antler 4.5 cms. long was made in a flattened cylindrical form and was probably used as a gambling stick.   The remaining objects found in the upper layers were twenty-five small water-worn pebbles and two larger pebbles of the same nature.   The larger ones could have been used for hand hammerstones, but none of these specimens had been worked.

When the floor level was reached two manos and a stone slab, that was evidently used as a lapstone, were found.   All of these specimens were made of close-grained sandstone, the last named specimen having yellow ocher on the surface. There was also in the floor layer a small fossil shell, a chalcedony concretion, and a small hand hammer made of petrified wood.

Pottery Trays.   Two fragmentary bowls of a very interesting form came from the floor deposit; they are of light-colored ware, corrugated on the exterior and smooth on the interior. They were made of a very hard compact pottery and are shaped like the basket trays used by the

Fig. 13   An Example of Cloisonné Work, Room 9.

Pueblo Indians of the present day.   When complete these vessels must have measured at least 25 cms. in diameter and their depth could not have been over 4 cms.   There is a partially smoothed band on the under rim and on the inner rim there is a painted band in black of about the same width.   Corrugated bowls of grayware are found to some extent in the Chaco region, but these incomplete bowls with a few other fragments from other parts of the ruin are the only evidences found of shallow corrugated vessels of this nature.

This room is the first one in which milling stones were found, but owing to the fact that there were no metates it would seem that the manos had been used for other purposes.   The finding of so many pipe fragments and especially the cloisonné object, suggests that the people who occupied this room were closely associated with the ceremonial life of the pueblo.

Room 10.

Room 10 was 13 feet 2 inches long on the north side, 12 feet 6 inches on the south, 8 feet 4 inches on the west, and 7 feet 3 inches on the east. The masonry was similar to that of Room 9. From the evidence obtained in excavating, it appears that the materials from one or more floors were piled upon that of the lower one. The layer containing specimens was over four feet in thickness. Through this, and on the floor itself, were scattered quantities of broken shells and other material.

Pipes. In describing the specimens from this room, the stone pipe, a portion of which was found in Room 9, will be the first to receive attention. Four fragments of the bowl were found in various parts of the room. These pieces have been assembled and with the stem from Room 9 complete the greater part of the pipe as shown in Fig. 12a. The material from which this pipe is made is a compact chert, probably from the cretaceous sandstone of this region. It is 8.2 cms. long and 4.7 cms. high at the bowl end. The stem is 2.7 cms. in diameter at the mouthpiece. The drilling tapers from the mouthpiece to the bowl, decreasing from 1 cm. to 4 mms. in diameter. The diameter of the top of the bowl is 3.2 cms. The peculiar angle of the bowl may be seen in the accompanying illustration. It bends backward upon the stem at quite a noticeable angle. This pipe is particularly massive for this region, but several of a similar nature were found in other parts of the ruin.

Another massive pipe (H-937) of the tubular type was also in a fragmentary condition, the five pieces having been scattered though the débris. Four of these pieces were discolored by fire. The greatest length of this pipe fragment is 5.3 cms., its greatest diameter, 3.9 cms.

Fragments of the bowls of seven pottery pipes, also from the débris, show what seems to be conclusive evidence that these objects were used in ceremonies and then broken. The finding of fragments of pottery pipes would excite no comment, but when massive stone pieces such as the tubular and large pipe with bowl, already described, are found, a reason is naturally sought. These pipes may have been broken in a sacrificial way during some religious ceremony and the fragments preserved either to keep them from being profaned by the hands of those who were not members of the priesthood or else for future ceremonies.

A pottery pipe of rather peculiar form is shown in Fig. 12d. Only a portion of the bowl remains. The fragment in its entirety measures 6 cms. in length; it has evidently been through the fire, but there still remains a broad band design in white on a dark background on the stem which is 2 cms. high and 1.5 cms. broad where it joins the bowl; from this point it tapers to the mouthpiece. Another fragment of a tubular clay pipe is 4 cms. long and 2 cms. in diameter at the bowl end. Unlike most of the tubular pipes, the opening of which tapers from the bowl end to the stem, this pipe has a separate bowl 2 cms. deep, from which a small hole extends toward the mouth end. This specimen is of dark gray and there are no decorations on the surface. Still another fragment of a pipe is represented by a pottery piece which may be a part of one of the long tubular pipes; it is light gray in color and the hole through the stem preserves a uniform diameter of 6 mms. throughout the length of the fragment.

There was another stone pipe of the tubular form (Fig. 19d). It is of easily worked stone, although of fine structure, 5 cms. in length and 2.3 cms. in diameter at the bowl end. The opening tapers from the bowl to the mouthpiece. This pipe was in three pieces when found and the fragments were in different parts of the room; the mouth portion and part of the rim are still missing.

Fig. 14 (977). A Bone Awl of Unusual Form, Room 10. Length, 9.7 cms.

Ceremonial Sticks. Further evidences of a ceremonial nature were the finding of a small ceremonial stick which had been painted a bright green, probably with paint made from malachite; the fragment of a small ceremonial stick, a portion of which is carved in the shape of an hourglass; and the end of one of the large ceremonial sticks, great numbers of which were found in Room 32 (p. 140). The carved portion of this stick was over 12 cms. long, but the specimen in its entirety must have been over 60 cms. in length. There is another stick bound with yucca cord, also a ball of wood 2.5 cms. in diameter. The only remaining object of wood to be noted is a stick 37 cms. long; it was quite thick and had a rounded end, but no evidence of its function could be found.

Miscellaneous Objects. Animal bones of various kinds were represented and there were two bone implements, presumably awls. One of these (Fig. 14) is an uncommon form and may have been used as a hairpin or for fastening garments, as similar objects were formerly used by the Inca of Peru. This specimen is 9.7 cms. long, the head measuring 1.3 cms. in width. The greatest thickness of this specimen is only 3 mms. If the lower or pointed half of this implement were cut off, it would be almost a duplicate of the other specimen mentioned.

The lower jaw of a beaver was made into a pendant, the condyle having been removed, the irregular edges ground smooth, and a hole drilled through the upper part. A large bear claw, found near the floor level, shows no evidence of having been used, but it may have been attached to some ceremonial object by means of a strip of buckskin.

A peculiar object made of antler is shown in Fig. 15a; it is 7 cms. long and 2.3 cms. in diameter at the central part. It tapers toward either end and is similar in form to the corks that professional runners carry in their hands. The use of this object by the Pueblo Indians is unknown. Fragments of turquoise objects and turquoise matrix, chalcedony concretions of small size, gypsum, chalcedony flakes, obsidian flakes, a mass of malachite, limonite, and a number of natural pebbles constitute the stone and mineral products as represented by this room.

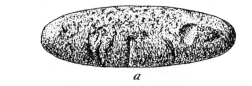

a

b

Fig. 15. Objects of Unknown Use: *a* (1065), antler, Room 10; *b* (5082), chipped stone, Room 37. Length of *a*, 7 cm.

The breast bones of nine turkeys were scattered in the débris, but none of them show signs of having been worked. Two pieces of limonite show evidences of having been worked and one was evidently intended for a pendant.

Sacrificial Breaking. It seems that the breaking of specimens was not confined to the pipes, for among the 180 arrow points found in the deposit there is hardly one that is not misshapen or broken. The majority of them show clean breaks as though the points had been snapped between the fingers. A portion of a chalcedony knife shows evidence of having withstood extreme heat, the break in this specimen also is clean as though it had been made intentionally.

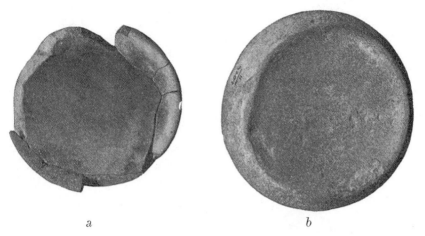

a   b

Fig. 16.   Shallow Stone Mortars: a (1150), Room 10;   b (5204), Room 38.

a   b   c

Fig. 17.   Grooved Hammers and an Arrow Polisher: a (1164), Room 10;   b (2733), Room 20;
c (4156), Room 29.

57

The breaking of ceremonial material is responsible for the fragmentary condition of a ceremonial mortar shown in Fig. 16a. This mortar was made from a cherty nodule and is 18.3 cms. in diameter at the top, the rim being 3.5 cms. high. It is beautifully smoothed on both the top and bottom, and the side slopes gently outward from the base. A slight depression near the edge of the upper part causes a rim, which would retain paint or other material that was being ground. Its last use prior to its destruction was the grinding of red ocher, traces of which still remain upon the surface. Shallow mortars of various forms are represented from this pueblo, but most of them are made of a much softer stone than that employed in making the specimen in question. The bottom and four pieces of the rim were found in Room 10; two of the largest pieces were found in the débris in Room 9.

There are several other stone objects evidently of a ceremonial nature, but as only fragments of them remain it is impossible to say what they represented. One, whose cross-section is wedge-shaped, having a length of over 12 cms., seems to have been a ceremonial knife. There are fragments of two other objects of similar form; other objects either broken or in a fragmentary condition, are two blade ends of a jasper implement, broken in three pieces and discolored by fire; a broken stone jar cover; fragment of a pottery shoulder, evidently of a human effigy vase; the broken handle of a pottery vessel; and a natural pebble which shows the action of fire.

Among the perfect implements were three crude grinding stones; one of fine grained sandstone which had been worn smooth on both sides, two rasping implements of white sandstone, two hand hammers, one made from hard compact sandstone, the other from a natural pebble, and a hard close-grained stone with grooves which had been used in sharpening bone and stone implements. Of the unworked objects there was a cup-shaped concretion, five natural pebbles, a piece of petrified wood, and a stone on the surface of which were rows of black crystals.

A lapstone whose surface has been used to such an extent that it is as smooth as though the polishing had been intentional was broken into three pieces. Fire has left its mark on this specimen, especially near the edges. The stone, when perfect, was over 28 cms. long, 16 cms. wide, and 4 cms. thick.

A large metate shows no evidence of fire, but one end has been broken in such a way that it seems intentional. It is of the usual slab form, common to the Chaco region, and the worn surface is not very deep; both sides, however, have been used. In one part of the room a thick red pigment was found; it had evidently been a covering for some ceremonial object, presumably on cloth; certain portions of this were painted with green. Pigments of the same color and consistency were found in place on the floor of Room 13 and will be described in detail with the other material from that room.

Problematic Objects. Ceremonial objects play a prominent part in the life of any Indian tribe and in the old ruins many objects of this nature are encountered. Their uses cannot always be determined, but the method employed in the manufacture of the material can as a rule be ascertained. Yet specimen H-968 presents an object, probably ceremonial in nature, that almost defies explanation. In shape it is like the basal end of an arrow point; it is porous and the specific gravity is so low that it floats readily on the surface of water. The inner structure is a pure crystalline white; the surface, however, presents a vitreous appearance and is slightly darker in color. The material is so light that it can be crushed between the fingers; from its appearance it would seem that it would fuse quite readily, but when put under the blow-pipe it required a heat of over 1500 degrees to make any impression on it whatever. Even then the result was merely the appearance of a few beads on the extreme edges of the detached fragment. The conclusion derived from blow-pipe analysis is that it is an extremely hard silica formation, volcanic in origin. From the appearance of the object it would seem that the material had been formed into this shape while in a fused condition. There are two points and fragments of two others of a similar material, but instead of being white they are black and have an appearance of porous volcanic glass. These objects float.

Stone Objects. A metate which was probably used for ceremonial purposes is shown in Fig. 18b. It is 45 cms. long, 26 cms. at one end, and 24 cm. at the other, with a uniform thickness of 3 cms. There is a groove for grinding which is 14 cms. wide and 28 cms. long at the narrow end of the stone. There is a depression which was no doubt used for holding the materials to be ground. The bottom and sides of this depression are worn perfectly smooth. The grinding trough still shows a pecked surface in all parts save the central. The rectangular depression at the narrow end may have been used as a mortar; if so, the grinding has been very uniform, as the bottom is quite regular. Ceremonial metates are not uncommon from Pueblo Bonito and a number of them will be described from other rooms.

A double pointed hammer is shown in Fig. 17. It is 14 cms. long and has a deep groove in the central portion. This object was made from a piece of volcanic rock and great care has been exerted in fashioning it. On either side of the groove is a ridge, flattened on three parts of its circumference, the flattened places being equidistant. One end of this implement is broken.

a   *b*

Fig. 18.   A Stone Slab and a Metate: *a* (2737), Room 20; *b* (1162), Room 10.

As though to account for the great mutilation of both the ceremonial and utilitarian objects in this room, we have twenty-three grooved hammerstones. Most of these hammers were made of natural pebbles, quite uniform in size. The greatest extremes in length are 12 and 6.5 cms. The grooves have been pecked quite deep and encircle the entire stone. In three of the specimens the groove is more shallow, only the edges being pecked deeply. Some of them have been used to a great extent, but most of them show no signs whatever of battering, they may therefore have been used for the ceremonial breaking or "killing" of the objects found in this and nearby rooms.

Among the objects which were undoubtedly broken to procure material for making ceremonial and other objects were over twenty-three fragments of *murex* and *strombus* shells, probably brought from the Pacific coast; most of them had been broken into small pieces. Associated with these pieces of shells were fifty-eight fossil shells composed of *spirifers* and other bivalves.

There was one piece of aragonite, worked to a considerable extent, the outer rim of which had been colored by iron-oxide through infiltration. It was concavo-convex in form, the convex side having received the greatest amount of polishing. It is similar to two other specimens found in this ruin. One of them, which was made of pottery, will be described under Room 80. It had been drilled for suspension, but whether the specimen from Room 10 had been drilled cannot be ascertained as the fragment is evidently but a small portion of the complete object.

Room 11.

Room 11, just east of Room 10, is another member of the series of lateral rooms under consideration. It was found to be 13 feet 5 inches on the north wall, 15 feet 8 inches on the south, 7 feet 9 inches on the east, and 6 feet 8 inches on the west. The upper rooms had fallen, leaving only the lower one to be considered. Its original height from the floor to the ceiling beams was 6 feet. Artifacts were found in the upper layers and it was not until the floor layer was reached that the few specimens found in the room were obtained.

Among these were two manos, one of which had been used for grinding red paint and a piece of calcite, two surfaces of which had been ground either to obtain the material for other uses, or else the stone had been worn away while the implement was being used as a polisher.

There were two pieces of turquoise matrix, a semicircular stick evidently used for ceremonial purposes, which was 8 cms. from end to end. Midway between the ends a hole had been drilled. There were a number of twigs bent in a circular form, but they were so rough and in such a broken condition that their use could not be determined. There was also the handle of a pottery dipper of the usual grayware, a number of bird bones, two bone awls made from splinters of deer bone, and the end of a pottery pipestem.

Room 12.

Room 12, directly east of Room 11, contained a mass of material, probably used for ceremonial purposes. It was rectangular in form, measuring 12 feet 6 inches on the north side, 12 feet 4 inches on the south, 9 feet on the east, and 8 feet 2 inches on the west. It may be well to state, before entering upon the consideration of the materials that were found in this room, that the walls of this series were standing to a much greater height at this point than in any of the other rooms described. The specimen-bearing layer was 5 feet deep, showing that the materials from two or more rooms had been added to the deposit on the floor of the lower room. When the lower floor was reached the distance from it to the top of the north wall was over 14 feet.

Pebbles and Fossil Shells. Of the great variety of objects in Room 12, fossil shells were the most numerous. There were over a thousand of these small fossils, many of them covered with red and yellow ocher. One of these shells (H-2552) had been drilled, no doubt for suspension, but it was the only one found in the room that showed any evidences of having been worked. The grooving of the hinge part may have been a secondary consideration, but in its present state it has the appearance of an owl's head. The openings formed by the drilling represent the eyes, the beak is formed by the point of the hinge, and the mouth represented by the hinge itself which had been accentuated by grinding. The feathers are represented by the natural fluting on the sides of the shell. The shells found in this room are from the coal measures and are composed of *spirifers* and other small bivalves. Another fossil that seemed to appeal to the Indians was the crinoid stem, over 300 fragments of this material being found. There are no evidences that these stems have been worked, but as is the case with the fossil shells, many of them still retain a coating of red and yellow ocher. A great many large and small water-worn pebbles had been collected and were found in the débris. There were over 140 of these stones, but very few of them had been used in any way that left its mark upon the surface. If they were used in a ceremonial way it must have been without any ocherous decorations as none of them show traces of this paint. Cushing states that water-worn pebbles were used as water-guides and that many of the old irrigating ditches in the Zuñi region had lines of pebbles along their banks, their office being to guide the water in the direction required. The pebbles found in rooms that contain ceremonial material may have been used in a similar way in some ceremony pertaining to the water supply or irrigation. Natural pebbles are used at the present time on the altars in some of the Pueblo ceremonies, but never in great numbers.

From the appearance of the stones found in this room it would seem that they had been selected for their peculiar forms, or for the beauty of their structure. There were between fifty and seventy-five pieces, including masses of quartz crystals, quartz containing iron pyrites, quartz crystals stained with copper salts, large quartz crystals in single form and in groups, large pyramidal calcite crystals, masses of iron ore showing iron pyrites and other crystals, a piece of goethite, iron-oxide belonging to the hematite family, and water-worn pebbles of chalcedony. These, with pieces of petrified wood and variously colored clays from the "Bad Lands," complete the list.

Chalcedony concretions were also well represented, there being more than 125 pieces, ranging in size from a mass weighing two pounds, to small delicately formed lace-like pieces. Shell fragments, mostly of the murex, were associated with these specimens. These shells probably came from the California coast. There were 125 fragments, but no whole shells were found.

A number of chalcedony and other stone chips were found, and six perfect arrow points and fragments of four others.

There were two clusters of quartz crystals, one of which was covered with red ocher and the other with some black material. Red ocher is sometimes deposited on quartz crystals by nature, but the appearance of this material suggests that it had been applied by the Indians. What the black material is cannot be stated, but there is a bubbling spring situated near the "Bad Lands," about twenty-five miles from Pueblo Bonito, which exudes a black liquid. The Navajo state that this material has been used by them in a ceremonial way for many years; it may be that the black deposit on these crystals is composed of the same material.

Broken Pipes. Five pipes were found in this room, all of them broken. Four were made of pottery and one of stone. The stone pipe is of tubular form and was found in a fragmentary condition as shown in Fig. 19f. It measures 5 cms. in length and 2.6 cms. in diameter at its widest part which is at the point where the bowl begins. The pipe is flattened, the shorter axis, at the point just mentioned, being 2.2 cms.; the material is aragonite. The hole in the stem maintains a uniform diameter throughout its length. The stem of another tubular pipe (H-2576) was found. It is 6 cms. long and 1.8 cms. in diameter at the bowl end.

Another pipe with a different style of bowl is shown in Fig. 20b. The pipe is of undecorated clay. The length of the fragment is 4 cms.; the stem is 1.8 cms. in diameter, and the flaring bowl measures 3.5 cms.

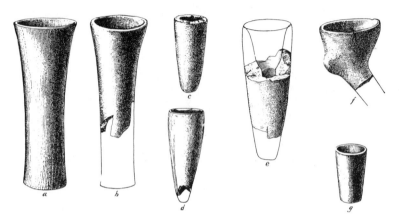

Fig. 19. Types of Stone Pipes; *a* (5110), Room 38; *b* (5112), Room 38; *c* (7209); *d* (952), Room 10; *e* (2570), Room 12; *f* (2880), Room 26; *g* (5109), Room 38.

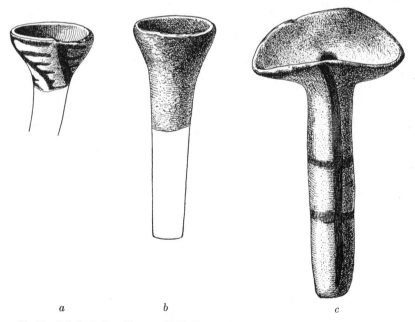

Fig. 20. Tubular Pottery Pipes: *a* (8117), Room 105; *b* (2571), Room 12; *c* (2569), Room 12.

at the rim. The bowl is very shallow, as the illustration shows, and from the discoloration it is safe to assume that it has been smoked.

A pipe of slightly different form is shown in Fig. 20c. It is made of clay covered with a white slip and has a decoration in black extending to the rim of the bowl. The decoration, as shown in the illustration, is composed of two lines which extend from the bowl to the mouthpiece on opposite sides of the stem and are joined by two other lines which encircle the pipe. On the under side there are additional lines, one set near the stem and the other near the bowl. The stem of the pipe has a decided curve and is flattened laterally. The measurements at its central part are 1.6 cms. by 1.8 cms. The bowl is flaring, but is flattened laterally in conformity with the stem. The rim is outlined with a line of black paint. The measurements of the bowl from rim to rim are 3.1 cms. by 5.6 cms., it is 1.5 cms. deep at the central part. The hole in the stem is quite large for a pottery pipe; it is irregular in form, its average diameter being 5 mms., the same size of opening being preserved throughout its length. The flaring bowl brings up a question as to the use of this pipe for ordinary smoking purposes. The flattening of the bowl would not admit of the use of much tobacco, and it is a question whether it could be smoked at all in such a shallow bowl. Again, the form of the bowl suggests the squash flower, the emblem used on the end of flutes and in certain ceremonial objects among the Hopi. The squash flower is a symbol of purity among these Indians and it may be that this pipe was used as a "Cloud-blower" in some ceremony of purification or in consecrating sacred paraphernalia.

A tubular clay pipe (H-2573) was found crushed into a score of fragments. The parts that could be put together give a fragment 8 cms. in length so that in its entirety it must have been several centimeters longer. From the fragments of the bowl it would seem that this part had been over 3 cms. in diameter. The clay is dark in color and the surface, a glossy black; its general appearance suggests pipes made by the Indians of some of the northern Rio Grande pueblos of the present day.

Miscellaneous Objects. A few bird bones were found in the room, also four bone awls. One of these was made from a splinter of deer bone and was very crude; two of the others were of the same material. One of them was merely a fragment, the point end, and showed that, like the other specimens in question, the point had been long and tapering. The fourth was a slender tapering perforator, made of deer bone, 12.2 cms. long and 3 mm. in diameter at the central part. This specimen

(H-2547) has been carefully smoothed and still retains a slight polish. The prong of a deer antler and the end of a crudely made ceremonial stick were found. The antler, at the point where it had been severed, had been ground until the end was perfectly flat.

Slabs of gypsum were found in the débris, also crystals of azurite and malachite. A piece of trachyte with a layer which had formed a part of a vein of turquoise attached; a peculiar sandstone concretion the base of which had been ground into circular form; a drilled limestone concretion, drilled for suspension and a torpedo-shaped piece of quartz crystal, ground into shape; two rectangular sets, or inlays, probably from a mosaic; a small shell inlay, probably for the same purpose; a fragment of a shell ornament; and a bead made of an *olivella* shell completes the list of smaller objects.

Fig. 21 (2548)
Drill Point, Room 12.

One drill made of chalcedony was found; it is 4.5 cms. in length and is shown in Fig. 21.

A dried frog was found in the débris, but whether it had been used by the old people or had found its way into the room after it had been abandoned cannot be stated.

There was one piece of pottery (H-2517) made of the usual gray material covered with a white slip. The vessel consists of three bowls joined together in the form of a clover-leaf. The rims of these bowls are outlined with black paint and there are decorations in the same paint on the interior of each bowl. The individual bowls average 5.5 cms. in diameter and 3 cms. in depth. One of these has a design composed of cross-hatching, forming a sort of lattice work figure. Another has a series of four rings which encircle the bowl; the third has a series of five triangles extending from the rim toward the center, each of these being filled with lines giving a hachure effect. Vessels of this nature are used by the Hopi at the present time for holding different colored paints, and this specimen retains a coating of green paint made from malachite.

Among the larger stone implements were two hammerstones of natural pebbles; a hammerstone of compact sandstone; a grooved stone hammer; a small lapstone made from a flat, water-worn pebble; a small sandstone slab; and the end of a moccasin-shaped stone. This was a large specimen, the rounding portion of the toe having the peculiar jog which is so prominent in specimens of this type from the cliff ruins of Utah and Colorado. It measures 15 cms. in width at its widest part and its greatest thickness is 1 cm. It is made of fine compact sandstone and has been carefully ground and smoothed (H-2577).

An object resembling a stone hoe was found. It is made of hard cherty sandstone and is shown in Fig. 22. It is 16.5 cms. long and 11 cms. in width at the widest part. It is made from a thin plate of sandstone, the greatest thickness being 1.2 cms. The cutting edge is slightly chipped, as are also certain other portions of the edge. The grooves in the edge of the stone for attachment to a wooden handle have been broken and left in a very crude state. The sides of the implement show no work whatever and from the condition of the edge it appears that it had not been used to any extent.

Fig. 22. Stone Hoes and a Dressed Stone: *a* (2606), Room 12; *b* (5220), Room 38; *c* (5101), Room 37.

Room 13.

Room 13 had suffered from fire, the eastern and part of the southern walls having crumbled from the effects of the heat. The room was 8 feet 6 inches long and 8 feet 4 inches wide. It contained a number of bird and animal bones, but none of them had been worked. Fragments of pottery bowls were scattered through the débris near the floor. They were bowls of small size, averaging about 12 cms. in diameter and of the type having a black design on the interior and outer rim. All of the fragments have dots or lines on the edge of the rim, and the pottery itself is of a very fine compact ware. One of the fragments has two handles near the rim which would show that originally there had been four. Fragments of another bowl bear painted designs in the form of bird feet. There was one fragment of red ware with black interior which seems to have been part of a very deep bowl of the type that widens gradually from the base to the rim.

There were eighteen arrow points in the floor deposit, all but two of obsidian. These points are of the usual tapering type.

Among the other objects of general interest was a natural quartzite pebble; a fragment of a highly polished stone object; a number of thin sheets of mica; a piece of cannel coal; and a small transparent quartz crystal.

Altar Painting. When the floor level in the eastern part of the room was reached, several detached pieces of red pigment were found; they bore on their under surface the imprint of cloth. Further investigation showed that these were the remains of a ceremonial object, oval in form. The greater part of the original pigment remained in position and it was thought desirable to endeavor to solidify the mass of sand upon which it rested in order to transport the object to the Museum. To do this the individual pieces which had curled from the heat of the burning room were moistened with a solution of gum arabic and allowed to fall back into place. When this was accomplished the entire surface was soaked with a solution of the same material. When the solution had penetrated to a depth of over an inch, layers of cheese-cloth were soaked in a solution of glue and applied to the surface, the cloth being carried to within an inch of the edge of the pigment area; the next step was the cutting away of the sides. When this was completed it was found that decayed vegetable matter formed part of the deposit which left openings which had to be filled with the cement composed of sand and glue. It required the greater part of a week for the solution to dry and before it was safe to turn the solidified mass of sand on edge. When this was accomplished the under part was covered with the cement of sand and glue and the whole mass, with the exception of the pigment itself, was covered with several layers of cheese-cloth which had been treated in the same manner as the ones previously used. When these had hardened the upper part was covered with layers of cotton batting and the mass enclosed in a box lined with sheepskins. In this condition it reached the Museum, where it is now on exhibition. The pigment-covered textile in its original form was no doubt used for some ceremonial purpose. The cloth was probably made of yucca although no traces of it remained. There are evidences that a band of green pigment had formed a border which encircled the object, but only a small portion of it remains, as before noted. In its present form the pigment averages 3 mms. in thickness.

Shell and Turquoise. Six inches below this object in the northwestern corner of the room a shell trumpet was found. It is the shell of a *strombus,* variety *galeatus* (Swainson) and was probably obtained in exchange from tribes living on the Pacific Coast. In making this trumpet the upper end of the columnella was ground off to form a mouthpiece. About 8 cms. of the lid of the shell was cut away and two holes were drilled near the edge of the remaining portion. These holes were no doubt used for the attachment of a cord by means of which the trumpet was carried. A mouthpiece made of clay, such as has been found on some of the *murex* shell trumpets in this pueblo, was found near by. A fragment of another mouthpiece of similar form was found near the floor level.

A number of fragments of *strombus* shells were scattered through the débris, many of them had been worked on the edges and some were drilled. One in particular has a design in hachure effect on the edge. A section of the edge of a basket bowl retains a covering of red pigment. This material had been applied to both the outer and inner surface of the basket, and may be a portion of one found in a fragmentary condition in an adjoining room.

Fragments of turquoise and small turquoise inlays were found associated with inlays of pink stone, forming rectangular and semicircular inlays, also flat pieces from which these specimens have been cut. There were two circular inlays of this stone. These specimens average 1.1 cms. in diameter. There was another made of jet which was about the same size; with it were a number of irregular jet inlays of angular form. There were three small beads made from azurite and one small bead made from an *olivella* shell.

Room 14.

Room 14, the easternmost of the series under consideration, proved to be one that had suffered greatly from fire. The material with which it was filled bore evidence of the great heat which caused even the walls to crumble. (See p. 283, where this room is numbered 85.) Work in this room was carried to the depth of five feet and then, owing to the ruined condition of the walls, it was decided to discontinue operations. The western part was the only section of the room that received attention, but in it a few specimens were found. One of these was a ceremonial stick with a carved head found in the uppermost layers, showing that it had been in one of the upper rooms and had thereby escaped the fire. There were three *olivella* shell beads, two blackened by fire, and a pottery bowl whose color had also been changed by the heat. This bowl (H-2703) is 12.5 cms. in diameter from rim to rim and 4.5 cms. in depth. The vessel was, no doubt, of the ordinary whiteware with decorations in black. The decorations retain their original color, but the vessel has changed to a dark red cream color. The design is in the form of meanders and dots, and extends to the rim which projects 3 mms. from the edge of the bowl.

Specimens of adobe showing impressions of cornstalks, reeds, and willow stalks which had been used as a part of the ceilings and floors, were taken to show the action of fire. Some of them are burnt to a brick red color, others to a black, probably from the action of dense smoke.

Room 14a. When work in Room 14 was discontinued, it was decided to devote the balance of the season to investigations in other parts of the ruin, but an accident caused the removal of the débris from the room between Room 10 and the room used as our storeroom and kitchen. There was a doorway in the south wall of the room, which will hereafter be known as Room 14b, and after each heavy shower there would be a pool of water on the floor of this room. Filling up the doorway with stones and masonry did not help matters, so the room into which this doorway led was cleared. Room 14a (over 14b) is shown in Fig. 23. The débris from the upper levels was cleared away, disclosing the floor and heavy beams that supported it. These beams spanned the shorter axis of the room, thereby causing them to lie in a north and south direction. The view shown in the photograph is toward the north. The wall in the foreground is of the old type, the stones being irregular in form with unworked edges. The north wall of the room is of a later period, the stones being shorter and thicker and having their faces dressed. Between these stones was chinking, composed of thin laminæ of sandstone. The adobe floor is shown to very good advantage in this picture. The surface was smoothed originally, but in falling from its natural position it cracked to the extent here shown. The material under the adobe was cedar bast, or shredded cedarbark. A very thick layer of this material had been scattered over the floor boards, before the adobe had been applied. These boards are best seen in Fig. 24. They are made of pine and the sides and ends have been carefully ground with sandstone rasps. The poles which upheld the floor boards may be seen directly under them.

The construction of floors of this kind is rather uncommon in Pueblo Bonito, due to the fact no doubt that the manufacture of boards of this nature was a somewhat tedious task. Most of the floors were sustained by poles, willow stalks, or branches with twigs. These are found in various parts of the ruin and will be described as the work progresses.

Room 14b. Room 14b is one of the rooms mentioned in the first part of this report as undoubtedly one of the last ones added to the pueblo before it was abandoned. A view of the north wall of the pueblo, showing the entrance into Room 14b, is shown in Fig. 5. A new type of masonry is shown in the photograph. The finishing of the larger stones and the chinking of the layers received the most careful attention from the old masons. In the section of wall shown, three doorways appear, which were closed at the time the wall was built.

Architecture. The ceiling of this room is worthy of attention. The room is rectangular and its longer axis is east and west. The beams ran in the opposite directions, their ends entering the north and south walls. The ceiling beams are made of pine and above them rested a layer of individual willow stalks. The ceiling as here shown (Fig. 25) is one of the most ornate found in the pueblo. The bark had been removed from the ceiling beams and also from the willow stalks, causing them to appear in strong contrast with the dark walls which surrounded them.

The southern wall was in a good state of preservation, plaster half an inch thick covered the greater part, and scratched into the soft surface were numerous names and dates, showing that the room had been open for years. Where the plaster had been torn off, the wall, thus presented to view, was made of large stones, the chinks being filled with thin pieces of sandstone. The doorway was plastered on the sides and the lintel composed of seven poles, 2½ inches in diameter and laid close together. The facing of the doorway was square, but the plaster had been rounded a trifle. The wall was bulged to some extent at the eastern end, but not enough to crack the plaster.

The northern wall was in good condition but almost all of the plaster had been washed off. This wall was similar in construction to the southern one, having large stones with the interstices chinked with smaller ones that often formed layers 2 inches thick, but it was not the regular layer wall. About 1 foot west of the doorway, and running from the floor to the ceiling in a zigzag line, was a crack that opened over 1 inch in some places. The doorway was a little to the east of the center and the bottom was 11 inches above the present floor level—the original floor was probably 1 foot or 1½ feet lower than the present one, which is the

Fig. 23. Interior of Room 14a.

72

Fig. 24.   Floor Boards in Room 14a.

Fig. 25. Ceiling of Room 14b.

74

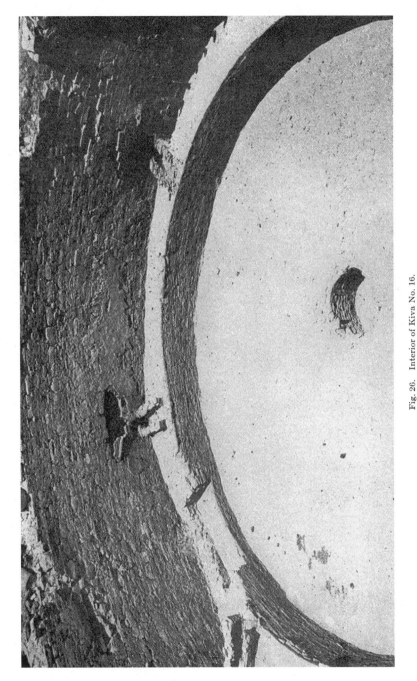

Fig. 26. Interior of Kiva No. 16.

75

Fig. 27.   Bench and Row of Sticks in Kiva No. 16.

76

Fig. 28.   Niche in Bench, South Side of Kiva No. 16.

77

Fig. 29. Metates in Room 17.

78

débris that has accumulated. All the measurements were made to the present floor surface; therefore, in order to get the exact height, the above-mentioned distance must be added. The lintel of the doorway was composed of logs about 2 inches in diameter and over 5 feet in length. Three of these are intact, and a fourth has part of the eastern end in position. The sides of this doorway are very even, the chinks being filled with such care that the present surface is almost smooth and devoid of open spaces. The sides had originally been plastered, as had also the bottom. The lintel was no doubt originally as it now appears.

The wall at the side of the doorway is 2 feet 4 inches thick, the outer part forming the exterior wall of the building. The eastern wall still retains most of its external plaster, but it is seared with marks, and water has greatly roughened the surface. It is composed of the same material as the sides of the room, and is built after the same fashion.

The lintel of the doorway is composed of round poles, 3½ inches in diameter, that reach across the room, the ends being buried in the side walls. Originally there were three, but only the front pole now remains intact; this doorway was also plastered, but only small pieces now cling to the sides. The wall at the side of the doorway is 1 foot 6 inches thick.

The western wall had a large crack running from the northern end of the upper part of the doorway to the ceiling; otherwise, the wall was in a fair condition of solidity. The plaster adhered to the stones over the greater part of the surface; the wall was of the same material and construction as the other three. The doorway, as in the other cases, had been plastered, but very little of the plaster remained. The lintel was composed of five sticks, about 2 inches in diameter, laid so as to touch each other. For some reason this doorway had been walled up and plastered to a distance of 10 inches from the present floor level, which would be over 2 feet from the original floor. The wall on the side of the doorway was 1 foot 6 inches thick.

Ceiling Structure. The ceiling of this room is composed of logs that measure from 4 to 6 inches in diameter. These run transversely and are from 2 to 3 inches apart. They are imbedded in the masonry with small pieces of sandstone packed around each end. The fifth and sixth logs from the western end have been removed; otherwise, the ceiling is in good condition. Above these logs, and resting on them, are small willow sticks, these measure from 3 to 4 feet in length, and most of them are but a trifle over ⅜ inch in diameter. These sticks are placed so close together that it would have been almost impossible to find a place large enough to insert a pencil when the ceiling was new. The number lying side by side in a section about the center of the room were counted and it was found that there were one hundred and sixty-three. Resting on these willows was a layer of cedarbark that supported the adobe floor of the room above.

The entrance to the upper room is situated in the southern corner. From the appearance of the ends of the two logs that have been cut off, one would be led to think that this opening had been made after the completion of the ceiling. The ends of the logs are very irregularly cut and on the under part are places where pieces have been stripped off as though the operation had been a difficult one.

Running parallel with the large timbers, but above the small sticks, are flat willows lying with the rounded side up; these are so placed that they occupy a space equidistant from the large beams; over these split pieces, at intervals of about 6 inches, are strips of yucca leaves, some of which have the ends tied. There are one hundred and fifty-one of these strings pendent from the ceiling, and it is highly probable that the room was used for drying meats or produce. The large beams were of pine and spruce, pine predominating. All of the pieces are bright and clean, and are entirely devoid of bark. They are all sections of young trees and were peeled while the bark was green. Some of them are badly checked, but the majority are quite solid. The small sticks are all individual willow growths, carefully peeled, and the butt end of each stick ground until it presented a flat surface. This was probably done with a piece of sandstone. Some of the willows measure ½ inch at the butt end, but most of them are under this figure. All of them taper, but each one has the whip end removed. In placing these sticks the butt ends were laid in a line, when the next layer was put in position, with a lap of about 2 inches. This form of ceiling was solid and compact, and, from an aesthetic standpoint, the finest found in the ruins.

Room 15.

Very little work was done in Room 15, in fact, only a few feet of earth were removed. Developments in Room 16 necessitated transferring the men from Room 15 and the ceremonial problems presented by this and nearby rooms and the attempt to ascertain the character of rooms in various parts of the ruin, employed all the time that remained in the season of 1896.

The investigations in the following years carried the work to the walls of Room 15, but the room itself, with the northern part of the ruin, has never received attention.

Room 16.

Kiva. The great central court of Pueblo Bonito is divided into two parts by a single series of rooms extending from an estufa (kiva) situated near the southern wall of the pueblo, northward to another estufa, directly in front of the semicircle formed by what was no doubt once the terraced part of the pueblo. This estufa will be known as Room 16; its exact position in the ruin may be seen in the diagram (Fig. 155).

This room was filled with débris when the work was begun, but it proved to be mostly of drift sand and portions of burnt ceiling timbers. Nothing of importance was found in the débris, with the exception of an obsidian arrow point of the usual tapering form; an ornament of stone made from a natural concretion; and a fragment of a mano made from honey-combed volcanic scoria. The room, after the débris had been removed, is shown in Fig. 26, which gives a general idea of its floor space, structure, and general appearance, but the individual parts can be seen to better advantage in the sectional photographs which precede. The diameter of the floor space was found to be 20 feet 6 inches; this, with the benches, gave a diameter of 24 feet 7 inches from face to face of the enclosing wall.

The room itself was well built, of the usual circular type; the wall was intended to be perpendicular and in most cases was almost so. Originally it was plastered, the coating which may still be seen in places, being half an inch in thickness. The bench that surrounded the entire circle was of uniform height, except on either side of the niches at the north and south, where it was slightly lower than the other parts, the descent being gradual and although not great, was readily seen. This bench was made of carefully selected stones; they range from 2 inches to over a foot in length and were on an average 1 inch thick. They were of the usual gray sandstone and were laid with a thin plaster, but so close that the space between them was hardly noticeable. On the surface of the wall face of this bench there was a layer of pure white plaster which was in some places fully 3 inches thick. The plaster on the main wall was of the ordinary brown variety and therefore the white must have stood out in strong contrast.

There were fourteen sticks imbedded in the bench at the southeastern part of the estufa. They were greatly decayed and had been broken to within a foot of the bench level. Their diameter, as near as one can judge from the decayed pieces that remained, must have been originally over 5 cms. These sticks stand in a line, following the contour

of the wall and are on an average about 18 cms. apart and 13 cms. from
the main wall. The use of these sticks cannot be given. Uprights in
pairs are used in some of the modern estufas as loom supporters, a great
deal of weaving being done by the men when no ceremonies are in progress, a use for such a series as is here presented does not suggest
itself.[1]

The southeastern part of the estufa showing the bench, two beam
supports, and the fourteen sticks is shown in Fig. 27. This picture gives a
good idea of the stones employed in the building of the wall and bench.

There were niches in the bench at the north and south side of the
estufa as shown in Fig. 28. The one in the north end was 20 cms. above
the floor, whereas the one at the south side started at the floor level
(Fig. 28). These openings virtually divided the bench into two sections
or semicircles and on each of these divisions there were three supports
for pillars. These supports average 65 cms. in length, 50 cms. in width,
and were 31 cms. in height. They were built around and over circular
logs made from trees having the heart intact and the sides and upper
part were plastered. These supports were built of small pieces of sandstone, thereby making a very compact mass, as the stones were readily
fitted to the rounding portion of the log and conformed to any irregularities that were presented. The logs were from 13 to 16 cms. in diameter,
and extended from the face of the support to a point nearly a meter
beyond the face of the estufa wall. Directly back of these supports there
have been rectangular openings which have had poles across the top
similar to the lintels of doorways. These openings may have been made
that the beams might be set in the main wall, but the reason for placing
the poles over them cannot be conjectured. All of these openings had
been filled with masonry similar to that of the surrounding wall area.
The openings averaged 81 cms. in width and the poles which spanned
their upper parts were from 47 to 63 cms. above the top of the bench.
Most of the poles had been destroyed by fire.

---

[1]One of the Navajo workmen employed in excavating this estufa, said that the meaning was quite
plain to him as he had heard the old medicinemen of the Navajo describe such poles as having been
used by the old Pueblo people. His explanation, although bearing little weight in a scientific way, was
nevertheless interesting.   He said that they had originally projected 1.26 m. above the bench level,
and then, regardless of the fact that he was supposed to be explaining a Pueblo altar, be proceeded to give
the Navajo names of the gods as represented by the sticks.   It is well-known that there has been an
interchange of ceremonies between the Navajo and the Pueblo, but it hardly seems possible that Navajo
god-names would be given to prominent objects of this kind in one of their ceremonial rooms.   He said
that beginning with the southern end their names were as follows: First *haste yalte*; second; *haste, yebecae*;
third, *haste yebaad,* and so on through the series using the gods already mentioned until the fourteenth
was reached and this one he named *tonilili,* who is the water-god of the Navajo.   This Navajo said that
the sticks formed the background of an altar, and that a mass of white sand found directly under the
row of sticks was used in making sand or dry paintings in front of the row of gods.

The logs in the supports on the bench, with one exception, had been destroyed by fire, but in the cylindrical openings which remained, a number of interesting objects were found. Beginning with the support at the east, which is numbered, one, the contents of each opening were sifted with the following results:—

No. 1 contained twenty-two turquoise beads, thirteen of which were cylindrical and nine of the usual flat form. There were also ten made from *olivella* shell beads, ten flat stone beads made in the shape of a figure eight, and five shell pendants. All of these specimens had been blackened by fire.

In support No. 2 there were seven cylindrical turquoise beads; ten of the flat circular form, half of which were turquoise; also thirteen stone beads of the figure eight form; seven *olivella* shell beads, and three shell pendants. The objects in this deposit had been so changed by the action of the fire that it was hard to tell in many instances just what the material was.

In support No. 3 there were twenty cylindrical turquoise beads; twelve flat circular beads; twenty-four shell beads of the figure eight form; seventeen *olivella* shell beads, and seven irregular shell pendants, all of which were blackened from the fire.

In support No. 4 there were three cylindrical turquoise beads, and two of the flat circular form, one of which still retains a bright green color. With these were fourteen *olivella* shell beads and twenty-one stone beads in the form of a figure eight. With the exception of the bead mentioned all of the objects were blackened.

In support No. 5 were five cylindrical turquoise beads; one flat circular turquoise bead; two stone beads of the figure eight form; one *olivella* shell bead, and one shell pendant. The specimens in this deposit had evidently been shielded in some way from the fire, for all of them preserved their natural colors, with the exception of a few pieces of turquoise which had become bleached to a certain extent by the fire; none of them, however, were blackened.

In support No. 6 there were two cylindrical turquoise beads; three of the flat circular form; three stone beads of the figure eight shape; fragments of two *olivella* shell beads; and two shell pendants.   The fire had blackened all of these objects, as was the case in most of the other supports.

On the bench between supports No. 3 and No. 4 there were four cylindrical turquoise beads; two of the flat circular form; ten of the figure eight form; ten of the *olivella* shell beads; and one shell pendant. These pieces were lying directly upon the surface of the bench, but originally they may have been covered with plaster. From various other parts of the bench there came one cylindrical turquoise bead; one of the flat circular type; two *olivella* shell beads; and three shell pendants.

Were it not for the fact that other estufas in this ruin had been investigated, the manner of disposing of the objects in the supports would be uncertain. From the investigations, it is safe to assume that these objects had been deposited in a ceremonial way in small openings or depressions which had been prepared for their reception in the top of each log; they were no doubt ceremonial offerings to the house-god, and will be described in detail when Room 67 is being considered.

From the objects found in these deposits it would seem that there had been a reason for selecting certain forms of beads. The cylindrical turquoise bead, although found in other parts of the ruin, is not at all common in this pueblo and yet there were several of these in each support. The *olivella* beads and those of the figure eight form are found in many of the rooms, but the only place in which the irregular shell beads were found in numbers was in one of the burial rooms known as Room 3.

The manner of roofing these ceremonial rooms is interesting to the student of primitive architecture. There were no evidences of ceiling beams save those in a fragmentary condition. They were found, however, in Room 67 where a study of this type of building as shown in Pueblo Bonito will be given.

Owing to the fact that rooms of this type were used for ceremonial purposes, objects, except of a ceremonial nature, are seldom found in the débris, unless as in the case of Room 67 where the estufa has passed into disuse and become a receptacle for sweepings from the rooms and terraces.

All of the estufas excavated in this ruin have a fireplace in the central part, or at least a point near the center of the floor area. The fireplace in this one is nearer the south side, about a meter south of the center. It was over 63 cms. in diameter and its sides had been built up with thin blocks of sandstone, the work being done in a very careful manner.

Room 17.

Metates. A little to the southeast of Room 16 and adjoining it at that side was Room 17. It was the first room on the north of the series that stretched southward across the court. The position of this room may be seen in Fig. 155. The eastern and southern walls had been carried away in the general disintegration of this part of the pueblo, leaving portions of the north and west walls standing. Owing to the fact that there was very little material covering the floor, it was not long after the investigations in the room were begun before the tops of two large metates or grinding stones were found. They proved to be very large ones and when the floor level was reached several others were found partly imbedded in the floor. The room in its entirety is shown in Fig. 29. This view is toward the west, showing the western and northern part of the room. The stone work indicates an intermediate period in the history of the pueblo. The stones are not faced to any extent, but greater care has been used in selecting them than is shown in the older type of walls. White plaster is still in evidence on the lower part of the west and north walls and there were evidences of white meal in all parts of the room.

This was essentially a grinding room and from the evidences it may well have been a room used for the grinding of material to be used in ceremonies. The floor space was almost covered with metates, used to such an extent that the central portions of the troughs had been broken. Three of these may be seen in the foreground; two of them had been placed in such a position that they would catch the meal from one of the larger metates. Between the large grinding stones, a stone slab was let into the floor; it was 94 cms. long, 67 cms. wide, and 3 cms. in thickness. The edges of this slab had been worked by grinding and the surface smoothed to some extent. Directly behind the large milling stone, at the left of the picture, was a small metate. It too had been used until a hole had been worn through the bottom. In its present inverted position it was evidently used as a bench upon which the grinder kneeled. Another broken metate is standing on edge upon this one, and resting against the west wall.

The two large metates seem to have been the only ones in use when the room was abandoned. The larger one, containing three grinding troughs, was a block of hard white sandstone, as were all the other metates in the room. Its length at the widest part is 94 cms., its width 71 cms., and its thickness, 18 cms. The mealing troughs had been worn to an average depth of 8 cms. This metate was covered with a thin layer of cornmeal and under the front part there was quite a deposit of the same material. The metate containing four depressions was 76 cms. long, 63 cms. wide and 18 cms. thick, the depth of the troughs averaging 8 cms. On the floor, which was made of adobe, two perfect and two fragmentary manos were found.

In the northwestern corner of the room directly behind the metate with four depressions, a trumpet made from a *murex* shell was found. The lip had been cut away to some extent and near its upper part two holes had been drilled; one of these had been filled with bitumen or some black gum which is still in place (Fig. 46). Four fragments of *murex* shell were found with the trumpet and judging from the fact that one of these is part of a mouthpiece, it may be the fragments are part of a second trumpet. These were the only small objects found in the room.

Owing to the fact that there is a depression in the court at this point, the southern end of the room has been washed away and its length, therefore, could not be determined. A short distance west of this end of the room, another large metate containing three grinding troughs was found. There is a possibility that it may have been originally one of the grinding implements of Room 17, but from its position it is hardly probable.

Room 18.

Room 18 is an angular room situated at the northeastern side of the square which surrounds Room 16. It is really a room which fills this particular corner. Its longest wall is that on the western side which measures 7 feet 2 inches long, the eastern is 4 feet 11 inches, the north which separates it from Room 19 is 6 feet 2 inches, and the south, where it approaches the arc of the estufa, is 2 feet 6 inches. The walls were standing to a height of 5 feet 7 inches above the floor level.

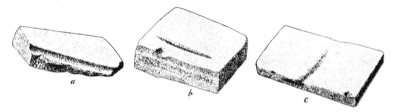

Fig. 30 *abc* (2802, 2804, 2800).   Rubbing Stones, Room 18.

Wood-working. This room was evidently one devoted to the manufacture of wooden objects. Only three specimens of wood were found in the room, one in the shape of a knife, the second a curved ceremonia game stick, and the third a fragment of one of the long ceremonial sticks with carved ends. There was a lapstone made of a hard fine-grained sandstone of a dark color, the surface of which has been smoothed from use. Another large piece of sandstone having a gritty texture and a light color was found on the floor; one surface had been worn as though it had been used for grinding objects of irregular shape. One of the sides, however, was flattened and had no doubt been used as a rasp in grinding the surfaces of wooden slabs or tablets. With these large stones were found twenty-six small implements made of the same gritty sandstone as that described. From their shape and from the various grooves and depressions in their surfaces, it seems quite evident that they comprised the outfit of a wood-worker. A series of these objects is shown in Fig. 30.

There is doubt concerning the use of these small rooms around the estufas. In this case it would seem that they had been devoted to the preparation of materials to be used in ceremonies in the estufa.

Fig. 31. View of Excavated Rooms, surrounding Kiva 16. The curved wall of the kiva may be seen at the left.

87

Fig. 32. Sealed Doorway, Room 20.

Room 19.

Room 19 is north of and adjoins Room 18. Its position in relation to the estufa (Room 16) may be seen in Fig. 31. The room was somewhat irregular in form and the walls were in a rather poor state of preservation. This part of the building had once been an old estufa which had passed into disuse and the space had been divided into small rooms. In these small rooms were found five manos, two large metates and three grinding stones; a small sandstone slab, probably used as a lapstone, one surface of which shows continued use; three sandstone jar covers; three hammerstones, such as are used for pecking the surface of stone implements; pieces of turquoise and azurite; a fossil shell; the fragment of a clay pipe; three arrow points; and two bone awls. There was a narrow passageway leading northward from the small rooms and in it four metates, two manos, and two rubbing stones were found. From the condition of the room it would seem that it was but little used.

Room 20.

In an endeavor to determine the character of the material in various parts of the ruin, the operations were shifted from the northwestern part of the pueblo to the eastern and southwestern parts. The first work was done in Room 20, which, as shown by the plan (Fig. 155), is situated in the northeastern part of the ruin. This room was almost square, the measurements showing the north wall to be 12 feet 6 inches long, the south wall 12 feet 3 inches, the east wall 10 feet, and the west wall 10 feet 7 inches. The masonry was of a solid compact form and was in many respects similar to that shown in the northern series of rooms; that is, the rooms of the later period. The stones employed were of the short thick form and the spaces between them were chinked with the same material, but the work in its entirety was not as carefully done as that shown in the outer rooms. The difference, however, may be due to individual skill, as the technique is the same. The walls retain a goodly portion of the original plaster. There was a doorway in the north wall, as well as one in the west. The one in the north wall was rectangular and steps made of stones covered with adobe were used as an approach to it. This was necessitated by the fact that the doorway was some distance above the floor level. These steps were still in place and were well preserved.

Doorways. The doorway in the west wall as shown in Fig. 32 had been filled with masonry and the interior plastered, forming a niche. This doorway is rectangular, having poles for a lintel and a slab of sandstone for a sill.   This slab projected some distance from the wall and thereby formed a shelf and was no doubt used as such after the doorway was closed.   The plaster on the sides of the doorway was thick and thus enabled the builders to round the corners in a very artistic way.   The greater part of this plaster was in place on the south side of the doorway. (The objects on the stone slab, as shown in the photograph, were found on the floor of the room).   The room was excavated to a depth of 12 feet before the floor was reached.   It seems to have been abandoned and used as a receptacle for refuse.

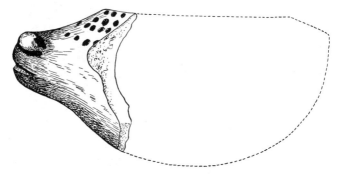

Fig. 33 (2731).   Fragment of a Bowl, Room 20.

Broken Metate.   Perhaps the most interesting object found in the débris was a broken metate of the usual form.   It was in a fragmentary condition and the seven pieces recovered were found scattered through the material that filled the room.   Some of the pieces were near the surface, others came from a point only a few feet from the floor level. It would seem that this metate had been broken and portions of it carried away to be finally thrown into this room.   This seems to be the only way to account for the widely separated fragments.   The stone itself is 65 cms. long and averages 45 cms. in width; there is however, a slight taper from top to bottom.   The trough is 47 cms. long, 26 cms. wide, and 3.5 cms. deep at it deepest part.   The area surrounding the central portion is decorated with a scroll design which has been pecked into the surface.   There are no decorations on the edges nor on the back.   The trough is covered with red paint showing that this material was probably the last to be ground, or perhaps mixed in the trough before it was broken.   The slab is of hard compact sandstone, and its greatest thickness is 5 cms.

Pottery. Among the pottery objects of special interest was a corrugated jar 5.5 cms. deep and 4.4 cms. in diameter near the mouth. This jar was made of light colored clay and is a perfect reproduction in miniature of the large storage jars made of the same material.

The head of a vessel made in the shape of a frog is shown in Fig. 33. The material is a light colored clay and the decoration, about the eyes and around the rim, is in black paint. The eyes and mouth are accentuated, the eyes having a bulging form common in the Chaco region.

Among the pottery fragments were several of bowls made of grayware, decorated on the inside and corrugated on the exterior. There were also fragments of corrugated bowls of blackware with a highly polished interior; one fragment has a figure of a snake, or worm, in relief near the edge; there were also fragments that had been worked. There was one object of pottery that had evidently been part of a vessel. This specimen is 24.5 cms. long and 1.6 cms. in diameter. On one side there is a ridge nearly a centimeter in height which is decorated with black dots. The entire length is not shown by these two pieces as there is a section missing. From the rounded ends and from the fact that the inner surface is devoid of the white slip which covers the remaining portions, it would seem that this object had been attached to some figure or vessel. In technique it is similar to the arms of the human effigy vases, but what the form of the vessel was of which this piece was a part, cannot be conceived. There was also an irregular piece of clay which shows the imprint of the hand that pressed it into shape.

Miscellaneous Objects. A great many animal and bird bones, also fragments of deer antler were scattered through the débris, many of them broken to obtain the marrow. These bones ranged from the large vertebrae of deer and elk, to rabbit and small bird bones; fragments of pottery vessels, such as one would expect to find in any refuse heap, were intermingled with the bones. There were nine manos of the ordinary rough form and four of fine-grained sandstone, such as are used in reducing meal to powder. There were also one natural pebble and a few obsidian and chalcedony flakes, two hammerstones made from natural pebbles, a grooved hammerstone, two pecking stones, a polished stone object of a half spherical form, and a stone slab in the shape of a jar cover, evidently used as a base upon which pigment or other materials might be ground. There were two fragments of sandstone implements, one of which was in the form of the end of a knife blade, the other the end of a small sandstone slab; a fragment of the toe part of a sandal stone was also found. Among the larger objects of sandstone was a slab probably used as a lapstone, which is shown in Fig. 18. This specimen is 39 cms. long and 21 cms. wide at the central part, and its average thickness is 1 cm. Both sides of this slab have been worn smooth from use. A sandstone sharpener is shown in Fig. 17. It has three deep grooves and a shallow one upon the surface; one of the deep grooves is carried over the edge to the base of the stone. There was an arrow-smoother, made of coarse-grained sandstone of light color, and another grinding stone of the same material having large grooves on the side. There were only two objects of wood that could be saved. One of these was the socket stick of a fire set, the other a fragment of a rectangular piece, flat, with rounded edges, and with a hole drilled through the center.

Among the mass of bones found in the room there were five sections of bird bone from which pieces had been cut for beads; five beads; and a fragment of a sixth which had been cut from these or similar pieces. There were three bone awls made from splinters of deer bone, also two bone bodkins, and the end of a bone implement shaped like a knife blade. One of the bone awls had a very fine tapering point and the larger of the bodkins had a hole drilled in the end by means of which it could be fastened to the belt of the worker.

Although this was a room used to dump the sweepings from the various houses, there was not the great variety of material in the débris that is generally found in such rooms. Local conditions no doubt account for this rather unusual state of affairs.

Room 21.

Room 21 is situated in the southeastern corner of the pueblo. Excavations were carried to a depth sufficient to enable accurate measurements to be taken of the walls, but owing to the fact that the room had been burnt out the excavation was not completed. The room was almost square, the north wall being 10 feet 2 inches long, the south wall 10 feet, the east wall 10 feet, and the west wall 11 feet. No specimens were found in the débris removed.

Room 22.

Room 22 was next to Room 21 in the southeastern part of the ruin. This room, like its neighbor, seemed unpromising, and was abandoned after a small amount of work had been done. In size it was about the same as Room 21. A number of potsherds were found in the material that was removed, all showing the action of fire. Most of the fragments were of the ordinary grayware decorated with black, but red and blackware were also represented. The only objects of a perishable nature found were a fragment of a carbonized sandal, and a section of an antler. This object, as shown in Fig. 46, had been worked to some extent, but whether it was made for ceremonial or utilitarian purposes is hard to say.

Room 23.

Room 23 is in the southwestern part of the ruin near Room 25. Work on this room was begun at the same time as that in Rooms 24 and 25. The results of the early stages of the work in the other rooms mentioned were so much more promising that Room 23 was abandoned. Nothing of interest was found.

Room 24.

Room 24, in the southeastern part of the ruin, was irregular in form, having a jog in the northeast corner. The north wall was 10 feet 6 inches long and then a jog extended into the room, 3 feet 5 inches southward, then 1 foot 4 inches eastward to the east wall which, from this point to the south wall, is 9 feet 1 inch; the south wall was 12 feet long and the west wall 12 feet 2 inches. The depth to the first floor was 6 inches; below this on the west side were two square rooms with a wall 1 foot 6 inches thick between them; the walls of the southern one had been whitened with a wash, no doubt made from calcined gypsum. The work in these lower rooms, however, was not completed.

Refuse Deposit. This room is another of the type that had been abandoned as a living room and used as a place for refuse. The specimens were scattered through the mass from the uppermost part to the floor level, and extended to the lower layers of the two rooms below. It is a typical refuse room, containing a varied assortment of articles.

Among the perishable objects were pieces of rush matting of a coarse type, all twilled. Two badly decayed fragments of a very fine mesh matting may have been the ends of pillow covers such as are found in the cliff-houses farther north.

Sandals. There were two sandals made of braided leaves of the broad-leafed yucca having yucca strands for fastening the sandals to the foot. The toe of these sandals was rounding and there was no evidence of a jog such as is shown in three sandals made of split yucca leaves probably of the narrow-leafed variety. All three of these specimens had the jog at the toe end, also two-strand yucca cords for fastening them to the foot. There is quite a difference in the manner of fastening these sandals to the toe as is shown in Fig. 34. In Fig. 34a there are straps of yucca which probably slipped over the great and the third toes. There is another cord at the heel which evidently tied about the ankle. In Fig. 34c there is a strap through which the big toe probably passed; from this two yucca cords were carried to the ankle and fastened to a strap which spanned the space directly above the heel. There were two fragments of woven sandals made of yucca fiber, one of these has a buckskin strap at the toe end and the other loops of yucca leaves on the sides. There is a two-strand yucca cord which passes through these loops. This may be a winter form of sandal which enabled them to cover the

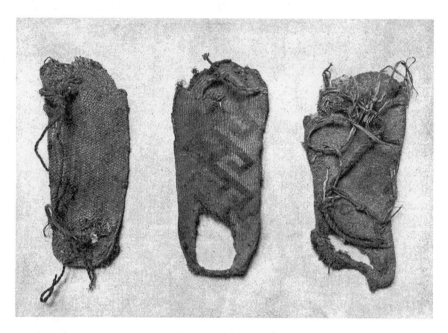

Fig. 34. *abc* (3949, 3942, 3946).   Sandals from Room 24.

foot with some warm material, which could be held in place by means of the lacing; both of these sandals had the jog at the toe end. There were seven fragments of woven plaited sandals, and a sandal of the latter type in course of construction, showing the manner in which the stalk end of the yucca leaf is carried to the under part of the sandal.

One of the most ornate sandals found in this ruin is shown in Fig. 34b; it is of the woven type, 25 cms. long, and 11.5 cms. wide at the toe. The warp is made of a three-ply cord of carefully selected yucca fiber and the woof is of some very fine white vegetable fiber. There is a cord over the toe end; the original fastening is shown on the right side of the sandal, but on the left it has been broken and a piece of buckskin passed through the sandal and tied to the strap. In this condition it has been worn for a considerable length of time, as shown by the flattened end of the buckskin on the under part of the specimen. A similar strap at one time spanned the heel, but only the ends now remain. There is a jog at the toe end. The sandal is intentionally cupped, and there is a reinforced piece where the back of the heel would strike. The surface bears a beautiful design composed of interlocking frets in two colors, brown and orange-yellow. The brown is well preserved and the yellow in some parts is quite bright. The toe of this sandal is frayed from use and there is a large hole in the heel resulting from the same cause, otherwise it is in good condition.

Pottery. A small bowl with crude but interesting designs was found in a fragmentary condition; it is 11 cms. in diameter at the top and 5 cms. deep, of grayware with rather complex black decorations on the interior. The first impression is that of a human figure with a peculiar balancing design on either side of it (Fig. 35). This rests upon the circle in the bottom of the bowl, a portion of which has been obliterated. The meaning of the roughly executed fret figures on either side, cannot be determined. Strange to say there is no design on the side of the bowl opposite the cross-like figure. The balancing design seems to have been a universal trait among the old potters in this region and it is seldom that an exception to the rule is found.

A dipper (H-3940) shows considerable use, as the outer edge of the bowl, that is the one farthest from the handle, has been worn. It is 21.5 cms. in length over all and the bowl is 4.5 cms. deep; it is of grayware with black designs. The decoration is divided into meander designs each of which occupies one of the spaces formed by cross lines, which divide the bowl into four parts. The handle is decorated with dots, possibly representing the spots on a frog. The handle is flat, of solid construction, with a slight bifurcation at the end.

A portion of an olla shows a handle which still retains a fragment of a yucca carrying cord. Other pottery pieces are in the form of a foot of some small animal, probably that of a deer. In addition, there were found, part of the hand and arm of another figure which has the hand painted black and a design in black dots on the arm; a fragment of a twisted handle of solid construction, possibly a dipper; a pottery disk with the edges ground; and pieces of unbaked clay.

Miscellaneous Objects. A small basket made of split yucca leaves, with a twig for the rim, measured 13 cms. in diameter with a depth of 5 cms. There is a jar rest 15 cms. in diameter made entirely of feather cord, that is, yucca cord over which feathers had been bound. A fragment of another jar rest made of braided yucca leaves was also in the débris. Associated with these specimens was a mass of two-strand yucca feather cord; cord made of human hair; and fragments of yucca cord of all sizes, but mostly of the two-strand variety. There was also a small

Fig. 35 (3941). Design upon a Bowl, Room 24.

piece of cotton cord. There were knotted pieces of yucca leaves in the form of a series of loops, probably for attaching ears of corn to the ceilings. There were in fact a great many specimens of knotted yucca leaves. There is a bundle of plant stalks enclosed in a harness, or net of yucca leaves, which may have been material for basket making. Two oblong objects were found, one of which retains a netting of yucca leaves. They are made of twigs bound together and may have been used as snowshoes by the boys or girls of the pueblo. These objects, with bundles of cornhusks tied with yucca cord, bundles of yucca leaves and yucca fiber with their original bindings, pieces of cedarbark rope, fragments of cotton cloth, some two-colored, and a number of pieces of rawhide, buckskin, and turkey feathers complete the more perishable objects found. One of the pieces of buckskin is marked with red paint which may have been the guiding line of the worker in cutting out some garment.

Among the wooden objects was a rather crude knife 32 cms. long, 3.5 cms. wide, and 1 cm. thick. One end had evidently been used to stir the fire, as this part is carbonized. Two smaller knife-like pieces made from splinters of cedar were also found; they were similar in shape to the one already described, but very much smaller. Both of these pieces showed use. There was also a branch, 8 cms. in length, stripped of its bark for half its length and a section cut from it. The object is interesting as showing the method employed in obtaining material for ceremonial sticks and other small wooden objects. A section of a cedar branch 8 cms. in length and 3.5 cms. in diameter may have been used as a kicking stick, although it may be merely the end of a branch from which a piece has been cut for the manufacture of some implement. A wooden slab, similar to the one described from Room 20, is 6.5 cms. long, 4.3 cms. wide, and 5 mms. thick. It has a little hole drilled through the center and the sides and edges are carefully worked. Part of a similar slab, although much smaller and not drilled, was found. The remaining objects of wood were: a portion of a half round ceremonial stick, covered with a green pigment; the hearth of a firedrill, a section of what may have been the end of a flute made of cottonwood; the end of a ceremonial stick; and several worked pieces of wood. There were also three cañon walnuts, one of which has the top ground off and the sides smoothed. There were fragments of six arrows made of reed; four of them retain the sinew fastenings; one showed the nocked end, another the foreshaft end; there were also three pieces that had been cut into sections as if for gaming purposes. One of these was painted red just above the feather binding.

Squash and pumpkin stems were found together with fragments of the rind of the latter and quids of yucca leaves and fiber.

There were a few fragments of pottery, pieces of gypsum, obsidian, azurite, malachite, large pieces of piñon gum, pieces of red ocher which had been ground to obtain paint; two sandstone concretions, two small sandstone disks, the largest of which was only 3.5 cms. in diameter; a chalcedony knife blade 4 cms. long; fragment of a jasper flesher of the type commonly found in the cliff-dwellings; and a piece of yellow ocher. Among the bone objects there are six short bodkins or blunt awls made from deer bones, one long perforating bodkin 20 cms. in length, with a fine point and with the surface polished, no doubt from wear; five awls, three of which are made from deer bone and two from bird bones; a small scraper 5 cms. long and 1.6 cms. wide at the blade; five beads made from bird bones; and one turkey bone 12½ cms. long, both ends of which had been removed. These objects, with a fragment of a bone implement 16½ cms. long and 6 cms. in diameter, carefully rounded and smoothed and tapering at one end, the calcined remains of a similar, though larger object, and a small bone die of a concavo-convex form with lines scratched on the concave sides, completes the list from this room.

Room 25.

Room 25, another refuse room, was situated in the southwestern part of the ruin. The measurements were as follows: north wall, 7 feet, 3 inches; south wall, 14 feet, 4 inches; east wall, 17 feet; west wall, 16 feet, 3 inches. The upper, or new part, of this room was built of short thick stones, chinked with small pieces, the north wall forming a break near the division line between the lower and upper room. In the upper wall a circular piece of sandstone appeared. Pieces of this kind were found in a number of rooms; they are irregular cylinders, having the face carefully smoothed. Their use in the walls cannot be determined, as the introduction of such a piece necessitates a break in the regular stratification of the masonry. No unusual conditions attend their presence in the walls and they do not seem to be placed in any particular position as regards their distance from the floor or adjoining walls. There is an opening in the lower part of the north wall which may have been a small doorway, but its appearance suggests that the masonry at this point had been torn away, possibly with the intention of making a doorway, and the work never completed. The east wall is built of selected stones which have been faced and the spaces between them chinked. It has a rectangular doorway in the center, with nine poles for a lintel. There are no other breaks of any size in this wall and all the plaster which formerly covered it has crumbled. The south wall was of the same construction and stood to the height of the ceiling beams. The west wall was made of similar stones and there is a break in the southern part, probably a doorway. There are four holes averaging 10.5 cms. in width, all of which are almost square and about 5 feet from the floor; they may have been used as pockets. There are no corresponding openings in the east wall, which would have been the case had small beams been stretched across the room for any special purpose.

Three feet ten inches from the north wall the face of the west wall crosses an old wall below the floor level of Room 25; this old wall runs northwest by southeast. The angular space thus formed was filled with masonry, making a support for the upper wall; this filled-in place was over 1½ feet thick. The old wall below the floor level is of very rough construction and may have been merely a foundation wall built to allow the north wall to be started on a level with the others.

West of Room 25 is Room 105. There is an angle wall forming a part of this room, which extends in a southeasterly direction and passes under the south wall of Room 25; it is built of large rough stones and chinked. One foot nine inches south of the room surface of the south wall and under it, is the south wall of the lower room. It abuts on the southwest wall and extends eastward past the east wall of the lower room. It is built of large uneven stones and in some places chinked, but the chinking is irregular. The east under wall is built in the same way. In the northeast corner there is an opening where a beam has rested; it is 4½ inches in diameter and extends 11 inches into the wall which is plastered and the plaster filled with pieces of sandstone which have been pressed into it while moist. This hole is about 2 feet 6 inches below the floor level. The east wall abuts the north one. The thickness of the south wall is 1 foot 3 inches, the other walls could not be measured. This under room was filled with stones and dirt to the level of the floor of the main room. The walls forming the upper rooms gave the following results when measured for thickness: north wall, 1 foot, 11 inches; south wall, 2 feet, 5 inches; east wall, 2 feet, 6 inches; west wall, 2 feet, 2 inches.

Pottery. In this room there were a great many potsherds, the majority of gray decorated ware. With these were many fragments of corrugated jars, also of red and blackware. No perfect pieces of pottery were found. One vessel (3042) in the form of a water jar has the upper part and a portion of the side complete; it is of grayware with traces of black decorations. The vessel in its perfect state must have been about 12 cms. in height with a diameter averaging 11 cms.

There were fragments of dippers, and over forty dipper handles. Some of these had the broken ends worked and two were of the rattle variety, having stones in the hollow part of the handle. One dipper of redware, with a black interior, had been broken and the outer edge of the bowl ground. Dippers of redware are not at all common in this region. The small forms with a solid tapering handle such as this are exceedingly uncommon.

Several fragments of small pottery vessels showing realistic modeling were found. One is the upper part of an effigy jar, showing a portion of an eye and what may have been a grotesque form of eyebrow for a mask. Another fragment of this figure, with a similar curved portion, may have been meant for an eyelid.

Another is a portion of a small vessel with handle. It is of grayware, decorated with designs in black. The handle part is broken, but it had been made to balance a long proboscis-like piece on the opposite side of the vessel. There are protuberances at the sides of this piece suggesting eyes. The tips of these are black and there is a circle of black paint at each base. The nose is rounded; the mouth has been formed by making a slit in the end of the projection; the nostrils are deeply indented and the tongue is represented by a broad black line in the central part of the under lip. This specimen is so grotesque in form that it is impossible to suggest the animal that it was made to represent.

The third is the handle of a jar in the shape of an animal figure represented as looking over the edge of the jar.

The fourth is a head, shaped like that of a deer. It is well modeled; the slip over which the design in black is painted, is a creamy white which forms a contrasting background for the design. The eyes are formed by balls of clay and are painted black; the mouth is a deep groove and the teeth are represented by eight dots on the upper and eight on the lower jaw, there being four on either side. The nostrils are drilled and there are remains of either ears or antlers directly back of the eye projections.

The fifth is a bird form made of solid pottery, evidently a part of some vessel. The wings are outlined in black and black dots represent the wing feathers. Two lines form a band across the neck portion, three bands cross the nose, and similar bands decorate the tail. This figure is 5 cms. in length and 3 cms. in width at the wing portion.

Three fragments of effigy jars were found.

One is a leg and foot of grayware having a decoration formed by two black bands and three wavy lines on the middle portion of the space between the foot and the knee. The foot is perfectly flat and the toes are represented by incisions in its upper part. This piece is of solid construction, 10 cms. in length and 1.5 cms. in diameter. It was no doubt the leg of a seated figure such as was found in Room 38.

The second is a portion of a figure showing the fingers of a hand, outlined with black paint.

In the last, two hands are represented as grasping some circular object. The hands themselves are 2½ cms. in width, so the figure in its entirety must have been a large one.

There is a neck of a jar of grayware decorated in black. The vessel has been broken and the lower edge of the neck ground smooth. In its present condition its appearance suggests an ordinary napkin ring. This specimen is shown in Fig. 36b.

One vessel the neck of which retained a wooden stopper was found. The neck was 4 cms. in width and was slightly flattened. The section of wood forming the stopper filled the opening completely; it was made from a branch of a tree and was perfectly preserved.

In Fig. 36c is shown a fragment of a dipper handle which was mended in a manner similar to that shown in the steatite pipe from Room 9. This specimen shows that the handle of the dipper had been broken and the edges ground until a perfect joint was obtained. At least this seems to be the case, judging from the ground surface of the specimen here shown. A small twig was then thrust into the hole in the center of the handle and a section of split cedar branch placed on the upper and another on the lower surface. The pieces of the handle were then put together, the central twig entering the opening in the fragment of the handle which was attached to the dipper bowl, the wooden splints resting upon its upper and lower parts. The splints were fastened at the handle end with two loosely spun yucca cords and then a space 3.5 cms. wide on the handle end and at least 3 cms. in width on the bowl end of the break was bound with a two-strand yucca cord. Just why they resorted to this method of lengthening the life of this dipper cannot be suggested, but it shows a very clever way of mending an object of this nature.

There were fragments of the smaller type of bird vessels made of very thin clay, having a rectangular or T-shaped opening in the upper part, and various fragments of corrugated jars with interesting incised designs. A few worked potsherds were in the débris, one in particular, a fragment of red corrugated jar, had the interior decorated in black. There were also two pottery handles which retained yucca carrying cords.

A number of small crude objects of unbaked clay were scattered through the débris. These objects are what Cushing called seed offerings; he claimed that they were the sacrificial forms of pottery from which the potters hoped that larger and perfect pieces would continue to grow. The largest of these figures is 6 cms. in width and 6 cms. long at the point where the object is broken; the smallest measures 1.7 cms. in

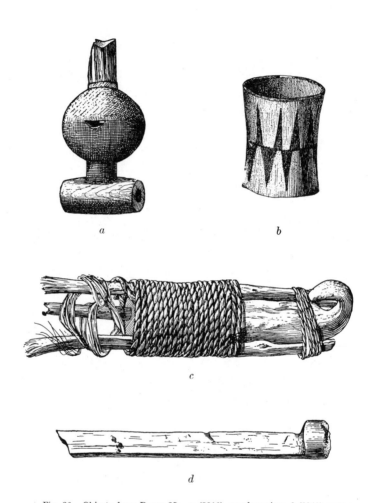

Fig. 36. Objects from Room 25: *a* (3016), wood carving; *b* (3042), pottery ring; *c* (2933), mended dipper handle; *d* (3068), wooden key to a trap.

width. They are flat pieces of clay having the general physical characteristics either incised or modeled in relief. Two of them have the
breasts modeled and the larger of the two has the nose modeled. Both
of these specimens have the eyes and mouth formed by incisions made
with the finger nail. The larger one has the upper part of the face
painted red and the lower part, that is, passing below the mouth and
ending at a point just below the breast line, painted black.

Bone and Antler. There were, comparatively speaking, few animal
bones in this room, but among those taken from the débris were fragments of deer antler and horn and antelope horn cores. There were no
unusual forms of awls or bodkins. Fourteen awls and perforators were of
deer and bird bones; only one of these was drilled for suspension. There
were also the blade ends of two of the large bone scrapers; two spatula-
shaped bones; and several fragments of bone implements. Four tines of
deer antlers had been made into bodkins; the points of three of them show
that they have been used, but the opposite ends of all are exactly in the
condition as when broken from the antler. Nine bird bone beads, one
section of bone from which a bead had been cut, with several fragments of
beads, were found; also three small-sized scrapers, made from the toe
bones of deer or elk. One shows a scraper in course of manufacture, the
work of grinding off the condyle of the bone is about half done; the other
shows a complete scraper. The use of these small implements has not
been definitely determined. They have been called scrapers, for convenience, but the appearance of some of the specimens suggests their
use as polishers.

There was a worked piece of antler 8.3 cms. long and .1 cm. in diameter at the larger end, although this part is somewhat flattened. It
tapers from this end so that the opposite end is slightly smaller. This
object may have been a game stick; at least, it is similar to the ivory
sticks used by the Indians of the Northwest Coast. A skeleton of a bird,
fragments of egg shells, probably those of the turkey, and two deer or
elk toes which had been used for rattles were also in the débris.

Skin Work. A number of very well-preserved pieces of buckskin
were recovered; most of them, however, were in a fragmentary condition and did not show the use to which they had been put. In Fig. 37
is shown a series of worked pieces which are as well preserved as any
pieces of similar material from this ruin. The upper one has a serrated
edge; just above the notches there is a broad line of red paint. The edge
opposite the notches is cut, showing that it had been detached from some
larger piece. The lower pieces shown in the figure are evidently parts of

Fig. 37 (3172). Buckskin from Room 25.

dresses and show the manner of fringing their edges. The larger piece still retains some of the original sinew sewing. This piece is at the present time as soft as when first tanned. There are fragments of bags such as were used for carrying paint and other materials, several pieces show cutting to good advantage, and one piece has a lacing of buckskin woven in and out on its edges.

Stone Work. In exploring a room of this nature objects such as are used for general purposes in the home are naturally expected, but here there were only two manos and not even the fragments of metates. There were several sandstone slabs with depressions in one side, for grinding paint and other materials. With them were grinders made of coarse friable sandstone; grooved sandstone slabs that had been used for sharpening tools; and two of the so-called pitted stones having depressions averaging 3.5 cms. in diameter and 1 cm. in depth. There were over forty hand hammers, or pecking stones, a number of flat pebbles, some of which have been used as hammerstones, others as smoothers; a few fragments of stone such as are used for making stone implements; small sandstone concretions which may have been used as sling stones; pieces of red hematite, the edges of which had been ground to obtain material for paint; red ocher, azurite, and malachite used in making paint; two water-worn pebbles, one of which had one side painted yellow, the other with its side painted red; small sandstone tablets used no doubt for grinding and mixing paint; eight stone jar covers, one of which had been used as a paint mixer; and the end of an object similar to a gorget, one end of which is perforated. One side of this object has scratches on its surface. There was a fragment of a mortar similar to the one found in Room 10. From the fragment it would seem that it had been about the same size, but the rim around the edge is very much higher in this than in the other specimen. The bottom of this object was flat and retains traces of red and yellow paint.

Fig. 38 shows a sandstone fetich in a fragmentary condition and was evidently discarded owing to the friable nature of the sandstone. It is 7 cms. long and 4.5 cms. high. There were a number of small sandstone implements and broken pieces of shells and other materials; the blade end of a jasper scraper; the end of a stone knife; an arrow point of chalcedony; and a few shell and turquoise beads, one of the shell beads having been made from an *olivella* shell. Piñon gum was also found.

Textiles. Of destructible material there was the usual variety of knotted pieces of yucca leaves; fragments of corn tassels; masses of feather cord; fragments of woven and braided sandals, one of the former

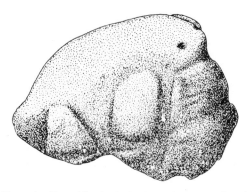

Fig. 38 (2957). Part of Carving in Sandstone, Room 25. Length, 7 cm.

Fig. 39 (3151). Piece of Cotton Cloth, Room 25.

of which has bands in brown which evidently crossed the sole when the sandal was complete; a sandal made from feather cord and quilted with a heavy cord of human hair; fragments of two stockings made of feather cord, the feathers being those of the turkey; a coil of feather cord tied in two places with a two and four-strand yucca cord; the usual variety of cords made from yucca fiber; quids of corn silk and yucca; squash and pumpkin rinds; yucca pods; corn and beans; and a section of squash rind that had been cut into the shape of the heel of a shoe. Had conditions been such in this pueblo that matting and similar objects had all decayed, we should still have had the record of the matting, at least, for in this room. there were several pieces of adobe which had no doubt formed a part of the floor of some room upon which are perfect imprints of mat sections.

Only three specimens of basketry came from this room; two of these were fragments. One was the bottom of a small oval basket, 7 cms. long and 4 cms. wide, of the three-rod coiled variety; the other, the bottom of a coiled meal basket of the same type. This specimen, however, was circular in form. A basket made of split yucca leaves, found in this room, was perfectly preserved. It is 19 cms. in diameter and 4 cms. in depth. The design on the bottom is in the form of a series of rectangles, one inside the other (twilling). Fragments of a number of jar rests were found, but none in a perfect condition.

Of special interest are some fragments of cotton cloth. Five pieces were found in the débris in a fine state of preservation. One piece (3139) is loosely woven, but the warp and woof are finely spun. The selvedges of two pieces have been sewn together with yucca cord. This weaving is similar to that seen in the kilts and sashes worn by the Antelope and Snake priests in Hopi ceremonies. The specimen shown in Fig. 39 is somewhat complex in weaving and is in three colors: white, black, and red. Work of this nature shows the high degree of culture attained by the old Pueblo people in the textile arts. In order to produce a figure of this kind careful adjustment and manipulation of the healds and heddles, or warp separators, is needed. The broad band running across the lower part of the fragment is white and three narrow bands which cross the broad one are red. The zigzag effect is in black and white. The old Pueblo people raised cotton to a greater or less extent, and the weaving art in the old days was developed to a high degree, especially among the cliff-dwellers. In the ruins in southeastern Utah have been found cotton balls which botanists claim to be a new species. It has been named *Gossypium aborigeneum* (Millspaugh). It is practically certain that this cotton plant was indigenous and the authority above-mentioned claims that it may be the progenitor of our tropical cotton. Note may be taken of a burden band made of cotton and yucca. The band is in two colors, brown and white. The fragment measures 21 cms. in length and 2.5 cms. in width. The eye-hole for fastening to the burden cord appears in one end. Also there is a braided cotton strip 21 cms. long and 8 cms. in width.

Wooden Objects. Comparatively few wooden objects were found in this room. There were some thirty sections of twigs, showing cut ends; some had been used for cutting buckskin, if we may judge from the cuts on their sides. Then there were five rectangular pieces of cedar with smoothed edges. There were two sticks such as are now used for the kicking game, one 7 cms. long and 4 cms. in diameter, and the other 7 cms. long and 3 cms. in diameter (H-2919, H-3004). There were three of the curved sticks to be described with the material from Room 32.

There were six wooden dice, made of half rounded pieces of twigs. The rounding portion of two of them has been ground, thereby making their surface somewhat flattened. Two small cylinders of wood, the ends of which have been carefully smoothed may have been used for gaming purposes; one of these is 2 cms. long and 1.3 cms. in diameter, the other 2.5 cms. long and averages 1.3 cms. in diameter; this one is slightly flattened. An object, shaped like the end of a bow, such as occurred in numbers in Room 2, was found; it is 6.5 cms. in length and made from the same material as those from the other room. Another type was the long cylindrical gaming, or cutting stick. One of these found in Room 25 was 17 cms. in length and 1 cm. in diameter. There were no marks from cutting on the surface of this specimen. Nine cañon walnuts were uncovered and two of these had been drilled for suspension, two holes in the upper part of each. Two utilitarian objects were a brush made of twigs, bound with a split twig, and the ends of a firedrill. One is a section of a branch, the greater part of one side having been cut away. Cushing identifies several such objects as keys for a figure-four deadfall. Among ceremonial objects may be mentioned one of the long ceremonial pieces which were found in pairs in Room 32. This one is 20 cms. in length and 5 cms. in diameter and has a line encircling it from end to end. A fragment of one of the ceremonial sticks with a curved end, the curved portion 12 cms. in length, was found; also the end of a smaller stick, which from the holes in one side was evidently used as a ceremonial firestick; and three fragments of heads of ceremonial sticks and a beautiful carved object in hard wood which is shown in Fig. 36a. This specimen, 4 cms. in length and a little over 1 cm. in thickness at its thickest part, has a flattened ball over the part which was no doubt meant to enter some other ceremonial stick, above this there is a barrel-shaped object connected to the flattened ball with a cylindrical piece. There is a hole drilled through the lower part and the tubular top piece has a hole 3 mms. in diameter drilled through it. This specimen is made from some very hard wood, presumably mesquite. The lower half is painted a rich orange, the upper half, that is, the neck portion which joins the two parts, seems to have been painted a dull red. The neck of the barrel-shaped object has been covered with green paint that may have extended to the orange area, as there are evidences of this color over the red. The object in its entirety is a beautiful piece of primitive wood carving; the work being so symmetrical and the general effect with the brilliant pigments making a ceremonial object worthy of any tribe.

Wooden flutes were represented by two pieces, one of which shows the distal end with part of one of the note openings. There were two fragments of squash rind on which a fine yucca cord had been attached and then a layer of thick red pigment applied. There is no decoration on this red layer.

Of great interest is a series of sections of reed arrows which have been cut; also several sections of reeds. In all, there are eighteen pieces which were probably used in games. Of these eight are proximal or nocked ends; three are distal ends which still retain the wooden fore-shaft, and the others are sections which retain their color or part of the wrapping, thereby identifying them as arrows. A number of these pieces still retain colored bands of red and green which in two cases alternate,—there being two bands of each color. The colored area is 6.8 cms. in length on one, but on the other it has been obliterated to such an extent that no accurate measurements can be taken. All of them retain a portion of the feather; one in particular (Fig. 40a) shows the interval between the sinew binding to be 9.2 cms. in length, the feathers themselves being 11.5 cms. long. There are three of these and they are placed equidistant, the feathering beginning 2 cms. from the end of the arrow. There were two sections of reeds averaging 3 cms. in length which had holes drilled, or burnt, in the sides.

Feathers. A number of eagle and turkey feathers were found and one of the eagle feathers was bound with yucca cord for attachment to some object. Three eagle feathers were bound side by side by means of a two-strand yucca cord (2938). There is also a small bundle of yellow and blue feathers tied in a bunch with yucca cord. The individual

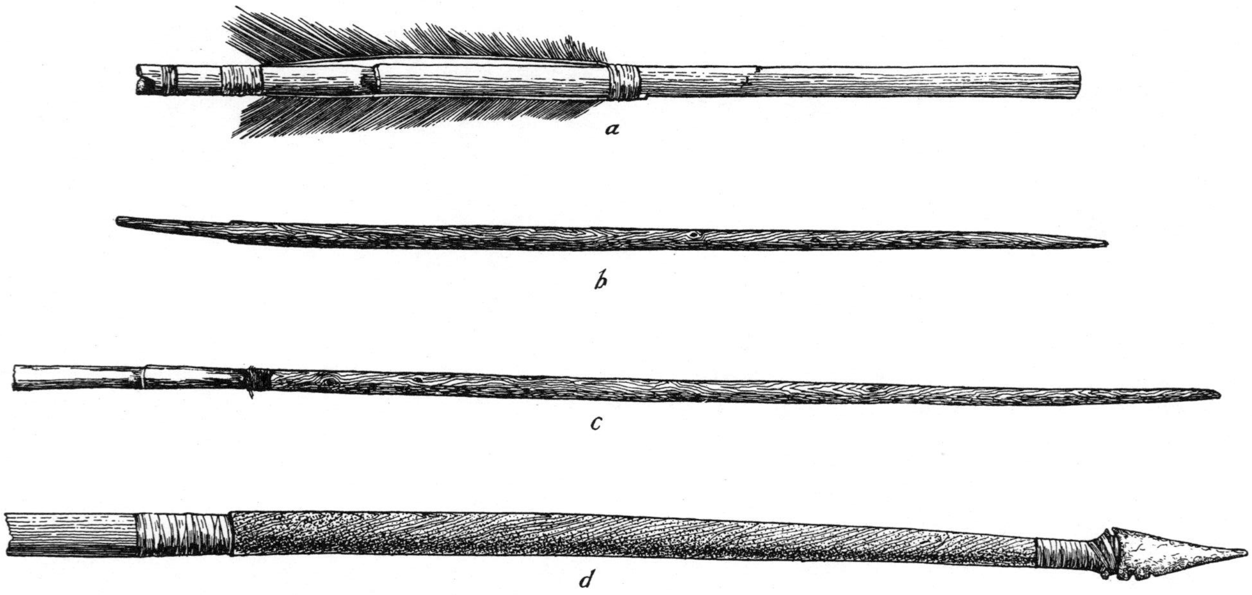

Fig. 40. Parts of Arrows: *a* (2916), end cut from shaft, Room 25; *b* (4474), Room 32; *c* (4472), Room 32; *d* (4572), Room 32.

110

colors seem to have been grouped into smaller bunches and their ends tied with a series of knots similar to those described as having been found in Room 1.

In general, this room contained a more varied assortment of material than any other room explored in Pueblo Bonito. Although it was an open room, the material had been preserved in a remarkable way. This is no doubt due to the fact that the specimens were lying in a mass of sand which allowed the water to percolate to the floor, thereby keeping the specimens in a completely dry state, which would not have been the case had they been lying in heavy soil.

ROOM 26.

Buried Kiva. Room 26 is really a mere excavation in the western court in which a few specimens were found. On reaching a certain depth the curved wall of an old estufa was found. The presence of this wall showed that the clearing of this estufa would be difficult, but an arc of the wall was uncovered. However, the following specimens were removed before the work was abandoned: twelve awls from splinters of deer bone; one awl from the leg bone of a deer; two awls from bird bones; two from splinters and one from a bird bone. The one made from a bird bone has an exceptionally fine point and one of the splinters has a very fine tapering point.

There was one scraper, from the tarsal bone of an ungulate, 13.5 cms. in length and 2.5 cms. in width at the blade end. This scraper had been worn on the under part of the edge of the blade as though used in scraping skins. There is also a fragment of a similar scraper, about the same size. Two sandstone jar covers, broken; a spoon-shaped object made from a potsherd; a piece of clay showing the imprint of a hand; a cylindrical piece of sandstone 5 cms. long and 3 cms. in diameter at the larger end; a shell bead; a piece of azurite; and the bowl of a pipe complete the list of the general specimens in this room. The pipe shown in Fig. 19 is made of clay and has an expanding bowl 3.5 cms. in diameter and 2 cms. deep. Near the base of the bowl there is a protuberance which may have been used in holding the pipe while it was in use. The inner part of the bowl is blackened and there is a deposit which appears to be the remains of tobacco.

In following out a portion of the arc of the estufa a support similar to those found in Room 16 was encountered. In the top of this support a deposit of turquoise matrix and two *olivella* shells were found, but there was no cavity in the support.

Room 27.

South of Room 17 there is an open space formed by the eastern part of an estufa, evidently associated with Room 16 (Fig. 26). At the southern edge of this depression the series of rooms which divides the Pueblo is continued. In Fig. 41 the room is shown after the accumulation of earth and stones had been removed. As shown in this picture, the room is 6 feet 10 inches long on the north side, 6 feet 8 inches on the south side, 11 feet 10 inches on the east side, and 11 feet 8 inches on the west side, the latter wall being the long one at the back part of the picture. The highest wall that remained standing was 4 feet above the floor level.

Altar Sand. This was evidently another of the ceremonial rooms associated with the estufas. In clearing away the stones from the fallen walls a mass of white sandstone was found in the southern part of the room and as it seemed improbable that this material had formed a part of a wall it was allowed to remain in place and the earth and other débris removed from about it. When the northeastern part of the room had been excavated to the floor level a stone mortar was found. There was a small grinding stone with a rounded surface on one side, which fitted the mortar cavity perfectly. This grinder had been made from a portion of the edge of a large metate; both of these objects may be seen in place in the photograph. It was quite evident that the sandstone had been brought to this room and had been stored there and ground for ceremonial purposes as needed. It is the type of white sandstone used at the present time in making sand paintings. The Navajo workmen were unanimous in saying that this had without a doubt been used by the old people in making their dry paintings in the estufas.

The mortar is made of an irregularly shaped piece of sandstone; it is 42 cms. wide at its widest part and 14.5 cms. thick. The mortar cavity is 26 cms. in diameter and 8 cms. deep. While metates are very abundant in this pueblo, mortars of this type are seldom found.

The only object found in this room, aside from the sandstone blocks and the mortar and pestle, was a fragment of a large corrugated olla; hence, it seems that this room had been used exclusively for grinding white sandstone as Room 17 may have been used for grinding meal.

Room 28.

In the north-central part of this ruin there is a well-proportioned room whose longer axis stretches east and west. The masonry is indicative of an intermediate period in the history of the pueblo. In appearance it differs little from other rooms; the upper strata brought forth

Fig. 41.   Room for preparing Altar Sand, Room 27.

113

Fig. 42. Pottery exposed in Room 28. A Bird'seye View.

114

Fig. 43. Cylindrical Jars in Room 28.

115

Fig. 44. Pottery in Northeast Corner of Room 28.

116

no evidence of rich deposits, nor was there anything on which to base a hope for unusual finds. Before the spade had disturbed the mass of fallen walls and the accumulated débris, this particular part of the ruin was a mound on which the greasewood thrived, and whose surface was covered with sand that rounded off the roughness of the fallen walls. The early stages of the work were productive of nothing of interest until a depth of two feet was reached, here, bits of worked turquoise and pieces in the matrix were found; then, a little deeper, a piece of hammered copper was unearthed. This interesting object was carefully examined, but it gave no evidences of having been a part of another piece. A foot deeper, in the western end of the room, there appeared a stratum of broken pottery; the pieces were collected and marked, and the work proceeded. The room now presented a very unpromising appearance, especially at the west end; here the walls were blackened, the posts, though in place, were but pillars of charcoal, the adobe burned to a terra cotta hue, and the sand and powdered adobe tinted a delicate red. Then fragments of a jar were found indicating a new form, which upon examination proved to be cylindrical. A pitcher was also found, but it too was broken. A little prospecting in the northeast corner of the western part, where these were found, served to locate another piece; this was over a foot and a half below the first ones. This part of the room was separated from the eastern section by a thin partition wall about a foot thick and four feet high. The lower portion of the western half was filled with sand that had drifted and washed in before the ceiling fell, and it is owing to this that the specimens were so well preserved. The sand was cleared away from the northeast corner of the western part, and a mass of bowls and vessels was found, Fig. 42. These were partly uncovered and a photograph taken, after which they were re-covered. From that time on, the work was confined to the western part of the room, the sand being thrown into the eastern part and then upon the bank.

A Pottery Cache. The work advanced rapidly toward the west wall, but, as it required the most watchful care, it was not until a day had passed that another piece of pottery was found, but after it was cleared there seemed to be no end to the cylindrical forms that the trowel and brush revealed. Pitchers and bowls were greatly in evidence, but the new form predominated, some on end, some in a horizontal position, and others presenting all degrees of angulation; in fact, there was a chaotic mass of pottery where once had been a well-laid pile, forced from their original places, and in many places crushed by the weight of the débris that the burning of the ceiling beams precipitated upon them.

Two days were spent in removing the rubbish from above the vessels and then came the delicate task of preparing the mass for photographing. A small steel stylus and a number of various sized brushes served to remove the earth from about and over the vessels, some of which were in twenty pieces and only held together by the equalization of pressure of the sand about them.

When this mass was ready for the camera, it was carefully covered with sheepskins as a precautionary measure against the possibility of stones falling from the overhanging bank above them, then the south side of the room received attention. Here a small four-handled bowl was found, also a pitcher and one of the cylindrical jars. Between the bowl and the other two pieces, there was a cache of stone jar covers, these in turn were covered, and the eastern and northeastern parts again became the objective point.

A portion of a pitcher was found near a post that rested against the eastern wall. From this point to the north wall, there remained a heap of sand 3 feet high and 3½ feet in width. When this was worked down, over fifteen pieces of pottery were added to those already found in this corner, and portions of others could be seen below them. These were cleared and brushed for photographing, and then the first that were found, which were a part of this corner deposit, were fully uncovered.

The room had now been thoroughly examined, the specimens brushed, but still in their original places, and the first layer made ready to be removed. The first picture taken at this stage of the operations was with a wide angle lense; the camera was inverted between boards and thus a bird's eye view of the room was obtained. This picture (Fig. 42) gives a fair idea of the pottery and its immediate surroundings, also the mass of débris upon which the western wall of the room is built. The base of this wall is outlined by a strongly defined break. It rests upon the remains of what was once a part of an old structure, whose material and workmanship are radically different from that of the upper part. Its age, or how long a time elapsed from its demolition to the day when new walls were built above its ruins, cannot be told, but it is self-evident that no pains were taken to form a foundation for the new wall. The pottery occupies the southwestern corner touching both the west and south walls, and seems to have been laid with cylindrical jars forming a row extending east and west, with the pitchers and bowls on either side.

The vessels in the northeast corner were the first photographed; they followed the north wall line, and, in fact, rested against it in some instances, even extending into the doorway where three bowls were lying upon the sill; from the western side of this door they stretched in a southeast line to the post in the center of, and resting against the east wall, and from this line to the northeast corner the space was completely filled. This group (Fig. 44) contains twenty-one bowls, one pitcher, and two cylindrical jars; all of these, with the exception of one of the jars, were ornamented, the scroll design in simple and conventionalized forms, prevailing.

A second layer was exposed and treated in the same manner as the first one. In this corner deposit, bowls formed the great majority, they were all of compact whiteware and ornamented in the interior with designs in black; handles were in evidence, but no exterior designs were found. These bowls varied greatly in size and capacity, the twenty-six that this corner produced, ranging from $5\frac{1}{4}$ inches to 1 foot 1 inch in diameter and $2\frac{3}{4}$ inches to 7 inches in depth. A résumé of the forms gives us but three distinct types: the circular bowl, the cylindrical jar, and the cylindrical topped pitcher; the former predominated to such an extent that it was practically a bowl deposit of twenty-six pieces with an intrusion of two jars and three pitchers. Thus we have in this one corner, on, or slightly above the floor level, thirty-one pieces, making in all, with the jar and pitcher that were found just above the mass, thirty-three pieces of pottery from the northeastern part of the room, the majority being in perfect condition.

The mass in the western part of the room occupied a space that extended four feet eastward from the west wall, and to a point five feet north of the south wall, thus covering an area of twenty square feet. In the first, or upper layer, there were forty-seven pieces, all but six of which were of the cylindrical type. An exposure was made with the specimens *in situ* (Fig. 43); not only the jars themselves were in place but in most cases the individual fragments. All the pottery that presented even a portion to view, was numbered, and then another picture taken, thereby following out the scheme that was started in the northeast corner and also continuing the number sequence. After the vessels in this layer were numbered, they were removed and another layer uncovered.

This layer disclosed thirty-seven specimens; the cylindrical form had thirty-one representatives, and there were two bowls and four pitchers. The third layer consisted of thirty pieces, seventeen of which were cylindrical jars, six bowls, and seven pitchers.

The fourth layer brought us to the base of the western limit of the room; most of the pieces were imbedded in the débris that formed the foundation of the western wall. There were fourteen vessels in all, of which thirteen were jars, the one exception being a pitcher. One of these jars (3378) is of redware, the only one of that color found in the room.

It seemed that this should exhaust the deposit, but on removing the jars, five more cylindrical pieces were found.

Thus in this deposit there were one hundred and thirty-six pieces of pottery, embracing one hundred and ten jars, eighteen pitchers, and eight bowls. There were also seventy-five stone covers, evidently for the jars and pitchers.

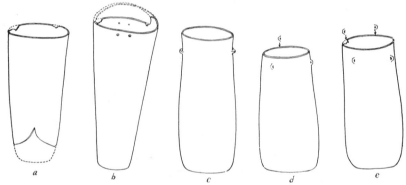

Fig. 45.   Forms of Cylindrical Jars, Room 28.   *a*, no handles; *b*, with a bail; *c*, two lugs; *d*, three lugs; *e*, four lugs.

Cylindrical Pottery. In considering the cylindrical or new form, we find that H-3378 is made of red material and, as stated, is the only piece of this ware that was found. This specimen has no handles nor even evidences of such appendages. It is 9⅝ inches in height with a diameter of 6⅛ inches by 6⅜ inches at the top, 5¹¹⁄₁₆ inches at the middle part, and 3¾ inches at the bottom. It has no decorations and no lines or markings of any kind appear on its surface. It is a darker ware than the usual red pottery of this region, and there is, therefore, a possibility of this piece having come from some other part of the country to serve as a model for the potters in making their whiteware. Two of the white jars are similar in form. The only embellishments on these pieces are four pairs of holes that served as handles. Among these people handles were used to a great extent, even the corrugated jars and ollas being fitted with them. The handle idea was developed. At all events the possible evolution of this cylindrical type is worthy of note. As these jars were no doubt used for ceremonial purposes the handles may have been for the attachment of feathers.

Summing up, we have one hundred and fourteen cylindrical jars. Of these sixty-six are ornamented. There is one without handles, two with sets of perforations through which cord handles may be passed, and one with a handle composed of a band of pottery that arched across the mouth of the jar. Then follows one with two handles, twenty-three with three handles, and eighty with four handles; three had an irregular arrangement of handles, and there were three whose tops were missing. making it impossible to classify them.

A number of the jars were marked, either on the bottom or the rim, with peculiar lines and figures, nor was this confined to the decorated pieces; their import, whether symbolical or decorative, cannot be determined. Over a dozen of the jars presented some line or series of lines, or some figure that was not one of the component parts of the decorative lines.

The subject of ornamentation cannot be taken up in this paper, but the types are shown in Plates 2–7. The extremes of height and diameter are, however, interesting. The highest jar in the collection is 1 foot $2\frac{1}{4}$ inches high, and the smallest $7\frac{1}{4}$ inches, the greatest diameter being $5\frac{1}{2}$ inches, and the smallest 3 inches. Of this form we have one hundred and twenty pieces, not counting the fragmentary ones that may be partially restored. One hundred and fourteen are from Room 28, and the other six from a sealed series of rooms just north of and adjoining Room 28.

Before closing a few words may be added concerning similar jars from Central America. One of the greatest nations of that vast country was the Cakchiquel, a branch of the Maya family. A large collection, showing the culture of this people, was collected by one Alvarado, the collection being bought by Dr. Eduard Seler. and a portion re-sold to the Duke de Loubat, who presented it to the American Museum of Natural History. There is a cylindrical form of pottery in this collection that is strikingly similar in form to the ones under consideration which was found at "Finca Pompeya", a ranch near Antigua, Guatemala. They vary in form as do the ones in the Hyde Collection, some being uniform throughout their length, others small at the bottom and wide mouthed; one has a somewhat flaring top. They range from 5 to 11 inches in height, and from 3 to 5 inches in diameter. One is of a light buff color and would readily pass as a specimen from Bonito, so nearly does it approach some of the specimens from Room 28. The ornamentation of this piece is confined to a band of decorative lines near the rim; in fact, almost all of the decorations are confined to this part, some have painted bands of solid color, some incised lines and figures, some raised lines. Most of the pieces are dark, either a dark red or a dull black, no handles are in evidence, but on one of the jars there are three knobs that are placed in the same relative positions as the handles on the three-handled specimens from Bonito.

The mass of pottery, found at a depth of 2 feet below the surface, was composed mostly of fragments of large cylindrical jars. There were fragments of large pitchers, also of a large decorated olla and a number of fragments of bowls, dippers, and corrugated jars; there were a few red-ware potsherds. Parts of eight jars of the cylindrical type were assembled, but yet these show no unusual forms in the way of ornamentation or the adjustment or styles of the handles. None of them were decorated on the bottom part nor were there unusual lines on the rim, such as were noted in the case of some of the pieces from the jar deposit of the lower room.

An unbroken vessel in the shape of a squash is shown in Fig. 47. A small portion of a bowl with peculiar decorations on the interior was also recovered. The decorations are in black on a gray surface and represent animals, probably deer or sheep (Fig. 46). The drawing of the figures is rather crude, but the specimen is interesting, owing to the fact that animal forms of this kind are seldom used in ornamenting pottery vessels, at least in the Chaco Region.

Miscellaneous Objects. In considering the specimens found in the upper layer of the room, a piece of copper first claims attention. It is a hammered piece of what seems to be native copper, 25 cms. long, 2 cms. wide, and averages 1 mm. in thickness, evidently hammered into its present shape and one side has scratches in the form of cross hatchings. The edges are irregular and there are cracks in the edge such as would naturally result from hammering.

A weather-worn shell bracelet and a fragment of a stone slab; eleven sandstone jar covers; several pieces of turquoise matrix showing veins of this material enclosed in trachyte and a number of small pieces of turquoise which had been broken from the matrix, were the only objects found with the potsherds in the upper deposit.

Scattered through the sand near the floor level of the lower room and intermingled with the pottery were seventy-eight sandstone jar covers; some of these may be seen in Fig. 42. They range from the crudest forms imaginable to carefully rounded and smoothed pieces, the majority of

Fig. 46. Decorated Potsherd, a Shell Trumpet, and Worked Antler: *a* (4093), Room 28; *b* (2621), Room 17; *c* (4738), Room 22.

Fig. 47. Pottery Forms: *a* (3581), Room 32; *b* (3564), Room 28; *c* (3583), Room 32.

Fig. 48 *ab* (3589, 3591). Pottery from Room 32.

them, however, very crude. Of the one hundred and twenty-one covers, sixty-eight were found in the sand, on, and slightly above the floor level; and six were found in a cache. These covers were evidently made to be used in connection with the cylindrical jars and pitchers with which they were found.

Among the other objects of stone found in the room was a large sandstone slab, broken into fragments, but upon which there still remain traces of red paint. There is also a peculiar globular concretion evidently of limonite, and, from the indications of the lower surface, used as a pestle. An obsidian arrow point; a small red jasper pebble, evidently used as a pottery smoother; and a circular piece of jet were found. The jet piece is 4 cms. in diameter at its widest part and flattened on one side; the under part is irregular in shape; the thickest part being 6 mms. The edges are beveled and the under part is covered with a layer of gum, probably piñon gum; the upper surface is smoothed and polished. It no doubt formed an inlay for some object. Scattered through the débris in the room were calcined fragments of chalcedony, many of them cracked into small bits; masses of sand which have been vitrified and formed into a slag were also found. Then too there were seven small fossil shells, and a small shark's tooth; three fragments of crinoid stems; two chalcedony arrow points, one of obsidian and one of chert; the point of a stone knife; a large calcite crystal; a small transparent quartz crystal; a piece of native sulphur; pieces of red and yellow ocher; a piece of silica of iron; and several thin laminae of mica.

Scattered among the bowls and jars on the floor there were ninety-three turquoise beads of the flat circular form; twelve turquoise pendants and a number of broken beads; turquoise inlays and pieces of turquoise matrix. Scattered through the general débris above the pottery were sixteen small circular turquoise beads. Among the shell objects found in the general débris were a number of fragments of murex most of which had been blackened by fire, and, on the floor level and scattered among the pottery vessels were sixty-nine of the figure-eight shaped beads; forty-three beads made from olivella shells; sections of shells; and nine fragments of shell bracelets, two of which are perforated for suspension of ornaments. Associated directly with the pottery vessels were four hundred shell beads, of these one hundred and five were olivella shells, one hundred and thirty were of the figure-eight form, and the balance were sections of olivella shells, flat circular beads and a few of irregular shape.

There were very few bone objects in the room, two bone awls made from fragments of deer bone being the only implements found, but there were fifteen fragments of deer antler, cut into lengths averaging 7 cms. Most of them had rounding ends and one of them has grooves in the side made by some cutting implement. These objects were so calcined by fire that pieces had scaled from the surface, therefore, it would be impossible to determine their original forms. A human tooth; a few fragments of wooden implements; a piece of knotted yucca cord, found in the upper levels; and a flat piece of wood 6 cms. square and 8 mms. thick having a perforation in the center were the only objects of a really perishable nature, found at the floor level. This was covered with sand and had in some way escaped the fire which had carbonized so many objects. The remaining specimens from this room were found in the vessels; a shell bracelet with a perforation through the valve of the shell was found in a bowl in the northeast corner of the room. A small circular turquoise bead was found in a bowl in the same corner; in another bowl there were two of the figure-eight-shaped beads and a small olivella shell bead; in a bowl four of the figure-eight-shaped beads, a flat circular bead of shell, a turquoise bead of the same shape, and a carved olivella shell bead were found. This carved bead has a series of elongated circles forming a band around the central part. There are five of these and each one has a dot in the center. Another bowl contained two shell beads, one of the figure-eight form, the other of an olivella shell, and another a small flat circular bead of turquoise.

Room 28a. This was a continuation to the eastward of Room 28 and separated from it by a wall of plastered stone 1 foot thick. This wall extended to the ceiling of the lower room which was 8½ feet from the floor at this end. The base on which the wall rested was composed of large stones. The room was floored at this depth (8½ feet) and had been filled in, and another floor put down at the bottom of the dividing wall or at a depth of 6 feet from the ceiling. The dividing wall was the only one on which the plaster remained; it was not very thick, but in good condition. The other walls of the lower room were roughly made, composed of large stones carelessly laid. There was a wall about a third of the way up on the southern side of the room, a foot wider than the balance of the wall and forming a bench extending from the east to the west wall. A little east of the center of the lower jutting wall a large ceiling beam had rested. From the size of the opening it must have been at least 10 inches in diameter. The northern and eastern walls of this room were roughly laid and the south wall had large stones projecting from the surface, particularly at the ceiling level. The walls of the lower part were in fact very crude as compared with the work shown by those of the upper room which had been laid with extreme care with selected faced stones that were in good condition when uncovered. In the eastern wall there was a sealed doorway of the usual type that led into Room 45; it had been damaged by fire, especially at the upper part where it bulged to a considerable extent.

The walls of the upper room showed no evidence of plaster. The stones of the southern wall are like those shown in the upper part of the wall in Room 28. The two parts which, for convenience, have been divided in the notes, really formed one room which extended the length of Rooms 28 and 28a; therefore, in studying the room the doorways and peculiarities of the upper walls must be considered as forming a part of one room only. There is a doorway of the old "T" shape in the western part of the south wall, one part of it is directly over the partition wall which separated the two lower rooms. This doorway led into Room 40. Owing to the fact that it was not cleared until this room was excavated, the measurements will not be given until that room is described. There was a doorway in the northern wall of the lower room, situated a little to the east of the center; it was very rough and higher than most rectangular doorways (2 feet 2 inches wide and 3 feet 6 inches high, the upper part being 2 feet 6 inches below the ceiling beams; its exact position was 7 feet 8 inches from the west wall). There was a place in the north wall, both at the west and east end, where a beam had been built into the wall, possibly for use as a support, but there were no corresponding depressions in the south wall. The one near the west end is 2 feet 2 inches from the partition wall, 5 feet high and 6¾ inches wide having a depth at the center of 3 inches. The one at the eastern end is 4 feet 2 inches high, 6½ inches wide and 2 inches deep. The concavity is such as might be formed by pressing a circular beam half its thickness into soft plaster. There were evidences of posts having stood on the south side of the room opposite these depressions, but fire had destroyed them. From the mass of vitrified sand at the end of this room one would be led to believe that it had been used as a storeroom for grain or other materials that would generate an intense heat as the timbers in the room would hardly cause enough heat to vitrify the surrounding material.

This room was 13 feet long, north and south, sides 7 feet 10 inches wide on the east and 8 feet 2 inches at the west end. At the eastern part of the room the walls stood to a height of over 19 feet above the lowest floor level. The upper room in its entirety is 25 feet 7 inches long on the north side, 25 feet long on the south side, 7 feet 8 inches at the west end, and 7 feet 10 inches at the eastern end.

One of the strongest evidences of the extreme heat generated in this room is the condition of the specimens. There were five stone slabs all of which had suffered greatly from fire, some had been burnt to a dull red, whereas others had been blackened by smoke; four of these had been carefully smoothed and used as grinding stones; two, in particular, had been used as metates. With them were found five sandstone manos of the heavy type used for coarse work, and one, that had been used for the finishing process, of fine-grained sandstone, one surface of which shows considerable wear   A small block of sandstone 9.5 cms. long, 5 cms. wide, and 3 cms. thick, had all of its surfaces carefully smoothed and one side covered with red pigment; it had evidently been used as a grinder. There was also a sandstone disk, 8.5 cms. in diameter and 2.8 cms. in thickness, plano-convex in form and the flat surface smoothed to such an extent that its use as a grinder seems probable. It had been cracked by fire to such an extent, that the flat surface has the appearance of pottery. A fragment of chalcedony; a very heavy handle, evidently of a large pottery bowl; two natural pebbles; fragments of the bowl of a clay pipe; and a sandstone jar cover of the usual form were also found. All of these specimens came from the lower room, on, or near the floor.

Room 29.

Room 29 was a small room west of Room 19. Its southern wall abutted the northern retaining wall of the estufa known as Room 16. Its walls were not well-preserved and comparatively few specimens were found in it. The specimens were mixed through the débris near the floor level. There was a flat slab of compact sandstone, measuring 34 cms. in length, averaging 15.5 cms. in width and 1 cm. in thickness; one side of this slab had been smoothed and the central portion shows considerable wear.

A sandstone jar cover had one surface polished and had evidently been made from a fragment of a grinding stone. In Fig. 17 a grooved hammerstone is shown, it is 10 cms. in length and 4 cms. in width at its broadest part; it is slightly flattened and one end tapers to a point, a form which is rather unusual in this pueblo. Among other objects of stone, were a piece of galena, a number of large flakes of obsidian, and a fragment of chalcedony. There were three bone awls, two made from splinters of deer bone, and one from the leg bone of a turkey. There were also pieces of feather cord, two-strand yucca cord, two sections of reed arrows, the end of a large wooden ceremonial stick, and a piece of pottery in the shape of an animal's paw.

Rooms 30 and 31.

Rooms 30 and 31 were merely shallow excavations in the eastern court of the building, started at the time Room 28 was nearing completion. The finding of a closed doorway in the north wall of Room 28 led to such a mass of material in Rooms 32 and 33, that it was deemed advisable to discontinue the excavations in other parts of the ruin and to devote the few weeks that remained to the careful study of the positions of specimens in the two rooms just mentioned.

Only two specimens were found in Room 30, one a fragment of a bone implement with two holes drilled in the end, and an arrow point of chalcedony. In the excavation known as Room 31, one bone awl was found. ˗

Room 32.

With the removal of the stones with which the doorway in the north wall of Room 28 was closed, a wall of drifted sand was encountered. Owing to the presence of an opening west of, and a little above this doorway, it had been possible to ascertain that there was an open space between the ceiling beams and the sand, in the western part of the room. To reach this open space a tunnel was cut through the sand. When the surface of the drifted sand was reached, a candle made it possible to examine the room. The drift had been from the eastward and the sand was piled almost to the roof at that end, but directly opposite the doorway in the northwest corner, was a mass of ceremonial sticks, many of which protruded over a foot above the surface. The sand was covered with various objects, carried in by pack rats, the most noticeable of which were spines from cactus plants.

In the western wall there was a doorway, almost filled by the sand. The ceiling beams had been crushed by the mass of débris above them, and in the central portion of the ceiling, following a line running east and west, the beams were cracked and splintered. There were supporting beams and posts in the northern side of the room.

As this room had been used for ceremonial purposes, each object as found, was located by measurements.

Pottery. The mug (Fig. 47a) is of grayware with black decorations in the form of bands, four of which encircle the vessel. These bands of black enclose cloud-terrace figures in white. Above the bands and near the rim is a series of lines and dots, and at the base of the vessel is a series of five narrow lines similar to those above the banded area. The handle is decorated with a design in black, with diamond figures in the center. This mug is 11.5 cms. in diameter at the base, 6 cms. in diameter at the mouth, and 11 cms. high.

Fig. 47c (3583) is a grayware mug decorated with black designs, found near the doorway. This specimen is slightly larger than the others, measuring 13 cms. in diameter at the bottom, 8.5 cms. at the top, and having a height of 12.2 cms. The design is in the form of a meander which starts in the central part of the mug near the handle, extends around to the opposite side, then passes to the lower part of the vessel, following the lower edge in a straight line to the handle again, then to the upper part of the vessel where the meander is resumed and circles the upper rim ending at the handle. The handle has a simple decoration of lines, some enclosed in rectangles, the effect being in keeping with the general decoration of the object. This is a pleasing decoration quite in keeping with the general decorative work of Pueblo Bonito. A little to the east and 2 inches north of the mug just described, a pitcher was found (3585); it was of grayware with black decorations which formed two bands, one extending around the lower part of the vessel, the other starting at one side of the handle and extending around the neck of the pitcher to the opposite side of the handle. These two bands are separated by a broad black line which encircles the vessel, but does not cross the part spanned by the handle. The handle which is composed of four half round pieces of clay joined together, evidently represents individual willow roots, which were employed in this manner in making handles for basket jars. The handle is decorated with lines which have small dots along the edge. There is a black line around the rim of the vessel, but it is not completed, there being an opening at the point directly above the handle. This pitcher is one in which the neck and the lower portion are joined, in such a way that there is a gentle curve at the point of juncture. The pitcher is 18 cms. in height and 17 cms. in diameter.

Before leaving the group found at the doorway, mention must be made of a whiteware jar decorated in black. It was lying upon its side and rested near the south wall of the room; it is of the cylindrical form, such as was found in Room 28. The slip on the surface is extremely white as compared with some of the other specimens; the design is in the form of two bands, one at the lower part of the jar, the other on the level of the handle. There are four handles. The jar is 11.5 cms. in diameter at the bottom and 10 cms. in diameter at the rim, and the height is 19.5 cms.

Two bowls were found 6 inches west of the doorway and 9 inches north of the south wall (3590 and 3587). These bowls were nested and rested against the western side of the basket. The former is of dull red-ware, undecorated, with a black polished interior. The diameter of the rim is 13.8 cms., and it had a depth of 6 cms. This bowl rested inside of the second bowl and contained remains of some material, probably food. It is of dull grayware, decorated on the interior with a band composed of a series of interlocking frets, and has ten dots on the edge of the rim. The bowl is 14.5 cms. in diameter at the rim and 5.5 cms. deep.

The next object encountered, was one of unusual shape for this region; it was found 8 inches west of the doorway in the south wall, one end resting against this wall. The specimen shown in Fig. 48a is of dull redware, with a black interior; it is undecorated and the rim has crumbled, evidently from age. In form it is rectangular with rounding corners; only a very small portion of the original rim remains, but it is enough to show that this portion of the vessel, as well as a part of the outer edge, had been covered with a black slip; it is 25 cms. long, 14.5 cms. wide, and 9 cms. deep.

After the last object was removed, the work near the doorway was carried eastward. At a point 6 inches east of the doorway, and 1 foot 1 inch north of the wall, a grayware bowl was found (Fig. 49) with an elaborate design in black, forming a band which covers the greater part of the vessel. A small area at the bottom has been left undecorated, save the center, which has a design in the form of a maltese cross. The central part, however, is in the form of a square and the arms of the cross are attached to its corners, the arms themselves, being pyramidal, with a series of short lines radiating from the base of each. This cross is similar to the one on a bowl from Room 24, Fig. 35. There were no decorations on the exterior of the bowl. This vessel which is of the type ordinarily used for general household purposes, is 27.5 cms. in diameter at the rim and 13 cms. deep.

One foot east of the doorway and resting against the southern wall, was found a water jar of the form common in the cliff-dwellings of Colorado and Utah. This vessel, as shown in Fig. 48b, is of grayware, extremely fine in texture, and the outer surface has been smoothed to such an extent, that there are practically no irregularities. The contour of the water jar is almost perfect, it tapers from the base to the point where the rim of an ordinary bowl would be, and from this point it is incurved toward the top, the opening left averaging 7 cms. in diameter. Two and one-half cms. from this opening, there is a raised band which rises on an average, 7 cms. above the surface of the vessel, and with a width at its top of 5 cms. This raised portion surrounds the opening. The opening itself has a broad band of black paint on its outer rim and then follow three smaller bands between the one just mentioned and the raised portion which is also painted black. Directly below this part of the jar there is a band composed of five curious figures. This vessel is 20.5 cms. in diameter at its broadest part and 12 cms. deep.

Fig. 49 (3575). Bowl of Grayware, Room 32.

Directly east of and resting against the water jar just described, was a bowl of redware with a black interior (3588). This bowl is of the usual type and was in a fragmentary condition when found; it is 20 cms. in diameter and 6.4 cms. deep.

Returning to the work in the western part of the room, that is, just west of the doorway, three bowls were found, the lowermost of which almost touched the end of the rectangular bowl. These (H-3580, 3575, 3579) were nested, and are all of grayware. A sandstone metate of the ordinary form was found 10 inches north of the eastern side of the doorway adjoining the level at the lower part.

After finding the metate, a number of objects were encountered west of the doorway. The first (3576) was a pitcher of grayware with a design in black in the form of interlocking frets on the upper part and two black bands on the lower part. The handle was of the usual form and was decorated with zigzag lines and there were black dots on the edge of the rim. This specimen was 16 cms. high and 11 cms. in diameter at its widest part. The specimen was found 1 foot 6 inches west of the doorway in the south wall, lying in a slanting position on the floor, the mouth almost touching the south wall.

Three inches west of this pitcher and 1 foot 5 inches from the south wall, a corrugated vessel of redware with polished black interior was found resting on the floor. This shallow bowl (H-3647) is very irregular in form, the corrugations are rough and the bottom of the vessel is indented in a number of places. The ends are rounded and there is a smooth rim, averaging 1 cm. in width around the oval edge. It is 18 cms. long and 13.8 cms. wide at its widest part. The sides are not uniform, one being comparatively straight, the other, quite slanting. It averages 5.5 cms. in depth. A jar (3577) was found 1 foot 11 inches west of the doorway, and 9 inches north of the south wall, lying upon its side upon the floor. This jar is of grayware with black designs and is of the tall cylindrical type; it was in a fragmentary condition when found. It is 26.5 cms. high and averages 6 cms. in diameter. There were originally four handles of the horizontal loop pattern, one of them has been broken and the fourth evidently broke while the jar was in use, or possibly before it was decorated; certainly before the present decorations was applied. There are two slight projections showing the place where the handle has been, but these have been ground almost to the level of the jar surface, and over them the white slip has been applied and then upon that the design has been drawn. The design is in the form of squares which are divided with a line running from corner to corner, one half of the spaces of each square being filled in with lines. This effect is carried out on all parts of the surface, with the exception of one side where the entire square is filled in with lines and directly below it another square has been divided into four parts, the opposite angles only being filled in hachure effect.

Continuing westward along the wall, a pitcher was found (3584). It was 2 feet 6 inches west of the doorway and lay bottom upward. This part rested against the south wall with the mouth slightly above the level of the door in the south wall. It is almost a duplicate of pitcher 3585, the design, the manner of forming the handle, and the general appearance of the vessel being the same. The life line on the rim of the vessel, which is somewhat flaring, is open, as was the case with the other pitcher, and it is quite probable that both pitchers were made by the same potter. It is 13 cms. high and 11 cms. in diameter at its widest part.

The next object found was another cylindrical jar of grayware. It was 2 feet 1 inch west of the doorway and 1 foot 3 inches north of the south wall. This vessel was standing in an upright position and in it were nine flat circular turquoise beads and two shell beads of the figure-eight form. The decoration on this jar was a series of narrow lines forming three broad bands which encircle the jar, all of them being below the handles. The handles were of the rope form and slanted upward. There were four in all, and they were placed on an average 3 cms. below the rim. The jar is 23 cms. high and averages 9.5 cms. in diameter.

After the removal of 3646 the work was carried northward in a small area west of the doorway. One foot west of this point and 9 inches north of the south wall, two sandstone jar covers were found, (3603 and 3600), about 2 inches below the door level. They were of the usual form, but 3603 was more carefully finished than the average jar covers from this pueblo, the edge being ground until it was at right angles with the sides.

Ornament of Hematite. While working in the southwest corner, a number of human ribs were found. They were 1 foot 6 inches north of the southern wall and 1 foot west of the doorway. They were mixed with fragments of wooden implements and other objects buried with the body. A little west of the ribs and 3 feet from the south wall, the right clavicle was found; a little west of this at a distance of 2 feet 9 inches from the southern wall, the left femur was located; and a few inches north of this a scapula. Near the femur mentioned, the main portion of the vertebral column was located.

In clearing away the débris in front of the human remains, that is, to the east of them, a bird form made of hematite was found. It was 1 foot 10 inches north of the south wall and 1 foot 9 inches east of the west wall, and was lying at a point 4 inches above the level of the southern doorway. This bird form is shown in Fig. 50. It measures 5.8 cms. from the tip of the bill to the tail, 2.7 cms. in width at the middle section of the wings and 1.6 cms. in thickness at the thickest part, which is directly back of the neck portion. The back is divided into two parts by bands of turquoise which have been sunk to the level of the surface. They start from either side of the neck, extend across the back, and end at either side of the tail. These divisions serve to accentuate the wings which are over 1 mm. higher than the general surface. In each wing three deep grooves have been cut and into these turquoise pieces have been inlaid. The turquoise lines extend to within 5 cms. of the edge and from this point a piece of shell extends to the edge. The tail is 1.5 cms. broad and a piece of shell 5 cms. wide has been attached to the end, the hematite having been cut away so that the shell would rest on the level of the stone. On the extreme edge of the shell three turquoise pieces were inlaid, but only one of them remains at the present time, as shown in the illustration. The head has been carefully rounded and the front part pointed to form the beak. A groove encircles the neck and in this a series of turquoise sets have been inlaid. The eyes are 3 mms. in diameter and are made of half round pieces of turquoise which have been glued into

Fig. 50 (10416). A Bird of Hematite, Inlaid with Turquoise, Room 32.
See Frontispiece, Plate 1.

holes drilled for the purpose. The under part is plain, with the exception of two holes which have been drilled through the breast. The manner of drilling these holes and a peculiar concavity between them is shown in the drawing. This figure evidently represents a water bird at rest on the surface of a pond or stream. The wings are folded over the back and the head is thrown forward as though the bird were swimming.

From the position of the holes drilled in the breast, it would seem that this object has been suspended in some way, and may have been used as a neck ornament in certain ceremonies. Its position in the room suggests that it had been buried with the body which was found directly west of and a little above it.

Miscellaneous Objects. The next object that was removed (3596) was a small mug; it was found 2 feet 6 inches north of the south wall and 2 feet 5 inches east of the west wall, standing in a natural position 6 inches above the level of the sill of the door in the south wall. It is of grayware decorated with black designs, 7 cms. high and 8.5 cms. in diameter at the bottom. The design is dim and almost obliterated in parts. The handle is extremely large for a jar of this type, and as in similar specimens, it extends from the rim to the bottom of the vessel.

One inch north of the mug just described and 2 feet 8 inches east of the west wall, the bowl of a coarsely made dipper was found. It is of rather peculiar shape, the handle was evidently of solid construction, generally cylindrical in form and attached to the bowl 1.5 cms. below its rim. It is 10.5 cms. wide at its widest part and 3.17 cms. deep. It is of grayware, but is discolored as though it had been through fire.

Three feet two inches north of the south wall and 7 inches from the west wall a bowl (3598) was found. It was about 6 inches above the floor level and rested in a natural position on a large flat stone. It is of grayware, decorated with black on the interior, having large black dots on the rim; it has two drilled handles. They are placed opposite each other and are 1 cm. below the rim of the vessel.

There was a mass of cloth, matted and partly decayed, in this part of the room, evidently part of the wrapping of the body. Water had poured into the room from the upper levels and had swirled about in this corner scattering the lighter specimens and the bones.

Fig. 51. Ornament of Lignite.

A large flat stone was found 2 feet 1 inch below the lintel poles of the doorway in the west wall. The débris below the stone had been caked from having been wet repeatedly.

Just below this stone, a pitcher was found; it was 2 feet from the south wall and 1 foot 4 inches from the west wall. It was lying on its side. It is of grayware with black decorations in the form of interlocking frets and half cloud terraces. The handle is also decorated and there is a series of dots around the edge of the rim. This specimen (3594) is 16.5 cms. high and 11.5 cms. in diameter at its widest part. On one side, near the rim, and on the opposite side, near the base, are areas that were blackened from fire.

Two feet five inches from the south wall and 1 foot 6 inches from the west wall and at a depth of 11 inches below the level of the large flat stone mentioned, fragments of a grayware bowl with black decorations and of a cooking vessel with a heavy corrugated handle were found; near them a human tooth, a number of vertebrae, and a fish bone were found.

Two stone jar covers were the next objects found, one of them on the same level as the large flat stone, and the other 6 inches below it. They are both made of sandstone and the sides of the objects have been ground and smoothed.

During the progress of the work a sketch was made showing the general stratification of the irregular layers at this part of the room. The measurements were made at a point 1 foot west of the southern door and 3 inches north of the south wall. The inflow of sand was from the east; hence, the sand layers increase in thickness from this point to the eastern wall of the room, which was no doubt carried into the room at the time that the burial was made and when the objects in the room were put in position. This gives a general idea of the character of the layers that were encountered, but it must be understood that there was no regular stratification, save in restricted areas where the water had not disturbed it to any great extent.

Layer A, sand	3 inches thick
Layer B, soil, charcoal, etc.	5 inches thick
Layer C, sand	$\frac{1}{2}$ inch thick
Layer D, black soil	1 inch thick
Layer E, sand	$3\frac{1}{2}$ inches thick
Layer F, soil	

A little below the western door level, 3 feet 4 inches from the south wall and 3 feet 9 inches from the west wall, small balls of red and yellow paint (4176) were found. From their form, which is rounding, it would seem that they had been retained in pouches, probably of buckskin. The yellow seems to be an ordinary ocher, but the red has a crystalline structure.

A circular object of jet, probably used as an ornament, was 4 feet 2 inches from the south wall and 2 feet 8 inches from the west wall and was found on the level of the lower part of the doorway of the west wall.

Just east of the mass of ceremonial sticks and near the north wall, several specimens were found. A sandstone jar cover was 7 inches from the north wall and 3 feet 3 inches from the west wall and was lying on the level of the large flat stone.

Three feet from the western wall and resting against the north wall, a broken bowl was found. There is a doorway in the north wall at this point and the fragments were directly in front of its western side, but 6 inches below the level of the sill.

Two sandstone balls were found 1 foot below the level of the north-ern doorway; they were 1 foot 9 inches from the north wall and 3 feet 10 inches from the west wall.

A Burial. The human backbone and pelvis which were found in the southwest corner (p. 134) were the next objects to receive attention. They were intact and were lying northwest by southeast, the pelvis being toward the northern point and 6 inches above the level of the western doorway. The vertebrae were lying in an almost horizontal position, ten of them were intact and in position, as were also the sacrum and the pelvic bones. Three vertebrae fell in removing the surface dirt, but they had probably been in place when the body was found. There were eight sticks in the sand at the right side of the body. From their appearance, it seems that they had been stuck into the soil of the sand at short inter-vals. One end of each is pointed and the opposite end is burned, as though they have been used as torches. The material is evidently cot-tonwood. They average 9.5 cms. in length and 1.3 cms. in diameter, although one of each is charred. There is no evidence of the action of fire on any other parts of the sticks. Scattered about in the sand were six pieces of similar size, but with squared ends; these, with two others with pointed ends, had the upper part charred in the same manner as those just described. With these was one which was larger than any of the others that have been mentioned, but owing to the fact that one end was missing, it cannot be determined whether it had been burned or not. What the office of these may have been is hard to say, but they may have been deposited with the body at the time of burial, and the ends burned for some special purpose. Wrapped about the bones and extending into the western doorway, there is a mass of burnt cloth, the greater part of which was simply woven textiles of finely spun yucca cord. The greater part of it was undecorated and shows no complex weaving, but there was one specimen, with a design forming broad bands and squares, seeming-ly stamped upon the cloth. In the center of each square, there is a raised portion caused by a deft manipulation of the threads during weaving. These small elevations have been dyed with the same dark color as that forming the bands and the squares.

Pottery. South of the body, a distance of $2\frac{1}{2}$ inches from the west wall and 1 foot 3 inches from the south wall, a pitcher was found. It was resting on its side with its base a trifle higher than its mouth, the base being on the level with the lower part of the western doorway. This pitcher (3953) is of the usual grayware with black decorations. It is 16 cms. deep and 8 cms. in diameter at the mouth. The handle and the edge of the rim are decorated, the former with a design similar to that shown on the upper part of the vessel, as in Plate 7 and the rim with a series of dots. One and a half inches east of the pitcher just described, with its base about the same distance from the south wall, a jar (3595) was encountered. It was lying on its side with the mouth pointing toward the southeast and was on the same level as the pitcher described above. This jar is of grayware with three bands of lines encircling it, two below and one above the handles which are of the loop form and placed perpendicularly. This specimen is 21.5 cms. deep and 9.5 cms. in diameter at the rim. The edge of the rim is decorated with a line of black paint, but there are no decorations on the bottom.

Another pitcher was found resting against the south wall, 10 inches from the west wall and 1 foot higher than the jar (3595). It is of grayware decorated in black. It is 16 cms. deep and averages 8 cms. in diameter at the mouth which has been somewhat flattened, owing to the careless handling during the firing process. The handle is decorated, as is also the edge of the rim. The line forming the decoration is open at the point just above the handle.

The three specimens just described were grouped about a post, 5 inches in diameter, which was 5 inches from the west wall and 5½ inches from the south wall; most of these specimens were within 4 inches of this post.

Another specimen (3609), a jar cover of sandstone was 10 inches north of the post and 8 inches from the west wall, causing it to lie very close to the pitcher (3593), but it was 2 inches lower than this specimen.

Another jar cover made of sandstone (3608) was found 3 inches under pitcher 3593 and the third 3607, was found 4 inches below pitcher 3592.

A small bowl of grayware decorated on the interior with interlocking designs in black was found 1 foot 1 inch from the north wall and 4 feet 10 inches from the west wall. It was lying in a natural position on the level of the sill of the doorway in the north wall and contained evidences of having been filled with some material, probably food. This bowl has had four handles near the rim, ranging in such a way, that they were equidistant; one of these, however, is missing. This bowl (3636), like many of the other specimens found in this room, has a series of dots on the edge of the rim. It is 9.5 cms. in diameter at the rim and 4 cms. deep.

The next object found was also a grayware bowl (3626); it was 5 feet 8 inches from the west wall and was resting against the north wall. It was lying in a natural position on a level with the bottom of the northern doorway. This bowl is the largest that was found in Room 32, it averages 29.5 cms. in diameter at the rim and is 13.8 cms. deep.   There are no decorations on the exterior.   On the edge of the rim there are six sets of dots, there being four in each set.   The design on the interior is composed of elaborate interlocking frets and bands of hachure work.

Just south of the bowl (3626) and touching it was a small pitcher (3633).   It was 9 inches from the north wall, and 6 feet 1 inch from the west wall, lying on its side and was a trifle lower than bowl 3626.   This specimen is of grayware decorated with irregular designs in black.   The handle is composed of two cylindrical pieces of clay joined together and their ends formed into one piece, where they join the vessel.   This specimen is 10 cms. in diameter at its widest part and has a depth of 12.2 cms.

In uncovering the specimens that have just been described an exceptionally large cylindrical jar was found.   It was 4 inches from the north wall and 6 feet 7 inches from the west wall.   It was lying on its side, the mouth pointing toward the northeast and was on the level of the base of the northern doorway.   This jar is of grayware, covered with a very fine white slip that had been applied to the interior as well as the exterior of the vessel.   The smoothing on the exterior has been carried to such an extent that the fine finish, in some places, has caused the vessel to look as though it was polished and is quite noticeable.   The vessel is absolutely devoid of ornamentation, the only embellishments being three heavy knob-like handles which are placed on an average of 1.8 cms. below the rim.   These handles are perforated, the holes being punched through from the base upwards.   This vessel (3638) measures 16.8 cms. in diameter at the rim, which is slightly irregular, there being a flattening on one side, and 28.6 cms. in depth.

Four jar covers were found 1 foot 6 inches from the north wall and 7 feet 8 inches from the west wall on the level of the base of the northern doorway.   These covers are of the usual form and size and are made of fine-grained sandstone.

A bowl of grayware (3643) found near the jar covers just mentioned was 1 foot 6 inches from the north wall and 8 feet from the west wall and 4 inches above the level of the base of the northern doorway.

A natural pebble of quartzite, which may have been worked a little on the edges, so that it could be hafted was found in the center of the rim, 3 feet below the level of the doorway in the north wall.   It resembles slightly the head of an animal and may have been used as a fetich (3648).

Ceremonial Sticks.   When the mass of ceremonial sticks in the northwest corner of the room was reached, it was found that most of the sticks had decayed, except in parts that extended above the surface of the sand.

Fig. 52.   Ceremonial Sticks, *in situ*, Room 32.

141

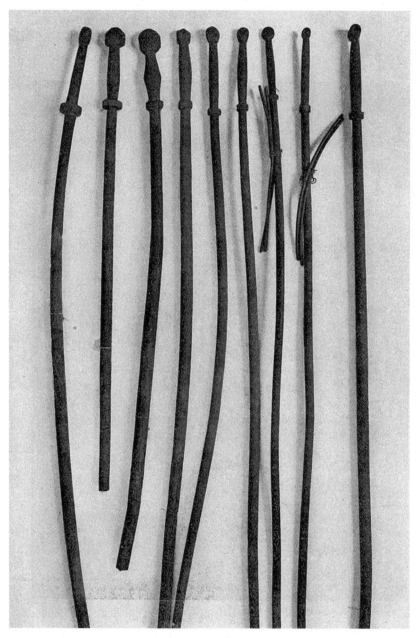

Fig. 53. Ceremonial Sticks, Type 1: *a* (4212), Room 32; *b* (4221), Room 32; *c* (4235), Room 32; *d* (4199), Room 32; *e* (4187), Room 32; *f* (4232), Room 32; *g* (4413), Room 32; *h* (4412); *i* (4522), Room 33.

In Fig. 52 the deposit is shown when the work of removal had begun. The work was slow and tedious, as many of the specimens were quite soft, evidently from recent rains. The crossing and interlocking of the sticks, and the necessity of bracing the ceiling beams added new obstacles. It was, therefore, impossible to remove many of the sticks in a perfect condition, but it was possible to mend a goodly portion of them after they reached the Museum.

Over three hundred were taken from this corner, but it is impossible to say how many of them had been lying beneath the surface and had decomposed to such an extent that it was impossible to remove them; but from the fragments that were found in the sand, it would seem that there must have been three hundred and seventy-five in all.

One end of each ceremonial stick is finished in some special manner so they can be divided into four definite classes, with certain subdivisions:-

1. The first has a carved end characterized by two knobs; the upper knob in one style being plain, whereas another of the same form, has an opening in this knob.

2. The second form has the end carved in the shape of a bear claw.

3. The third form has the end flattened in the shape of a broad spatula.

4. The fourth form has a wedge-shaped end; some of the specimens are bound with buckskin and cord.

Type 1. A series of specimens showing the type of form 1 is shown in Fig. 53. It may be seen that the main characteristic of this form is the carved end, formed of an irregular piece at the extremity of the stick and a circular band raised above the surface at a point averaging 10 cms. below the end of the stick. There is great variation in the manner of carving the ends of these sticks, but all of them follow a general form. The intervening space between the raised portions is, in some specimens, almost uniform in diameter, while in others it increases in size from the end to the central portion, decreasing again to the raised band, thereby forming a spindle-shaped piece. The general form of the ends can be seen to good advantage in the figure mentioned. Some of them are rounding, others flare on the sides and come to a point at the end; but all of them are flattened and in no instance has one been found, whose end is perfectly rounded. In only one specimen of this type has a hole been found in the carved piece at the end. This peculiarity belongs to a subdivision of this type, the difference in the two forms being in the formation of the raised band. In this type the surface of the band is perfectly flat, whereas in the subdivision, there is a slight groove in its surface. The stick mentioned as having a hole drilled through the upper part may have been grooved slightly when it was new, but it is well-preserved and it hardly seems that this could be possible. These sticks are of cottonwood and range from 1 cm. to 1.7 cms. in diameter. None of these specimens is intact, the lower end of each having been broken off. The longest, however, measures 1.1 m. in length.

Six of these sticks have the remains of cords tied at the upper end, all seemingly of yucca fiber; four of them are tied between the knobs, two just above the lower knob, that of the third directly below the knob at the end of the stick, and the fourth had cord tied just above the middle portion. One of these is knotted at the end, in a similar fashion to that found about the quills of feathers, showing that these cords were no doubt

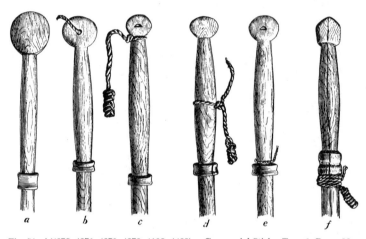

Fig. 54a-f (4375, 4371, 4379, 4378, 4185, 4433).   Ceremonial Sticks, Type 1, Room 32.

used to fasten feathers to the ends of these staves. The other two sticks had the cord bound directly below the carved band. These specimens are shown in Fig. 54. There are three specimens of exceptional size which are shown in Fig. 53b, c, h. In the first two specimens, the band at the end of the carved space is 2.8 cms. in diameter, whereas in all the other specimens, the average is greatly below this figure. The other specimen shown is rather roughly finished and the slope of the central portion has been strongly accentuated.

With this group were found three sticks with two slender ceremonial sticks fastened to their sides, directly below the carved end. These sticks may be seen in Fig. 53. In one of these the sticks are bound with a loose two-strand yucca cord, the pieces being bound side by side and running parallel with the main sticks. There is also evidence of a cord fastened directly below the carved end which is perforated, this being the specimen mentioned as being the exception in this type. The second stick having the smaller sticks bound to its surface has a yucca cord tied loosely below the carved band. Its end has been knotted and still retains a portion of the quill of a feather. The third stick had the binding cord in place when the specimen was uncovered, but it had decayed to such an extent that it could not be retained. The specimens are, however, tied to the stick in the same position as when they were found. This stick has the remains of a cord directly below the carved end and another just above the carved band, this being the only instance noted in which two cords were found on the same specimen.

The use of these small sticks which have been found in a number of rooms in Pueblo Bonito, as already noted, cannot be definitely determined, save that they are used in a ceremonial way and are no doubt similar to the prayer sticks used by the Pueblo Indians at the present time. They are found in many of the rooms of the pueblo, but this is the first instance in which they have been found associated with ceremonial sticks. Cushing claimed that they were scalp stretchers and that their ceremonial use was secondary. They are generally found in pairs and are almost always curved, but it would hardly seem from their form, that it would have been possible to utilize them for stretching human scalps.

There were fifty-seven sticks of Type 1 that could be removed, although a number of them are represented merely by the carved head piece, but in each instance a part of the head piece has been preserved to show conclusively that it belonged to this particular form. The ends of four of these sticks are burned, but as there was no evidence of a fire in this room, it may be that the sticks were burnt before they were put in place. Two of the burnt sticks are the ones having the small ceremonial sticks attached to their sides.

The subdivision of this type, as already noted, differs from the others in having a hole drilled through the end and having the lower raised band grooved; there are however, eighteen exceptions. These pieces have the groove around the lower band, but no hole drilled through the upper part. Save for the difference noted, these specimens are the same as the form already described. Fourteen of them had the cord attached to their upper parts and one has a band of cotton cord tied at a point 10.5 cms. below the grooved band. One of these had the cord passed through the hole in the end, as shown in Fig. 54.

Type 2. This type is represented by fifty-four pieces. This form has a curved end, carved to represent the claw of an animal; its appearance suggests the claw of a bear. In Fig. 55 a series of these sticks is shown; it may be seen that they vary considerably in the size of what, in an animal claw, would be the basal part. In some, there is a very slight enlargement at the end of the stick; the other extreme is a very broad heavy piece from one side of which the claw-like projection starts. The widest is 3.7 cms. broad and the narrowest, 1.5 cms. The claw part in some is flattened on the inside and rounded on the outer surface; on others it is rounded throughout its length. In size and material these sticks are similar in form to Type 1.

If these sticks had cords for the attachment of feathers there is no evidence of them at the present time. The only one showing remains of a cord, had the band in such a position that it seems to indicate that a small ceremonial stick rather than a feather had been fastened to it.

Type 3. Type 3 differs radically from those already described. Types 1 and 2 were cylindrical throughout the greater part of their length, some of them tapering toward the plain end. All of the specimens in Type 3 are half rounded; some of these taper slightly toward the end, but they preserve a uniform plano-convex form throughout their length.

There were fifty-four specimens of this type, representative forms of which are shown in Fig. 58. The end corresponding to the carved end in the other specimens, is flattened in this type. In the widest blade, the stick measures 2 cms. in width, on the flat side, and tapers generally to a width of 3.4 cms. at the end of the blade. The blade averages 8 cms. in length. The sticks average 1.2 cms. in thickness and decrease to 3 mms. at the end of the blade. Some specimens, however, are almost twice this thickness at the end, whereas others taper to a very thin edge.

Three of these sticks show evidence of attachment of feathers, two have yucca cords attached, and one has a cord made of cotton; these cords are placed near the blade end of the stick. Another stick shows evidences of having been bound at the blade end with a cord, probably of buckskin; the area that was bound extends from the point where the blade begins, 6 cms. toward the end of the blade itself. Two of the specimens have been found with strips of buckskin over a centimeter in width (Fig. 58); one of the specimens has the yucca cord for the attachment of a feather. Both of these sticks are split at the point where the wrapping was adjusted and it was evidently for some such defect in the stick that the wrapping was applied; but if used in certain games, as the consideration of other specimens found with them would tend to show, it may have been applied in order that a firm grip might be obtained in handling the stick. Few of these sticks have been preserved in their entirety, the end opposite the handle being missing in most cases; however, some specimens show this portion, which might be called the distal end. These give a good idea of the taper of this end of the stick; one of them is almost a counterpart of the small gaming sticks found in Room 2 and it may have been from sticks of this kind that the small dice-like pieces, were cut (p. 35). Most of the pieces were in a fair state of preservation.

One of these sticks has an object carved on the flat side at a point 30 cms. below the blade end. This is in the form of a raised figure, 3.7 cms. long, 1.1 cms. broad at the end toward the blade, and tapering to 5 mms. at the opposite ends. This end is raised 3 mms. above the surface of the stick. It is evidently made to represent the rattle of a rattlesnake. The stick is perfectly straight below this figure, but directly above, it curves backward, the curvings being evidently intentional.

In the Zuñi ceremonials, there is a game played with sticks that might be called an Indian golf game. The clan of the south meets the clan of the north and the game is waged with all the ardor of a battle. Before the game, both sides pray to the ceremonial representatives of their sticks and carry miniature sticks with them. The game is to decide the fate of the year. Should the south win, it would rain, but should the north be victorious, there would be a windy season. In deciding the outcome of a battle, a band of braves is selected to represent the enemy; an equal number oppose them, then a battle royal ensues. Should those who represent the enemy be vanquished, the braves will go forth to the conquest with light hearts, for they have won the spirit battle, which assures success in a physical one; thus, by divination, according to Cushing, many great events were decided.

Another ceremonial stick that belongs to Type 3, is shown in Fig. 58a. This stick has the half round form of the others, but the end has been finished in a unique way. The rounded portion of the end of the stick was cut away to allow a broad spatulate piece to be lashed to it. This piece is 15 cms. long, 6.5 cms. wide at the blade end, and 4 cms. thick. It tapers gently towards the point where it is bound to the stick. At this end there is a projection which fits into a groove and over it a band of sinew 1.4 cms. in width has been wrapped. At the extreme end of the main stick, a groove has been cut and directly below it, two holes have been drilled into the flat portion. By means of these holes and the groove, the pieces have been joined together with sinew, making a neat, and at the same time, a very substantial finish. This is the only instance in which two pieces were employed in making one of these ceremonial staves.

Type 4. Type 4 is represented by twenty-two pieces; they are cylindrical sticks, but are as a rule greater in diameter than those in types 1 and 2. They are rougher in finish than those in the types just mentioned; some of them have knots projecting from their surface and others are very irregular in form. The care shown in the selection of the other pieces has not been carried out in selecting this material. The largest of these specimens measures over 2 cms. in diameter; two of the perfect ones measure 1.135 m. and 1.11 m., respectively. The ends of the sticks corresponding to the worked end of the other pieces show a flattening on one side of the stick which divides it in half at the end and tapers back until the general level of the stick is reached. The worked area averages 14 cms. in length; in some however, it extends backward over 20 cms. Fig. 58 shows a series of the more perfect of these sticks and gives a good idea of their form.

A variant or subtype of this form is shown in Fig. 60. There were ten of this form and they differ from the others inasmuch as they have bindings of sinew at the end of the blades and, in two instances, at the point where the ground surface begins. On one of these specimens there is a broad binding of sinew which originally covered a space 4.5 cms. broad. A part of the sinew has disappeared, showing that the portion toward the blade end, over a distance of 1 cm., was painted black. The remaining portion to within 5 cms. of the end of the binding was painted a bright orange color, all of the colored area having been covered with the thick binding of sinew. There was evidently a defective space in the middle portion of this stick as it had been bound with a strip of buckskin which was over 1.5 cms. in width. The specimens were similar to those already described, the only difference being in the handling of the blade end; they had been bound at the tip with sinew, as in the specimens just described, evidently to strengthen this point. Over the entire blade a grillwork of rawhide strands was adjusted. The technique of this work is rather interesting and is shown in Fig. 60. It may be noted that in all of the specimens but one, the rawhide covers the entire worked space, with the exception of a narrow place averaging 5 cms. at the point and extending beyond the worked area on the face of the stick. In the third, a similar technique was found; in place of the buckskin, a finely spun cord was employed. There were ten of these specimens, three of which are shown in Fig. 58. In two of these a finely spun yucca cord was used which covered the blade in the same manner as did the buckskin, the only difference being that the cord does not extend to the plain surface of the stick and does not completely cover the blade end. The third

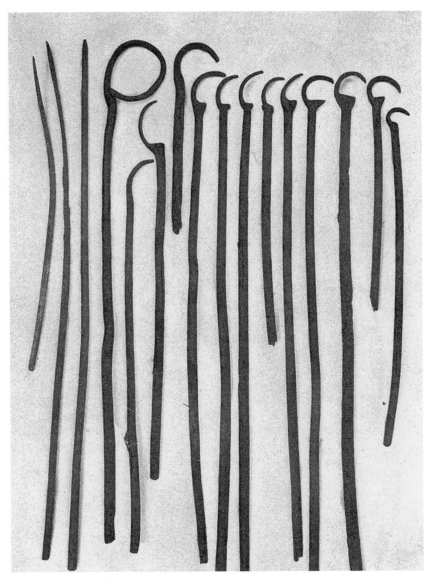

Fig. 55. Ceremonial Sticks, Type 2: *abc* (4504, 4438, 4437), Room 32; *d* (4539), Room 33; *e-p* (4332, 4331, 4358, 4384, 4367, 4342, 4360, 4385, 4386, 4428, 4355, 4363), Room 32.

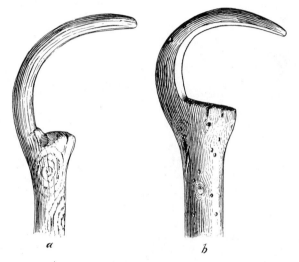

Fig. 56. Ceremonial Sticks, Type 2: a (4348); b (4428).

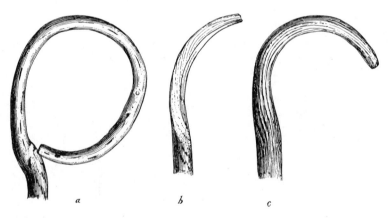

Fig. 57. Ceremonial Sticks, Variants of Type 2: a (4539), Room 33; bc (4332, 4358), Room 32.

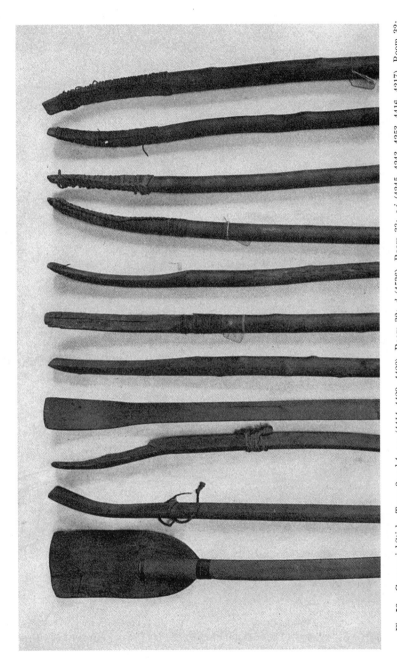

Fig. 58. Ceremonial Sticks, Types 3 and 4: *a-c* (4414, 4420, 4422), Room 32; *d* (4536), Room 33; *e-i* (4245, 4243, 4253, 4416, 4217), Room 32; *j* (4512), Room 33; *k* (4418), Room 32.

151

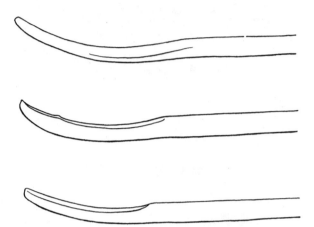

Fig. 59.   Ceremonial Sticks, Type 3: a-c (4327, 4301, 4397), Room 32.

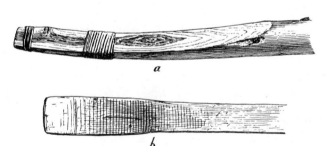

a

b

Fig. 60.   Ceremonial Sticks, Type 4: a (4514), Room 33; b (4301), Room 32.

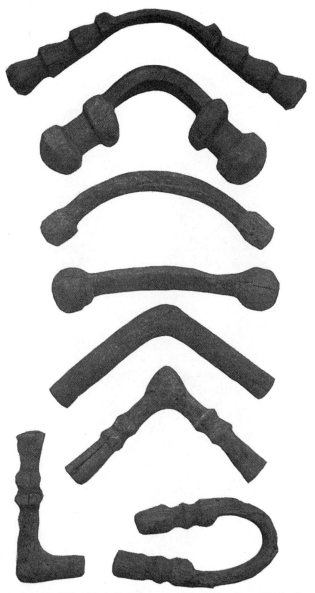

Fig. 61 *a-h* (4477, 4478, 4480, 4490, 4488, 4489, 4481, 4493).   Curved Sticks, Room 32.

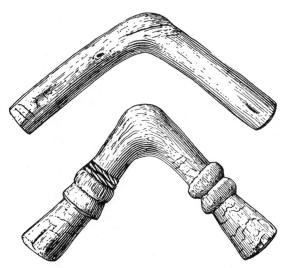

Fig. 62.   Curved Sticks: *a* (4488), Room 32; *b* (4551), Room 33.

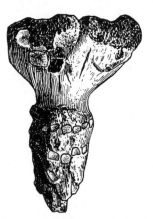

Fig. 63 (4368).   End of Ceremonial Stick, inlaid with Turquoise, Room 32

154

Fig. 64. Curved Sticks: *ab* (8795), Room 55; *c* (4618), Room 33; *d-f* (4507, 4506, 4440), Room 32.

155

Fig. 65 (4500).   Design on a Painted Board, Room 32.
See Plate 8.

specimen was covered with cotton cord, bound with buckskin at the point where the blade begins and reinforced 3.5 cms. from the end with a band of sinew. The knotting of the cord on the edges of the stick is the same as that shown in the rawhide covered pieces already noted.

Associated with the game sticks were a number of branches of greasewood and other sticks which, because they had not been finished, could not be classed as game sticks; two of them had evidently been used for stirring fires, as their ends were burnt. There were other sticks, of the curved form shown in Fig. 64, many of them in a fragmentary condition when found. The use to which these sticks were applied cannot be suggested, but evidently they had some connection with the game sticks. In the illustration (f) appears a stick with worked ends. It is 55 cms. long and 3.2 cms. in diameter. Its appearance suggests that it might have been used as the rung of a ladder, but there is no evidence of wear to show that it had been used for this purpose.

In Fig. 55a-c (4504, 4437–4438), two carefully finished sticks of cottonwood and one of deer antler are shown. All of these objects taper at one end; in the case of the antler piece, the opposite end is slightly tapered. The cottonwood pieces are 79.5 cms. and 77.5 cms. in length, respectively, and average 1.2 cms. in diameter at the butt end. The piece of deer antler has been ground and is 57.5 cms. in length and 1 cm. in width at its widest part. There are no markings upon the surface of these sticks to indicate their use. Associated with the game staves were twenty-three complete sticks, such as were found attached in pairs to the larger staves, and fifty-six fragments of these slender curved pieces. There was found with the large game sticks, a series of curved sticks, more or less elaborate, which may have been tossed by means of the large sticks. In Fig. 61 a series of these specimens is shown. Fig. 61b is 13.5 cms. long and the knobs at the ends, which are irregular in shape, have an average diameter of 3 cms. The band which separates the ends is 2.6 cms. broad and 1.3 cms. thick. It is made of cottonwood. Fig. 61a is 18 cms. long and is flattened on the under side. The three cone-shaped pieces on either side of the flat central part average 2 cms. in width. Fig. 61b and 61c show a simple form of Fig. 61a; they are about the same size and average 13.5 cms. from end to end. This form reminds one of the bags filled with sand and tied together with a piece of buckskin, as used by Indians in a game. There were three other specimens of the type just described. In Fig. 61g a variant of this form is shown; it is 12 cms. from end to end and the balls on either end measure 1.5 cms. in length, whereas the others average nearly 6 cms. in length. There was one other specimen of this form. Fig. 61d is of the dumb-bell form; it is 14 cms. long with a flat band connecting the balls which average 2.7 cms. in diameter. Fig. 61e is a cylindrical stick, 1.2 cms. in diameter, and 14.5 cms. from end to end. It is curved, but there has been no carving on the surface. Figs. 61e and 62a show another stick, angular in shape, which is also simple in form. There was another specimen of this form, but it was in a fragmentary condition. Figs. 61f, h, and 62b are elaborations of the angular type, with the arms carved in a manner similar to that seen on some of the larger ceremonial sticks. There was one other fragment of this carved angular type. Fig. 61 shows those with a ball on either end and a raised portion from which the narrow separating band started. This type seemed to be the most common, as there were nine in a fragmentary condition, both ends of which were found. One of these was decorated with cross-hatching which covered the entire surface. There was one fragmentary piece with three cones on either side of the central portion. There were also fourteen ends, the opposite portions of which could not be found; most of them were similar to those that have been described, although there were a few showing slight variations.[1]

Finally, note should be taken of the fragment shown in Fig. 63. This is the knobbed end of a wooden stick, inlaid with small pieces of turquoise.

Design Board. Among the ceremonial sticks in the northwestern part of the room, a slab was found which, from its weight, was evidently of wood; it was completely covered with plant mould and no special attention was given to the object until it reached the Museum; it had been dried to some extent and faint outlines of designs could be seen upon the flat surfaces. It was subjected to a careful brushing and washing, with the result that elaborate designs were found to cover both sides and one edge of the slab.

The slab itself measures 16.5 cm. in width and 17.5 cm. in height. It averages 1.7 cm. in thickness at the decorated edge and widens to 2.5 cm. at the opposite edge. The decorated edge has been carefully smoothed, but the opposite one is somewhat irregular; the upper and

---

[1]Some of these sticks resemble the wooden bars used by the Zuñi belt weaver to hold the warp series to her belt. Quite similar objects have been found in ruins in northern Chile and Argentine [See, Ambrosetti, Juan B., "Exploracionòs Arqueológicas en la Ciudad Prehistórica de 'La Paya' (Valle Calchaqui-Provincia de Salta)," Segunda Parte, Descripción del Material Arqueólogico (Buenos Aires, 1908), 465–466], which from the signs of wear upon their surfaces must have been used as rings or toggles. Curiously enough, both the angular or elbow type shown above and the more extended curved forms are found in Chile. The suggestion, therefore, is that originally these objects from Bonito were practical instead of ceremonial.—Ed.

lower edges have been rounded. This object was no doubt meant for suspension, and may have been an altar slab. In the corner, at one end of the decorated edge, a hole has been drilled through the face of the slab, thence upward to the center of the upper edge, thereby leaving one side free from defects.

The designs on the sides of the slab differ. On one side, as may be seen in Plate 8, there is an interlocking fret design, the major portion of the lines which form it being serrated. These lines are in black and green on a red background, the designs themselves being edged with a narrow line of orange. The opposite side of the slab which is shown in Fig. 65 has the same red background, and the design in general is similar to that shown on the obverse, but on this side the lines are straight and none of them have the edge serrated. The colors of the bands forming the designs on this side of the slab are black and a deep carmine or plum color. The latter are outlined with orange as were those on the other side. The design on the edge is a continuation of that on the side just described and it seems to be carried to the edge on the side opposite.

There still remains enough of the designs to give a general idea of their former appearance, but in order to develop them to the extent shown in the accompanying illustrations, it was necessary to keep this surface wet during the greater part of the time that the artist was at work. The figures are the usual geometric elaborations found in this pueblo.

Arrows. Standing upright and resting against the walls in the northwest corner of the room, a quiver of arrows was found. Thirty-two of these became detached from the main mass when the quiver was uncovered, but over half of the arrows were removed in the condition in which they were found, and may now be seen in the Museum, where they are on exhibition. It seems that the arrows were divided into groups which were tied with heavy two-strand yucca cord. One of these cords is still in position, the others had decayed to such an extent, that they could not be preserved. In the mass that was removed intact, there were forty-nine arrows that can be counted, that is there are forty-nine points which project to such an extent that they can be seen, others may be imbedded deeper in the mass; but, owing to the fact that the opposite ends of the arrows are in such a poor state of preservation, it is impossible to check up the count from that end. The actual number of arrows therefore, cannot be decided upon, but with the ones that were detached, there are eighty-one arrows, the points of which could be examined.

These arrows are of the compound form, made of reeds with a wooden foreshaft; they average 77 cms. in length, including the foreshaft and point. The foreshafts are made of some hard wood which has the appearance of greasewood, although it may possibly be mountain mahogany; they average 18 cms. in length from the point where they enter the reed to the end where the stone point is attached, 8 mms. in diameter at the base, and taper gently toward the point. They are fastened to the main shaft, that is, to the reed, with bindings of sinew, and the points are attached with substantial bindings of the same material. The points are mostly of transparent chalcedony and are of the tapering variety, a number of them have double notches on the side, as may be seen in Fig. 40d.

Owing to the fact that the room has contained so much water at times, the feathering of the arrows was not preserved. Still adhering to some of them, there are fragments of the quills, which show the manner of feathering; they have a line of black paint on the notched end; but aside from this, no painting, such as has been noted on some of the arrows from other rooms in Pueblo Bonito, was in evidence. Most of the arrows retained the notch, in fact the greater number were complete, the only blemish being the loss of the feathers, and a partial decomposition of the surfaces, which rested upon the ground.

In studying the workmanship on these arrows, there is one point that is quite apparent, that is the manner of straightening the solid wooden foreshafts; although they have been ground and smoothed after the straightening process was complete, the marks of the teeth may still be seen on the surface. Indians may be seen at the present time in the Southwest straightening sticks which are to be used for arrows in this manner. The work is accomplished by grasping the ends of the stick firmly with either hand, bending it, and biting the surface at the same time. On some of the foreshafts from the ruins, indentations which are quite deep, may be seen.

The finding of arrows in the ancient pueblos, is not uncommon, but seldom, if ever before, has a complete quiver been encountered. A great many fragments of arrows of similar form to those just described were found in the ruin; but strange as it may seem, no perfect bow, nor even a large fragment of one was found.

Three foreshafts of wood and a fourth with a section of the reed arrow attached, were found (Fig. 40). These foreshafts are of the usual form, with the exception of the end which is carried to a point. These are what Cushing called "self foreshafts," meaning that they were complete and were not intended to hold a stone point. These specimens were found among the ceremonial sticks, but not near or associated with the quiver of arrows. It is rather interesting to find this type of foreshaft in the room, as all those in the quiver that could be examined had been fashioned for the attachment of a stone point. They measure 27.3 cm. in length, the part that enters the reed shaft being on an average 2.7 cms. long.

Miscellaneous Objects. Directly behind the mass of ceremonial sticks in the northwest corner and resting against the north wall was a club of elk antler lying with the butt end toward the north. This specimen is 48 cms. long and has a hole drilled through the small end for the attachment of a thong. Very little work has been done upon the antler, with the exception of the grinding off of a prong directly above the handle and a general grinding away of the base of the antler. The surface has been smoothed to some extent, but there are no decorations.

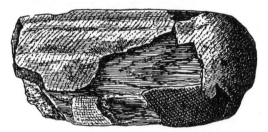

Fig. 66 (4181).　A Cloth-Covered Object, Room 32.

Another object of interest found under the body in the southwest corner of the room is shown in Fig. 66. It is a piece of what seems to be a section of a cactus stalk. In its present fragmentary condition it is 8.5 cms. long, 5 cms. broad, and 3 cms. thick. The lower part is intact, but part of the upper end is missing; the upper part has been bound with yucca cord, the remaining part of which is over 1 cm. in width. This binding circled the upper part of the object and from a layer of cloth which covers the greater part of one side at the present time it would seem that the whole object had been enclosed in a similar layer. Owing to the fact that the specimen is not complete, it is impossible to say what its use had been, but it may have been used as a badge of office such as is carried by priests at the present time among the Hopi and Zuñi and used also on ceremonial altars.

Two wooden slabs were found in the general débris in the western part of the room. Both are of cottonwood; one is 20.6 cms. long, 8.5 cms. in width, and 2.5 cms. in thickness, the sides and ends are rounded. Boards of this nature were used, according to Cushing, for stretching the skins of animal heads that were to be used for ceremonial purposes. The other slab is 27 cms. long, 9 cms. wide, and averages 1.5 cms. in the center, it tapers, however, toward either side. Two holes have been drilled at the upper edge near one of the corners, and one of these has been closed with a wooden plug. There are also two holes near the lower edge of the piece, but there is nothing either in form or in the positions of the holes to indicate their use. One of the ordinary kicking sticks was found in the northwest corner. It is 13 cms. long, and averages 4 cms. in diameter; it is of the usual form, but slightly larger than the average stick of this nature.

A small section of reed was found in the western part of the room. It is 4.7 cms. in length and has the ends cut at right angles with the reed. It may have been used either as a die or as a drinking tube.

Among the fragments of ceremonial sticks from the northwestern corner was one painted black and orange, similar to that noted in one of the perfect sticks. In this case as in the other one mentioned, the orange occupies the major portion of the band, but both colors had been perfectly preserved.

Among the other objects found in the western part of the room, were three sandals of the braided variety, the material used being narrow strips of yucca leaf. There were also fragments of finely woven sandals made of yucca fiber. Fragments of a number of small and at least one very large basket were also found. These objects, with a large piece of galena, a piece of calcined gypsum, an irregular mass of piñon gum, a chalcedony flake with a very sharp cutting edge, a number of pieces of squash rind and squash and pumpkin stems, a piece of squash or pumpkin rind cut into a circular form, drilled in the center, the remains of a fiber cord with which it was no doubt attached to some object still in place in the hole, and a number of pieces of reeds finish the list of objects.

Room 32 proved to be 8 feet 11 inches long on the north side, 8 feet 8 inches long on the south side, 4 feet 7 inches wide at the east end, and 7 feet 3 inches wide at the west end. There were doorways in three of the walls and all of the walls were plastered. These doorways were of the usual form and had poles for lintels. The one in the north wall was 1 foot 9 inches wide and 1 foot 9 inches high; it was open and led into a room which, upon investigation, proved to be another of the burial series. This doorway was 3 feet from the west wall. The southern doorway was 1 foot 10 inches wide and 2 feet 10 inches high; it was 4 feet 2 inches from the west wall. The western doorway was 2 feet from the southern wall. It was 1 foot 9 inches wide and 2 feet 9 inches high. The floor was about 1 foot below the level of the doorways, which were about an equal distance above it. The distance from the ceiling beams, in their present condition, to the door sills averaged 4 feet.

Room 33.

Room 33 is directly west of and connected with Room 32. When the latter was first entered, it was found that the sand had almost filled the western doorway, but there was enough space remaining to allow passage through it, and into Room 33. Entrance was gained by the writer, and, with the aid of a candle, certain objects were seen which were in keeping with the ceremonial sticks that protruded from the sand in the room already examined. The room proved to be somewhat smaller than Room 32; but the sand had not filled it so deeply as the other room. A full account of its contents has been published in "The Exploration of a Burial Room in Pueblo Bonito, New Mexico."[1] The unique feature of the room is that it was a burial place and with the bodies were deposited very interesting objects fully described in our earlier publication.

The room under consideration is very small compared with the rooms in the northern part of the building. It is situated in a section where there evidently was a great deal of reconstruction work, to which fact, no doubt, may be attributed the presence of so many small rooms grouped about Room 33. The length of the northern wall of the room is 6 feet, of the southern wall 6 feet 3 inches, of the eastern wall 5 feet 10 inches, and of the western wall 6 feet 10 inches; that is, the room is almost square. The doorway in the eastern wall is 2 feet 3 inches from the southern wall. It is of the ordinary rectangular type,—1 foot 10 inches high and 2 feet 3 inches wide,—provided with poles for a lintel. This is the only entrance to the room. The sides of the doorway are plastered, as are all of the walls. There are no decorations on the walls, nor are there evidences of the room having been made for a burial chamber. In the southwestern corner is a post that was placed under the crossbeams, which extend north and south, as a precautionary measure. These beams enter the northern and southern walls; but, in adding new

---

[1]*Putnam Anniversary Volume* (New York, 1909), 196–252.

rooms above this series, the builders evidently thought it advisable to strengthen the floors with posts. The top of the post mentioned had fallen against the western wall. Its base stands about a foot from both the western and the southern wall. The largest post in the room was found under the beam in the northwestern corner. Its distance from the walls is about the same as in the case of the post in the southwestern corner. In the northeastern corner are two posts, one of which supports the ceiling beam, standing 5 inches from the eastern wall and a foot from the northern wall; the other post is four inches west of the one just mentioned, about the same distance from the northern wall, and extending through the ceiling into the room above. A post in the southeastern corner at the base is six inches from each wall, but has fallen against the eastern wall. The ceiling is composed of thirteen beams, of various sizes, over which is a layer of cedarbark. In the southwestern corner, at a distance of 1 foot 6 inches from the ceiling beams, were five willow sticks protruding from the wall, and forming a sort of rack; but nothing was found in it. The room in its entirety is in a very good state of preservation, the only defect being a slight bulge in the ceiling.

Though the specimens found have been adequately described elsewhere[1] some of the more important may be noted here. Among these are six flageolets shown in Fig. 67. One of these was highly decorated, Fig. 68. The types of pottery found are shown in Figs. 69–70. Ornaments of turquoise and shell were abundant. One of the most striking was a basket covered with a turquoise mosaic (Fig. 71). It is described as follows: At first, in clearing away the surrounding sand, the small turquoise pieces seemed to be in place; subsequently, as the sand was brushed from about them, many fell from their original position. It required several hours to determine the shape of the object covered by these turquoise pieces; but, owing to the fact that fragments of the material on which the turquoise had been fastened still remained, it was possible to ascertain that the object had been a cylindrical basket, 3 inches in diameter and 6 inches in length. The basket work had decayed; but the fragments showed conclusively that it had been made of very slender splints over which a layer of some material, probably piñon gum, had been placed, this being the medium that held the turquoise pieces in position. A restoration of this specimen is shown in Fig. 71, the individual pieces being represented as adjusted in the manner noted by the writer in uncovering the specimen. The cylinder was practically

---

[1] *ibid.*, *Putnam Anniversary Volume.*

Fig. 67 *a–f* (4560, 4559, 4557, 4558, 4561, 4562). Flageolets from Room 33: *a*, From the northeastern corner of the room; *b, c, d*, From the south-eastern corner; *e, f*, Carved flageolets found with *bcd*.

165

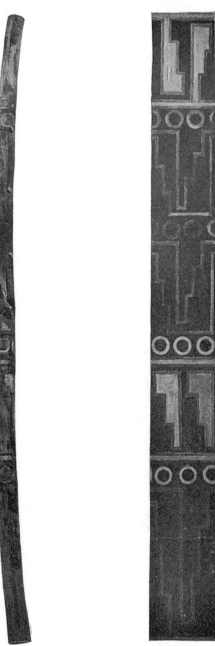

Fig. 68 (4563).   Painted Flute from Room 33.

Fig. 69 a-l (3610, 3617, 3627, 3618, 3624, 3675, 8628, 3656, 3645, 3635, 3630, 3612). Mortuary Pottery from Room 33.

Fig. 70 *a-k* (3637, 3621, 3676, 3620, 3616, 3623, 3619, 3622, 3616, 3614, 3678). Mortuary Pottery from Room 33.

Fig. 71 (12758). Restoration of Cylindrical Basket covered with Mosaic of Turquoise, Room 33.

169

Fig. 72. Large Turquoise Pendants, Room 33.

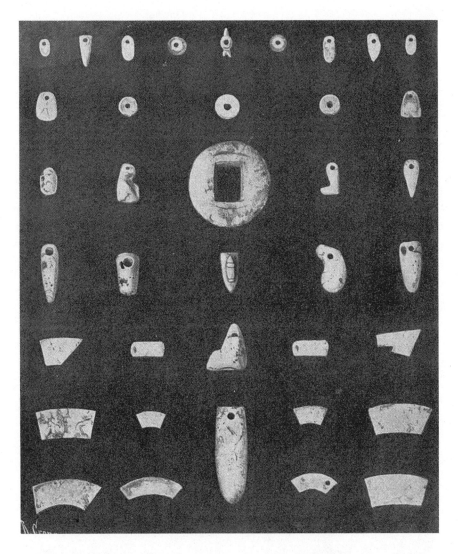

Fig. 73.   Examples of Turquoise Beads, Pendants, and Inlays found with Skeletons in Room 33.

Fig. 74.   Large Turquoise Pendants found in Various Parts of Room 33.

filled with sand, and was also covered by the same material, which had drifted over it. Thus, though the basket work had decayed, the several inlays were held in place by an equalization of pressure. This condition made it possible to determine, not only the general form of the object, but also the irregular arrangement of the various pieces of turquoise. In his legends concerning the Navajo Indians, Dr. Washington Matthews shows that several references to "turquoise jewel-baskets" are made by them. But whether their traditional knowledge of the subject is of mythical origin, or whether their ancestors saw such baskets in use by the Pueblo Indians in the early days, cannot now be stated with certainty; but the Navajo legend is none the less interesting on this account.

There were 1214 pieces of turquoise forming the mosaic which covered the cylinder, and so closely were these placed, that hardly an opening was left in the whole surface. Partially filling the cylinder, and lying directly below its mouth, was a mass of turquoise and shell beads and pendants. In this deposit there were 2150 disk-shaped turquoise beads. With these were 152 small turquoise pendants, of various forms, and twenty-two large pendants of the same material, the largest of which measured 3.6 cms. in length, 2.7 cms. in width, and 3 mms. in thickness. One of these (3769) is of irregular form, having the edges on all sides notched. Another (9250) is carved so as to give the appearance of a bird with a crest. A third pendant is crescent-shaped; this was made from a fragment of a disk-shaped bead. Still another (3852) is in the form of a bird, the head and bill being outlined by a deep incision; there is also an incised line about the neck.

Associated with the turquoise beads and pendants were 3317 shell beads and small pendants. Among these were a few beads made from olivella shell, but most of them were disk-shaped. There were also seventy shell beads of cylindrical form, and eight specimens of the same kind having holes drilled in the sides, in which turquoise sets no doubt had been inlaid. Still other objects unearthed were sixty-eight large shell pendants of irregular shape, most of them of the flat form; nineteen of these have holes drilled in the sides for the reception of turquoise inlays. This fact might be deemed purely conjectural, were it not that a pendant of similar form still retains one of the turquoise sets in place. Two of the shell pendants found in this deposit are in the shape of moccasins; these are drilled for suspension. Three cylindrical beads of shell, averaging 3 cms. in length and 8 mms. in diameter, were found. These beads are similar to specimens discovered in the same room, each provided with a bird bone passing through the central opening. The deposit contained also four shell pendants representing bird forms: one of these specimens still retains a piece of turquoise inlaid in the side. A fifth specimen is of the ordinary form of pendants drilled for the reception of an inlay, and still retains a piece of turquoise in a groove cut just below the drilled portion.

In the center of the mass of shell and turquoise ornaments, below the turquoise mosaic cylinder, an object having an animal form was found. This figure (Plate 1, 3657) is made of soft but very compact stone. The greater part is of a light pink color; but there is an area of chalky white on the under side, extending through to the tail. This latter part is so much disintegrated that the material rubs off at the slightest touch. The object in its entirety is 8.7 cms. in length, and 3.3 cms. in width at the widest part, that is, across the shoulders. It is 1.6 cms. in thickness at the shoulder, tapering from this point to the nose, also to the wedge-shaped tail. The general form of the object is shown in Fig. 76c. The body is marked off from the head by a deep groove on each side. The head is carefully carved. One feature is a shovel-like projection, evidently made to represent a flat nose. There are pits forming eyes, which evidently were once inlaid with pieces of turquoise. A band of the same material passes across the neck. This object was obviously made to be used as a pendant. To prevent the cord from wearing away the very soft material, the makers inserted a bird bone in a hole drilled just above the neck; the opening on each side was countersunk, and the space was filled with gum. Over each end a large turquoise bead was placed, one being in position when the object was found. These completely covered the ends of the bone, which otherwise would have detracted from the finish of the figure. Whether this object was made to represent a real or a mythical animal is not determined.

Near skeleton No. 14, but not associated with the deposit just described, were the remains of another object made of turquoise and shell mosaic inserted on basket work. Owing to the fact that the basket work had been woven over a wooden body, or at least over a form of fibrous material (as a piece of cactus stalk), several fragments of the object still retained their form, and could be removed. From the contour of the largest fragment, the object must have been 4 cms. in diameter and more than 6 cms. in length, although the length of the portion found is but 3 cms. Unlike the mosaic cylinder above described, this specimen is made of turquoise beads and ovoidal thin pieces of shell. The beads were strung on a cord and placed on edge against the body of the cylinder, in parallel rows separated by two rows of the thin shell pieces which overlapped like shingles. The number of beads in each transverse row was from six to seven, according to the thickness of the pieces. There are the remains of three of these rows of beads, and of three of the alternating rows of shell which occupy more than half the diameter of the object. With this specimen were a number of beads very much larger than the ones which remained in place, the former averaging 6 mms in diameter, while the latter are under 4 mms. Sections of the larger beads were found, showing that they had been strung

Fig. 75.   Turquoise Frogs and Tadpoles, Room 33.

in the same manner as the smaller ones. How they were applied is, of course, conjectural: possibly they formed a row at each end of the specimen. There were discovered more than five hundred loose beads that had formed a part of this interesting object, which was no doubt used ceremonially.

In addition there were many turquoise pendants and ornaments, types of which are shown in the illustrations. A detailed description will be found in a former publication.

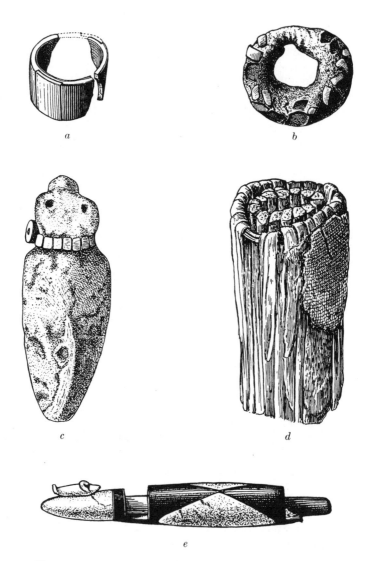

Fig. 76.   Specimens from Room 33:   a (12794), Jet ornament, natural size;
b (12787), Mouthpiece for a shell trumpet, Fig. 77, natural size; c (10418), Encrusted
stone ornament, length, 8.7 cm.; d (3673), Object made of reeds, length, 9.4 cm.;
e (10420), Hematite cylinder inlaid with turquoise, length, 5.4 cm.

a

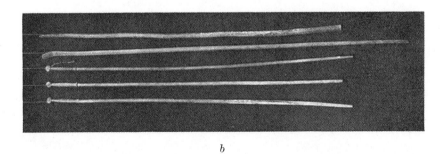

b

Fig. 77. *a* (3653), Shell Trumpet found with Skeleton 14, Room 33; *b* Ceremonial Sticks found between Ceiling Beams in Southwestern Corner of Room 33.

Room 34.

Directly south of Room 27 and the series of rooms separating the main courts in the pueblo was Room 34. This was rectangular in form, 6 feet 7 inches wide at the north end, 6 feet 6 inches wide at the south end, and with a length of 17 feet 7 inches on the east side and 18 feet on the west side. The eastern wall had been almost completely destroyed, but the other walls were still standing to a height of 7 feet. Two small wall pockets were found in the west wall; the fireplace in the floor also had two circular depressions near it.

Fig. 78 (3682). Bead of Shell with Section of a Bird Bone Inserted, Room 33. Length, 3 cm.

This fireplace was 8 inches from the west wall; almost circular, the longer axis, north and south, measuring 2 feet 3 inches, and the shorter one, 2 feet 1 inch, its depth being 6 inches. The floor was carefully smoothed adobe. The circular places near the fireplace were made of adobe; they average 10 inches in diameter on the outside and 4 inches in diameter on the inside. These depressions, appearing as they do, in a room of a series which connects estufas, are rather interesting. No specimens were found in this room.

Fig. 79. Turquoise Pendant and Set Showing Inlays of the Same Material, Room 33.

Room 35.

Room 35 was one of a series extending east and west as may be seen in the plan, Fig. 155. It is rectangular in form and shows the following measurements: the east wall, 12 feet 3 inches; the west wall, 12 feet 5 inches; the south wall, 11 feet 11 inches; the north wall, 12 feet.

The upper walls are of poor construction, but the lower ones seem to have been made with greater care. There is a doorway in the western part of the north wall of the usual rectangular form. In the south wall, there are two large ceiling beams projecting from the surface. When the débris was cleared from this room, it was found to be the remains of two rooms. The lower one measured 6 feet 2 inches from the floor to the ceiling and the upper one was not complete, but the distance from the lower floor to the top of the wall in the northwest corner was 12 feet. The floor of this room, that is, the upper one, was composed of sticks ranging from two to four inches in diameter. These ran east and west and were supported by four beams which ran in the opposite direction. They were in pairs, each pair touching and being $2\frac{1}{2}$ feet from the east and west sides of the room. These logs were 5 inches in diameter and were well imbedded in the masonry. Above the sticks a layer of brush had been placed and over this adobe which formed the floor of the room. The floor had caved in from the extreme weight that had rested upon it, and the lower room was filled with débris. The floor beams were broken and most of them were badly decayed.

The walls of this room were composed of large stones set in mortar, but none of the interstices were chinked with smaller stones. It had originally been plastered, but the only place which retained the plaster was a portion of the south wall; here it was quite thick, the surface being very irregular and showing finger marks over the greater part of its area.

The lower room was a trifle smaller than the upper one. The walls were composed of smaller stones and all but the west one retained the greater part of the original plaster. In the northeast corner the plaster was very thick and filled with finger marks.

The east and west walls were not joined to the north and south walls, they simply rested against them. They were really partitions that had been built at the convenience of the owners after the long hall-like place had been completed. In this way they could divide it into the sizes desired and change it without damaging the north and south walls.

Directly below the place where the two beams protruded from the south wall, near the east side, there was a small wall pocket, half a foot square and running back into the wall about the same distance. This pocket was 1 foot below the ceiling beams. In the western wall of the upper room, 4 feet from the south wall and resting upon the floor timbers, are two layers of stone marking a well-defined place, a foot and a half on the bottom and about 6 inches wider on either side of the top where the wall is broken. This was probably one of the old T-shaped doorways. The room contained a few specimens scattered about in the débris. It was completely cleared and the excavations carried to a distance of 3 feet below the lower floor. The specimens from the débris were the following: three bone awls made from fragments of deer bone, two fragments of ceremonial sticks, one with the end shaped like a bear claw, a number of turkey quills, fragments of shell, red ocher, obsidian, and turquoise; also a turquoise bead and pendant and a shell bead, a stone arrow point, fragments of a charred basket and corncobs, a ball of clay, pieces of yucca cord, three hammerstones, and two smoothing stones.

Room 36.

Room 36, just west of Room 35 and south of Room 2, was almost square. It measures 11 feet 9 inches on the north, 12 feet 10 inches on the south, 12 feet 4 inches on the east, and 12 feet 1 inch on the west. There were two stories, as in Room 35, the lower room being 7 feet high. The walls of both rooms were plastered. There was a doorway in the north wall, 2 feet below the ceiling beams and 4 feet from the west wall; it was 2 feet 6 inches wide, and the top and bottom were rounded with mortar, the upper part covering the wooden lintels. There were also the remains of a small doorway in the eastern part of the same wall.

In Fig. 80, the northern and eastern part of this room is shown, giving a general idea of the masonry and the floor beams. The north wall was rough as compared with the other walls of the room, the east and west walls being merely partitions.

In the south wall, there was a pocket 4 inches below the ceiling and 11 inches square. There was also a corner doorway in the southeast corner of the lower room. It was flush with the east wall and 1 foot 6 inches below the ceiling; it was 1 foot 4 inches wide and 2 feet high. The wall of the upper room on the south side was blackened by smoke and many of the stones had been calcined from heat.

The specimens found in this room, were in the débris, on, or slightly above the floor level. They are as follows: a lapstone 37 cms. long, 20 cms. wide, 3.5 cms. thick (its use as a lapstone was evidently secondary, as there are evidences that it had been used as a baking stone); a small metate and mano found together, the metate is 44 cms. long and 25 cms. wide at the widest part, made of fine-grained sandstone, as is also the mano; the mano is 14.5 cms. broad and is of the short type, such as are used with the small metates; two rectangular grinding stones; a mano that had been used to such an extent that only a small portion of it remained; a small sandstone slab, probably used as a lapstone; two sandstone jar covers; pieces of shell that had probably been used in making ornaments; fossil shells; pieces of gypsum; a portion of the jaw of a beaver, with a tooth in place, which has been worked and had probably been used as an implement; pieces of azurite and malachite; turquoise matrix; a fragment of a turquoise pendant; shell beads; and three bone awls.

There was a pointed stick, evidently a fire stick, also one of the cylindrical sticks of the long type as described under Room 2.

There was the stem of a clay pipe which was roughly made, the clay being of the micaceous type used in making the cooking vessels.

Fig. 80. North and East Walls of Room 36.

181

Fig. 81. Masonry in Room 37.

182

Another pipe, similar to Fig. 20c, is also of clay, but of the ordinary gray-ware. A portion of the stem of a steatite pipe was also found. Great care had been taken in fashioning this piece, the surface still retaining a high polish.

Among the pottery pieces found were fragments of two small gray-ware mugs which averaged 7 cms. in height. They are extremely small for this region and it is interesting to note two specimens of this size from one room. There was also a portion of the rim of a corrugated grayware bowl of flat form almost a duplicate of one described from Room 12 and a fragmentary bowl of peculiar from, somewhat in the shape of a broad-mouthed crucible.

Room 37.

Room 37 was west of Room 36 and south of Room 4. It was 11 feet 9 inches long on the north side, 12 feet 10 inches on the south, 12 feet 4 inches on the east, and 12 feet 1 inch on the west. The general style of masonry in this room is shown in Fig. 81.

The north wall of the lower room had been heavily plastered. In this there was a doorway, made circular by the abundance of plaster applied. The lintel of the doorway was made of flat stones; it was 4 feet 1 inch from the east wall and 2 feet below the ceiling beams, and measured 2 feet in height and 1 foot 10 inches in width. The east wall was very crudely built, but had been covered with a thick layer of plaster. The south wall was also rough and bulged in places. The west wall was built of selected stones, carefully laid, but there was a slight bulge near the southwest corner. There is a doorway of the rectangular type, in the western wall, 6 feet 4 inches from the north wall and 1 foot 6 inches below the ceiling beams; it was 2 feet in height and 1 foot 9 inches in width. The wall at the north end of the room was standing to a height of 13 feet above the lower floor. The specimens found in this room were scattered through the débris.

There was one large sandstone metate and twenty-five sandstone jar covers, most of which had been carefully smoothed. There were also a number of fragments of jar covers; two of the perfect specimens are plano-convex, a rather unusual form, and made of a very compact sandstone. There was one stone slab probably used as a lapstone; also two large slabs used both as lapstones and for grinding; a small metate; a mano; and a lapstone formed of a large irregularly shaped water-worn pebble, such as are found in the cliff-houses. There were two sandstone grinders and a fragment of a sandstone implement, 6 cms. wide and 3.5 cms. thick at the small end, gradually increasing in width up to the point where it is broken, the fragment measuring 25 cms. in length. All surfaces of this fragment are perfectly smooth and in some places the smoothing has been carried to such an extent that it has almost become a polish. What the use of this object (5101) may have been, cannot be stated. There was one large natural pebble that had probably been used for polishing purposes and a great many small pebbles and fossil shells. With them were chalcedony concretions, fragments of chalcedony, a mass of fragments of murex and strombus shells, three fossil shells of unusual form which still retain evidences of red paint, a small pebble, one surface of which had been worn smooth from use, a piece of galena, a large fragment of murex shell which had been drilled, a small irregular shaped ball of pumice stone, a stone cylinder made from a natural concretion, evidently used as a bead, and two bone awls, one made from a deer bone, the other from a turkey wing bone. There were also three pink stone inlays, pieces of azurite, pieces of turquoise matrix, a stone bead of cylindrical form made from jasper, a mouthpiece made of gum which had been used on one of the shell trumpets, and two fragments of designs in blue and black painted on red pigment which had been spread over some stick foundation.

There were two objects, one chipped from petrified wood, the other from chalcedony. They are roughly chipped, and as shown in Fig. 15, measure 9 cms. in length with a general thickness of 2 cms. Their shape and size suggest that they may have been carried in the hands during races.

There were four small billets of wood measuring 6 cms. in length and 2.5 cms. in diameter, which may have been used for the same purpose as the stones mentioned above; the sticks however, may have been used in playing some game. With these billets were several fragments of ceremonial sticks, also one of the so-called gambling sticks, shaped like the end of a bow, such as were found in numbers in Room 2. The skull of a dog was also found in the débris.

Room 38.

After finishing Room 37, the scene of operations was transferred to the room just east of Room 35 and south of Rooms 8, 9, and 10. In shape, this room appears to be rectangular, but closer inspection shows that the longer walls, those on the north and south sides of the room, are rounded, the curve following the regular contour of the outer wall of the pueblo. It measures 32 feet 2 inches in length on the north side, 27 feet 8 inches on the south side, 10 feet 2 inches on the east side, and 13 feet 9 inches on the west side.

The walls had been well plastered; on the lower portions, especially in the northwest corner, finger marks are in evidence. The southern wall is plain, there being no doorways or other openings in its surface. Near the western end of this wall, at a distance of 5 feet 5 inches from the west wall, a projection jutted into the room. It was made of stone and had a plastered surface. It averaged 6 inches in thickness and extended 1 foot 1 inch into the room, and was angulated toward the northwest, instead of being at right angles with the south wall. This extension evidently served as an anchorage for a beam which formed a support for a platform. As though to verify this supposition, there was found, partly imbedded in the plaster of the south wall at this point, a portion of a heavy beam which extends from the anchorage to the west wall. This beam was 2 feet below the ceiling beams of the room. The south wall was not well preserved, no doubt due to the fact that it was comparatively thin. The mortar was cracked and in patches as though the ends of the sandstone slabs had been but slightly covered.

The west wall was rough and irregular, but the plaster was intact when the room was cleared of débris. It presented an unbroken surface, and, as in the case of the south wall, there were no doorways leading into the adjoining room.

The north wall was rough and unsymmetrical as though it had suffered from some severe shock. A large block of sandstone protruded from the surface, which was bulged and unsightly, as compared with the walls of most of the rooms examined. Near the west wall, was a slight protuberance in the form of a slender pillar projecting a few inches from the wall. It was opposite the angle wall on the south side of the room, and formed the northern rest for the supporting, or easternmost beam of the bench before-mentioned. The rounded side of a doorway extended to the point where the pillar begins. This doorway is built in such a manner that the opening is some inches from the general surface of the wall. The sides were heavily plastered and rounded from the opening outward, forming an ovoid niche in the wall. It was 2 feet 4 inches below the ceiling beams, 1 foot 6 inches wide, and 2 feet high. This doorway was open and connected the room with Room 9, which is directly north of it. In the eastern end of the north wall, at a point 5 feet 2 inches from the east wall, there is another doorway of the regular rectangular type, with straight sides and a wooden lintel. It was in a part of the wall that had suffered to a great extent, and was closed with masonry, but owing to the sagging of the wall at this point, the sides of the doorway are somewhat irregular and the stones misplaced. It was 1 foot 10 inches below the ceiling beams, 2 feet 2 inches wide, and 2 feet 2 inches high.

The east wall presented a more uniform surface than the north wall, although the plaster was cracked like that of the west wall; it is of the division type, extending nearly from the surface of the north wall to the south wall. There is a doorway in the lower part near the south end, the distance from the south wall being 3 feet 2 inches. This doorway is rectangular in form, and has lintels for poles. It was 1 foot 10 inches below the ceiling beams, 2 feet 2 inches wide, and 3 feet high.

The north wall is intact to a height of 4 feet in some places, above the ceiling of the lower room; the average height of the lower room walls is 6 feet. The east wall extended about the same height above the ceiling beams; the south wall was about a foot lower, and the west wall was $4\frac{1}{2}$ feet above the ceiling beams, at its highest point.

The platform at the western end of the room may have been separated from the main room, but there were no evidences of a partition wall, nor were there any marks of a post in the room at this point. From the position of the partly decayed beams it seems that there had been an ordinary platform, the space beneath which was open.

Turquoise Ornaments.   The eastern end of the room was excavated to a depth of several feet and the work was then carried westward. Nothing of particular interest was found in the upper layers, but the removal of the stones and the fallen beams was still in progress when a platform was uncovered. The first evidence of this structure was a peculiar projecting wall, 6 inches thick and extending in a northwesterly direction. It was attached to the south wall and had been used as a support for a beam that entered the north wall at a point opposite. The western support of the platform was upheld by posts, but these and the poles that had formed its upper surface were no longer in position; they had been crushed by the weight of the débris and, when uncovered, were greatly decayed. Other unusual objects soon came to light: a frog of jet, inlaid with turquoise; a jet tablet and a buckle; turquoise birds and many pendants and beads. These have been fully described and illustrated in a former paper.[1]   (Frontispiece.)

Miscellaneous Objects.   The general material other than that which has been described as having been found on the platform, and that which will be described from the floor level of the room was found scattered through the débris, many of the smaller objects being found in what must have been the refuse from the upper floors.

---

[1] "Ceremonial Objects and Ornaments from Pueblo Bonito, New Mexico," *American Anthropologist,* N. S., vol. 7, 183–197 (1905).

There was one large sandstone metate and twenty-five manos, ranging in size and thickness from the small manos used with the light slab
metates to the very thick ones, used in the first process of crushing the
corn. They also varied in their composition, some being of the very fine-
grained sandstone, while others were made of coarser materials. There
were seven large sandstone slabs which had been used for grinding purposes, also three small slabs of sandstone that had been used as hand
stones in grinding. There was a fragment of a slab of black slate which
must have been a good-sized lapstone. There were three blocks of
coarse-grained white sandstone and one slab of red sandstone of the same
coarseness which had probably been used as rasps in working wood.
There was also an irregular piece of coarse sandstone that had evidently
been used for the same purpose as the larger pieces. Hand hammers were
represented by twelve specimens made of natural pebbles and sections of
petrified wood and quartzite. These are the hammers used in pecking the
troughs in metates, and in working away the irregular surfaces of stone
implements.

There were eleven grooved hammers, all of which were made from
natural pebbles, also a fragment of a twelfth. Four large stone mauls
were found. The largest of these (5224) is made of a natural pebble and
measures 36 cms. in length, 17.5 cms. in width, and 5.5 cms. in thickness.
This maul has two deep grooves, one on either edge. It was probably
hafted at the end of a very heavy handle and used, as were the other
mauls found here, for quarrying the sandstone blocks for use in
building their houses. The second one (5253) is made of a cherty nodule
which measures 29 cms. in length, 16 cms. in width, and 7.5 cms. in
thickness. The third (5252) is also made of a fine hard-grained sandstone. It is 25 cms. long, 14 cms. wide, and 8.5 cms. thick. The fourth
(5225) is made of a natural pebble, and is 21 cms. long, 13 cms. wide, and
5 cms. thick. All of these specimens have the edges deeply grooved, but
in no case does the groove cover the sides of the stone, being confined to
the edge only. This interesting series of hammers and mauls was scattered through the débris.

In Fig. 16 a circular stone is shown. The upper part is slightly concave and shows evidences of pecking and grinding. The side seems to be
the natural surface of the original cherty nodule. The under part is
smooth and has evidently been used to some extent. The specimen
averages 21.5 cms. in diameter at the bottom and 17.5 cms. at the top,
the sides being sloping.

In Fig. 22 one of two stone implements is shown. They are made of sandstone, and were evidently used as hoes or shovels. The old Cliff-Dwellers hafted large pieces of horn on the end of sticks, no doubt using them for shovels in digging; it may be that these stone implements were hafted in the same way. The thin section of the handle would lend itself very readily to such mounting. The larger specimen measures 21.5 cms. in length and 17.5 cms. in width at the widest part of the blade, the average thickness being about 1 cm. The smaller specimen is only 9 cms. in length and 16.5 cms. in width.

There were three sandstone jar covers of the usual size and shape, also a fragment of a fourth.

Scattered through the débris were a great many small water-worn pebbles, fragments of shells, fragments of chalcedony and other stone material, such as would be used in making arrow points. Some of these were in the form of flakes that have been used as scrapers. Pieces of limonite; chalcedony concretions; gypsum; cañon walnuts; red ocher that had probably been used for paint, four perfect arrow points and a number of fragmentary ones, were also found. There were also a few stone and shell beads, crinoid stems, and fragments of turquoise. With these were three fragments of shell bracelets.

There were two implements made from chalcedony, one had probably been a bodkin, and the other a wedge. There were very few bones and only five objects made from bone. Three of these were awls. There was one scraper made from the humerus of a deer, and a bone bead.

There were four objects made of wood, two were ceremonial sticks; one of the type having a knob on the end was found on the floor of the northwest corner of the room, as was also the other one which is of the type with the end carved like a bear claw. There was a third ceremonial stick found slightly above the floor level of the northwest corner, Fig. 85. This stick seems to be complete. It is of the type having a knob and collar on one end, the knob is flattened and has a hole drilled through it. It is 36.5 cms. long, and between the carved portions, there is a wrap of yucca cord which fastens what seems to be a small branch with juniper leaves attached. Lying against the juniper branch are the ends of cords showing a series of knots, which would indicate that they had once held feathers. From their position it would seem that a cord which had once been used with feathers was here represented in a secondary use, that of binding the branch to the stick. The fourth stick mentioned is one of the long cylindrical type with cuts on the surface, as described from Room 2.

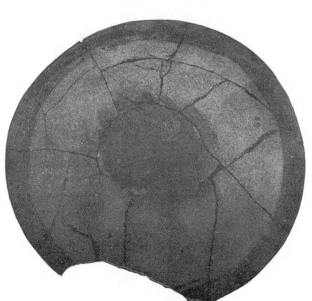

Fig. 82 (5111). Corrugated Bowl, Room 38. Diameter, 25.5 cm.

189

There were a great many potsherds in this room, both of red and grayware. They were principally of bowls and bowls of dippers. No perfect pieces were found, but there were three bowls of grayware averaging 13.5 cms. in diameter which could be mended. These bowls were decorated on the interior, the decorations being in black and of a type common to this pueblo.

The greater part of a corrugated bowl of grayware was found scattered through the débris. The fragments were brought together and the bowl, with the exception of a small portion of the rim, is shown in Fig. 82. This bowl is of the same type as described from Room 10. The whole outer surface is corrugated; it is painted white on the inside and has a broad band of black on the inner rim. It had evidently cracked while it was in use, as there are two holes near the rim, one on either side of a break. These holes had been drilled from the outside, showing conclusively that they had not been made at the time when the vessel was in course of construction. This bowl

Fig. 83 (5205). Beak-like Object made of Chaledony, Room 38.

averages 25.5 cms. in diameter and 6.8 cms. in depth. There were portions of the rim of another bowl of the same shape and character, but only three small pieces were found. There was one fragment of pottery in the form of an animal head. It was of grayware and had the ears and face decorated with black lines. There was also a fragment of a grayware vessel in the shape of a human breast (4737).

There were four shell trumpets made from murex shells, also the mouth end of a fifth; this mouth end still retained portions of a gum that had formed the mouthpiece (5106, 5107, 5108, 5105). The first three specimens were found near the center of the room, at a depth of 3 feet below the surface. The first two specimens have the lips drilled for suspension and there are remains of gum around the mouth end. Gum has also been used in several places to fill up holes in the surface of shells. The third specimen has the opening for the mouth end, but it is so large that the work was no doubt given up, as the lip of the shell shows no drilling and there are no evidence of there having been a mouthpiece. The fourth specimen was found in the southwest end of the room, 2 feet below the surface and 4 feet from the west wall. The lip is drilled for suspension and the gum about the mouth opening is still in place.

A fragment of an object, shaped like the beak of an eagle, was found in this room. It was in three pieces, two of which had suffered from the effects of fire. This specimen is made of chalcedony and is shown in

Fig. 83. It is a little over 5 cms. in length and 1.2 cms. broad at the head part. Great care has been shown in making this object, and it is to be regretted that the major portion of it was destroyed by fire.

Three pieces of a glass-like slag were found, similar in surface appearance to the arrow points found in Room 10. Whether this slag was brought from some other locality, whether it is the remains of Indian work, or whether it is the result of the fire that must have raged in one part of the room, cannot be stated, but it is an interesting find in view of the fact that the arrow points, which have been described and which are mentioned above, present characteristics quite similar to these pieces.

Pipes. There were three fragments of clay pipes. One of these was in such a fragmentary condition, that the parts could not be assembled. It had been, however, of the type with the bowl at right angles to the stem. It was of dark brown clay and the surface had been covered with a black slip and highly polished. The second fragment shown in Fig. 19b is 9 cms. in length, 2 cms. in width, and 1.5 cms. in thickness. There is another fragment over 2 cms. in length which evidently was joined to this piece; as there was no evidence of the bowl on either piece, the stem in its entirety must have been 12 cms. in length. Unlike most of the pipes in this Pueblo, it is of light clay. Another pipe is made of a dark brown clay, similar to the first fragment mentioned. It is 7 cms. in length and averages 3.3 cms. in diameter at the bowl end. This was evidently a tubular pipe.

In Fig. 19a a stone pipe similar in form to that just described is shown. It is similar in form to the pipes found among the Klamath Indians of California. It is 9.8 cms. in length, 3.7 cms. in diameter at the bowl end, and 2.6 cms. in diameter at the stem end. The bowl begins to taper outward toward the rim, at a distance of 2.5 cms. from the end; here the hole contracts to 1 cm., holding this size until it reaches a point 2.5 cms. from the stem end. It then begins to widen and at the opening it is 1.5 cms. broad. A depression 5 mms. in diameter and 2 mms. deep has been drilled near the center of the pipe on one side; this may have been done for the insertion of an inlay, possibly of turquoise. This pipe has evidently been through the fire, as there are two large flakes, resulting no doubt from the heat. All parts of the pipe have been carefully finished, and the outer surface still retains a high polish.

Another stone pipe of the cylindrical form is shown in Fig. 19g. It was found a few feet below the surface, in the center of the room. In general technique, it is similar to the one just described; the formation of the bowl being similar to and the widening and boring of the stem end being the same as in the other stone pipe, the greatest difference being that it tapers gradually from the bowl to the stem end. It is 3.2 cms. long, 2 cms. in diameter at the bowl, and 1.4 cms. by 1.1 cms. at the mouthpiece, the measurements showing that there is a flattening at this end of the pipe. The bowl end, however, is practically circular, there being but very slight difference in the diameter.

A fragment of the stem of a pipe was found in the general digging a few feet below the surface and near the eastern part of the room; later the bowl of the same pipe was found. The two pieces were joined with the result shown in Fig. 84. This pipe is made of a very soft stone. The bowl is at right angles to the stem and raised upon a platform bifurcated in front as shown in the figure. The general appearance, from a three quarter view, is that of a figure with the torso bent upward and the arms doubled under the body, the remaining portion extending backward and forming the stem of the pipe. Directly back of the platform, there is a ridge which conforms to the angle of the back part of the bowl. If the pipe is held by the stem and viewed from the base in a three quarter position, it has the appearance of an animal form, the head being represented by the platform, the ears by the upper part of the platform; this part being the portion that is divided and the bowl forming the body. What it was made to represent is however problematical. The pipe measures 14.5 cms. in length, the stem 9.3 cms., the platform 4.3 cms. in length and 3.3 cms. in width. The bowl is 4.6 cms. high in front and 3 cms. above the stem. The height of the pipe from the base of the platform to the edge of the bowl is 7 cms. The diameter of the bowl is 3.5 cms., the opening in the same being 2.5 cms. in diameter. The hole in the bowl tapers from the opening to a point at the extreme bottom; the hole in the stem meeting it at a point fully 1.5 cms. above the bottom of the bowl drilling. The hole in the stem at the mouthpiece is 8 mms. in diameter. This pipe is a very unusual one and is unlike any other that was found in the pueblo. It has evidently passed through the fire so that the exact nature of the material from which it was made is hard to determine. The outer surface is black and has been highly polished; the interior at the present time has the appearance of soft, very friable sandstone, dull pink in color.

Effigy Pottery. In removing the débris from this room, a number of fragments of the face of a human effigy jar were found. Some of them were discolored by fire, but most of them retain their natural color. It was not until the floor level was reached that these fragments ceased to appear. Most of them, however, were found in the northeast end of the room, about 3 feet below the surface.

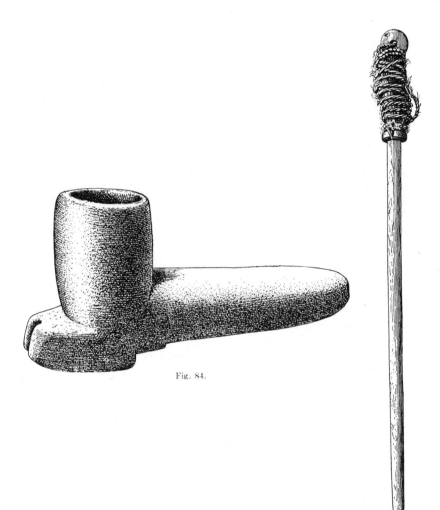

Fig. 84.

Fig. 85.

Fig. 86.

Fig. 84 (5208). Soft Stone Pipe of Unusual Form, Room 38.
Fig. 85 (5217). Ceremonial Stick, Room 38.
Fig. 86 (5145). Inlaid Scraper, Room 38.

The distribution of human effigy vases in the Southwest presents an interesting problem. The Pueblo country has furnished but few such objects for comparison and any new locality in which they are found, especially when situated in the northern boundaries of the culture area, is worthy of consideration.

The subject has been fully covered in my article in the Boas Anniversary Volume.[1]

Macaw Skeletons. When the floor level was reached, it was found that there was a fireplace near the center of the room. It is circular and made of flat stones placed on edge, the interior being plastered. The upper ends of the stones were on a level with the adobe floor, and most of the stones were in place. The work of excavation extended from the west, eastward, that is, when the floor level was reached; the floor was cleaned, exposing the fireplace, and there remained a mass of débris in the east end of the room. In working through this with hand trowels, a mass of bird droppings were found. An accumulation of this material fully 10 inches thick extended over the greater part of the width of the room. Upon, and partly imbedded in this mass, were the skeletons of twelve macaws (*Ara militaris*). They were massed in such a way, that the individual skeletons could not be determined, but all of the bones were removed. From the evidence it would seem that there had been cages or perches for these birds, and that they had been kept alive. When the entire floor had been cleaned, the adobe was broken and a search below the floor level begun. At a point 9 feet 4 inches from the southeast corner and 10 feet 6 inches from the northeast corner and at a depth of a foot below the floor level, a circular cavity had been dug in the floor and in this the skeleton of a macaw was found. The hole had been carefully formed, filled with adobe, and the surface finished so that there were no evidences of its position.

In the southwestern part of the room near the projecting wall, another macaw burial was found. It was 7 feet from the southwest corner and 12 feet 4 inches from the northwest corner. It was slightly below the floor level, but not as deep as the one just described, although it had been buried in the same manner and with as great care. A careful search of the remaining portion of the stratum directly below the floor level failed to reveal other skeletons.

---

[1] "Human Effigy Vases from Chaco Canon, New Mexico" (*Boas Anniversary Volume*, pp. 320–334. New York, 1906.)

Thus there were fourteen macaw skeletons in this room, two birds that had died and been buried, no doubt in a ceremonial way, and twelve that were killed when the room was deserted, or were the victims of an accident. Had these birds been left in the room and had starvation been the cause of death, their bodies would have been more scattered, unless perchance they were confined in cages as suggested. At all events, it seems that the room had been deserted, as the greater number of birds had not been accorded as careful a burial as had the bodies of the two found below the floor. This may have been a Macaw clan room.

Most of the objects found in this room point to the fact that it was used for ceremonial purposes, or for the reception and storage of articles that were used in ceremonies. The pipes found in the main part of the room are such as would be used in sacred observances. The large human head of pottery, with symbols on the face and chin, was also an object of a ceremonial nature, to say nothing of the carved and encrusted turquoise pieces that were found on the platform in the western part of the room.

In removing the mass of macaw bones, skeletons of a smaller bird were found. These proved to belong to the bluejay family. They are called in the west piñon birds (*Cyanocitta Stelleri diademata*). There were four skeletons.

Portions of parrot skeletons and skeletons of other birds have been found in other rooms of Pueblo Bonito, but never in such quantities nor *in situ*, as they were found in Room 38. The *Ara Militaris* or green macaw is found at the present time in certain parts of Mexico and there is strong evidence that it was at one time quite common in the northern part of Mexico and extended even to the southern parts of New Mexico and Arizona.

Room 39.

Room 39 was a long rectangular room, south of Rooms 35 and 36. It was narrower at the west end than at the east, the measurements of the floor level being as follows:—The north wall 21 feet 1 inch, the south wall 20 feet 3 inches, the east wall 9 feet 8½ inches, the west wall 8 feet 3 inches. The south wall was well plastered and finger marks were in abundance near the eastern end. Near the west-central part of the wall there was a large doorway, not well-defined, that had been closed with large pieces of sandstone.

At a distance of 4 feet 9 inches from the eastern wall and 1 foot 2 inches below the ceiling beam, was a wall pocket. It was 11 inches wide at the bottom and narrowed to 7 inches at the top. Its height was 1 foot and it was 1 foot 5 inches deep. It had a small beam across the top in the southeast corner about 1 foot below the ceiling. There are beams protruding from the masonry, which no doubt formed the top of a closet. There was a post approximately 3 feet from either wall which had evidently formed the corner post of this storage place. On the floor inside of this space, there were quantities of piñon nut shells, suggesting that the closet or bin had been used for storing food.

The eastern wall was well plastered and there was a doorway, 1 foot 4 inches from the north wall. This doorway was 1 foot 3 inches below the ceiling beams, 2 feet in width, and 2 feet 1 inch high.

The north wall retained some of its plaster, but most of it had disappeared. The stones used in the masonry were large and rather roughly laid. The doorway was 6 feet 10 inches from the west wall, 1 foot 7 inches below the ceiling beams, 2 feet 2 inches wide, and 2 feet 5 inches high. It was of the ordinary rectangular form. This doorway was open and led into Room 36.

The western wall was merely a partition between the rooms, the ends abutting on the north and south walls. This wall had originally extended to the ceiling, but had partially fallen.

The specimens found in this room were from the débris from the upper floors and also from the floor of the lower room.

Arrow Points. In the material from the upper floors were 211 perfect arrow points and 112 fragments. These points were of the delicate tapering type and were made of obsidian, chalcedony, and jasper. The largest of these points measure 4 cms. in length and 1 cm. in width at the widest part. They range from this size to very small ones. All of them are of the notched variety and quite a number have secondary notches on the sides. (See Fig. 40d.)

In the débris were also turquoise and shell beads, turquoise matrix, fossil shells, a small slab of hard compact shale of a greenish color, half of the bowl of a clay pipe, a stone jar cover, a small pottery bowl measuring only 6 cms. in diameter, two large bone awls made from deer bones, fragments of shell bracelets, three large stone slabs, and a grinding stone. There were also a great many fragments of pottery vessels and animal bones; with the latter were several pieces of deer antler.

On and just above the floor level of the lower room, were fourteen large sandstone metates, fourteen manos of the same material, a block of coarse sandstone that had been used for sharpening bone implements, a large stone slab which had evidently been used as a door, two sandstone concretions in the form of cups, one sandstone ball, deer and other animal bones. Among the animal bones was a scraping tool made of bone. The surface of this bone is worn to a considerable extent, showing that it had been in use for some time. The skull of a dog was found in a fragmentary condition, also the lower jaw of another dog skull; a deer vertebra was found which had been worked to a considerable extent, the condyles at one end having been ground; the whole object showing the process employed in grinding off the ends of bones that were to be used in making implements. There were four bone awls made from deer bones, the blade end of a bone scraper that had been highly polished, the top of an antler point which shows the cutting to very good advantage, a small bowl of grayware only 5.5 cms. in diameter, and a small stone cylinder. This is a plain cylinder, 4 cms. in length and 1.7 cms. in diameter. The surface is perfectly smooth and the stone, evidently gypsum, is semi-transparent.

The most interesting feature of the work in this room, was the finding of the delicate worked arrow points. They were scattered through the débris in such a way that it was impossible to tell whether they had been attached to arrows when they were left in the upper rooms or whether they had been in one group and scattered when the upper floors fell. It is, however, the largest number of points that was found in any of the rooms in the ruin and represents the highest type of chipping that is known in this region.

Fireplaces. When the floor of Room 39 was cleared, two irregular fireplaces were found. The largest of these was 10 feet 7 inches from the southeast corner and 8 feet 2 inches from the northeast corner. Its greatest breadth was 1 foot 11 inches, its greatest length 1 foot 4 inches, and it was 1 foot deep. The other was 2 inches to the northeastward of this one. It was 1 foot 2 inches by 1 foot 4 inches and was 11 inches deep.

Room 39a. Room 39a was directly west of and adjoining Room 39. It was 7 feet 8 inches long on the north side, 7 feet 6 inches on the south, 8 feet 5 inches on the east, and 8 feet 10 inches on the west. The partition wall at the east end was composed of stones and crossed beams, and at the southern end, about 1 foot 6 inches from the south wall, there was a post that had helped to support the wall, as it had been built into it. This wall, from its appearance, had been a hastily built partition wall and was very rough. The north wall was well plastered and at the western end, 1 foot 6 inches from the western partition, there was a post. It was built into the plaster and was one of the supports for the ceiling. Fifteen inches northeast of this post, was a second one, its diameter being 6 inches; a foot northwest of this post, was a third, a trifle smaller than the second. All of these posts had evidently acted as supports. The western wall, or partition, was composed of two poles running north and south across the room. There were no stones across the poles, the ceiling having remains of cord or matting which may indicate that a mat or piece of cloth was used as part of the partition. These poles were about midway between the floor and ceiling. The distance from the floor to the ceiling beams at the north end, was 5 feet 10 inches and at the south end 5 feet 8 inches. The walls at the north side of the room were standing to a height of 2 feet above the ceiling beams, and were about 6 inches higher than those at the south side. Only the extreme western end of the room is shown and the sticks which had formed the partition between this room and the one west of it.

Room 39b. Room 39b was west of and in reality a part of Room 39a, the dividing wall being formed merely of the poles and whatever material had covered them, as described when the last room was under consideration. The north wall was plastered, as was also the case with the west wall; the south wall still retains some of the plaster but, in places, the masonry was in evidence. There was a doorway in the south wall, the eastern wall forming the eastern part of it. It was 2 feet 10 inches wide, 3 feet high, and 10 inches below the ceiling beams. It had a lintel of poles and was of the regular rectangular form. In this part of the room were two poles that had been placed across the corner, one end of each being imbedded in the eastern wall. These sticks, on being removed, proved to be a portion of a ladder. There was a fireplace in this corner, the northeast, which was directly under the poles just mentioned. It was shallow and shaped like a pan with flaring sides, made of small stone slabs, and one side of it touched the east wall. It was 1 foot 7 inches from the north wall and averaged 1 foot 8 inches in diameter, and was 7 inches deep. One foot, three inches, from the east wall and 1 foot below the ceiling beams, was a rectangular doorway; it was 2 feet 6 inches wide and 2 feet 10 inches high.

The measurements of this room were as follows:—The north wall 7 feet 4 inches, south wall 7 feet 6 inches, east wall 8 feet 10 inches, and the west wall 8 feet 7 inches. The distance from the floor to the ceiling on the south side was 6 feet and on the north side, 5 feet 8 inches. A small area in the northwestern corner of the room had been disturbed by a party who were working in the room during the winter months of 1896-97, but little if any of the material in the room, was removed.

Cylindrical Jars. This room contained a mass of cylindrical jars and other material as shown in Fig. 87. These jars were on the upper floor: there were nineteen specimens, all of which were broken, also a bowl, twenty-nine stone jar covers, two hammerstones, an elkbone club, and many potsherds. In the débris below the floor, just mentioned, there were a number of stone arrow points, turquoise beads, shells, a bone button, and potsherds.

The jars seem to be larger than those found in Room 28, but are otherwise similar.

Room 40.

Room 40 lies directly south of Rooms 28 and 28a. It has the same type of masonry as these rooms and was of the same period. It was slightly shorter than the two rooms just mentioned: its length on the north side being 22 feet 6 inches and the east side 11 feet; the south side is the same as the north and the west end the same as the east. When the work in this room was begun, the surface was slightly below the level of that of Rooms 28 and 28a. The débris that filled the room was composed of the fallen wall, stones, fragments of flooring, and decayed ceiling beams. When cleared, the north wall proved to be standing to a height of 11 feet above the floor level. At this point the roof had been, but all evidences of it had vanished, save the opening in which the roof timbers had rested. These openings show that the timbers had been of large size, at least 10 inches in diameter. Owing to the fact that the north wall was described as the south wall when considering Rooms 28 and 28a, it will not be necessary to treat it in detail at this time. It was composed of thin stones and almost devoid of chinking.

Doorways. An old fashioned T-shaped doorway in the north wall was 10 foot 9 inches from the east wall, the lower part was 1 foot 8 8 inches high, that is, from the sill to the point where it widens, and was 2 feet 4 inches wide. The widening of the upper part caused the main portion of the doorway to be 3 feet wide; this part being 3 feet 2 inches in height. This doorway had been closed in a methodical way with heavy sandstone slabs.

Directly west of this doorway and on the same level, and only 1 foot 2 inches away, was a second doorway of the same type. It was closed, as was the case with the one just described, but owing to the fact that the wall had been broken somewhat at this part, the outlines of the upper section could not be defined, the lower part, however, was quite distinct. The stones with which it was filled protruded, thereby causing the outlines of this part to be very noticeable. The masonry of the south wall was similar in style to that of the north wall, and owing to the lack of time this wall was not entirely uncovered.

The east wall was made of thin slabs of sandstone and in the upper part a number of openings appeared. Four feet below the ceiling beams of the upper room, there was a bench made of comparatively thin pieces of sandstone. This bench was 2 feet in height and 2 feet wide, and had evidently been built upon a mass of débris. Heavy ceiling beams pierced this thick wall; these beams were 6 feet below those shown in the north wall. The west wall was similar to the east wall and there were no openings or doorways in its face.

Bins. Three feet from the west wall, there was a small stone enclosure. The east and west walls of this bin-like place were built against the north wall and extended southward a distance of 7 feet; the distance between them was 6 feet 2 inches. The walls were about a foot thick; the southern wall was slightly curved. The distance from its center to the north wall was 7 feet 8 inches. The inner surface of the walls was carefully faced and there was a small closet in the center of the southern wall, a few inches from its top. These walls extended to a height of 3 feet 6 inches above the floor level. In this room there was a large stone slab, also a number of shell beads and small fragments of turquoise which might indicate that it had been used as a workshop.

Room 41.

Room 41 is south of Room 54 and east of Room 45. It is rectangular in shape; the walls were irregular and of rather poor construction. The first floor room is 5 feet 9 inches high; a small portion of the walls of the upper room is still standing. After digging through the floor of the lower room, the second floor was found 6 inches below the first one, both floors being made of adobe. There was a shelf in the northeast corner of the lower room, its exact position being 2 feet 9 inches below the ceiling. This shelf was made of stone and projected into the room a distance of 1 foot 6 inches. In this corner, below the shelf, there was a semicircle of sticks which had been set into the adobe floor. Only vestiges of the wood remained, but from the form of the enclosure, it may have been a small cage for storing corn or other large objects.

In the center of the room were three posts with a number of broken ones about them. They may have formed a support for the ceiling, but from their fragmentary condition, nothing definite could be learned concerning their real use.

The room measured 7 feet 9 inches on the north end, 7 feet 11 inches on the south, 13 feet 6 inches on the east, and 11 feet 4 inches on the west side. The highest part of the wall, measuring from the lower floor,

Fig. 87.   Cylindrical Jars in Room 39b.

201

Fig. 88. View of Room 42, looking northwest, showing closets and passages in north wall and fireplaces and bins in the floor. The bin in the foreground is the one lined with metates.

was 8 feet 10 inches. The only doorway in the room was in the east wall of the lower part. It was 1 foot 8 inches wide, 2 feet 3 inches high, and 1 foot 3 inches below the ceiling beams.

Most of the objects found in this room were on the lower floor, but a few of them were scattered through the débris and no doubt came from the upper floor levels. The following may be noted: two bone awls, stone hammer, two stone axes, three stone jar covers, two metates, nine manos, two stone slabs, a grinding stone, two stone door sills, and a quartzite knife.

Room 42.

Room 42 is southwest of Room 41. The walls of this room were of large stones and showed but little chinking. The most noticeable characteristic of the room was the number of doorways and openings, most of which were in the south wall. There was a doorway of the ordinary rectangular type, but one just west of it and on the same level slanted towards the northwest, forming an acute angle with the wall on the west side. These doorways were in the lower room and were a trifle lower than those in the northeast corner. This one had been damaged to such an extent that no measurements could be made (Fig. 88).

The floor of this room presented a rather complex appearance. Near the north wall, and almost in the center of the room, was a depression 10 inches deep, which may have been a fireplace. It was five-sided, the sides being composed of flat stones set up on edge. The bottom of this depression was made of adobe, and had evidently been subjected to fire, as it was very hard.

South of this depression, with one edge against the south wall, was a sort of pit. For a bottom it had a large flat stone; the sides were composed of four metates and a thin stone slab. They stood upright; above them was a layer of small stones forming a wall that brought the sides of the pit on the floor level. The metates were placed with the grinding surfaces facing the inner part of the pit. There were a number of small bin-like enclosures in this room, one of which was near the northwest corner. The walls were standing to a height of 2 feet. There were evidences, however, that at least certain parts of the walls had extended to the ceiling. There was a doorway in the south wall of the main room. It was of the ordinary type and had wooden lintels, as had all of the doorways in the room.

There were doorways in the upper part of the north wall, i. e., in the second story room. They were of the rectangular type and had evidently been filled in at the top. The wall was broken to such an extent, however, that their exact shape could not be determined. The ceiling beams extended from north to south and averaged 3 inches in diameter.

The measurements of this room, taken at the floor level were as follows: east wall, 9 feet 5 inches; west wall, 9 feet 10 inches; north wall, 14 feet; south wall, somewhat indefinite, but slightly under 14 feet in length. The specimens found in this room were as follows, all of them, unless otherwise noted, being from the débris which covered the

Fig. 89.   Closed Doorway in East Wall of Room 43.

floor: in the southwest corner at the floor level, a large metate was found; from the doorway in the northwest corner a number of pottery fragments; two manos; five small stones; a small stone mortar; two sandstones; a grooved mano; a sandstone concretion in the form of a cup; fragments of obsidian; a fossil shell; a number of turquoise beads; bone beads; and a stem of a clay pipe; pottery olla; eight bone awls; a bone implement; a bone scraper; a piece of deer antler; two breast bones of turkeys; arrow points; strombus shell; end of an arrow-shaft; fragment of a moccasin; and a number of potsherds.

Room 43.

Room 43 was southwest of Room 42. This room was small and almost square. It measured 5 feet on the north, 5 feet 8 inches on the south, 6 feet 4 inches on the east, 7 feet 11 inches on the west. There was a doorway of the rectangular type in the east wall of the lower room (Fig. 89). This room was 7 feet in height and the walls of the second floor were standing to a height of 5 feet. No specimens were found in this room.

Room 44.

Room 44 was directly west of Room 43. This room was long and narrow. The south wall of the lower room was built of medium-sized stones and chinked irregularly, thereby giving the surface a rather crude appearance. There were no doorways in this wall, as the opposite side abutted on the circular wall of Estufa 16. The east wall was heavily plastered and had been blackened by smoke. In this wall there is a doorway of the usual rectangular form. As a sill it had a flat stone, which averaged ½ inch in thickness and extended to the edge of the doorway and about 3 inches into the room. The lintel was of poles which averaged 1½ feet in diameter and on either side of the doorway logs had been built into the wall. They were placed in a perpendicular position and completely covered with plaster.

The north wall was well plastered and at the western end it was rounded so that the corner of the wall projected over an inch from the point where the stone walls joined.

Fig. 90 (5520). Shell of a a Walnut, inlaid with Turquoise, Room 44.

The upper room retained the major part of the plaster on the north wall; west of the central portion it was very smooth. A number of layers of plaster had been applied and the scaling at certain points was quite noticeable. There was a doorway near the center of this wall which had a stone slab for a sill. The west wall had a doorway in the upper part. It had a beam 1½ inches in diameter, used as a lintel. This doorway had been sealed up. The south wall was similar in appearance to the others mentioned, but the greater part of it had fallen. This room was 13 feet 10 inches long on the north side, 14 feet on the south side, 5 feet 1 inch on the east, and 5 feet 2 inches on the west side. Very few specimens were found in this room. Those worthy of mention were a large metate, a game stick, a stone slab, a broken bowl, and a cañon walnut (*Juglans Rupestris*) which had been covered with gum and inlaid with turquoise (Fig. 90).

Room 45.

Room 45 is directly north of Room 42. This room was smaller than Room 44, being long and narrow. The north and east walls were made of large stones and heavily plastered. The south wall was broken and crushed to some extent. Near the western end of the south wall, there was a doorway with a large beam 6 inches in diameter for a lintel. This doorway was somewhat rounded at the top and the sides were slanting. It connected Room 45 with Room 42. Just west of this doorway there was a post which had been built into the wall, probably as a support for the ceiling. Opposite from this post, and 1 foot 6 inches from the north wall was another post 6 inches in diameter, which was intact. The top was on the level with the ceiling beam openings in the north wall. The measurements of this room were as follows: north wall 19 feet, south wall, 17 feet 8 inches, east wall 7 feet 5 inches, west 6 feet 10 inches.

All the specimens found were in the débris near the floor level. As will be seen in the following list, stone implements predominated. There were: one metate, ten manos, five stone hammers, two grooved stone hammers, two stone slabs, one stone pestle, a sandstone grinder, an arrow point, fossil shells, obsidian, jet, galena, and potsherds. There were also a bone gouge, three bone awls, a bone scraper, two dog skulls and other animal bones. A pottery bowl was found in the eastern end of the room.

Room 46.

Room 46 was west of Room 45. The only prominent feature of this room was its well plastered walls. They were irregular, however, and all, with the exception of the western one, were devoid of doors. The doorway of this wall was of the ordinary rectangular type and led into Room 39.

This room was dug to a depth of 3 feet below the floor level. The eastern wall was not over 10 inches thick in its thickest place, and at some points not over 6 inches. It seemed more like a temporary partition between this room and Room 45, than a permanent wall. No specimens were found. The measurements were as follows: north wall 5 feet 6 inches, south wall 6 feet, east wall 7 feet 2 inches, west wall 7 feet 2 inches.

Room 47.

Room 47 is directly south of Room 46. This room was rather peculiar in shape, the corners being of a rounded form. The walls were composed of large flat stones to which a portion of the plaster still adhered. Nothing of interest was found, although as in most of the other rooms, it was dug to a depth of over 3 feet below the floor level. There was a doorway of the usual type in the east wall. The measurements were as follows: north wall 6 feet, south wall 6 feet, east wall 10 feet 9 inches, west wall 10 feet 9 inches.

Room 48.

Room 48 belonged with a rather peculiar series, comprising Rooms 48, 49, and 50. This room had well plastered walls, but only the south wall was standing to any height. It had twelve thicknesses of plaster, but in most places the outer layers had fallen off. One of the ordinary rectangular doorways led from this room into Room 44, but it had been closed with stones and plaster. The eastern wall had fallen within 2 feet of the floor level. The north wall was rough and irregular, and for about half its length at the eastern end it had fallen. The west wall was built on a large beam which was on the level with the ceiling beam of the lower room. This wall was very crude and it fell when the earth was removed from the front of it. The lower part of this room was well plastered and the walls were in better condition than in the upper room. There was a bench at the western end. The measurements were as follows: north wall 5 feet 4 inches; south wall 5 feet; east wall 8 feet; west wall 7 feet 3 inches. The specimens found were four metates, seven manos, a hammerstone, a stone pestle, a stone slab, two flint nodules, part of a human pottery figure, a pottery leg and foot, a number of potsherds, turquoise beads, and animal bones. All of these specimens were from the upper room. In the lower room 102 perfect arrow points and fifty-two broken ones were found. Most of these points were made of chalcedony and obsidian.

Room 49.

Room 49 was north of Room 48. It was long and narrow and may have been used as a storage room. The walls were rough and only certain portions of them were faced. In the middle of the north wall, on the level with the floor, was the southern end of a closet-like opening, mentioned in the description of Room 39. Nothing of interest was found in this room. The measurements were as follows: north wall 9 feet, south wall 9 feet, east wall 1 foot 10 inches, west wall 2 feet.

Room 50.

Room 50 was a small room over the western end of Room 48. The western wall was rough and unplastered and a bench 2 feet wide extended into the room. It was 2 feet above the floor beams. This bench extended to the eastern edge of the west side of the passageway at the north side of the room. The eastern wall was rough and fell when Room 48 was cleared. The northern part of the room was taken up with a passageway, the eastern side of which was solidly built. The western wall was 1 foot 3 inches thick, and with the eastern wall of Room 51 formed a solid piece of masonry, 3 feet 9 inches thick. Rooms 49 and 50, and the upper part of Room 48, formed a rather complex arrangement above a large first story room below Room 48. Room 50 was 4 feet 3 inches wide on the north, 4 feet 8 inches on the south, 7 feet 8 inches on the east, and 7 feet 9 inches on the west. Five arrow points were found in the débris. The bench on the northeast corner measured 5 feet by 1 foot 4 inches. The passageway for this bench at the eastern end of Room 49 was 2 feet 4 inches wide.

The lower Room 48 measured 13 feet 5 inches on the north, 11 feet on the south, 7 feet 11 inches on the east, and 6 feet 10 inches on the west.

ROOM 51.

Room 51 was directly west of Room 50. The walls of this room were composed of medium-sized stones and were chinked with very thin ones. The chinking, however, was not very regular. The western end of the room was rather roughly built and was intact to the north wall of Room 52. From this point to the north wall it had disappeared, having been torn down by a working party during the winter of 1896–97. The lower room had been burnt out on the eastern end. The walls of this room were well plastered. The western wall was simply a partition which divided the lower room into two small rooms. It extended to the ceiling beams and the plaster which covered its entire surface was blackened with smoke. This wall was 10 inches thick. The measurements of Room 51 were as follows: The north wall, 11 feet 6 inches; south, 10 feet 9 inches; east, 9 feet 2 inches; west, 8 feet 4 inches. In the débris the following specimens were found: one large metate, two small hammerstones, a grooved ax with double edge, a stone showing drilling, pieces of turquoise, turquoise beads, chalcedony flakes, a clay ball filled with turquoise chips, a bone awl, a dog skeleton, a number of animal bones, fragments of shell bracelets, a crude pottery bowl, a pottery incense burner (Fig. 91), and a number of potsherds.

Room 51a. Room 51a was a small room of a lower series and was just west of Room 51. The walls were practically the same in construction as those mentioned in the description of the last-named room. There was a rectangular doorway in the south wall. This doorway connected with Room 28. Another doorway in the northeast corner of the north wall was of the rectangular type, as was the case with the one in the south wall. The room measured as follows: north wall, 7 feet 9 inches; south wall, 6 feet; east wall, 8 feet 2 inches; west wall, 8 feet 2 inches. The following specimens were found in the débris: three large metates, two stone door sills, a stone hammer, animal bones among which were several dog jaws, two bone awls, three fragments of shell bracelets, pieces of shell, two fossil shells, a wooden game stick, and a number of potsherds, one of which was worked.

Fig. 91 (5590).   Pottery Vessel suggesting an Incense Burner, Room 51.

Room 52.

Room 52 was directly west of Room 51 and was of irregular shape, the west wall being much wider than that of the east side. The eastern wall was roughly built and had been partly demolished by other investigators.

The south wall was strongly built and presented a very compact and uniform surface and approached in appearance the closely chinked walls, being formed of large dressed stones and chinked with small flat pieces. This wall slanted towards the south. The west end of this room was roughly made and had been plastered. There was a rectangular doorway in the lower part of this wall which connected with Room 58. It had a flat stone for a sill and the upper part of the doorway was somewhat rounded. The north wall was made of large flat stones which were regularly laid, presenting a strong contrast as compared with the south wall. There were two other doorways in this room, one in the west and the other in the north wall. The room measured as follows: north wall, 6 feet 4 inches; south wall, 5 feet 11 inches; east wall, 9 feet 3 inches; west wall, 9 feet 6 inches.

There were very few specimens found in this room, the most interesting, however, were a number of fragments of cylindrical jars, such as were found in the large deposit in Room 28. These fragments, the deposit in Room 28, and those in Room 39b, were the only ones found in Pueblo Bonito. Isolated jars of cylindrical form were found in Rooms 32 and 33 and the Moorehead party obtained one or more from the rooms adjoining this group. Among other objects found in the débris was a stone hammer, two sandstone slabs, a pitted stone, a stone jar cover, a cylindrical pipe, fragments of shell bracelets, a bone awl, potsherds, also fragments of matting and cloth.

Room 53.

Room 53 is directly north of Room 52. This was one of the two rooms explored by the Moorehead party. The south wall of this room was standing to a depth of 6 feet at the western end. It is poorly built and evenly plastered. There is a beam extending the full length of the wall; probably for a support. It was about 4 inches in diameter. The western wall was similar in construction to that of the south. There was a doorway in the center of this wall, but the sides have been torn down and its outline was almost obliterated.

The northern and eastern walls had been torn down by previous workers. The lower or first story room had very rough and uneven walls. The south wall was made of large stones and had a doorway of the ordinary type, with a wooden lintel. The western wall was similar to the south wall and there was a doorway of the ordinary type near the central part. This doorway led into Room 56, which was also worked by the Moorehead party.

A Deposit of Beads. The Moorehead party excavated the greater part of this room. When our workmen began to clear the débris from the south end of the room, an almost complete human skeleton was found. The skull was missing, but near the middle of the room, the lower jaw was found. Continuing observations along the eastern wall, a post was found at a distance of 6 feet from the south wall. Near this post two pitchers and a small bowl were found, also a portion of a large cylindrical jar. Near the east wall the skull of a child was found, and near it was a deposit of turquoise and shell beads. There were over

Fig. 92.   Stone Implements in Room 54.

211

Fig. 93. Walls of Room 54.

4000 flat circular turquoise beads and about thirty shell beads or pendants in it, and they had no doubt formed a necklace. The débris on the floor was then cleared away and the work was carried below the floor to a depth of 3 feet. Nothing of importance was found below the floor level.

This room was 11 feet 6 inches wide on the north end; 10 feet 5 inches on the south end; 14 feet 2 inches on the east; 13 feet 5 inches on the west. Resting on the floor, about midway between the end walls, at a short distance from the east wall, there were two pottery pitchers, a bowl, and a stone jar cover. In the southwestern part of the room, fragments of feather blankets and two end boards of baby carriers were found. In the débris there were a number of fragments of wood including ceremonial and game sticks and a wooden slab. Fragments of pottery vessels, turquoise beads, and animal bones were also found. These, with the child's skull, the human bones, and the deposit of turquoise and shell beads, completed the list of objects found in the room.

Room 54.

Stone Implements. Room 54 is directly east of the adjoining Room 38. The excavations in this room had been carried to a depth of about 4 feet when a layer of stone implements was found (Fig. 92). These implements extended to a depth of several feet below this point and had evidently been stored in one of the upper rooms. In this deposit there were two metates, sixty-four manos, thirty-seven hammerstones, sixteen stone jar covers, two grooved hammers, three smoothing stones, two sandstone grinders, eleven stone slabs, two grinding stones, two stone knives, nine worked stones of various shapes, a hoe-shaped stone, grooved maul, five bone awls, a bone scraper, a pipestem, an arrow point, pieces of turquoise, fossil shells, potsherds, two wooden knife handles (Fig. 94), and fragments of baskets.

After the stone objects had been removed and the débris cleared from the floor, it was found that practically nothing had been left on the lower floor, the only object of interest found was a piece of coal, which was lying against the north wall.

The photograph (Fig. 93) of this room gives a comprehensive idea of the manner in which it had been constructed. Near the middle of the western section was a projecting wall which extended in a northeastern direction. This wall was 4 feet 8 inches long and the end was 7 feet 5 inches from the southwest corner. Between this projection and the western wall of the room at a distance of 7 inches from the south wall, were two posts. A third post may be seen in the opposite corner. This

Fig. 94 (5650).   Wooden Knife Handle, Room 54.

Fig. 95 (5651).   Hafted Stone Knife, Room 54.

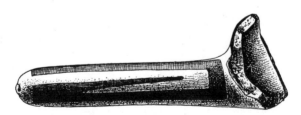

Fig. 96 (5647).   Handle of Pottery Vessel, Room 54.

214

post, with the other two, no doubt formed a support for a platform similar to the one noted in Room 38, which adjoins this room on the west. East of the projecting wall were five posts, two near the south and three near the north wall. Three of these may be seen in the photograph. These posts evidently formed supports for another platform. There are two doorways of the usual type in the north wall, also one in the south and one in the west wall. In the foreground of the photograph, another wall may be seen. This one, however, extended from one side of the room to the other. Near the corners of this small division of the main room, two posts were in evidence. These may have extended to the ceiling, but from the condition of the ends it would seem that they had not decayed to any extent, and that they had no doubt served, as in the case of the others, as supports for a platform. The measurements of Room 54 are as follows: north wall, 24 feet 7 inches; south wall, 25 feet, 3 inches; east wall, 10 feet; west wall, 8 feet 5 inches.

Room 55.

Room 55 was directly west of and adjoining Room 28. It showed two distinct types of masonry. The west wall was built of small slabs of sandstone which had been closely laid. At the base of this wall, which was very compact, could be seen a portion of a beam 6 inches in diameter. This beam was built into the north wall and acted as a support for the west wall, as the foundation would otherwise have been insecure, built as it was on the débris of one of the walls. About 3 feet below the ceiling beams, at the north end of the wall, there may be seen a beam over 9 inches in diameter. This beam also extended to the northern face of the wall and the west wall is built around it. It evidently extended to the south wall and no doubt acted as a support to the upper story. The face of the west wall was unbroken, save for the places where the crossbeams showed and where the ceiling beams protruded from its surface. At this point there were six sticks showing that the ceiling beams ran east and west. The upper wall stood to a height of 4 feet at the northern end and a broken doorway of the rectangular type was in evidence in the center, but the southern part of the wall was only 2 feet high.

The north wall was rough and composed of thin stones. There was a space in the upper central part of the wall where there had been a beam running north and south, that had acted as a ceiling support. At the northeastern part of this room, the northern wall had a secondary wall, filling the space between it and the east one. This wedge-shaped portion was a continuation of the well-built wall described in Room 51a and formed the south wall of Room 52. The joint made by the two walls was by no means perfect, but comparison as regards the masonry was striking. The upper part of the north wall was built of large stones and presented a solid appearance. The foundation, as in the case of the western one, was simply the débris of the burnt-out portions of the rooms, which had formed a part of the old building.

The south, like the western wall, was made of small flat stones closely laid. The surface of this wall was unbroken, save for the upper part where the cross-beams had entered. The north wall of the lower, or old, part of the building was well plastered and had been blackened by fire. The eastern wall of this lower part was simply a pile of débris that separated Room 55 from Room 28. The southern lower wall was composed of large flat stones, laid without any regard to order, and projected beyond the main wall over a foot. The western lower wall, as mentioned, was simply a pile of débris. About 4 feet below the western wall were the remains of a floor. The beams had been forced from their original places, but had formerly run from east to west. Above them was a cedarbark floor covering and pieces of the adobe floor were also in evidence. The upper room had evidently been built over an old part of the building without any clearing or leveling of the old walls. The new wall at the southeastern corner was built against the old north wall. The remaining portions of the old structure had been utilized, but no particular pains were taken to restore the old parts and no use had been made of the old material. Excavations were carried to a depth of over 4 feet below the old floor beams, but nothing but clean sand was discovered.

The room measured as follows: north wall, 7 feet 2 inches; south wall, 6 feet 4 inches; east wall, 8 feet; west wall, 7 feet 3 inches. The total height of the walls at the northwest corner was 18 feet 9 inches. The following specimens were found in the débris; two ceremonial sticks and fragments of others, hammerstone, arrow point, small basket, bone awl, foot of a deer, mummified prairie dog, and a piece of shell.

Room 56.

Room 56 was directly west of Room 53 and was worked by the party under the direction of W. K. Moorehead.[1] It contained two graves that had been opened by this party and the bones were scattered throughout the dirt that was piled in the northeastern part of the room. There was also a mass of human bones in the northwestern corner, so it was impossible to determine how many bodies had been buried here.

---

[1]During the winter of 1897–8, Mr. Warren K. Moorehead directed some additional excavations, opening a number of rooms as designated in the text.

The walls were well plastered and presented an unbroken surface, save in the northern end of the east wall, where there was a doorway. This opening was 1 foot below the ceiling and measured 2 feet 2 inches in height and 1 foot 10 inches in width. This doorway led into Room 53.

The ceiling was composed of twenty-five rough poles that ran from east to west. These were covered with brush. Above this covering was the adobe floor of Room 63.

There was a jog in the northwestern corner where a wall had been torn out and a new one built just west of it. The corner was rounded to the old wall site, forming a marked concavity from this point to the western wall. From the eastern wall to a point where the curvature of the north wall begins, the distance is 4 feet at the place where this rounding ends; where the old wall begins, 5 feet 3 inches, leaving a space of 1 foot 4 inches that was added to the room by the erection of the new wall.

The two graves under the floor of this room had been separated by a stone wall, the top of which was on the level of the floor, and extended from the east to the west wall. Its width at the top was 1 foot 2 inches and extended to a point below the lower level of the graves. This wall was evidently a part of an old room, for on the western side, under the western wall of the room under consideration, there is another wall which extended the whole length of the western one. Its top was on the level with the floor, and as in the case of the cross wall, its lower limits extended some feet below this point.

The grave in the northern part of the room extended from the cross wall to the south wall. It was 7 feet 3 inches long, and 4 feet 9 inches wide on the southern end, and was evidently the same in width at the north end. This grave was uncovered by the Moorehead party and it could not be ascertained whether it had been boarded up or not; it was 2 feet deep.

The grave at the southern end of the room was smaller than the first one. It was 6 feet 7 inches long on the western side and 6 feet 4 inches on the eastern side, both ends, however, measuring 3 feet in width. The north end was formed by the cross wall. This grave was 3 feet deep and the bottom was composed of sticks. The sides were made of four boards, the upper and lower ones were set at an angle, thereby giving a rounded appearance to the grave. This grave was probably covered with boards, but it may have been covered by matting, for fragments of both were found in Room 53, where the greater part of the débris from this room was thrown. The measurements of this room were as follows: north wall, 6 feet 7 inches; south wall, 5 feet 3 inches: eastern wall, 16 feet 3 inches; western wall, 13 feet 10 inches. The average distance from the floor to the ceiling beams was 5 feet 6 inches.

Aside from the human bones and a number of animal bones, gathered from the débris, which had not been thrown into the adjoining room, only two specimens worthy of mention were found. One was a stone jar, the other a broken stone jar cover, and a few potsherds.

Room 57.

Room 57 was west of Room 55. This room was particularly interesting as it showed a perfect division between the old and new parts of the building. This condition of affairs was noticeable in Room 55 and extended into Room 28. The upper or new walls of this room at the east and south sides were made of thin flat pieces of sandstone and were laid so closely that very little mortar was needed to form a solid wall. They were so even and so well laid, that at a short distance, they appeared to be plastered. They reminded one of the closely built eastern wall of Pueblo Chettro Kettle. The southern wall was uniform in appearance, but was slightly rounding. There was a doorway in the center of this wall about $2\frac{1}{2}$ feet above the floor. For a lintel it had five beams strapped together with a piece of bark. This doorway was closed with flat stones which had been carefully placed, but at the upper part on the eastern side, some of the stones had been removed, exposing to view a beautifully plastered surface, as smooth and even as any in the building. The south wall may have been plastered, but there was no evidence of it. The eastern wall presented practically the same appearance as the south wall, the surface being neatly finished and compact. There was no break in the surface of the eastern wall in the lower room. The ceiling beams ran east and west and rested upon a large beam which ran in the opposite direction. Above the ceiling in the east wall, the wall was somewhat rougher than the others that had been noted, and stood to a height of 4 feet. In the center was a doorway of the usual rectangular type. Only a portion of it was to be seen as the wall had fallen, carrying away the top and most of the south side. The north wall presented a rough surface, the stones were undressed and laid without regard to evenness or symmetry and patches of plaster still adhered in places. There was no break in the surface, but near the eastern end there was a log a foot in diameter which no doubt supported the ceiling. There was a second log slightly smaller than the one mentioned, on the same level and about 2 inches from the western wall.

The remaining north wall stood to a height of 5 feet above this beam and was of the same material and construction as the lower one. The western wall is composed of faced stones well laid, with the interstices chinked. Built into the wall, at a point south of the center, is a pole 4 inches in diameter. A portion of it protrudes from the surface, its upper part being buried in the masonry. This pole runs down through the old part of the building, on which this room was built. This beam was probably standing when the new part was constructed and was utilized as a support for the new wall.

Below this room was a mass of burnt logs and stones and a fallen ceiling of an old room. The beams ran east and west, but had been crushed and broken. Above them were the remains of a brush covering. At the north side of this lower space was a well-plastered wall that had been left standing when the other part of the room had been destroyed, and upon it the wall of the upper room was built. The eastern and western walls of the upper room were built upon the débris of the old part. When the wall was cleared at the northeastern corner, the débris fell from under the east wall, leaving an open space over 2 feet in width, but owing to the fact that the wall was wedge-shaped and the rooms on the north and south sides had not been cleared, it acted as a keystone and therefore remained intact.

About 1 foot west of the upper or new wall, on the western side of the room, was a wall composed of sticks. This was part of the old ruin and in building the upper room they had missed it by the above-mentioned distance. This old wall was made of upright posts against which stones had been laid. These had been covered with plaster, which gave the wall a rounded appearance.

The south wall of the upper room had a firm foundation, as it rested upon a solid wall, composed of posts and projected over 1 foot to the north of the upper wall. These posts were firmly set in the ground and across them at intervals of about 1 foot, were poles which were lashed to the upright pieces. The spaces between the poles were then filled with plaster and mud and the surface plastered.

The lower room was smaller than the one built above it, but the exact measurements could not be taken as we dared not clear away the débris under the east upper wall. The upper walls widened towards the top, the flaring sides being very noticeable. The measurements of this room were as follows: north wall, 7 feet 8 inches; south wall, 6 feet 10 inches; east wall, 7 feet; west wall, 7 feet. The following specimens were found in the débris: three manos, two hammerstones, a stone jar cover and fragments of another, fragments of dog skulls, and pieces of turquoise and shell.

Room 58.

Room 58 was north of Room 55 and directly over Room 33, where the turquoise and ceremonial objects were found. Part of the third story of this room was standing; the highest portion was at the southwest corner, where it ran to a height of 5 feet to the ceiling beams of the second story. The south wall was of very thin stones laid in mortar and slanted towards the east until at the eastern corner, it was only 2 feet above the ceiling beams. The eastern wall was a little over 1 foot high and of rough construction. The north and west walls were of the same type of masonry.

The eastern wall of the second story room was well plastered, as was the case with the other three. It had a doorway in the central part near the floor, was of rectangular form and connected with Room 52. In the southwest corner of this wall, level with the ceiling, a portion of

Fig. 97 (8794).   Handle made of Bone, Highly Polished, resembling Ivory, Room 58.

the wall had been broken away when forming an entrance to the open series of rooms, which extended in a northeastern direction from Room 3. In the northeast corner of the room, about 6 inches from the east and 3 inches from the north wall, there was a post 5 inches in diameter, which was mentioned in the description of Room 33. It extended from the floor of the lower room through the ceiling into the upper one. The measurements of this room were: north wall, 6 feet 1 inch; south wall, 6 feet 1 inch; east wall, 5 feet 7 inches; west wall, 6 feet 2 inches. The average height of this room, from the floor to the ceiling beams was 6 feet 9 inches. The specimens found in the débris were: two hand hammerstones, a grooved hammer, a reed brush, several ceremonial sticks, also potsherds and animal bones.

Room 59.

Room 59 was in the southwestern part of the ruin, southwest of Room 23. This room was circular in form, with an angular offset at the southern end. The walls were composed largely of large stones and had been well plastered. Several layers could be counted. The angular part at the south end was covered with plaster. There was a fireplace in the center of the circular part, made by placing stones on edge. The specimens were as follows: six hammerstones, three smoothing stones, a stone ax, a worked stone slab, a pottery bowl, a pottery handle of a jar cover, a bone awl, two lower jaws of dogs, animal bones, and potsherds.

Room 60.

Room 60 was directly east of and adjoining Room 20. This room was of the angular type, the south wall being much shorter than the other three. All of the walls of this room were fairly well preserved, although there were evidences that a fire had raged in certain parts of the room and some parts of the walls showed the effect of the heat. In the lower part of the north wall was a doorway of the usual rectangular type with a stone slab for a sill. There was a doorway in the west wall at a point 1 foot above the floor level and 3 feet 6 inches from the north wall. This doorway, which is of the usual type, has a double lintel composed of poles. The layers of the poles are 8 inches apart and the spaces between have been filled in with sandstone. The measurements of this room are as follows: north wall, 15 feet 5 inches; south wall, 6 feet 5 inches; east wall, 13 feet 5 inches; west wall, 10 feet 3 inches. Resting on the floor within a few inches of the south wall, near the central part of the room, a large corrugated jar was found. In it was a thick layer of red paint, also some seeds. A red bowl and one of plain ware were found near the jar. Other objects which were found in the débris included three dipper handles, a number of potsherds and a pottery animal, nine hammerstones, a broken moccasin-shaped stone, a worked stone slab, seven manos, a stone jar cover, a stone cylinder, an arrow point, fragments of chalcedony, turquoise, and shell, two bone scrapers, two bone awls, a bone implement, an animal bone showing cutting, a bone bracelet, a number of animal bones, fragments of sticks, squash rind and seeds, pieces of matting, and a deer skull.

Room 60a. Room 60a was a small angular room, southwest of Room 60. It had evidently formed one of the corner rooms of an old estufa, a part of which will be described as Room 76. This room measured as follows: south wall, 5 feet 3 inches long; the east wall, 6 feet; west wall, 7 feet. The west wall is the hypothenuse of a right-angled triangle, the other two sides being formed by the east and south walls. Nothing of interest was found in this room.

Room 61.

Room 61 was directly east of Room 37, and north of Room 53. This room was comparatively small. There were two stories standing. The lower room was well plastered, but it bulged near the ceiling beams, evidently from the accumulated weight above it. A little to the east of the center of this wall was a doorway. It was 2 feet 6 inches below the ceiling beams and of the rectangular type, but it had been plastered to such an extent that it was semi-oval in form, the plaster being rounded out to the surface of the wall at the sides of the opening. It had a wooden lintel. This doorway led into Room 6. On the west side of the doorway was a wooden loop fastened in the plaster. This was one of the loops used in barricading the door. Very few of these were found in Pueblo Bonito, but they are quite common in the cliff-houses in southwestern Colorado and southeastern Utah. Fragments of ceiling beams protruded from the wall, showing that they had originally extended from north to south.

The north wall of the upper room stood to a height of 6 feet and was well plastered. It had a doorway of the usual type with a large stone for a sill, which projected over 3 inches beyond the wall surface. The lintel was made of poles.

The eastern wall was built of large dressed stones and presented a very solid appearance. The stones were not closely laid, there was no chinking, the stones being laid with plaster. There was a doorway of the usual type in this wall. It was 2 feet 9 inches above the floor level. It had a wooden lintel and had been closed with plaster. The walls of the upper room had fallen, the remaining portion at the north end standing to a height of 3 feet 6 inches.

The south wall was roughly constructed and the western end had been torn down by other workers. There was a doorway near the west-central part, but this was destroyed when the wall was demolished. This wall was built around upright stakes, the corners being rounded with plaster.

The western wall was well plastered. In the north-central part there was a doorway of the usual type with wooden lintels. One interesting feature in connection with this doorway, was the fact that it was 2 feet above the floor and that it had a step in front of it which was composed of flat stones which projected 8 inches into the room. The upper western wall stood to a height of 5 feet above the ceiling of the lower one. The measurements of the lower room are as follows: north wall, 11 feet 1 inch; south wall, 9 feet 4 inches; east wall, 11 feet 6 inches; west wall, 10 feet 4 inches. Most of the specimens found in this room were in the débris covering the floor; fragments of a human skull, scattered about in the southeast corner; pieces of a jaw with teeth and fragments of the cranium, blackened and charred to such an extent that it seems hardly possible that it could have been accidental. There was no evidence of there having been a fire in this room. The only piece of charred wood found was a section of a post 2 feet long and 2 inches in diameter. This had evidently fallen from one of the upper rooms. The pieces of the skull lay as if they had been scattered by hand. Had they fallen with the débris from the ceiling above, they would not have been lying in the positions they occupied in the accumulation of floor material. There were a few fragments of human bones beside the skull, but these showed no evidence of having been burnt. Among the other objects found in the débris was a grooved stone ax, two stone slabs, a stone slab evidently used as a cooking stone, a stone pestle, fragments of a stone jar cover, pieces of petrified wood, and natural pebbles. There was also a bone awl, a bone showing cutting, three rabbit skeletons, a number of animal bones, two wooden implements, a stick which may have been used in hunting rabbits, a game stick, a section of a whip cactus stalk, and fragments of shells.

Room 62.

Room 62 was very interesting. At the western end was a flooring that rested on cross beams, running north and south, which were about 3 feet above the general floor level of the main room. The western beam entered each wall about 1 foot east of the west wall; the next beam was inserted in the south wall, but at its northern end, it rested upon a post that was 2 inches in diameter. The eastern beam was inserted in the wall at either end, and at the north end was about 1 foot south of the doorway. These beams averaged about 4 inches in diameter.

Resting upon these beams, and running east and west, was a series of poles averaging 2 inches in diameter. They had evidently been of uniform length, with the exception of the one nearest to the south wall which projected about 2 feet beyond the others and rested upon a jog in the southern wall. Over these poles, running north and south, a reed matting was fastened by means of small branches and strips of wood which ran across the mat at right angles to the reeds and were fastened to the poles with strands of yucca (Fig. 98).

The floor had been crushed and the beams broken by the weight of the débris, but was intact enough to give a good idea of its original appearance.

The southern end of Room 62 presented a very irregular appearance, not only in its irregularity but in the general aspect of its surface.

The western part of this wall was composed of small stones closely laid and the greater part of the surface was covered with plaster. Two feet, five inches from the west wall, and 5 feet from the floor, was a small circular pocket about 5 inches in diameter and extending 10 inches into the wall. It was well rounded with plaster, there being no break in the general plaster about its rim. These beams projected from the surface at a height of 3 feet 7 inches from the floor. These were the beams that supported the reed floor as described in another place.

Nine feet east of the west wall and 3 feet 7 inches from the floor was a jog in the wall, 10 inches long and almost 3 inches wide. Upon this rested the long pole, which was the southernmost one of the reed floor series. The depression for this jog ran from the point 3 feet 7 inches above the floor to the upper part of the wall below the jog, the wall rounded toward the west. From this point, that is from the eastern edge of the jog, the wall was rounded for a distance of 6 feet 11 inches. Its eastern end was continued toward the southeast, forming the outer wall of the northeast part of the circular estufa just south of Room 62. Just west of the upper central part of this circular portion of the wall, was a portion of a doorway. It was 7 feet 3 inches from the eastern wall and the sides were 1 foot 3 inches high, of the usual square type, and was 2 feet wide at its base. The wall had fallen on this side of the room, carrying the upper part of this doorway with it.

This circular wall was composed of stones that were somewhat larger than those in the southern part, but they were no less firmly laid. Most of the surface was covered with plaster, which, in places, showed the various layers that had been applied.

At the extreme eastern part of this section of wall was an opening about 6 inches in diameter, about 3 feet 8 inches above the floor, that marked the places where a cross beam had once been, as there was a corresponding opening at the same height in the north wall.

The remaining, or eastern portion of this wall, was 5 feet long, its surface was almost devoid of plaster, which presented to view a compact, but rather uneven plane. At a point about 3 feet 8 inches above the floor and about 1 foot east of the western edge of this part of the wall, a small beam protruded, ranging east of this and on the same level were four more beams about the size of the first one, which was $1\frac{1}{2}$ inches in diameter. These logs had been broken off flush with the wall and had no doubt formed a floor similar to the one at the western end of the room.

Fig. 98.   View of Room 62 showing the Fallen Ceiling and Construction of the Wall Pockets.
A new layer of plaster is shown by the line running across the wall.

Fig. 99.   Wall Pockets in Room 62.

Fig. 100.   Baskets and Pockets under the Floor of Room 62.

227

Fig. 101 (9159). Design on a Painted Board found in Débris near Room 63.

228

These beams seemed to divide the eastern portion of the south wall into two parts, the upper portion of which was composed of much smaller stones than the lower part, and the surface was much more even. This 5 feet of wall was evidently the base of a right-angled triangle of masonry, whose perpendicular followed the continuation of the eastern wall of Room 62 and whose hypothenuse was concaved in conformity with the outer wall of the estufa. The general height of this southern wall was 7 feet 11 inches, it having suffered more than the others when this part of the building fell.

Wall Pockets. The western wall was very interesting from the fact that no less than four pockets were found (Fig. 99). The greater part of this wall was covered with plaster, the only portion where it had been detached being at the lower northern end and a small space at the south end against the south wall. The wall itself, at least the point that was visible, was composed of large dressed stones, the spaces between which were chinked with small flat pieces, forming a very compact and pleasing surface.

The upper part of the wall had suffered by fire, the stones being calcined and the plaster blackened. No beams projected from this wall to mar its general appearance; the closets, or wall pockets, were well finished, which caused them to add to rather than detract from the beauty of the wall.

Near the ceiling level at the southern end of the room, a pocket almost square in form, was encountered in the early stages of the work. Pocket 1 had boards for its sides, the upper and lower part and the back being plastered. The wall plaster was broken about its edges, but seemed to have been square at the edges of the pocket; if rounded at all, the curvature must have been very slight. The box-like opening was 1 foot 3 inches wide at the top and 1 foot 4 inches at the bottom, the sides being 1 foot ½ inch high; the cross measurements were 1 foot 6 inches and 1 foot 9 inches, respectively, the former being from the lower south to the upper north corner. The pocket extended 1 foot into the wall, and therefore formed a receptacle for quite large articles.

The triangulation was as follows, the measurements being taken from the floor: from the lower corner at the northern end to floor at the northwest corner of the room was 9 feet 1 inch and from the opposite corner of the pocket to the southwest corner of the room, 4 feet 8 inches.

Pocket 2 was a small orifice with well-rounded edges. It was simply a plastered depression in the wall surface 9 inches long and 6 inches high with a depth of 6 inches. The corners were rounded to such an extent, that it presented a semi-oval appearance. The triangulation of this pocket to the same points as the former one, was 7 feet 1 inch at the north side and at the south, 6 feet 2 inches. Just below these pockets the wall was divided transversely by the lower limits of a layer of plaster that had been applied to the upper part of the wall, this line was on a level with the upper part of Pocket 3. This closet was well made and looked firm and solid, owing to the fact that the lower part was composed of a flat board over an inch in thickness, that not only extended to the back part of the pocket, but projected under the masonry at the sides. This board was well dressed and had been smoothed ere it was put in place.

The upper part was composed of five poles laid side by side, as are the lintel poles of a doorway. There were five of them and their average diameter was about 1½ inches. These poles were built in the masonry at the sides of the pocket and served as a support for the narrow strip of wall between this and Pocket 1. The northern side of this opening had a thin layer of plaster for a facing, but on the southern side most of it had become detached. The plaster about the edges had been broken to such an extent that its original form could not be determined, but it had probably been nearly square.

The length of this lower part was 1 foot 9 inches and of the upper 1 foot 6 inches, the right (north) side being 1 foot 1 inch and the south, 11 inches. The diagonals were respectively 1 foot 10 inches and 2 feet, the former being from the lower south to the upper north corner. The triangulation from the points previously used was 7 feet 6 inches at the north side and 3 feet at the south, the depth was 1 foot 3½ inches.

The symmetry of this pocket was spoiled by the dip of the lower board, which gave it an irregular form. Why it was placed in this position is not apparent and seems strange in view of the fact that most of this work is uniform and in strict observance to planes and angles.

Pocket 4 was in general form like Pocket 2; the lower part and sides were well rounded with plaster, concealing whatever may have been used for the base. Possibly nothing was used but the plaster, but at the top a portion of the plaster had been knocked off, revealing a board ½ inch thick, that formed the upper part of the pocket and extended into the wall on either side of the pocket.

The length of this closet was 1 foot 1 inch and the height 8 inches and it extended into the wall 7 inches. The triangulation from the same points as the previous ones, was, from the north side, 4 feet 2 inches and at the south, 4 feet 10 inches. The plaster at the edges of this pocket, and especially at the lower part, was gently rounded outward to the general wall covering.

Doorways and Walls. In the southern part of the wall and 2 feet 7 inches from the south wall was a small opening that led into the next room to the west. This opening, Pocket 5, was 1 foot high and 7 inches wide; its top was rounded with plaster, but it had a small board for a lintel. Its base was formed of a dressed board which was flush with the floor level. The sides of this opening were plastered and on the edges the plaster was still intact and very slightly rounded.

At the upper part of the wall, just above and north of Pocket 1, was the base board of an old doorway that had been filled up and covered with plaster. From the outlines it seemed to be of the general square type, but the upper part had fallen.

Just above the ceiling, in the northwest corner, a wall crossed this room, its diameter northeast and southwest. It was standing to a height of 3 feet but was in a crumbling condition. The north wall presented a rough uneven surface and the greater part of the plaster was blackened by smoke. On most of the surface the plaster was in place, but around the places where beams had been, it had fallen. The only large break in the surface was the doorway which was 1 foot 9 inches from the east wall. This doorway was of the square type, but the top was beautifully rounded and the plaster was in good condition. The height of this opening was 2 feet 4 inches and the width 1 foot 9 inches. These dimensions held good to a point about 6 inches from the surface at the top and 2 inches at the bottom. Here a thick layer of plaster commenced at both sides and rounded to the lintel, which was composed of five large beams, this plaster continued to the other side of the wall; across the top of this plastered part were two sticks, evidently put there to hold the plaster in place, but it had either fallen from its own weight or been knocked off.

These layers of mortar decreased the size of the doorway to such an extent that the sides were only 1 foot 10 inches high and the width, 1 foot 4 inches; the base of this doorway was composed of a stone slab that projected a little beyond the masonry. About a foot west of this doorway and 4 feet from the floor, one of the cross beams supporting the reed floor entered the wall. There were two more places between this point and the west wall where beams had evidently entered, the second was supported by a post, but originally may have entered the wall.

Just over the opening nearest the door, a wall had run to the ceiling, and no doubt was supported by the beam that crossed the room at this point. Whether it ran to the opposite wall or not, could not be ascertáined, as it had fallen. Judging from the place in the plaster, it could not have been much over 6 inches in thickness.

In the western end of this wall, and with the floor for a starting point, were three places that were devoid of plaster; they were no doubt part of the general surface at first, but the plaster had worn off by use. These places, which were about 1 foot wide, and the same in height, probably marked the points where metates had rested.

From the west wall to the center of the first one was 7 inches, to the center of the second 2 feet 4 inches, and to the center of the third, 3 feet 10 inches.

Just above the two western places described above, there is a depres-·sion that has been plastered, but which may have been a door.

At the eastern end of this wall, is a wall pocket, 2 feet 7 inches from the floor and 9 inches west of the east wall. It is 1 foot high and 1 foot 2 inches wide. It runs through to the next room, and therefore, is more like a passageway than a closet, but was probably made in this way so that it could be used from both rooms, or as a means of conveying articles from one apartment to the other. The upper part was composed of eight poles laid like the door lintels; the sides were plastered but were slanted a little toward the top. The wall above it was badly bulged and the plaster had fallen from quite a large area.

Just to the east of this opening a beam protruded and west of it, on the same level, were the places where three more had been. These are the ones mentioned in the description of the southern wall and probably supported a floor similar to the one at the western end of the room, as was suggested in the other description.

The ceiling beams projected from the wall 9 feet 10 inches above the floor at the eastèrn end of the room, and 11 feet 8 inches at the western end. There were seven in all and they averaged about 8 inches in diameter. Above these beams was a mass of débris which was fully 5 feet high near the western end.

Across the northwest corner and just above the ceiling beams, a wall crossed, as before mentioned, and just above the corner itself was a doorway. This was tilted and in poor condition and little could be gathered from it from the work done in Room 62.

The eastern wall was composed of selected stones and the places between the large stones were chinked with flat pieces of sandstone. The lower part of the wall retained most of its plaster, but from the upper part, large patches had fallen.

There was a doorway of the square type in the lower southern part of the wall that had for a lintel a board nearly 1½ inches thick, it extended beyond the side of the doorway at the southern side, over 2 inches and at the northern side about 3 inches. This doorway was 9 inches above the floor and 1 foot 7 inches north of the south wall. It was 1 foot 9 inches wide and 2 feet 2 inches high. The sides were plastered and the wall plaster was rounded slightly at the edges.

The wall was standing at the northern end to a height of 9 feet 10 inches, but at the southern end only 7 feet 1 inch was intact.

A Buried Floor. The floor plan of this room presented a length of wall at the north side of the rectangle 19 feet 11 inches in extent, the east wall having a length of 7 feet 5 inches, and the west wall, 10 feet. The south wall, including the contour of the rounding part was 21 feet 9 inches.

Diagonally from the northeast to the southwest corner the distance was 22 feet 2 inches and the distance between the opposite corner proved to be 22 feet 9 inches. The floor in the western part of the room was torn out and under it was found another well-plastered floor. At the western wall the second floor was about 1 foot 2 inches below the first and the eastern end of this lower room, where the wall crossed, 7 inches at the southern side of the room. This lower floor rested upon a rounding projection of the main wall which was originally about 1 foot wider than the upper wall at the west end, but being rounding in form a piece had been added to square the surface, making it protrude from the main wall about 1 foot 6 inches.

This jutting wall was a continuation of the rounding part of the south wall described in another plan. Instead of following out the contour, the upper wall was squared. This bench decreased in width as it neared the eastern end of the room and was about 4 inches wide where it joined the square piece of masonry that extended northward from the southern wall at a point 7 feet 7 inches east of the west wall and extended to within 11 inches of the eastern cross wall. This projection was on the same level as the bench and was well built and plastered. It was 2 feet 1 inch long at the western side and 1 foot 10 inches long on the opposite side, having a width of 2 feet 8½ inches.

The western wall crossed at the lower floor level, resting simply on the hard sand that filled this western part of the room. The northern wall ran to a point about 4 feet below the lower floor level and the east, or division wall, was only 1 foot thick, the top being on a level with the upper floor.

The southern wall was well built and extended to a depth of over 6 feet. The western wall from the northern edge of the bench to the north wall was 8 feet 6 inches long. The north wall was 10 feet 4 inches long; the east wall, 7 feet 5 inches; while the southern wall presented a surface 11 feet 2½ inches in length.

The diagonal lines showed a distance of 13 feet 6 inches from the northwest to the southeast. A line from the northwest corner to the junction of the square of masonry at its west side, and the south wall was 10 feet 7 inches in length.

On breaking through this second floor, a pocket was found near the northwest corner of the square piece of masonry. A triangulation from the eastern or partition wall, placed it 7 feet 9 inches from the northeastern corner and 5 feet from the southeastern corner. The opening of this pocket was a trifle below the floor level; the pocket itself was circular in form. It was about 10 inches deep and 1 foot in diameter and was filled with broken pottery. The sides were not plastered and from appearances it had simply been scooped out of the hard packed sand, and pottery thrown in. As further work brought more of these pockets to light, the one described was called Pocket 1 (Fig. 100).

Basket-Covered Pockets. Pocket 2 was found a little to the northeast of the first one. It was also circular in form; the diameter both east and west and north and south was 3 feet; the triangulation was taken from the east wall and proved to be 5 feet 2 inches from the northeast corner to the center of the pocket, and 6 feet 2 inches from the southeast corner to the same point. This pocket was covered with a large basket, but the greater part of it had decayed. From the size and shape of this basket, it must have been almost a counterpart of the "Basket Peoples" large baskets as found in the Grand Gulch region in Utah. In burying the people in pockets and covering them with the large baskets, we have a custom analogous to that employed in this case, but whereas, the pot-holes of the "Basket People" were plastered, these were simply holes in the level sand.

Under the large basket at the southern side of the hole, were two smaller baskets. The remaining part of the hole, even under the small baskets, was filled with broken pottery. This pottery may have been broken after being placed in the holes, but as the pieces of various vessels were widely separated, it is more than probable that the bowls and pitchers were broken before they were placed in the pocket.

Pocket 3 was to the southwest of Pocket 2 and joined it at the northeast edge. This pocket was circular, the north and south and east and west diameters being 3 feet 2 inches. The triangulation was taken from the western wall to the center of the pocket, the line from the north corner being 6 feet 10 inches and from the south, 6 feet 10 inches. In this pocket there were only two pieces of pottery, a small pitcher at the southern side, and a very large one. Just opposite this was the largest piece of its kind that had been taken from the ruin up to the time of its discovery; it measured, when restored, 1 foot 1½ inches in height and 11 inches in diameter. The triangulation from the west wall to the center of the pocket from the north end was 4 feet 6 inches, and from the south end, or corner, 9 feet 11 inches. The pottery from this pocket consisted of a broken bowl that rested against the southern edge of the opening.

Pocket 5 was partly under the western wall. It was probably circular, but only one measurement could be taken with any degree of accuracy, as its western limit was not readily defined. The diameter from north to south was 3 feet 2 inches and the distance from the southern wall to its center was 5 feet 6 inches. This pocket contained the remains of a large basket and broken pitchers and bowls. At its western rim, it had a bowl that was perfect, save for a crack in its side.

These pot-holes were all hollows in the hard sand that filled the room below the floor level. The sand was so firmly packed that the sides of the holes remained intact, even though no plaster had been applied.

The upper part of all the pockets was just below the floor level and though the sides were carefully rounded, the bottom was merely an irregular flat surface. The average depth of these pockets was 3 feet 9 inches.

The space between the upper and lower floor of this room was filled with sand and large stones, it was therefore, not an accumulation of material, but had been filled intentionally; in the northwest corner of the room, 10 inches from either wall, and resting on the lower floor, was the bowl of a pitcher, but no other material worthy of mention was found on this floor.

The partition wall was 1 foot 3 inches wide and a little over 1 foot deep, and ran from the north to the south wall, the ends simply abutting on the side walls. This wall was well made and the surfaces were very even.

The eastern room, or that part east of the wall, was 9 feet 2 inches long at the north side and 10 feet 3 inches at the south, the ends being 7 feet 4 inches at the eastern part and 7 feet 3 inches long at the western.

The diagonals were run from the eastern corner to the western junction of the cross and side walls. In making the northeast and southwest measurements, the distance proved to be 11 feet 6 inches, the opposite line being 12 feet 10 inches long.

When this floor was taken away, a mass of dirt and stones was encountered, as in the other side. These were thrown out and a second floor encountered about 1 foot below the first. This second floor was hard and well defined.

About 1 foot from the south wall and built against the partition wall was a semicircular piece of masonry, the radius of which was 1 foot and the length 1 foot 3 inches. It was well plastered, but its use was not apparent.

This second floor was torn up and under it four pockets were found, three along the partition wall and one in the northeast corner; they were so poorly defined that no measurements could be taken. They seemed to have been about 1½ inches in diameter, but the sides had crumbled. Had we not encountered the one in the western part of the room, these would no doubt have passed unnoticed, the only way they could be detected was by the sand that was so much softer than in the other parts of the room. Nothing was found in these pot-holes.

The walls of this part of the room were well plastered, and at the eastern end of the lower part of the wall flared somewhat toward the east.

Room 63.

Room 63 was west of Room 53. This room was rectangular in form and had its corners plastered, giving them a rounded appearance. The west wall was composed of thin stones and there were no doorways or other openings in it. It was 16 feet 1 inch in length; the ceiling beams were 7 feet 7 inches above the floor. This was the second story; the wall of the third story was standing to a height of over 6 feet. There was a doorway in the upper part of the wall; the wall itself was of the old type, being built of thin slabs of sandstone. The plaster that had at one time filled the spaces between the slabs had entirely disappeared, and the wall presented a very weak appearance. The north wall was broken and did not reach the ceiling level at any part. The east wall was composed of upright posts and stones, the surface being well plastered. At a point 7 feet 1 inch from the north wall was a rectangular doorway 1 foot above the floor and with poles for the lintel. The south wall was also covered with a thick layer of plaster and stood to a height of 7 feet 5 inches. This room was directly over Room 56. The dimensions were as follows: north wall, 6 feet 2 inches; south wall, 5 feet 9 inches; east wall, 16 feet 1 inch; west wall, 16 feet 1 inch. No specimens worthy of mention were found.

Room 64.

Room 64 was southwest of Room 62. This room is of irregular shape and will be described in detail when rooms of this class are under consideration. When this room was cleared of débris, a series of walls was found under the floor, showing that this part of the building had been constructed from an old portion. The following specimens were found in the débris: at the south end, near the floor level, a pottery ladle, a corrugated jar, and a broken pottery bowl; in other parts of the room, thirteen hand hammerstones, three sandstone balls, two stone slabs, a stone maul, two grooved hammers, a grinding stone, two stone jar covers, six manos, chalcedony, obsidian, and other stone fragments, a piece

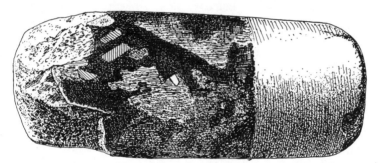

Fig. 102 (5961).   Painted Stone Pestle, Room 64.

of hematite, a piece of iron ore, and a stone pestle. The pestle is cylindrical and painted with geometric designs, Fig. 102. Among the bone specimens were seven bone awls, a worked animal rib, a bone bead, a bone scraper, a number of animal bones, and fragments of deer and antler. There were fragments of a small pottery bowl, a worked pottery jar bottom, a pottery bowl, and handles of vessels. There was also a stick used in a kicking game, an arrow point, and a worked piece of clay. In the lower room, that is, below the floor level, only animal bones were found.

Room 65.

Room 65 was one of a series of rooms formed by partitioning a passage running east and west, the side walls simply abutting against the north and south walls. The room really extends northeast and southwest, but for convenience in description, the northeast wall will be known as north and the other walls will be treated in a relative order.

The west wall was simply a partition between Rooms 65 and 66. It was built of small chunky pieces of sandstone and a sparse sprinkling of thin slabs; its surface had been covered with plaster at one time, but at the upper southern end most of it had fallen. That which remained was blackened by fire; this was particularly noticeable at the northern end where the plaster was quite thick.

There were no doorways or pockets in this wall and its ends were not built into the other walls, being as before mentioned, built up to, or against them. This wall was a little over 1 foot thick.

The north wall was rather peculiar, both from its irregular shape, as well as from the pockets and door that broke the surface at the east and west ends. Over the doorway in the western end, this wall was built of large stones, but in the other parts of the wall, smaller stones were in evidence. Originally, the whole surface was plastered, as shown by the blackened patches that are to be seen in various parts.

The northeast corner of the room is filled with masonry from a point above the ceiling beams to the top of the closet. The surface of this masonry was 3 feet 4 inches in width and commenced at a point 6 feet 9 inches from the west wall. It was well laid and had a finished surface, selected stones having been used in its construction; it too had been plastered. It ran into the next room.

Doorways and Wall Pockets. There was a doorway in the western end 11 inches above the floor. Its western side was a continuation of the general north wall, and was on a line with the west wall of this room, as though it had been a part of it. In fact the plaster had made it a uniform surface, but on clearing part of this room, the plaster was torn off, bringing to light a point that proves almost conclusively that the western wall made two rooms of what had originally been only one. When the pieces of plaster fell they disclosed a rounded corner of plaster, which, on close inspection, proved to extend along the surface of this part of the north wall toward Room 66. It was not merely a mass that might have been forced in when the room was plastered, but as far as could be seen, it presented a smooth blackened surface. This plaster was from $\frac{1}{2}$ inch to over 1 inch in thickness. This doorway had been plastered on both sides, although the stones were small and well laid. It was 4 feet 8 inches high, 2 feet 4 inches wide at the top, and 2 feet 2 inches in width at the bottom. A pole 2 inches in diameter ran across the top about 3 inches back from the surface, but this had been broken from the eastern end by the weight above it.

Directly back of this doorway was a smaller one with its sill on the same level as the first. It was 2 feet 2 inches high and 1 foot 11 inches wide and had two small poles for a lintel. The space above the lintel was filled with well laid small stones, and presented an even surface. The wall that narrowed the opening slanted toward the north; at the bottom of the doorway it was 8 inches from the general surface of the north wall; at the lintel level of the second doorway, it was 1 foot 5 inches, and at the top 1 foot 7 inches. The entire surface of this opening had been covered with a heavy coat of plaster and, as in the other parts of the room, the surface of the plaster was blackened.

In the northeast corner was a sort of closet, 1 foot 7 inches above the floor level; the east side of this pocket was 2 feet 2 inches high and was comparatively perpendicular. The west side slanted eastward a trifle and presented a surface 2 feet 3 inches high, and was 1 inch longer than the perpendicular from the same point. The opening at the bottom was 4 feet 9 inches long and at the top, 4 feet 4 inches. It was semicircular and the whole surface was plastered; at the upper back part stones protruded and this surface was also covered with plaster which still adheres to it.

The radius, measuring to the outer surface of the room wall, was 2 feet 10 inches. Six inches above the front wall of the pocket and 10 inches north from the surface, there projects from the west side of the pocket a beam 2 feet 6 inches long and 4½ inches in diameter. At its eastern end it is partly covered with plaster and its end almost touches a large plaster-covered stone that projects from the wall. Six inches back from the surface of the general wall, there projects from the west wall of the pocket, a stone 2 inches thick and 8 inches long; it is covered with plaster and extends into the pocket 5 inches; this helps to support a beam that projects from the wall just above it and extends to another stone that projects from the north wall. This stone is only 1 inch thick and it protrudes 5 inches from the wall. This would seemingly make a very poor support but that is evidently its purpose. This beam was 2 feet 2 inches long and 3 inches in diameter, and only 1 inch of its end rested upon the before-mentioned stone. This beam ran parallel with the wall forming the front of the pocket, while the other one was parallel to the general north wall. These beams showed very little blackness, whereas the plaster was jet black. This state of affairs may be accounted for by the nature of the two materials, the porous nature of the plaster affording the soot a better resting place, and allowing it to get a more tenacious hold than on the wood.

Fig. 103.   Floor Pockets in Room 65.

This pocket extended below the general floor level of the room and was 2 feet 3 inches deep. This wall, the north, was standing to a height of 11 feet 6 inches at the west end and 11 feet at the east end.

The peculiar masonry in the northeast corner was rather puzzling, for it seemed to extend in a northeast direction into the next room. In its lower part there were still to be seen the outlines of a doorway, although some of the wall had fallen at this point. There were two circular places in the north wall where ceiling beams had protruded; they were about 8 inches in diameter and 9 feet above the floor.

The east wall was well plastered on its lower surface, but near the top, most of the plaster had fallen. This wall was pierced by two pockets and one closed doorway; it was 12 feet 7 inches long at the top, 9 feet high at its north end, and 7 feet 8 inches in height at the south end.

The pocket near the northern end was 2 feet 8 inches above the floor level; a triangulation from the lower corners of the pocket to the lower corners of the wall, gave a distance of 8 feet 9 inches on the south side and 3 feet 5 inches on the north. It was 1 foot 5 inches long at the bottom and 1 foot 7 inches at the top, the right side being 1 foot high and the left 11 inches. The lower corners were rounded with plaster and the diagonals were, therefore, less than if these had been square corners. From the upper north corner to the lower south corner was 1 foot 7 inches and from the other corners 1 foot 9 inches. The greatest depth was 10 inches, but stones protruded from the back and sides, and in some places the depth was only 3 inches. There was a flat stone $\frac{1}{2}$ inch thick that extended the whole length of the pocket, forming its bottom; the sides and top were very irregular, but were plastered. On the north side are marks of three fingers running horizontally in the plaster.

There is a doorway that has been closed with large stones and plastered 1 foot 3 inches south of the upper corner of this pocket and 2 feet 5 inches above the floor. It is 2 feet 10 inches high, slightly bottle-shaped, the bottom being $6\frac{1}{2}$ inches wider than the top, and the sides tapering quite symmetrically. Six inches above the bottom of this doorway the width is 1 foot 10 inches; 14 inches higher, it is 1 foot $6\frac{1}{2}$ inches, and at the top it is 1 foot $3\frac{1}{2}$ inches wide. The peculiar part about this doorway is the fact that it is not closed even with the surface, but a space averaging $5\frac{1}{2}$ inches intervenes between the stones and the general wall surface, forming a bench which was probably used as a pocket. The whole surface was covered with plaster and the lower corners were rounded. The filled part was not even and large stones projected from its surface; these also were covered with the blackened plaster.

Three feet, seven inches south of this doorway is a pocket. Originally, it may have been another doorway, but if so, it has lost its identity by being plastered over a well-laid wall that fills the back part. It is very irregular and its base is 11 inches above the floor; its north side slants outward a little and is 2 feet 7 inches in length; the opposite side also slants outward and is 2 feet 9½ inches long. The perpendiculars measured from the same lower point were in the former instance 1 foot 6¼ inches and in the latter, 1 foot 9 inches. Its greatest depth is 10 inches; this maintains along the greater part of its northern side, but it gets narrower as it extends toward the south and at some points is only 5 inches deep. The width at the top is 1 foot 8 inches and at the bottom 1 foot 4 inches. The perpendicular measurements were taken from a flat stone that ran across the corner; this stone was 8 inches wide, 1 foot 7 inches long and 1¼ inches thick, and extended 7 inches from the corner. This pocket was well plastered and most of it was intact. This wall extended 2 feet above the ceiling beams at the north end, making it 11 feet high at this point.

The south wall was built of medium-sized stones, the majority of them slabs. They were well laid, giving the surface a very even appearance. This wall had been plastered, but the only portion where it still remained, were the central and lower parts. The only break in this wall was at the western end where there had been a doorway; this space, however, had been filled with stones and plaster even with the surface of the main wall. It was 1 foot 6 inches wide at the top and 1 foot 5 inches in width at the bottom, and 3 feet 10 inches in length from the base stone to the lintel, which was composed of poles. Only fragments of the poles remained, however. The side of this doorway had been plastered and the stones, along the outer edge, were well laid and even. The southern part of the western wall of this room covers up part of this doorway, but the western side is fully 2 inches west of the wall in Room 66. This seemingly verifies the statement and theories deduced from the evidence gained from the plaster in the northwest corner concerning a long use of this part of the building, or one large room, ere the partition wall was erected. This doorway was 3 feet 9 inches above the floor; the stones below it had been loosened and some of them had fallen.

In the eastern part of this wall, a stone, mentioned in the description of the corner pocket of the east wall, is embedded in the plaster. This wall is 7 feet 8 inches high at the eastern side and 8 feet in height at the western end, and save for the place below the closed doorway, is firm and solid.

Buried Floor and Pockets. The floor of this room was composed of adobe. There were two breaks in the surface, both on the west side; one was a fireplace of the ordinary circular type. A triangulation from the eastern corner placed it 10 feet 9 inches from the southeast corner and 8 feet 9 inches from the northeast, the measurements being made to the center of the fireplace. The other opening was a doorway or air passage in the southwest corner. This passage was in the floor and ran under the west wall into Room 66, it was directly in the corner and was 1 foot 6 inches wide and the same in length. The northeast and southwest diagonal of this room measured 14 feet 6 inches and the opposite one, northwest and southeast, 15 feet 4 inches.

The north wall was 6 feet 9 inches in length, from the western wall to the point where the wall pocket commences, and from this point to the eastern wall 3 feet 4 inches, the eastern wall was 12 feet 7 inches long, the southern, 8 feet 5 inches, and the western 11 feet 7 inches in length. A line from the south wall to the point in the north wall where the pocket begins, was 13 feet 7 inches. This floor was torn out and about 1 foot below it (10 inches) another floor was encountered. This floor had a large complicated fireplace at its western side and just below the floor level the space was honeycombed with pockets. In the northwest part, or corner, of the floor space is a circular pocket that measures 2 feet 2 inches one way and 2 feet the other, and is 1 foot 3 inches deep, it is 2 inches south of the north wall and 6 inches east of the west wall. Its sides are plastered and the bottom is also covered with a thick layer of the same material.

One foot five inches south of this pocket, the north wall of the fireplace extended in an east and west direction. The back part of this fireplace was composed of four stones standing on end; the two toward the south rested against the west wall, but the others were about 1 inch away from it. The wall space covered by these stones was 2 feet 6 inches in length. The stone nearest the south wall was 11½ inches long, 3 inches thick, and 7 inches deep, and formed the back part of a box-like place that was 9 inches long at the western end, about 10 inches long at the eastern, and about 1 foot wide; it was about 1 foot deep, the bottom being of adobe. The sides and ends were of stones stood on end.

Just north of this place and separated from it by a large stone 4½ inches thick and 6 inches wide, which ran to the bottom of the pocket, was another pocket or portion of the fireplace. It was 1 foot 5 inches long, north and south, and 1 foot 2 inches wide at the north end; the southeast corner was rounded by laying the stones in a semicircle. Two large stones on end formed the back part of this place; between them and the southernmost stone of the four, was a narrow stone that formed the end of the division wall. The north wall of this pocket was composed of slabs of sandstone about 1 inch thick. This pocket is also 1 foot deep.

Just east of the eastern walls of these pockets and only separated by the stones forming the wall, there is a fireplace, or a place in which a fire had been, judging from the calcined stones, 2 feet 3 inches deep, 1 foot 2 inches wide, and with an irregular surface formed of stones and adobe. There is a bench above and to the east of this fireplace that is 1 foot wide and 1 foot 4 inches deep. This end of the rectangular space, enclosed by stones set on end, is semicircular and is 2 feet 2½ inches east of the central part of the east side of the east wall of the two small divisions near the west wall, this measurement being made to the center of the circular part.

This fireplace, or at least the top of the stones surrounding it, was on a level with the floor and the interior of the eastern part had been plastered. A stone wall formed the eastern side of the deeper place or fireplace and extended to the level of the bench at its eastern side. The length of the northern side from the west wall to the turn at the east end was 3 feet 4 inches, and on the opposite or southern side 3 feet 9 inches. From the western wall to the center of the inner section of the circular part, or the eastern end of this fireplace, was 4 feet 1 inch.

One inch south of this place and 2 inches east of the western wall was an oval pocket 2 feet long by 1 foot 5 inches in width; it was 6 inches deep and the sides and bottom had been plastered. It was of somewhat irregular egg shape, the small end being near the west wall; it slanted toward the southeast and at a point on the south fireplace wall 1 foot 3 inches east of the west wall; its southern edge was 1 foot 5 inches south of this south edge of the fireplace wall.

About 3 inches southeast of this pocket was an irregular fireplace composed of seven stones stood on end. It was irregular in form and the stones may have been displaced a little in measuring this portion of the floor, but as they stood, there were five in place. It measured 1 foot at the eastern end and 9 inches at the western, the southern end was about 1 foot long and the north about 1 foot 1 inch. These are inside measurements and show the general size of what appeared to be a fireplace, but there was no evidence of its having been used. The stone at the eastern side was 2 inches thick and 7 inches high, the others averaging about 4 inches in height.

The eastern stone of this fireplace rested on the edge of a large deep bin that was in the shape of a horseshoe. At this point it was 1 foot 7 inches southeast of the oval pocket near the fireplace. This pocket, or pot-hole was 3 feet wide, east and west, and 3 feet 6 inches long, north and south. In height or depth it was 3 inches; the stones forming its top slanted downward a little at the north end, thereby giving it the appearance of being lower at this point, but the measurement given is about the average depth. At the north end the hole is squared with a stone wall. The north face of this wall is 2 feet 1 inch long and on either side 8 inches to the perpendicular surface of the circular wall; the circular wall is only 1 foot 3 inches high at this point and from it to the top of the squared part is 1 foot 9 inches.

This pocket, which may have been a granary, was well plastered, both the bottom and sides having a layer of plaster $\frac{1}{2}$ inch thick over the stones that formed the well-like opening. These stones, from what could be seen, were well laid and extended to the bottom of the hole. As the plaster was intact on most of the surface this could not be ascertained for a certainty. The bench at the northern end was plastered, as was also the square surface and the sides. The pocket was larger at the top than at the bottom; the measurements were taken 2 feet above the floor level, thereby giving average dimensions.

In the southwestern corner there was an opening or passageway that led into Room 66. It was 1 foot 10 inches long, north and south, and 1 foot 4 inches wide, east and west, and had a wooden lintel composed of poles. Its south and west sides were formed by the walls of the room, while its north and east sides were walls of small slabs well laid and reaching to the lower floor level. This opening was over 2 feet deep and the doorway leading into Room 66 was 1 foot 2 inches wide. In the southeast corner there was an oval pocket 1 foot 4 inches wide, east and west, and 1 foot 10 inches long. It was 1 foot west of the east wall and 6 inches north of the south wall. Its eastern side runs parallel with the east wall and in its lower part the adobe is plastered on the wall itself.

The north wall of this pocket is straight east and west and is composed of slabs of sandstone 1 inch thick, laid in such a manner as to present a very even surface. At the northwest corner, this wall forms a right angle with the west wall of the pocket. From the east wall to the point where the west wall joins it this wall is 1 foot 2 inches long, but it extends beyond this point $6\frac{1}{2}$ inches.

All the walls are composed of stone and are plastered, but on the north wall most of the plaster has fallen. This pocket was 1 foot 1 inch deep at the north end and 11 inches deep at the south end.

Three feet one inch north of the face of the north wall of this pocket, on the eastern wall line, is another pocket, that was originally almost rectangular in shape with rounding corners. At the time of writing the only part standing was that against the east wall and about 6 inches on the southeast side. This was composed of small slabs of well-laid sandstone that extended to the lower floor level, the depth at the eastern side being 10 inches. This measurement was made to the stones that composed the bottom of the pocket; there are two of them, the one nearest the south wall being the larger. This one is 1 foot 2 inches long, 9¾ inches wide, and 14 inches in thickness; the other is 1 foot ½ inch long, 8 inches wide, and about the same thickness as the other.

The wall on the southeast side covers the stone nearly 1 inch, so in taking the measurements north and south, this distance was allowed for at the north end; on the west end the measurement was to the edge of the stones. The southeast side of this pocket was 1 foot 1½ inches long and the northwest was 11 inches; it was 1 foot 3 inches long on the southwest side and 1 foot 4 inches in length on the northeast side. It was built against the east wall, as its southern end and its northernmost point were about 2 inches from the wall. Originally its sides had been plastered.

This pocket was in another pocket of irregular shape and with sides of large stones. The sides were rough but had been plastered. This pocket measured, from the northeast to the southwest end, 2 feet 11 inches, and a line at right angles to this one from the point where the southeast wall of the small pocket ends to a point on the east side, 1 foot 5 inches, from the point in the southeast, and where the last measurement was made, 1 foot 7 inches. The northwest corner of the smaller stone was 3 inches from the side of this pocket; the northeast end of the same stone was 4 inches from the edge of the same. This pocket was only 7 inches deep, but originally it probably extended to the floor level.

Five inches north of this pocket on the eastern wall line, was a large pocket or bin, no doubt for the storing of grain. This bin extended along the eastern wall 4 feet 3 inches; the main wall of the building or room formed its eastern side. This pocket was narrow at the northern end and from this point the sides flared outward as they ran south and met a semicircular part that formed the southern end.

South of this rounding part there was a bench, the east side of which, from the junction of the eastern wall and the south curved wall to its south corner, was 1 foot 4½ inches. Its length at the south end was 3 feet 1 inch and its western side to the curve, 1 foot 3½ inches. Its central part from the center of the southern wall to the center of the curved wall, was 1 foot. The diagonals of this bench were northwest and southeast, 3 feet 2½ inches and northeast and southwest, 3 feet 4 inches. The height at the eastern corner was 1 foot 5 inches; at the western, 1 foot 4 inches; and at the center, 1 foot 5 inches.

The eastern wall, from the north corner to the point where the southern wall begins, is 2 feet 10½ inches long. From the junction of the east and south walls it is 2 feet 11 inches; the west, from the latter point to the north wall was 3 feet 1¼ inches; and the north wall was 1 foot 9½ inches in length. The length of the bin, from the center of the north to the center of the south wall, was 3 feet 4½ inches. A line at right angles to this one from the center of the side walls was 2 feet 6½ inches in length.

The measurements were taken 6 inches below the surface of the pocket and give the accurate dimensions at this point only. The top itself is a little larger and the bottom is smaller, and as in almost all aboriginal work, the sides are somewhat irregular.

The north and south line on the floor is 3 feet 3½ inches long, the east and west is 3 feet 5 inches; and the width 2 feet 6½ inches, which gives an approximate idea of the sides. The average depth of this bin is 2 feet 11 inches; the bench at the southern end is 1 foot 6 inches above the floor of the pocket at the eastern wall, 1 foot 3 inches high at the center, and 1 foot 4 inches high where it joins the west wall.

The north wall of the bin is plastered to a height of 7 inches above the floor level of the bin; above this and to the top of the bin, the wall is rough and large stones protrude from the surface. The floor of this bin is composed of flat stones over which a layer of plaster was laid. The sides of the bench as well as the circular place, were well plastered; in fact, the whole bin, with the exception of the upper part of the north end, was covered with a thick layer of plaster.

The side ends and the bench were composed of thin slabs of sandstone laid with great care, as the surface, where pieces of this plaster had fallen, was even and the stones closely laid.

The specimens in this room were scattered through the débris, most of them, however, being near the floor level. Among the objects found were: four metates, eight manos, nine hand hammerstones, four stone jar covers, fragments of others, a stone slab, an arrow point, a polishing stone, a piece of red hematite, an iron pyrite nodule, seven pebbles, fragments of stone implements and cooking stones, fragments of chalcedony, azurite, and malachite, a grooved ax, agate nodule, nine bone awls, a bone scraper, fragments of deer antler, deer teeth, animal bones, and pieces of sheep horn, two pottery heads, a pottery disk, two rough clay dishes, a pottery foot, a base of large pottery jar, a number of fragments of pottery vessels, a piece of painted wood, fragments of shell, and a number of fragments of sandal-shaped stones.

Room 66.

Room 66 was a small and almost square room west of Room 65. The most interesting feature of this room was the eastern wall; it contained a series of pockets. One of these had a square opening, 4 feet 4 inches from the north wall and 10 inches above the floor level. There were three pockets above this one, but these were irregular in shape. There was also a doorway in the south corner of this wall, the lower part being 9 inches above the floor level. The main part of this wall stood to a height of 9 feet. Another wall of much better construction towered above this one to a height of 6 feet, making the entire height of the two walls 15 feet.

The north and west walls contained no features worthy of special mention. There was, however, a fireplace, which was 3 feet 6 inches from the south wall and 3 feet 10 inches from the east wall. It was a shallow depression of rectangular shape, the dimensions being 1 foot 9 inches by 2 feet.

After removing the floor, a wall was found extending from the southeast corner toward the center of the room. It was 1 foot in width and 1 foot 2 inches deep. Another wall had crossed this at right angles. These walls were evidently a part of the old building, which had been destroyed, or at least had passed into disuse before the present rooms were built.

The measurements of this room taken at the floor level were: north wall, 11 feet 1 inch; south wall, 9 feet 9 inches; east wall, 9 feet 4 inches; west wall, 9 feet 9 inches.

The following specimens were on or above the floor level; one metate, eight manos, six hammerstones, four stone jar covers, a worked piece of sandstone, nine arrow points, two stone slabs, chalcedony scraper, fragments of stone implements, fragments of chalcedony, obsidian, and gypsum, six bird bones that showed cutting, six bone awls, a bone skin dresser, a split animal bone, animal jaws and several bones, a painted stick, a piece of pottery worked into the shape of a moccasin, pottery fragments worked into various shapes, and potsherds.

Fig. 104   West Wall of Kiva, Room 67.

249

Fig. 105.   Hole in End of Kiva Post, Room 67, containing Turquoise Beads.

ROOM 67.

Kiva. Room 67 is an estufa under the western court. The estufas of Bonito are characterized by a circular wall forming a room, the roof of which is usually below the general level of the surrounding rooms. At the base of this wall there is a bench of solid masonry from two to four feet high that projects from two to three feet into the room. On this bench there are invariably a series of low pillars or blocks of masonry, six of which have been found in each estufa in this pueblo, and as far as I am aware this number obtains throughout the cliff-dwellings. But in the cliff-houses the estufa bench and pillars are much higher than in Pueblo Bonito and the pillars are so close together that Baron Nordenskiold in describing them says: "The upper portion" of the estufa wall "is divided by six deep niches into the same number of pillars." In Bonito they are simply details of the masonry, being very low and separated by intervals of nearly ten feet.

Ceremonial Deposit. The estufa in Pueblo Bonito, where the ceremonial deposits were found, is situated in the western court. When the work of excavation was begun the surface was apparently level and there was no evidence of walls until a depth of 2 feet was reached. Then a mass of masonry was encountered which proved to be a circular wall composed of faced blocks of sandstone laid with thin layers of adobe enclosing a room 25½ feet in diameter. This room was filled with refuse material and had apparently been abandoned and used as a dumping-ground. When all the débris had been removed and the floor level reached, 15 feet below the surface, it was found to be composed of adobe, perfectly smooth and level except in the center where the fireplace was situated. In the angle between the floor and the wall and extending entirely around the room, lay the usual bench; in this case 2 feet 2 inches wide by 2 feet high. Built up across this bench to a height of 1 foot and placed at regular intervals around it, were six oblong masonry blocks or pillars. On the western side, just before reaching the pillar level, a hollow clay cylinder was found 6 inches in diameter, with the top broken in and with the ends resting on two of the pillars. On the bottom of this cylinder and clinging to the inner face were fibers and strips of bark which showed that a log once occupied this position. From its position we naturally conclude that this was one of the roof beams, and on turning to the cliff-houses, where such beams are better preserved, we find, in the estufas similarly placed beams supporting a roof. Hence, we may assume that the roof of this estufa was built in a manner similar to one found in the "Square Tower House" of the Mesa Verde region and described by Baron Nordenskiold as follows:—

Two estufas, the roofs of which are partly preserved, are of interest, for, to the best of my knowledge, this is the only cliff-dwelling where these cliff rooms retain their roofs. * * * The roof rests on six stone pillars between the niches, and was built in two parts, the lower consisting of five courses of poles laid horizontally in a circle, and thus increasing the height of the estufa by some feet. These poles supported a flat roof of beams.[1]

This description would probably apply, in a general way, to the roof of the estufa, in which the remains of the log were found. It is practically certain that the lower part of the structure was the same, but the beams probably extended to a higher point than in the one in the "Square Tower House," in order to allow sufficient room to stand upright. The sloping exterior was probably covered with matting or brush (charred fragments of both of which were found) ere the roof was covered with earth. It is evident that a layer of earth must have covered a part of the roof, for below the refuse material there was a stratum that contained pieces of burnt roof beams that had been converted into charcoal.

Directly under the mould of the log before mentioned, was a thin layer of adobe, on the upper surface of the roof supports. The support of the southern end of the log at the left of Fig. 105 was barely covered, and the adobe had cracked in places revealing a log beneath embedded in the masonry. When the adobe was removed a circular piece of the same material about 2 inches in diameter was found resting on the log, as shown in the above illustration. It was a plug that covered a deposit of turquoise and shell beads, pieces of crude shell, and turquoise matrix. These were taken up and their resting-place proved to be a well-rounded cavity. Before the earth from over and around this support was removed, the one at the north end of the log was examined. A similar deposit was found, but there was no special cover for this one nor was the cavity in the wood carefully worked—its form being elongated and in appearance more like a natural depression caused by dry rot. After these deposits had been taken up the supports were uncovered and the logs enclosed in them removed. (The supports were simply rectangular blocks of sandstone laid in adobe, about a log which extended from the edge of the bench to a point several feet under the main estufa wall).

The log from the first support examined was taken out and is now in the Museum. There were six of these beam rests or supports on the bench of the estufa, over which the ceiling beams crossed, each containing a log which held an offering; but the one at the south end of the

---

[1]Nordenskiold, G. *The Cliff Dwellers of the Mesa Verda, Southwestern Colorado, their Pottery and Implements.* Translated by D. Lloyd Morgan (Stockholm, 1893), 57.

mould of the ceiling beam, was the most carefully prepared and contained the greatest amount of material. Practically the same conditions
were presented in Room 16 (p. 84), but the manner of deposition may
have differed.

Deposits of materials of this nature are generally considered to be
sacrificial. Since these were found at a critical point in the structure of
the room, where they literally supported the entire roof, that is, exactly
under the six points where the lowest roof beams rested, we may infer
that they indicate some ceremonial connected with the construction
of the estufa.

No definite conclusions concerning the prevalence of similar sacri-
fices, can be drawn from such meager evidence, but the discoveries in
the two estufas suffice to show that a certain form of sacrificial offering
was, at one time, in vogue in this pueblo. Whether in the other estufas of
Bonito there is an absence of such deposits or a variation in the place or
manner of depositing the material will remain an open question until
more data have been obtained. Dr. J. Walter Fewkes, of the Bureau of
Ethnology, in commenting on this discovery, stated that he had the
good fortune to observe the dedication of a house in one of the Hopi
villages in northern Arizona. He said that in constructing the house, a
small opening was left in the outer surface of the front wall, at the left
of the doorway, and about 5 feet from the ground. When the day for
the ceremonies arrived a feast was prepared, but before anyone partook
of the food, a small portion of each kind was placed in the opening; then
shell fragments and beads were added to the offering, after which the
place was carefully covered with adobe and plastered in the same manner
as the other parts of the wall. He said that a similar ceremony takes
place in the dedication of each new house, and possibly a more elaborate
one when the kivas are built.

Deposits of the kind here described have never been reported from
the Pueblo ruins and these are probably the first to be discovered.

The following specimens were found in this room. These specimens,
unless otherwise stated, were found in the débris with which the estufa
had been filled; twenty hand hammerstones, four stone jar covers, a
sandstone grinder, three sandstone balls, a stone knife, four worked
stones, several natural pebbles, which had evidently been used in pottery
making, a flint knife and points of two others, red hematite, obsidian
flakes, chalcedony cores and flakes, fragments of iron ore and red paint,
thirty-one bone awls, six bone beads, six bone scrapers, a number of
animal bones, three pottery disks, three pieces of pottery in animal form,

a pottery foot, a small pottery ladle, stone and pottery pieces, containing paint, several balls of sun-baked clay, a broken dish, a bowl with an animal form painted in the bottom, two pottery feet, a piece of pottery in the form of a bird, a pottery jar cover, small pottery pestle, fragments of an incense burner, numerous potsherds, a few small arrow points, fragments of malachite, shell, and turquoise, a number of animal skulls, fragments of human pottery faces, four clay cylinders, and a number of other fragmentary pieces.

Room 68.

Room 68 was southwest of Room 20 and directly west of and adjoining Estufa 75. This room was one of the series running east and west, forming the fifth series from the north wall. When the débris had been removed a fireplace was found near the central part. It measured 2 feet 9 inches by 2 feet 11 inches high and at its southwest corner there was a circular place, about 1 foot in diameter, that was connected with the fireplace by a small opening. This part was 1 foot deep and was made of stones and well plastered. Around its edge there was a wall averaging 3 inches in height and at the point where it joined the fireplace proper, there had been a stone. The fireplace had been walled with stones and plaster, the depth being the same as that of the adjoining depression just described.

In the northeast corner of the room, at the floor level, there was a pocket. A wall 6 inches high had been built across the corner, its length being 2 feet 3 inches and an opening had been made in the corner forming a pocket which measured 1 foot 3 inches in depth. This pocket extended below the floor level and had a rounded top. It was well plastered.

The south wall was roughly built and was composed of medium-sized stones and pierced by two doorways. There was a doorway 3 feet 10 inches west of the east wall. Its sill was on the floor level; its height and width were the same, 1 foot 8 inches. It was of the ordinary rectangular type, as were all of the doorways in this wall. Two feet four inches west of this opening there was another doorway somewhat irregular in shape. There were no doorways in the west wall, but there were two of the usual shape in the north wall. There was a pocket in this wall, as well as in the eastern wall.

About a foot below the general floor level a number of walls were uncovered. When the earth was cleared from above them, it was seen that they formed the enclosing walls of a series of angular bins, but were in reality the continuations of walls which extended under the rooms adjoining this one, and had once formed a part of an old series of rooms. One of these walls was 3 feet 3 inches in width and extended northward from the south wall. Upon this the fireplace of the above-mentioned floor was situated. The average depth of these walls below the floor level was 6 feet. The measurements of this room were as follows: north wall, 14 feet; south wall, 13 feet 8 inches; east, 14 feet 2 inches; west, 11 feet 10 inches. The following specimens, unless otherwise stated, were found in the débris from the main part of the room: two metates, thirty-nine manos, five hand hammerstones, a polishing stone, a grooved stone hammer, three stone slabs, a stone pestle, a stone jar cover, a grooved stone ax, a stone mortar, fragments of jasper, azurite, mica, petrified wood, turquoise beads, fragments of clay pipes and pebbles, fragments of a wooden distaff, and a clay ball. There were also a number of potsherds and animal bones. In one of the bins formed by the angular walls, below the floor of this room, there were twenty-four hand hammerstones.

Room 68a. Room 68a was directly west of Room 68. It was a narrow passage-like room with unplastered walls. At the south end and 1 foot below the level of the broken south wall, was a wall of solid masonry that extended northward from the south wall, a distance of about 3 feet on the eastern side and 2 feet 10 inches on the western. The north end was 3 feet 7 inches wide. This wall or body of masonry was composed of medium-sized stones carefully laid. Its top was even with the floor level and was over 2 feet thick. Just north of this mass of masonry was an open space that extended 1 foot 10 inches below the floor level. This space was floored and was 4 feet 1 inch long on the western side and 4 feet 8 inches in length on the east. Its northern limit was defined by a mass of masonry similar to the one in the south end. Unlike the southern part, this mass was composed of two walls, but owing to the fact that their surfaces touched, the general appearance was the same. These walls were composed of stones which were laid with the same care as those in the southern mass of masonry and extended to about the same depth. The central or open part of the room may have been plastered originally, but there was no plaster in evidence on the walls when the débris was cleared. There was a closed doorway of the rectangular type in the center of the north wall, but the other walls presented an unbroken surface. This room measured over 3 feet 2 inches in width on the south and the same at the north end. The west wall was 11 feet 4 inches long and the east 11 feet 7 inches long. Nothing of interest was found in this room.

Room 69.

Room 69 was directly west of Room 68a.   Its longer axis, unlike that of the room just described, was east and west.   There was nothing of special interest noted in this room until the floor was removed.   There was a doorway in the north wall and another in the south wall.   There were two cupboards in the northeastern corner, one in the north wall, the other in the east wall.   The room measured as follows: north wall, 18 feet; south wall, 18 feet 7 inches; east wall, 10 feet 6 inches; west wall, 9 feet 10 inches.   After the floor was removed a rather intricate series of walls was found.   There was a fireplace in the western end below the floor level and a U-shaped bin near the central part.   The following specimens were found in the room: fragments of stone jar covers, seven turkey bones with ends cut, fragments of azurite, malachite, potsherds, and a worked fragment of a small olla in the bin under the floor.

Room 70.

Room 70 is northwest of and next to Room 62.   This room is irregularly shaped and rather peculiar in its construction.   In reconstructing this part of the pueblo, several walls had to be built in some places and in others various methods had to be adopted to adjust the old walls to the new conditions.   One particularly interesting feature of this room was the northeast wall which is supported on poles.   Directly below it is a doorway of the rectangular type.   There was a peculiar bevel to the front of this doorway, the inner part having been built in such a way as to allow a stone door to be built against it in a slanting position.   The lower end, that is, the first floor, had been built in by the old people.   There was a good old south and west wall, but the east wall had been built on a mass of roughly laid stones.   There was a doorway of the rectangular type in the north wall.   The measurements of this room are as follows: north wall, 2 feet 10 inches; south wall, 14 feet 10 inches; east wall, 7 feet 10 inches; west wall, 9 feet 10 inches. The following specimens were found in the débris: six hand hammerstones, two stone slabs, two stone jar covers, a smoothing stone, a fragment of a stone celt, a bone implement, pieces of charred cord, four large game sticks, a stick used in the kicking game, a ceremonial stick, a wooden knife, worked pieces of pottery, potsherds, and animals bones.

Room 71.

Room 71 was just west of Room 69. The masonry was similar to that noted in the description of Room 69. There was a doorway of the usual type in the north wall and another in the west wall, the latter being filled with large stones. There was a pocket built in the south wall in such a way that the east wall formed its eastern side. About 6 inches below the general floor level was a fireplace. It was 2 feet 7 inches in diameter and built of small sandstone slabs. Extending from the fireplace to the wall in the southeast corner was a passageway which was 1 foot 2 inches wide at the point nearest the fireplace. It was built of stones, had been plastered and may have been used as an airshaft either for the ventilation of the room or as an outlet for smoke. The measurements of the room at the floor level were as follows: north wall, 18 feet 8 inches; south wall, 15 feet 11 inches; east wall, 8 feet 4 inches; west wall, 10 feet 2 inches. The following specimens were found in the room, most of which were on or near the floor; two metates, twenty manos, five stone slabs, twenty-three hammerstones, a grooved stone hammer, a grinding stone, a polishing stone, a stone jar cover, part of a jasper knife, other stones and fragments, a rectangular pottery dish, a fragment of pottery containing paint, a rough pottery animal form, and numerous potsherds. Two parrot skeletons were found in the southeast corner at the floor level. Other objects found in the general débris were a bone awl, a piece of wood painted blue, and animal bones.

Room 72.

Room 72 was south of Room 20. This room was somewhat irregular in shape. The north end was rectangular, but the southeast end was semicircular in form. In the eastern wall were five pockets. Aside from this there was nothing of special interest in the construction of the walls. Before the floor level was reached a mass of metates was found. These were placed on edge as though they had been stored in this room. Some were finished and had been used. Others were in course of construction, while some had merely been roughed into shape from sandstone slabs. The measurements of this room at the floor level were: north wall, 5 feet 3 inches; south wall, 2 feet 8 inches; east wall, 10 feet 3 inches; west wall, 20 feet 7 inches. The curve of the wall in the southeast corner is 12 feet 2 inches in length.

After the floor of this room had been removed a series of walls was found beneath it.

There were twenty metates found in the deposit on the floor. With them were twelve manos, four hand hammerstones, two stone jar covers, a rectangular and a circular stone slab, fragments of stone slabs, chalcedony flakes, turquoise beads, fossil shells, seven bone awls, a bone scraper, an implement made of horn, animal bones, a shell bracelet, a pottery pitcher, and a number of potsherds. Nothing of interest was found below the floor level.

Room 73.

Room 73 was in the southeast part of the building. It was east of Room 24. The upper part was rectangular in form, but had a jog at the northwest corner. In the upper central part of the east wall, was a closed doorway with a wooden lintel. Inside of this, with the south wall of the first doorway for one side was a small one also with a wooden lintel, and in the center of this, the second one, there was a small opening 6 by 12 inches, with a stone sill and a wooden lintel.

In the southeastern part of this room, placed directly in the corner, was a doorway with a wooden lintel. There was another doorway of the rectangular type in the central part of the south wall. A small opening in the upper west corner of the south wall had small poles for a lintel.

The lower floor had been divided into four rooms, the walls of which had been plastered, but presented perhaps the best masonry that was found in this part of the ruin. There were stones projecting from the facings of the walls of this lower room. These may have been used as stepping stones in going from the lower to the upper floor. The jog in the northwest corner extended only to the floor level of the upper room. The measurements of this room were as follows: north wall, 15 feet 11 inches; south wall, 18 feet; east wall, 13 feet 6 inches; west wall, 9 feet 3 inches to the beginning of the jog. This extended 2 feet east and then 3 feet 2 inches north, making the west wall in all 12 feet 5 inches in length. Only a portion of the lower part of the room was worked. The following specimens were found: one mano, one hammerstone, a stone arrow smoother, pieces of azurite and malachite, an arrow point, wooden foreshaft, two bone awls, bone implement, potsherds, and animal bones.

Room 74.

Room 74 is a small angular room, which formed the southwest corner of Estufa 75. This room is similar to Rooms 79 and 81, both of which are on the northern part of the estufa. The following specimens were found in Room 74: three bone awls, fragments of a shell bracelet,

Fig. 106. Kiva, Room 75.

259

Fig. 107. Part of Room 76.

Fig. 108. Northeastern Corner of Room 78.

261

fragments of a ceremonial stick, a circular potsherd, the knob of a pottery jar cover, a few small arrow points, also potsherds and animal bones.

Room 75.

Room 75 is of circular form, and lies between Rooms 68 and 72. Owing to the fact that this room was a typical estufa, no description of it will be given (Fig. 106). The following specimens were found in this room: six hand hammerstones, a smoothing stone, two stone slabs, stone jar cover, ten bone awls, a bird bone showing cutting, a bone implement, turquoise beads and fragments of turquoise, animal bones, and potsherds.

Room 76.

Room 76 is south of Room 60. The following specimens were found in the débris or on the main floor of this room: six manos, eighteen hand hammerstones, a stone used for polishing implements, a stone jar cover, fragments of chalcedony and obsidian and a crinoid stem; also twelve bone awls, a bone scraper, a bone showing cutting, a clay ball, charred bones, pieces of skin, a number of worked potsherds, a pottery jar, found in the southwest corner, potsherds, and animal bones.

Below the main floor level the following specimens were found: fragments of turquoise and malachite, some chalky material probably used for paint, pieces of red stone probably used for the same purpose, fragments of obsidian, animal bones, decorated potsherds, and pieces of squash rind. Three inches below the floor level a small pottery bowl was found.

Room 77.

Room 77 was a small rectangular room, north of Room 68a. It was similar in construction to Room 68a and presented no features worthy of special mention. Under the floor of the room there was a series of old walls. This room measured: north wall, 5 feet 8 inches; south wall, 6 feet 7 inches; east wall, 10 feet 3 inches; west wall, 10 feet 3 inches. The following specimens were found in the room: two manos, fragments of a stone slab, a chalcedony knife, a broken flint knife, two bone awls, and potsherds.

Room 78.

Room 78 was north of Room 71. This room was particularly interesting owing to the fact that it differed in many ways from the rooms heretofore described. It was of the usual rectangular shape and the walls were well plastered. The north wall was irregular and had been blackened by smoke. There is a doorway in the north wall with a flat stone for a sill and poles for a lintel. The south wall is merely a facing laid against an old wall. It is 1 foot thick at the east end and gradually decreases in thickness towards the western end of the room. This wall was rather roughly laid. In the central part of this wall there is a doorway which connects with that in the original wall. This secondary wall fell at the eastern end of the room. There was a doorway in the north wall but there were no openings in the east or west walls. A bench extended 1½ feet north of the base of the south wall. The floor was on the level with the top of this bench. In the northeastern corner was a large olla which was half buried in the floor (Fig. 108). The fireplace in the southeast corner was under the secondary wall. It was circular and built of stones, the top being well plastered. It was filled with lignite. The large fireplace, northwest of the one just mentioned, was built of thin slabs which stood on edge. West of this there was a post and still further west, another large fireplace made of slabs. It was closed when found, with a flat stone, and was only 1 foot in diameter. It was built of stones and had been carefully plastered. This one, as was the case with the one under the south wall, was filled with lignite. There were no evidences of old walls under the floor, but some of the fireplaces had evidently passed into disuse and had been covered before the room was abandoned. The measurements of this room were as follows: north wall, 21 feet; south wall, 18 feet 8 inches; east wall, 8 feet 1 inch; west wall, 10 feet 10 inches.

A great mass of material was found in this room, the major portion being scattered throughout the débris. At a depth of 6 feet 5 inches below the ceiling beams and at a point 3 feet 6 inches from the east wall a parrot skeleton was found. Most of the bones were against the south wall. At a depth of 7 feet 2 inches another parrot skeleton was found at the floor level in the center of the room. As already mentioned, a large olla with a stone cover was found in the northeast corner; a pitcher was found in the east corner near the floor level. The following specimens were found in the northeast corner: nine bone awls, twelve bone beads, and a bone die. The following specimens are from the general débris: ten manos and fragments of others, six stone slabs, sixty hand hammerstones, a flint knife, a chalcedony knife, a grinding stone, part of a stone ax, a stone disk, natural concretions, natural pebbles, chalcedony chips and cores, arrow points, turquoise beads, pieces of petrified wood, gypsum, a ball of white chalk-like stone, a polishing stone, two stone knives, a stone ax, a pottery animal head, a small pottery ladle, a number of worked potsherds, a pottery dipper, a pottery clay ball, potsherds, pottery feet, a pottery pipe, a number of potsherds with worked edges, a clay jar stopper, fine clay used in preparing the slip for pottery vessels, arrow points, part of a bone scraper, a turtle carcass, three bone awls, and a number of animal bones. The following specimens were found over a foot below the floor: a hammerstone, obsidian, arrow points, turquoise beads, yellow ocher, pieces of jet, turquoise matrix, two vessel handles, a fragmentary bowl, a number of worked stones, squash rind, and animal bones.

Room 79.

Room 79 is the angular room forming the northeast corner of Estufa 75. This estufa is built in a square enclosure, the circular wall touching the wall of the enclosure at four points. The remaining space forms angular rooms in the corners of the square. The estufa wall formed a convex side to these rooms. The other two sides are straight. As a rule, very little was found in rooms of this nature.

The northern part of this room was rough, but covered with plaster. There was a doorway in this wall but it was practically covered by the east wall of the room, which shows that this part of the building had been reconstructed. West of this was another doorway of the same type, that had been closed with masonry. West of this doorway and near the western corner were two oval pockets. The east wall is exceedingly rough and has stones protruding from the surface. Some of these protrude over 5 inches and there are stones similar to these in the convex wall on the southwest side. The only objects found in this room were two manos, a fossil shell, a stone flake, and a few potsherds. Below the floor level, in the center of the room, a skeleton of a child was found. With it were a number of potsherds. The burial of children below the floors of rooms seems to have been a custom among the people who inhabited this pueblo.

Room 80.

Room 80 is north of and next to Room 69. It is of rectangular form and is one of a series running east and west. The walls are practically the same as those mentioned in the descriptions of Rooms 77 and 78. Work in this room was begun at the eastern end. Near the west wall and at a depth of 3 feet 6 inches, a painted stone mortar was found. The accompanying photograph (Fig. 109) shows this specimen *in situ*. This mortar is also shown in Fig. 110. It is the most elaborately decorated

Fig. 109.   Painted Stone Mortar in Room 80.

a

b

Fig. 110 (6828).   Design on Painted Stone Mortar, Room 80.

266

object of this nature that was found in the pueblo. On the same level, but east of the mortar, a number of human bones were found. They were scattered throughout the débris and had evidently fallen from one of the upper rooms. These bones show evidences of having been burned and they were broken, as is the case with other human bones found in the pueblos of this group; from the fact that they had been in one of the upper rooms, it may be that they had been used for some ceremonial purpose, as it was not the custom to bury even portions of bodies in the upper rooms. At least no other evidences of such a practice were found. Very little material was found in the general débris, but when the floor level was reached, a mass of stone implements was encountered. Most of these were found on the south side of the room, and some of the larger specimens rested against the south wall.

The measurements of the upper rooms were: north wall, 18 feet 5 inches; south wall, 18 feet 5 inches; east wall, 10 feet 2 inches; west wall, 9 feet 11 inches.

The specimens found were as follows: five metates, thirty-one manos, four stone slabs, fifty-three hand hammerstones, a sandstone grinder, a stone mortar, a grooved hammer, a stone jar cover, a smoothing stone, a number of natural pebbles, fragments of chalcedony and other stones, and fragments of stone slabs. Other specimens associated with the stone implements were as follows: seven bone awls, a bone implement, two cut bones, a number of deer bones and fragments of antler, a number of worked animal bones, and a porcupine jaw.

A specimen was found in the south side of the room which was probably used ceremonially. It was made of pottery and was concavo-convex, being drilled on the edges, Fig. 111. Other objects of pottery were a handle of a vessel, a pottery foot, fragments of pottery probably used as smoothers, a number of worked potsherds, a fragmentary corrugated jar, a great many fragments of pottery vessels, and pieces of adobe showing finger impressions.

After the floor was removed, a series of walls were found; some of these formed small rectangular rooms. In these rooms the following specimens were found: eleven hand hammerstones, an adobe ball, a natural pebble, and a number of potsherds, some of which were worked.

---

[1]Painted mortars of less elaborate design were found by Hough, Bull. 87, p. 31, in the upper Gila Region. The colors were red, yellow, and black.

Room 81.

Room 81 is an angular room forming the northwest corner of the square which surrounds Estufa 75. It is the room which corresponds with Rooms 74 and 79. The masonry was practically the same as that of Room 79, but the walls had been more carefully finished at the north side. This one especially was well plastered and smooth. In its lower part there was a closet, the opening of which measured 1 foot by 6 inches. This closet extended 1 foot north and 2 feet in the opposite direction. The opening had a sandstone slab for its base. A little above and to the west of this opening, was a smaller pocket with an oval opening, the plaster having been rounded at the edges. It was 4 inches high and 7 inches long. The west wall was well plastered and contained a large

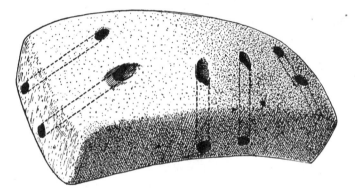

Fig. 111 (6991). Curious Pottery Object with Perforations, Room 80.

pocket similar to the one in the north wall. Near its south end the plaster was over an 1½ inches in thickness. The southeastern wall corresponded to the southwestern wall of Room 79, and like this one, was oval in form. This room measured as follows: north wall, 5 feet 10 inches; southeast wall, 8 feet 10 inches; west wall, 7 feet. Nothing of interest was found in this room.

Room 82.

A small patch in the center of the north wall of Room 82 marks the only evidence of the plaster that once covered this well-laid wall. Near the western wall is a large closed doorway of the old type. The east wall was also well built, but entirely devoid of plaster, and had no openings. Though the south wall bulged, it showed traces of having been well built, composed of small thick slabs. It may possibly have had a doorway in its center. The west wall still retains some remnants of plaster and its upper part shows the action of fire. Under the floor was uncovered a partition wall which proved to be the continuation of the room found below Room 77 and formed a right-angled triangle. These lower walls bore no trace of fire. The partition wall extends to the bottom of the lower room on the side of Room 82. There are two additional small angular rooms inside the floor.

Room 83.

In 1897 a copper bell was found in the southwest corner of this room. (Fig. 112.) A section of the first floor level was left in the corner above mentioned and this was removed before the second floor was disturbed. On removing the second floor, which was composed of adobe and flat stones, a multiplicity of walls and fireplaces was found. Near the east wall was a fireplace composed of flat stones around which had been loosely laid a ring of irregularly shaped pieces of sandstone. In the center of the room was a stone wall, part of which formed a fireplace and in the southwest corner there was still another fireplace.

Fig. 112 (7081). Copper Bell, Room 83, slightly enlarged.

The space occupied by the different floor levels amounted to about 2 feet. The south wall was built upon a foundation of large stones that extended from 6 inches to 1 foot beyond the main wall. At this, the foundation level, a semicircular layer of stones was encountered and investigation proved it to be the outer wall of an old estufa. Excavation in this southwest corner uncovered a well-formed estufa of the circular type. The upper wall sloped outward to some extent and was well plastered. It was composed of large stones and was very crude as compared with the estufas of a later period in other parts of the ruin.

The bench was 3 feet 2 inches high, approaching in this respect, the type found in the cliff-houses. Those previously found in the ruin contained a comparatively low bench. This bench was well plastered and its edges were rounded. The eastern section of the bench was quite level, but the western end of the exposed arc dipped to such an extent that it left a regular ridge at the edge. In the construction of the bench a boulder had been utilized, its position being almost in the center of the arc. The floor of this estufa is 8 feet below the first floor level of Room 83.

Its western wall was lost beneath the foundation of the west wall of Room 83, where it passes the southeast corner of Room 84. Beyond this no explorations have been made. Its eastern part passes southward under the south wall of Room 83 and it too is lost in an unopened room. This estufa is but one of the evidences of a lengthened occupation and belongs to the series that stretches westward as far as Rooms 57 and 58. Below the floor of the estufa the virgin sand was reached, this point being 20 inches below the level of the ceiling beams of the first room.

Room 84.

The walls of this room were plastered and their lower portions were blackened by fire. The north doorway was rounded at the top, had wooden poles for a lintel, and a metate, with the grinding side exposed, for a sill. The south doorway, also rounded at the top, had plastered sides. The east and west walls were unbroken, but in the southeast corner of the east wall there is a depression about 3 feet wide which runs to the second story; the lower wall north of this bulges a trifle and extends to the plastered section in the northeast corner. This place was overhanging, was built of stones and mortar, and bore no evidence of fire. It was probably a support of some kind for the upper walls; at least it supported the cross beams at this end of the room. As evidenced by the contour of the plaster, the beam did not enter the wall; hence, the floor was supported at the east end by this projection. Near the west wall, at the same level with the plastered section, there is a hole in the north wall where a beam 7 inches in diameter had entered. The fireplace, built of stone and plastered on the inside, is about 1 foot deep.

The upper room had also been plastered and its walls showed no blackening. The doorways in the north and east walls were of the square type; in the north wall the doorway was near the center; in the east wall it was at the south end, about 2 feet from the south wall. The west wall simply abuts on the north and south walls. The east wall is solid at the corners.

Room 85.

In the southeastern corner of Room 85 there were two bins or small rooms, probably used for storing grain, Fig. 116. The one in the corner was formed by a wall that formed the arc of a circle, the radius of which was about 3 feet 9 inches, taking the corner as the center. The south wall of this bin, formed by the south wall of the room, was well plastered and its surface unbroken, save five depressions that had been

Fig. 113. North Wall of Room 83.

271

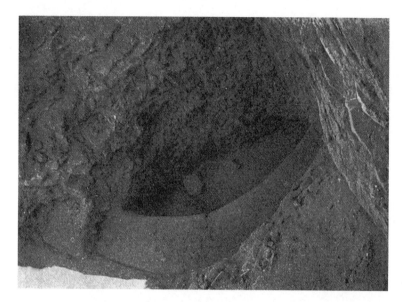

Fig. 114.   Under Wall, Room 83.

Fig. 115.   Sandal Figures on North Wall of Room 83.

272

Fig. 116.   Bins in Room 85.

273

Fig. 117.   North Wall of Room 85, showing Calcined Surface.

Fig. 118. Specimens *in situ*, Room 85.

275

Fig. 119. A Large Wooden Slab, Room 85.

276

Fig. 120.   Pottery in Place in West End of Room 85.

Fig. 121 (7282).   Large Vessel from Room 85.

made for beam rests; the largest of these was near the west wall and was over 5 inches in diameter. The other four were near the east wall, three of them being in a group; one of them was circular with a diameter of $3\frac{1}{4}$ inches, while the other two were simply depressions, lengthened as though the plaster had been removed with the cupped fingers; the fifth was 1 foot 1 inch above the highest of the group and was not very deep.

One inch from the south wall and 4 inches from the east, is a post $3\frac{1}{2}$ inches in diameter and 4 feet 5 inches high. Another post 6 inches in diameter stands in the northeastern part of the bin. Its top has decayed and part of it has probably fallen, but as it stands, it reaches a point $\frac{1}{2}$ foot above the ceiling beams. Another post 7 inches in diameter and 1 foot 6 inches high stands in the northern part of the bin. The top is smooth, as though from use, and, as it is directly under the doorway to the bin, was evidently used as a step.

Fig. 122 (7270).   Wooden Flute, Room 85.

The east wall of the bin is well plastered, the plaster being intact over the entire surface. There are four depressions for poles that are on the same level as those in the south wall; three of them were but slight places that had been picked into the plaster, the fourth is deeper and still retains a thin layer of plaster that had been applied to the wall after the hole was made.

The quarter circle that forms the third boundary of the bin is made of rough stones over which a thick layer of plaster was spread. It extends from the floor to the ceiling beams where it joins the south wall and may have extended to that height throughout the southeastern part of the circle, but the northern part of the circle does not point to such a possibility. On a line with the highest depression in the south wall there are in the circular wall three charred beams about $2\frac{1}{2}$ inches in diameter. These ran east and west and no doubt rested upon a cross beam that was supported by the depression in the south wall and the northern part of the curved wall.

One foot six inches from the south wall there had been a doorway, but only the sill and part of the south side remain to show its form. The plaster on the side is thick and rounded and the base is composed of a large flat stone that has a rounded end; on this had been placed another stone that was covered with plaster to form a surface for the sill. The sill is a flat piece of sandstone with notched ends for the insertion of the upright side posts. The north side of this doorway abutted on the end of the circular wall of the next bin.

The wall on the northern part of this bin is very thin and, judging from its formation, only extended a short distance above the present level, which is 1 foot 7 inches above the floor. No corn or other cereal was found in this bin to point to its having been used as a receptacle for produce, nor was there anything to give a clue to its use. The circular wall ranged from 5 to 8 inches in thickness and was well plastered.

The bin just north of this was of the same form, with the exception of the south wall which is the convex part of the north wall of the other bin. Using the southeast corner as a center of a circle, the rounding wall would be the arc of a circle, the radius of which was 3 feet 1 inch.

The east wall is formed by the main room wall and is well plastered. There are three depressions for the reception of beams, two of which are on a level with the top of the north wall of the bin, the third about $1\frac{1}{4}$ feet below them.

The circular wall is solid and well built, having for its inner base support three large metates, or slabs, that stand on end and slant a trifle toward the north. These are on the north side and the edges almost meet. There is still another large slab in a similar position, on the west part of this bin. Between the slab at the northwest part of the bin and the one against the south wall is a well-built wall, just above it there are evidences that a doorway had been at this point.

The plaster at the top of the north wall is very thick and is rounded, and, at this point, is on a level with the beam supports in the east wall. The north wall is from $\frac{1}{2}$ to $\frac{3}{4}$ foot thick at the top, but much thicker at the bottom.

There is a post below the point in the west wall where the old doorway probably stood; it is broken now, but evidently served as a step, although it may have been a support.

The western part of the circular wall is nearly 2 feet thick and has served as a support for the cross beams from the east wall. About 1 foot 3 inches above the support holes in the east wall, there is a line on the plaster that defines the roof limit of the two bins. It extends from a point where the circular wall of the north bin joins the east wall to the south wall; its lower limits are on a level with the upper part of the highest support hole in the south wall, and with the charred beams in the circular part of the south bin. The lower series of holes in the east wall are the same height in both bins and perhaps formed a second floor or shelf for stowing goods.

These bins had evidently been built after the room had passed into disuse and become partly filled with rubbish, for the walls are simply a facing against the débris. It was therefore essential to have a firm surface to hold back the loose material; hence, the stone slabs and metates on edge in the lower part of the circular wall of the north bin.

A little over 2 feet above the floor level at the northwest part of the north bin the plaster is cupped, showing the point where it was rounded out over the débris. Below this place there is nothing to be seen but the rubbish that covered the whole floor of the room.

There are two steps composed of large flat stones that lead to the doorway in the south bin. These rest upon the débris as does also tha large metate with a hole in the bottom that lies against the south well of the room and near the west wall of the south bin.

In the west end of Room 85 is a series of bins that stands above the floor level of the main room. There are three double tier bins against the west wall of the room and a large one east of this series. The one in the southwest corner of the upper series is a small pocket-like place, with the plaster of the sides rounded at the base, thereby forming a cupped bottom. In the south wall of this bin where the ceiling beam had passed through there is an opening 9 inches in diameter and about $8\frac{1}{2}$ inches from the west wall. This beam must have been a long one, for there is a hole on the same level, in the south wall of Room 83, and another of the same size, in the north wall of the bin and directly in line with the other two. The plaster and stones have fallen where it would have entered the north wall of Room 85, so it is impossible to say whether it crossed the entire width of both rooms.

The west and north sides of this bin were unbroken, but presented an irregular, although well plastered, surface. They are all blackened and had suffered considerably from the fire that ruined this part of the room.

The entrance to this bin is on the east side. At one time there had been a good doorway, as evidenced by the south side which is fairly well preserved. Outside of the original east wall of the bin and against the south wall of the main room, is a piece of masonry that is 6 inches thick against the south wall, but tapers down to nothing at the edge of the doorway. It had probably been placed there some time after the inner wall was built, for this under wall was blackened by smoke. On the north side of the doorway the order was reversed, the thick part being near the doorway and tapering toward the north.

The floor of the bin is plastered and supported on beams 3 inches in diameter; two of these extend into the main room. The walls of this bin are still standing to within a few inches of the ceiling level.

The two bins to the north of this one and on the same wall line and level, are broken to such an extent that nothing can be gathered as to their original appearance. The walls are of large rough stones. At the south end of the one next to the southwest corner there is a large sandstone boulder that runs east and west; one end extends under the west wall of the room and the other forms the northwest corner of the large bin.

The large bin just east of and adjoining the wall series is a spacious affair that extends from the floor of the room to the ceiling, at least at its western and northern parts. About 4 feet 9 inches above the floor level there are remains of ceiling beams in the north wall of the bin, and these poles, judging from the angle, must have run to the south wall of the bin. The east wall, however, is rounded at this height and therefore, could not have extended above this level. Again, there is a hole in the south end of the west wall from which a beam may have extended eastward, so there may have been a cover over the entire bin. Beyond this all is speculation, as there is no mark on the west wall whereby one may define the limits of the upper bin.

The west wall of this bin is rough and irregular; in the northwest corner there is a large sandstone boulder, or more properly speaking two, for there is a broad seam in the top that seems to divide it. There is a wall in this corner that stands 1 foot 6 inches in height and has a beam 3 inches in diameter across its top, then the bare stone is in evidence for 2 feet 6 inches where the wall begins again: this upper part of the wall is supported by poles that rest against the rock.

South of the second stone, which is part of the west wall proper, for about 8 inches, there is a plain stretch of masonry, then a doorway is encountered that should open into the lower part of the bin in the southwest corner of the room. It has been filled and plastered over and was almost obliterated, the only evidence of its having been a doorway being the depression in the plaster and the stone sill that projects 2 inches beyond the wall. The balance of this wall is plastered and in good condition, but the surface is irregular. The beam hole before mentioned, may have been where a floor beam from one of the west bins protruded, but from the angle of entrance it seems hardly probable. This wall stands to within a few inches of the ceiling timbers.

The south wall of the bin is in a fair state of preservation and retains all of the plaster with which its surface was covered. There is a little seat or step in the southwest corner, 1 foot 2 inches above the floor, which extends along the south wall a distance of 1 foot and along the west for 8 inches. It is 7 inches wide from the corner to the center of the edge. It is seemingly composed of plain plaster and may have been used for a number of purposes.

There is a doorway in the central part of this south wall. Its sides are well plastered and rounded; it has a flat stone for the sill. The doorway extends from a point 2 feet 7 inches above the floor level to the top of the standing wall which is on a level with the ceiling beams in the north wall of the bin.

The east wall is plain and has suffered by fire; its top is a brick red. The plaster has fallen to a height of about 2 feet above the floor level, but over the balance of the surface it is intact. As mentioned before, this wall extends only to the level of the ceiling beams in the north wall and was rounded at this point, in the same manner as the north wall of the north bin against the east wall of this room. The surface of this wall is unbroken on its upper part save by the cracks that seam its surface.

The north wall is rough, bulged, and burnt, but the extreme heat had extended but a few inches below the ceiling beams, Fig. 117. Five or six beams had entered this wall; above their level the plaster is burned to a terra cotta color. This upper wall had extended to the ceiling and made a turn at the northeast corner, but how far it extended over the east wall could not be ascertained.

The floor was smooth and hard. About 2 inches below it was an adobe floor that was so hard that it must have been baked. It was nearly 2 inches thick and one could hardly make an impression in it with a trowel. Embedded in the upper floor, directly under the doorway in the south wall, was a dressed stone that had evidently served as a step, but the falling débris had pressed it against the south wall.

We turn now to the main part of Room 85. This was a long spacious place just north of Room 83, east of Rooms 84 and 13, and west of Room 78. A small portion of it was worked in 1896 and has been described as Room 14 (see p. 69). In re-numbering at the commencement of the work in 1897 it was taken for granted that there were two rooms between Room 13 and Room 76; hence, the eastern part was numbered Room 85. Thus the room has two numbers. This room has suffered greatly through the agency of fire and the heat was so intense that sand and plaster were vitrified and glazed; the north wall suffered more than the others, and the upper part of the room more than the lower. To cause such a furnace corn or grain must have been stored in the room, but no evidence of these could be found.

The north wall above the ceiling beam level is burned, warped, and generally destroyed. There is a doorway of the rectangular type in its western part, with a stone slab at the top and with its sill and the sides rounded and plastered. It is of the same style as that in the north wall of Room 99, where the stone door rests against the sloping space at the sides. The plaster about this doorway is still in place, but is black, white, and red from the action of the fire.

About 3 feet east of this doorway there seems to be an old doorway that has been closed with plaster and stones, but the wall is in such condition that it is impossible to tell. The wall east of this place has fallen northward, but is still held in place by the débris in the next room. Holes in this wall and corresponding holes in the south wall show where two large ceiling beams have entered. They are fully 1 foot in diameter. There is a large square doorway in the northeast corner just below the ceiling level, it has boards for the lintel, and strange to say, the fire did not devour them. It seems that the fire limit extends only to a point 6 inches west of the east wall; the plaster in the area east of this line is only slightly blackened, probably by the smoke. West of this line the heat must have been terrific, judging by the condition of the wall.

From a point on a line with the east wall of the large bin, to the west wall, this wall is in a fallen condition and we dared not remove the stones and débris for fear that the wall might topple over.

The south wall is of two thicknesses, above the ceiling level it is fully 6 inches wider at the west end than the lower wall; the projection decreases in width as it advances toward the east until it is barely 3 inches where it passes the east wall. This wall abuts on the west wall and is still quite solid, although the massive top wall looms over one in a top-heavy manner that is anything but pleasing to one at work in the room below.

There are two closed doorways in the upper wall. The one near the west end is smaller and has more rounded sides than the other, but both are of the rectangular type and have their sides well plastered. Both are filled with carefully laid stones and the surface has been covered with plaster.

The lower wall is solid and in good condition, it was only slightly damaged by the fire and retains all of its plaster. There is a doorway of the rectangular type, in the central part the sides have been well plastered. Five poles formed the lintel, two of them are still in place.

About 1 foot above the east side of this doorway is a depression for the reception of a beam, it is 3 inches in diameter and has a mass of plaster around its upper and west side, into which pieces of sandstone have been forced to chink the end of the beam. Between this and the western wall of the eastern bin there are three other depressions in the plaster that have probably served the same purpose. Of the two ceiling beam holes mentioned, one is just west of and really rested against the west wall of the east bin, and the other was about 7 feet 6 inches west of it.

The bins in the east and west part of the room took up quite a portion of this wall. Descriptions of its surface, as included within these confines, will be found in the descriptions of the bins (p. 279).

The east wall abuts on the north and south and presents an unbroken surface, save where the beams over the bins entered the wall. The ceiling level is well defined by the ceiling beams, or poles, over thirty of which are visible. The plaster on this wall is blackened somewhat by smoke, but is intact and in good condition.

The wall above the ceiling beam level has a heavy coat of ordinary plaster, and over it there has been placed a layer of white. This upper wall stands to a height of about 3 feet.

The west wall, or at least what may be seen of it above the bins, presents a very dilapidated appearance. About 1 foot from the south wall is a closed doorway that has had rounding sides. It is covered with plaster but its ovoid form can be defined. North of it the wall has fallen to such an extent that no special features can be recognized.

After removing the stone steps, mentioned in the description of the east bin (p. 281), a small bin was uncovered. Its northeastern part was formed by the metate that was mentioned as being in the southwest corner of the north bin. The clearing of this bin proved that the slab was a metate, as the marked side was in evidence in the small bin. The southeast part of this bin was formed by the northwest wall of the south bin and the balance was simply the walls formed by the sand and one of the stone steps. From its appearance, it seems that it was either never finished, or else used only for a short time ere the place was filled in and the stone steps put in place.

There is a large post in the south part of this bin that stands almost under the doorway leading into the south bin. It is about 10 inches in diameter and stands about 2 feet 9 inches above the old floor level.

The top is burned and in making the bin it was covered and served as a support for the masonry.

One foot, eleven inches west of this post there is another, it is about 6 inches in diameter and stands 1 foot 6 inches above the old floor level. Five feet, five inches west of this one is another, about the same size as the last, but standing 4 feet 2 inches above the floor. Whatever the use of these posts, which are in line with the one in the northeast part of the south bin, on the east side of the room, they evidently formed a part of the room ere the visitation of the fire. All but the one in the bin are burned and their tops are now a mass of charcoal.

There is a post 6 inches in diameter that supports the stone sill in the south wall of the large bin in the west part of the room, and another 4 inches in diameter serving the same capacity under the sill of the doorway into the lower bin in the southwest corner. This doorway was heavily plastered and the sides were rounded; two flat stones formed the sill but the top had fallen in, as was the case with the doorway in the large bin. The sill of this doorway, southwest, projected 6 inches from the bin wall and this space from the floor up had been filled with solid mortar. All of the posts examined below the floor level were backed with the dark colored slabs, like those found in the large estufa in the west court, and around the logs in the supports dug out in the estufa of Room 16. These were packed around to a height of from 6 to 10 inches, and from its firmness, was evidently used as a tamping. Just west of the bin on the east end of the room, in fact part of it is under the largest of the stone steps, it is over 1 foot deep and is below the old floor level. There is a large stone slab standing on edge in the northeast part of the fireplace, its edge must have reached just to the floor level. Another slab, on the southeast side, reached from the last mentioned stone to within 4 inches of the second post west of the bins. This post, it seems, was put in place after the fireplace had been in use, as one of the stones is missing on this side and the coal, stone, and mortar, used as packing, extend fully 1 foot over the floor of the fireplace. Nine inches northwest of this post stands the third stone. All of these are calcined and blackened, as is also the stone bottom. The stones on the north side were broken and fell to pieces when the earth was removed.

Six inches west of this fireplace is a second one which was probably built after the post spoiled the utility of the first. This one is 1 foot 8 inches deep and is composed of five large slabs of sandstone, one stands on edge at the east, one at the northeast, one at the northwest, one at the west, and the fifth at the south. The bottom is composed of a large

287

Fig. 123.   Remains of a Charred Rope, Room 86.

Fig. 124.　Walls of Angular Room under Room 87.

stone slab. The stones were blackened and calcined, and were therefore exceedingly friable and delicate. The new or upper floor level was over 1 foot above the sill of the doorway in the south wall, and upon this rested the large double metate with a hole in the center.

A number of interesting specimens were found in the floor, Figs. 118–122.

ROOM 86.

Room 86 is bounded on the north and west by unworked rooms; on the south it joins Room 78 and on the east, Room 87. It is one of the second series of rooms south of the north wall and is built much in the same manner as the outer wall at this point.

The north wall seems to have been repaired at its upper eastern part, since the western and lower part, composed as it is of large flat stones, conforms to the old style of building. This wall is still standing almost to the height of the third story.

The east wall abuts on the north and south walls and shows the same class of work as the eastern part of the north wall, the three stories being composed of well-laid selected stones.

The south wall is new at its east end; it is made of faced stones, presenting an oval appearance and these are chinked with smaller stones. This style of wall was apparently restricted to the second story; the lower part was strong, but not as well built as the upper part. In the lower part of this wall was a doorway; west of the doorway the wall is composed of rough stones and is evidently old. There is evidence that it was faced with small pieces of sandstone. This wall extends to the second story where it joins the east wall. The western part of the wall is in a state of decay which stands out more forcibly when compared with the well-built wall at the east end.

The west wall is composed of large flat irregular stones, such as are generally found in the old walls. It abuts on the north and south wall and its surface is very rough and uneven.

The north wall is 1 foot 10 inches thick; the east, 2 inches thick; and the south, 1 foot 11 inches thick. The room was cleared to the floor level and then dug to a depth of several feet below that plane. A number of large stones and metates were found below the floor level.

ROOM 87.

On the north Room 87 is bounded by an unworked room; on the south it joins Room 80. It is really one of the several series of rooms south of the north wall, but there is a small angular space between the north wall of the room north of this one and the outer wall, that is formed by a wall that runs southeast from the outer wall and joins it at a point just abreast of Room 86.

Room 87 is standing to the height of the second story on the north side and also the north part of the east and west walls. The floor of this room rested upon a foundation of old walls and was, therefore, not as deep as Room 86.

The north wall is built mostly of well-laid small stones. The surface stones are a facing for the rough inner wall and are laid without mortar, giving an appearance similar to the east wall of Chettro Kettle.

In the center of the first floor wall there is a doorway of the rectangular type, the sides very straight and even for unplastered surfaces. There is a weak place above this doorway that marks the only real defect in the wall. At either end of this wall, 1 foot 6 inches below the ceiling beams and about 8 inches from either end wall, are square openings. The opening in the eastern end is the better of the two, but this is in poor condition. They were probably about 1 foot by $1\frac{1}{2}$ inches and may have been ventilators.

The ceiling beams ran north and south, as shown by the large beam holes in the wall. The upper part of the wall, above the ceiling beams, was made of the same sized stones and built in the same fashion as the lower part. There was a rectangular doorway in the upper part, but the top of it had fallen with the wall.

Near the east wall were three beam holes about 6 inches to 1 foot in diameter; a large one was about 1 foot 4 inches and two small ones about 8 inches in diameter in the center. There were two large beam holes midway of the eastern and western wall.

The south wall was built like the north wall and had a rectangular doorway in the center. This is closed with carefully laid stones. The wall is in good condition and at the west end extends to the ceiling beams.

The east wall also has the same technique as the two previously described. At one time there was a doorway in the center of this wall, that is now entirely devoid of shape; the stones at the top and sides have been displaced and the opening filled with débris. The wall stands to the height of the ceiling beams and, at its north end, to the height of the north wall which is fully 7 feet above the ceiling beam level.

The west wall, built like the other three, presents a solid unbroken appearance. At its south end it stands to a height of 4 feet above the ceiling beams and at its north end, fully 8 feet above that level. The respective measurements of the walls, showing their thickness, are as follows: north, 2 feet; south, 1 foot 10 inches; east, 2 feet; west, 2 feet.

On a level with the floor, as before mentioned, are the tops of a number of old walls. On removing the floor it was found that the space was occupied with these walls, save for an angular space in the center and the narrow end of another in the northeast corner. These walls were thick and massive and were built of the large flat, rough-edged stones that characterize the material of the old walls. The north and west sides of the large angular room still retain a good portion of the plaster with which they had been covered and which was blackened as though by long use. A wall runs parallel with the south wall of the room and joins another that runs northwest and southeast, near the east wall; this second wall abuts on the west wall of this lower series, as does also the first mentioned. The west wall does not rest against the west wall of the room, but the space between them is almost filled by the stones on which the upper wall rests (Fig. 155).

The north wall seems to act as a support for the upper wall, as is the case with the south wall; the east wall is built squarely across the top of the old walls. The room, or pointed space, in the northeast corner, extends under the east wall and forms part of the network of rooms below the floor level of Room 88. The east and west walls of this upper room, abut on the north and south walls, as do all of the end walls of this series, which extends to Room 99.

ROOM 88.

Room 88 lies just east of and adjoins Room 87. To its north is an unworked room; on the east lies Room 89; and on the south it is flanked by Rooms 77–82. This room has the same general appearance as Room 87. The walls are of the same material and built in the same manner. The north wall has a rectangular doorway in the central part, about 1 foot above the floor; in the upper part, near the east and west walls, there are square openings like those found in the north wall of Room 87. These openings are like those in the outer wall of the pueblo and it is more than possible that this was at one time the outer wall of the building. The lintel poles were still in place in the square opening near the east wall. These poles were fully 3 inches in diameter. The wall stood to a height of over 8 feet above the ceiling beams and had a doorway in its upper part. Only a portion of the sides of the doorway is still in place. Large pieces of the wall above the square openings have fallen, but the greater part is in good condition.

The east wall is solid, not even a doorway breaking its surface. It is somewhat bulged near the floor, but is otherwise in good shape. The south wall is in a good state of preservation near the east end; in fact the only bad place is near the west wall where a large section has fallen out. There is a closed doorway of the old T type with well-defined lines, in the east center of the wall. The stones with which it is closed are well laid.

The west wall shows the same broken place in the center as on its side in Room 87. This may have been a doorway, but there is absolutely no evidence of it on this side. Barring this defect, the wall is in good condition, and stands to the height of the ceiling poles, which may be seen at its north end where the wall towers 8 feet above them. This high section is only 2 feet 6 inches wide at its lower part.

The east and west walls abut on the north and south walls and all are devoid of plaster. In this room there is a continuation of the walls found at the floor level in Room 87; they form four places in this room all of which extend into other rooms. The one in the west end extends under the west wall of the room and ends in an acute angle in Room 87 (Fig. 124).

The southwest wall of the central room passes under the south wall of the upper room, as does also its southeast wall. Just southeast of the large space, with the same wall for its base, is another angular room; its northeast and northwest walls form a right angle, the south upper wall is the hypothenuse, the acute angle is lost under the east wall.

The fourth space is in the northeast corner and, with the east wall of the room as a perpendicular, forms a right-angled triangle with the base on the north side. Unlike those in Room 87, these lower walls are only 1 foot thick, although their width is about the same.

The wall running northwest and southeast seems to end where it meets the north upper wall and extends under the east wall at its other end. The wall in the southeast end abuts on this wall and passes under the south wall. The wall running parallel to it in the west central part of the floor area abuts on the same wall as the others, and also abuts on a mass of masonry in the southwest corner. These walls are all built upon the natural yellow sand.

There is a bench a little over 1 foot wide that runs along the north wall; in it are four places where posts have probably rested; they average about 10 inches in diameter. The upper walls show the following thicknesses: north, 2 inches; south, 1 foot 10 inches; east, 1 foot 10 inches; west, 2 feet.

Room 89.

Room 89 is also one of the series of rooms running east and west of which Room 99 forms the eastern limit. It is bounded on the north by an unnumbered room, on the south by Room 90, on the east by Room 98, and on the west by Room 88.

The north wall is built of various sized stones, no continuity of size of material or manner of laying is shown. The lower part is in good condition and still retains the greater part of its plaster, but the upper part is warped and in places stones have fallen out. At one place, near the ceiling beams and only a few feet from the west wall, a few stones have fallen, disclosing a timber built into the wall. It is laid horizontally and was evidently used as a strengthening medium. It is just above one of the square holes and no doubt served as a lintel to the ventilator, which, however, seems to have been closed with stones. There is another of these square places near the east wall, thereby following out the same order as in Rooms 87–88.

A doorway in the lower part of this wall is of the rectangular type and has eight poles for the lintel; these average 2 inches in thickness. At the northern limit of this doorway, 1½ inches below the main lintel, are two poles the space between them being filled with stones. The doorway was half full of débris, the lower part, however, was closed with a well-laid plastered wall. Judging from the holes in the wall at the ceiling level, there must have been eight large beams running north and south.

The second story wall is of the same style of masonry as the lower story, but was evidently built after the lower wall, for it is fully 3 inches north of the lower wall surface. This may have been because the upper wall was built over the roof of the lower room and thereby made a perfect joint impossible. The story is in good condition and has a doorway in the center. It is rectangular in form and has a peculiar jog on either side; near the north end the top of this doorway has fallen. At the east end of the room the third story is in evidence, a pile of wall about 8 feet long and 6 feet high being still in position. From the floor to the second story ceiling beams is a distance of 19 feet, thereby making over 22 feet of wall on the west side of this room.

The south wall is bulged and buckled to such an extent that it is almost a wreck at the west end. It is similar to the north wall in its masonry, and retains a great portion of the plaster, most of which is, however, in patches.

The only intentional break in the surface is a doorway of the old wide-topped type near the east end; the lower part is closed with large stones and the upper part filled with débris. The outlines are fairly plain, but the height could not be ascertained owing to the falling of the wall which carried part of it away.

The east wall is solid and presents an unbroken surface, the masonry being the same as in the other walls. Over fifteen poles can be counted at the ceiling level, and above them the wall of the second story rises to the height of the beam holes in the north wall. The surface has no opening in it, and although warped laterally at its center, is still in fair condition. This wall abuts on the north and south walls.

The west wall stands almost to the first ceiling level and abuts on the north and south walls; it has quite a patch of plaster on the lower part and the masonry does not form that of the other walls. There is not a break in its surface, all the stones being intact.

The floor of this room was rather uneven; no fireplaces were found in it. The measurements of the walls gave the following thicknesses: north, 1 foot 9 inches; south, 1 foot 10 inches; east, 1 foot 10 inches; west, 1 foot 11 inches.

Room 90.

Room 90 is in the northeastern part of the ruin and is bounded on the north by Room 89; on the south by the estufa, Room 75; on the east by Room 20; and on the west by Room 82. It is one of a series extending east and west and its walls, except at the east, have fallen so that not even the entire first story remains.

The north and south walls are only a trifle over 7 feet in height. The walls are rough and in poor condition, especially the west end of the north wall which contained two pockets and a doorway. The latter was of the rectangular type and was filled with débris from the fallen wall. The wall directly above it was completely destroyed, the space being filled with débris. The pocket in the western part of this wall was rectangular in shape, its larger side ran parallel with the floor and a flat stone served as the bottom. It was about 1 foot 10 inches long and 10 inches high, extending into the wall a distance of 1 foot 9 inches. The back of the base was composed of flat stones which looked like manos; these were laid side by side, their ends pointing north and south.

The pocket in the eastern end of the wall was 1 foot 3½ inches long by 9 inches high, and 1 foot 4 inches deep. It too had a flat stone extending the full width of the pocket and forming a base for the front part. Both of these pockets were comparatively rough but probably presented a better appearance when the plaster was in good condition. At one time the whole wall had been plastered but most of it on the upper part had fallen.

The south wall was in good condition and was composed of small stones; these were particularly small at the upper part of the west end. There was a doorway of the old broad type in the center that had been carefully closed with large stones and covered with plaster. This was the only break in the wall. As was the case with the north wall, only the lower plaster remains.

The east wall was rather rough in construction and its center was pierced by a rectangular doorway that led into Room 20. Most of the plaster had disappeared and the wall had bulged a little on either side of the doorway. The lintel of the doorway was composed of six poles in an advanced stage of decay.

The west wall was strongly built and well faced, the only defect being a slight bulge in the center. There was a small pocket in the lower part of the north end which looked as though a few stones had been pulled out, as there was no evidence of its having been used or plastered. A small patch of plaster showing evidences of fire and smoke remained near the central part of the floor.

The room is not due east and west, the east and west walls being 20° east of north. Nothing of great interest was found during the removal of the débris. The usual potsherds, bones, etc., were encountered and when the floor level was reached a great many metates and stone slabs were found. When the dirt was cleared away the upright slabs were found to be the walls of bins. To the north of one series was found some plaster that had once contained a series of metates. A large metate had probably fallen from the floor above, as it rested on a layer of dirt that was over the best-preserved metate rest. There was a pile of stones near the central part resting against the south wall; these too had probably fallen from the upper floor like the flat metate in the northwest corner. A large metate, with a hole in the bottom, rested upon the floor and was probably a part of the furniture of the room.

When the floor was cleared a series of bins was uncovered. They ran parallel with the walls at the sides of the room and extended from the west wall to within 1½ feet of the east wall. There were ten in all; the row was not straight but formed an elongated arc, the convex side of which was toward the north wall. All the bins, with one exception, had flat stones for the bottom. These were surrounded with mortar that was rounded at the corners and sloped upward to the sides. The distance

Fig. 125. Mealing Bins, Room 90.

from the edge of the metate slope to the bottom of the bins was from 2 to 3 inches. (Fig. 125).

Room 91.

This room is situated over Room 3. An opening was made in its southeast corner in 1896 to make an entrance to the series of open rooms that run northward from Room 3. The lower part of Room 3 was heavily walled, the plaster in some places being fully 2 inches thick. The room may have been used as an estufa or council room, but if so, the usual bench was missing. The opening in the room was in the southeast part and on the wall beams was surrounded with bunches of cedarbark tied with yucca cords.

The floor was laid upon four large timbers that ran east and west; they were natural logs which measured nearly 1 foot in diameter. They extended about 1 foot into the western wall and protruded fully 8 feet beyond the eastern wall. The two northernmost logs were surrounded at their eastern ends with strips of cedar that extended the whole width of the wall which was 2 feet thick. These pieces were used as packing in the same way that small flat stones are used around smaller beams. The strips were not only in evidence on the lower part of the beam, but completely encircled it.

The western wall of this room was rather uneven and had tipped towards the west until there was a distance of four inches between it and the top part of the northern wall. It had been covered with a thick layer of plaster which remained in place over the greater part of the northern half, where numerous layers could be noted. There was a closed doorway near the south end, or at least an opening that had been filled after the wall was built, but the lines could not be definitely ascertained, owing to the dilapidated condition of this part of the wall.

The north wall was completely covered with plaster, all but the outer layer being in good condition. A square doorway in the west central part was closed and completely covered with plaster. This wall presented a very uniform surface and was 1 foot thick.

The northeast corner was in good condition, the plaster being intact and solid. The east wall was 2 feet thick and made of good-sized stones that were laid in the general way, no special plan being carried out so far as specialized manipulation is concerned. It was well plastered and presented a flat surface, the joint with the south wall being firm and strong, although the south wall was not built into it.

The south wall was solid and in good condition, the surface had been plastered but the greater part had fallen. The doorway in the west central part was of the square type, and extended about 6 inches above the ceiling beams to the top of the standing wall. As there was fully 6 inches of adobe above the floor, the door evidently commenced at the floor level.

The stones in this wall were somewhat smaller than in the east wall, but were laid in the same manner as were those in the other walls as near as could be ascertained. The walls of this room were standing, on an average of about 5 feet above the floor beams and were about the same level as those of the rooms west of it.

The beams forming the support for the floor were in good condition save where they extended into the room east of Room 91. In clearing out Room 3, an opening was found just east of the fireplace, but at that time the outlet was not found. However, in digging down to the beams in the room east of Room 91, a square opening was encountered that was probably the upper end of the air passage from Room 3. It was near the southeast wall of Room 91 and was left for investigation when the room in which it is situated was worked.

Room 92.

This room is directly north of Room 91; its exact direction is northwest and southeast. This room was filled with the stones and dirt of the fallen walls to within about 2 feet of the floor. Here the material from the upper floor was encountered; it could be kept separate from the deposit on the main floor as a stratum of sand had washed in and covered the floor to a depth of from 5 inches to 1 foot, until the floor of the upper room was buried.

The charred ceiling beams of the room were found throughout the débris and a great deal of corn was found on the fallen floor. A bunch of bean bushes was found in the west central part of the room and masses of beans from the same plant, that were still green; corn on the cob; and beans in the pod were encountered. After the material from the fallen floor had been examined, the layer of stratified sand had to be removed to reach the main floor. The sand was almost as hard as mortar and a pick had to be used to remove it. The flow had been from the southwest.

In the material on the main floor a jaw of a cinnamon bear was found, also fragments of two claws and a quantity of hair besides the general material from such a room. The room was very dry and the finds were, therefore, well preserved. The floor was covered with adobe and there was a large flat fireplace in the west-central part. The bottom of this fireplace was well smoothed and only a trifle below the floor level. At one time it had probably been surrounded by a ridge about 3 inches high and 8 inches wide, but only a portion on the north remained intact.

The beam that supported the center of the room was broken and had let that part of the floor down several inches, causing a very pronounced slant toward the west wall.

The west wall (northwest) was in about the same condition as the corresponding wall of Room 91, of which it was a continuation. It had retreated from the end of the south wall about 3 inches and from the north wall about 2 inches. The surface had been covered with a thick layer of plaster, but the greater part of it had fallen. The wall itself was very poorly constructed; it was composed of small slabs laid in mud with no attempt at facing. In the finished room the plaster was relied upon to cover up these defects.

Fig. 126 (7662).   Stone Pointed Drill, Room 92.

The doorway in the central part was of the old type, narrow at the bottom and broad at the top, possibly, as has been suggested, to allow a person to enter with a bundle on his back. This doorway was filled with stones and dirt that might have been placed there by the old people, but which is probably the débris from the fallen walls. The north wall was probably originally plastered, but hardly a vestige of it remains. This wall is solidly built, being composed of large faced stones chinked with smaller ones; it simply abuts on the east and west wall and is nearly 3½ feet thick. The only break in its surface is at the west end where there is a doorway. It is about 4 inches above the floor and of the usual rectangular type. The plaster on its western side is still intact, but on the opposite side most of it has disappeared.

The wall at this side (east) back to the wall of the next room, which is a distinct and individual wall, is 2 feet 2 inches. The lintel is composed of four heavy well-preserved beams, each 5 inches in diameter. The places where they have been let into the walls are chinked with small stones and mud, as though the door had been broken through after the wall was built. The first lintel beam runs eastward from the eastern side of the doorway to a distance of 5 feet 4 inches; its entire length may be traced by a series of small stones that were placed around and in front of it. The chinking, on closer examination, shows that it had fallen out. Very little care had been taken in replacing it, as the stones protrude beyond the side walls. A portion of the upper part of the wall, over the doorway, has fallen, but the other parts of this wall are in good condition.

The east wall is composed of good-sized stones, which are well laid. Almost all the plaster has disappeared but the wall is in good condition save at a point below the doorway, where the stones are displaced. This doorway is of the rectangular type and is filled with débris.

The south wall is very solid and exceedingly well made. It is composed of medium-sized stones chinked with smaller ones, the chinking being forcibly noticeable around the doorway. This doorway is of the rectangular type and the sides are well laid. The wall had been plastered, but very little of it remained. Below the door the wall had fallen, and, at the west end there was a space of about 3 inches where the west wall had fallen away from it. This wall is 1 foot thick and is separated by a large log that rests upon a comparatively thin wall.

Room 93.

Room 93 is the second room south of the darkroom and is one of the outer rooms at the northwest corner of the ruin. The longer axis of this room is northeast and southwest. The walls of this room were well made and were thicker than the average wall.

The north wall (northwest) was composed of large stones chinked with smaller pieces of sandstone and had a doorway of the usual rectangular type, in the northeast end, with ten poles for a lintel. This wall was unbroken, save for the doorway; the wall was broken below the level of the ceiling beam at the southwest end, but at the northeast end it reached a height of 20 feet above the floor. The ceiling poles were about 1 foot in diameter as evidenced by the openings that still remain in the wall.

The southeast wall was composed of large dressed stones, the chinking being done with very thin pieces of sandstone. There was a doorway in the central part of the room and about 1 foot $1\frac{1}{2}$ inches below the ceiling beams; it was of the rectangular type and had poles, about 2 inches in diameter, for a lintel. In the northeast part of the wall is a nearly square opening, 1 foot by 16 inches, that has a flat stone for the top and was probably used for passing things between the rooms.

This door opening was in good condition, but the doorway was broken at the top. The wall was standing to a good height at the southwest end, but at the northeast had fallen to the level of the ceiling beams. This wall was 1 foot 6½ inches thick.

The southwest wall is built in the same firm manner as the other two and has the same form of chinking. There is a doorway of the rectangular type in the center; it has poles for a lintel and is in good condition. The wall is standing to a height of 1 foot above the doorway and is 1 foot 4½ inches thick; it is not built into the southeast wall, but simply abuts on it, as it does on the northwest wall.

The northeast wall presents an unbroken surface. It is one of the walls that radiate from the outer wall, and stands to a height of 20 feet above the floor; it passes the southeast wall and extends southeastward, forming the northeast wall of Room 101 and the southwest wall of Rooms 100–104. It is built of the same large stones as the other walls of the room and chinked in the same manner; it is 1 foot 7 inches thick.

The northwest, or outer wall, of the room is 2 feet 2 inches thick and since it forms the outer wall of the ruin is solidly built. All the walls were devoid of plaster, but may have been covered when the room was new. Because this is one of the outer rooms of the ruin, the walls on the northwest and southeast sides are rounded to some extent.

A well-smoothed floor was found, but very little of interest was brought to light from the débris.

Room 94.

Room 94 is one of the outer rooms at the northwest end of the pueblo; it is southwest of and near Room 93 and is bounded by Room 102 on the southeast. The north wall (northwest) was in fairly good condition at the northeast end, but the southwest end had fallen and was simply a mass of débris. There was a doorway in the upper part of the northeast end that was almost square, but it too had suffered by the falling of the wall.

The northeast wall was in fair condition and was built of large faced stones which were chinked with small pieces of sandstone. This was the typical wall of the outer series and stood out in strong contrast to the rough inner walls. There was a decayed, rectangular doorway in the upper central part.

The southeast wall was in fine condition and was built in the same manner as the other walls. It was intact, but bulged somewhat near the top. There was no doorway in this wall and its surface was practically devoid of plaster.

The southwest wall had fallen at its northwest end, but its southeast part was in good condition and showed that it had been of the same workmanship as the other three. There had been a doorway in the upper part; although still definable, it was badly damaged. The floor of this room was well plastered, but about its center was a wall 2 feet wide that ran parallel with the end walls, its surface being on the floor level.

Room 95.

Room 95 is fourth, southwest of the old darkroom, its true position by the compass is northeast by southwest, its longer axis being the one in question.

The walls of this room were almost completely destroyed, as though forces other than natural elements had played a part in their destruction.

The north wall (northwest) was completely demolished and only a portion of the oppposite wall was in evidence. This was at the floor level and showed that it had been a strong well-built wall at one time. The wall was built like the others of the outer series, being the chinked form.

The east wall had fallen, save at the south end, where it was still intact; it was 1 foot 6 inches thick and abutted on the north and south walls. It was, however, carefully built and was of the same type of masonry as the other walls of the series.

The west wall was standing to a considerable height where it joined the south and north walls, but was only about 1 foot high in the center. It was 1 foot 7 inches thick and composed of the same faced stones as the main walls. This wall abutted on the north and south walls and had suffered with the others when this part of the building fell, as shown by a large crack in the center.

Room 96.

Room 96 is the fifth of the outer series that stretches southwest from the old darkroom. Its larger axis is 22° east of north, but for convenience' sake, the walls are given as north, south, etc.

The north wall is composed of large faced stones which are chinked with thin pieces of sandstone. It is 5 inches high where it rests against the east wall, but has fallen at the center and west end. This wall is 1 foot 7 inches thick and is built upon a foundation of sand that is thickly sprinkled with charcoal.

The south wall is of the same solid character as the others, but instead of abutting at the east end it passes on and is embedded in the east wall; at the west end it abuts on the outer wall. There is a doorway in the center of this wall which is narrow at the top and flaring at the bottom. The sides are 1 foot 7 inches thick and present a very even surface. Eight poles form the lintel and they range from 2 inches to 3 inches in diameter. This wall extends about 5 feet above the ceiling level.

The east wall presents an unbroken surface, composed of the same faced stones and chinked in the same style as the other walls. Evidently it stood in as good condition as when built, save for the slant toward the west, which gave it a rather uncanny appearance to one at work below it. It stood to the height of the ceiling poles for over two-thirds of its length, but at the north end, about 2 feet of its height had disintegrated.

There is a wall about 7 feet in height standing above the ceiling level at the south end of this wall. It is about 3 inches east of the room wall surface at the south end, and fully 1 foot east of the surface where it ends, a distance of 7 feet 6 inches north of the south wall of the room. This upper wall is 1 foot 8 inches thick.

The west wall was massive in appearance at its south end and re-tained this characteristic for a distance of over 8 feet. Beyond this point the lower part of the wall could be traced for a few feet, but further on there are no evidences that a wall had ever been in place, the space it had occupied being simply a mass of débris. Very large stones were used in the construction of this wall and it almost seems as though there must have been some other force besides the falling upper walls, to cause such an utter annihilation of so strong a piece of masonry.

At a point 8 feet 5 inches from this south wall there is a perpendicular line of stones that evidently mark the site of a doorway; its bottom stone is about 2 feet above the floor level, and above it, for 6 inches, there is a regular chinked wall, therefore this doorway must have been closed. The south side of the doorway stands to a height of 3 feet above the stone base or sill, and at this point the wall has fallen. The wall stands to the height of the ceiling beams for a distance of about 4 feet from the south wall and is 1 foot 9 inches thick, being the outer wall of the series it passes on toward the south.

The east wall of this room is the eastern limit of the new walls. At the point where the south wall of Room 96 joins the east wall, the old and new walls are only 1 foot 4 inches apart. At the end of the upper wall, 7 feet 6 inches north of the south wall, the distance from the old wall to the inner room is 6 feet 6 inches. The upper wall is 1 foot 8 inches thick and the bench formed by the top of the east wall of Room 96, west of the upper wall, is over 1 foot; therefore, the east wall of Room 96 must be over 2 feet 8 inches thick, or else the upper wall is built partly upon the filling between the walls. The old wall behind Room 96 is made of flat undressed stones and appears to be almost a dry wall. At this point it is 1 foot 2 inches thick. This outer series of rooms commences at the northeast part of the ruin and extends to the extreme southwest part. It was evidently built to round out the contour of the pueblo.

Room 97.

This room is directly under Room 92 and is of the same form. It is almost due northwest and southeast on its larger axis, as shown by the compass.

The southwest wall of this room is the northeast wall of the square estufa, Room 3, and extends to the ceiling timbers where its top is formed by a beam about 8 inches in diameter, that extends its whole length, and enters the northwest wall. Near the southeast wall, it is supported by an upright timber. This wall was roughly built and heavily plastered, the plaster in some places being 2 inches thick. This covered the irregular stones and gave the wall a fairly even surface. The wall was blackened with a grimy soot and its surface was almost covered with finger marks. To the northwest of the doorway there were bear tracks, made by pressing the closed fist against the plaster and then adding the toes with the end of the finger; nail marks were also to be seen and these were succeeded by snake-like lines. The whole face of this part of the wall had seemingly served as a blackboard when the plaster was still moist. (Fig. 126.)

The surface southeast of the doorway had also received attention. There were two perfect impressions of a hand that gave very good paper casts, also a snake-like series of finger-nail marks, and numerous other finger marks and scratches.

The doorway in this wall was peculiar, owing to its narrowness and great height. It had extended from the cross beam at the top of the wall to within 2 feet of the floor, but it now has its upper part closed with large stones and mortar; its sides are rounding and it has a flat stone for the sill. The southeast side is comparatively straight, but the opposite one is concaved near the bottom.

This is a dividing wall and simply abuts on the northwest and southeast walls. The part to the southeast of the doorway is in good condition, save in a few places where pieces of plaster had fallen, but the northwest part was bulged and cracked. Near the top was a crack about

1½ inches wide between the northwest end of this wall and the north-west wall, but at the bottom it is intact and not separated.

The northwest wall had also been covered with a heavy coating of plaster but it had fallen in many places, exposing sharp edges of irregularly shaped stones. The fallen plaster had been displaced while the room was still occupied, for the exposed stones are covered with the same scales of grimy soot that blacken the plaster.

The doorway in the southwest central part is of the rectangular form and has five two-inch poles for a lintel. These poles, as well as the sides of the doorway, have received the same layer of soot as the wall, and therefore, present a very dirty appearance.

The wall itself is solid and well preserved, the fallen plaster, however, gives it a very rough appearance.

The northeast wall of this room presents a surface that stands out in strong contrast when viewed in connection with the walls just described. It is made of large stones chinked with smaller ones and is about the same type of wall as that seen in the outer series of the west side of the pueblo. The stones have been selected and the surface is, therefore, quite even, though the wall is devoid of plaster.

There is a doorway in the northwest corner that proves conclusively that this, the northeast wall, is a new one, and that the other two, the northwest and southwest, are older. The northwest side of this doorway is a continuation of the northwest wall, has the same blackened plaster, and all the characteristics of that wall. It ends in an old smoke-begrimed doorway that was the doorway of the old room. The lintel poles, and in fact the whole opening, is black, whereas the lintel poles and the southeast side of the new doorway are bright and clean, as though but a few years old. There are six lintel poles in the new opening, ranging from 2 inches to 4 inches in diameter. The outer one extends 5 inches beyond the side of the doorway, its whole surface being exposed in the face of the wall. A place was dug in the southwest wall for the insertion of the lintel poles and the space about them was filled in with small stones and plaster, whose whiteness stands out strongly against the blackness of the wall. It is a rectangular doorway and the unplastered southeast side is 2 feet 2 inches thick. The old wall beyond it is about 1 foot 4 inches thick and the doorway joins the new one at an angle, the slant being toward the southwest.

The surface of the northeast wall had evidently never been plastered; it is bulged in some places and depressed in others, but not enough to weaken the upper wall.

There is a beam about 6 inches in diameter, that can be traced for a distance of about 6 feet from the northeast wall; it evidently runs the whole length of the wall, as did the one on the opposite wall. As this is one of the old blackened timbers, it could not have been put in when the new wall was built, nor could it have served as part of the northeast wall of the old lower room; therefore, it must have supported an upper wall which was torn down when this part of the pueblo was being re-modeled. At the northwest end of the new wall it emerges and passes northwest at an angle until, where it enters the northwest wall, it just rests against the northeast wall. This beam supported the ceiling poles which ran northeast and southwest, and its northeast end, judging from the angle, probably enters the old wall near or in the northeast corner.

The southeast wall was irregular and of the wattle type. Its north-east end was exposed, showing the upright poles and the bundles of willows tied to them. The space between the cross bunches of willows had been filled with stones and clay, and the surface plastered. This had been part of the old room and had been plastered over when the new wall was built. The old blackened plaster may be seen where the wattle wall that juts into the room joins the southeast wall.

There was a bench that ran from the northeast wall to the jutting wall. It was built like the northeast wall and, as it is unplastered, was probably a part of the new structure.

The portion of the southeast wall to the southwest of the jutting piece had been filled in with a new unplastered wall. The old blackened poles were in place on either side of it, and in the southwest corner the old blackened plaster was in place. There was a doorway in the ceiling in this corner and in the plaster near the top of the corner, there was a depression in the plaster to help in making an exit. The wattle beams, at the ceiling level, were tied with split willows and yucca cord.

The wall that jutted into the room was of the wattle type and ran to the ceiling level at the southeast end, but was lower at its northwest limits. (Fig. 127). It was a part of the old room and its sides still show the soot and smoke, but not as much as the side and end walls. It is composed of seven or eight upright poles that are bound laterally with bunches of willows, and tied with withes of the same material. At its northwest edge there is a bundle of willows resting against the upright pole and over these is the thick plaster. The whole surface is thickly plastered; on the southwest side there are nail marks and scratches in its surface.

Fig. 127.   Wall of Wattle Work, Room 97.

307

On the opposite side, about 1 foot from the southeast wall and the same distance from the ceiling beams, is a cup-shaped place similar to the one in the southwest corner of the southeast wall. There was a bin in the southwest recess, formed by two flat stones placed on edge.

There is a large fireplace in the center of the room and another in the recess in the northeast corner. Just northwest of the latter there is what had evidently been a support for a post. It is composed of a platform of plaster on which rests a ring of thin pieces of wood that stand on end, and which probably formed the packing about the post: these sticks are enclosed in a jacket of plaster.

Fig. 128.   View of Room 97, looking Northeast.

Room 98.

Room 98 is next to the east one of the series that stretches east and west in the north part of the ruin and of which Room 86 is the most western one worked. It is bounded on the north by an unworked room, on the south by Room 20, on the east by Room 99, and on the west by Room 89.

The north wall is in a fair state of preservation, the masonry of the lower level is built up of stones, seemingly used regardless of size or appearance in the wall. There is a doorway of the rectangular type in the lower central part that has had what seems to have been a board lintel. Only a layer of wood dust remains to judge by, so it may have been built of poles. It is filled with stones and débris and the lower part is plastered.

There are two ventilators in this wall situated 1 foot below the ceiling beams and near either end wall. The one near the east wall has been filled with stones and the lintel poles may still be seen.

The second story is about the same as in Room 89. In the center is a rectangular doorway that has three lintel poles in place at its northern limit. There are two poles in place below the lintel. These form the top of a secondary opening made by building a narrow wall against either side of the original doorway and formed a rest for the stone door. In building this second story the joint was made so that there is only a trifling difference between the surface of the two walls, but not so with the third story wall part of which, including the side of á doorway, is still standing. The face of this top wall is fully 4 inches north of the second story wall. This top wall is standing a little higher than its neighboring part, over the next room, Room 89.

The south wall is more compactly built than the north wall and has more faced stones in its surface. It is in very good condition, save over the doorway in the center, and still retains the plaster on the lower part.

There are two doorways, both in the eastern part, and only a little over 1 foot apart. The one near the east wall is very small and of the "T" type, the lower part was a little over 2 feet high and only 1 foot 3 inches wide, while the bar section was only 2 feet 8 inches wide by 11 inches in height. The lower portion is filled with a well-laid wall, while the upper part is full of débris.

The doorway just west of this is of the rounded rectangular type; it is in the center of a square of masonry about 3 feet 10 inches by 4 feet. This place had been left, it seems, when the wall was built. A pole running along its top may have served as a lintel, but, at all events, this space has been filled in with a solid wall and only a small doorway left, under which are two steps. The wall above this square place has fallen, but at the north and west ends it stands from 1 foot to 4 feet above the ceiling level.

The east wall is standing to the height of the second story ceiling level. The masonry is the same as in the other walls and the lower part is still plastered.

There is a closed doorway near the floor at about the center of the wall; it is rectangular in form and filled with large stones and covered with plaster. At the first ceiling level the ends of the poles may be seen

Fig. 129.   East and South Wall of Room 99.

in the wall above these poles. The wall is weathered and most of the chinking has fallen from between the stones. This wall abuts on the north and south walls.

The west wall presents an unbroken surface from floor level to top, save where the poles have rested at the ceiling level. The masonry is about the same as in the other walls, although in the lower part there has been more of an attempt to alternate layers of large and small stones.

Fig. 130. Doorway in Room 99.

This wall abuts on the north and south walls and stands almost to the height of the second story ceiling level.

The floor of this room is rough and uneven and no fireplaces were noted. The floor was calcined in a great many places which may mark the old cooking places.

The steps under the doorway in the south wall are worthy of special mention, as they are about the finest and best preserved found in the ruin. There was a similar step in the opposite side of the wall in Room

Fig. 131. Pitchers in Corner of Room 99.

312

20. The step in this room is built of stones and entirely covered with plaster. There are two steps in the block, the first or lower one, is 1 foot high and 8 inches deep and 2 feet 1 inch wide over all; the second one is 1 foot 1 inch high, 11 inches deep and 2 feet wide, making the whole step a little over 2 feet high. Two stones project from the wall that seems to have been a part of it and which would have made it 2 inches higher.

The measurements of the thicknesses of the four walls gave the following results: north, 1 foot 6 inches; south, 1 foot 10 inches; east, 1 foot 10 inches; west, 1 foot 10 inches.

ROOM 99.

Room 99 is one of the series of rooms that runs east and west along the northern part of the pueblo. It is bounded on the north by an unexcavated room, on the south by Room 60, and the northeast by an unexcavated room, on the southeast by Room 70, and on the west by Room 98. This room, on its shorter axis, is about 20° east of north, but the walls are mentioned as north, south, east, and west for convenience. (Fig. 129.)

The wall is built of various sizes of sandstone slabs; in the lower part of the wall they are mostly small, but above the ceiling level large stones predominate. The lower story, at least, was well plastered at one time, as shown by the plaster that is still in place on the lower part of the wall. There is one of the ventilators, post holes, or whatever they may have been, about 5 feet 6 inches above the floor level and 10 inches from the west wall; it is about 1 foot 6 inches high and 1 foot wide, and is now filled with a well-laid wall of small pieces of sandstone.

There are evidences of a second opening at the point where the northeast wall joins this one, but its limits are undefinable, owing to the fallen condition of this part of the wall.

One of the finest doorways (Fig. 130) thus far observed in the ruin is situated about midway of this wall, its extreme measurements show 2 feet 1 inch at the top and 2 feet 4 inches at the bottom, and a height of 3 feet 3 inches on the east and 3 feet 3½ inches on the west side. The sill is made of two large slabs of sandstone, one at each side of the wall, the small space between them being filled with small slabs and plaster. The lintel was composed of poles, but only a few burned pieces remain in place. The stone sill protrudes into this room about 2½ inches, but the mortar had been applied to the under part, which was almost on the floor level, thereby making a solid front. Four inches north of the face of the wall, the doorway lessened in width by a wall on either side. This wall averages about 4 inches in thickness and slants towards the north. The base is, as before stated, 4 inches north of the face of the wall, while at the lintel level it is a little over 1 foot from the same plane. The lintel beams are 2 feet 7 inches above the sill and seem to have extended only a few inches south of the jog in the sides of the doorway. The whole doorway, with the exception of the sill, had been covered with plaster, and that on the sides was quite thick and in almost perfect condition. The sloping sides were the means employed for holding the stone door in place, as the sloping surface would preclude the possibility of its falling, and then too in case of an attack, could be readily applied to prevent intrusion. The slanting wall extends to the northern limits of the main wall and the plaster is there rounded to form the sides of the doorway. As this side, the north, is so much smaller than the south side of the doorway, and, as there is seemingly no way of fastening this side, and again as the openings in the upper part are the same as those in the present outer wall, it seems highly probable that this wall was at one time a part of the north wall of the building, or main pueblo.

The south wall, or at least that portion below the ceiling beam, is built in the same manner as the north wall, the spaces between the large stones, however, show more chinking than in the other wall.

There is a rectangular doorway in the center of the wall; the sill is a stone nearly 2 inches thick, that extends the whole width of the doorway. The lower part of the sill is 1 foot 4 inches above the first floor level. The doorway has been closed with large stones and the surface was plastered as in Room 60. The sides are of the regular form and still retain a good coat of plaster. The wall above this doorway has bulged a little, but where the upper wall joins it, forms a bench nearly 6 inches wide. The bench tapers toward the east and west and is lost in the wall at a point 3 feet west of the southeast wall, but is still in evidence at the west end.

The greater part of the surface, below the ceiling beam level is covered with plaster; west of the doorway it is black and crumbling from the fire that raged in this end of the room.

The second story wall is built of smaller slabs than the lower part and there are evidences of three doorways in its surface. The one near the west end is of the rectangular type and is still standing. The one in the center is only recognizable by a portion of the west side that remains. The third is a corner doorway about 4 inches from the southeast wall. It runs northeast and southwest, and its sides are built of large faced stones; it is standing to a height of about 2 feet. This wall abuts on the southeast wall and thus shows the eastern limit of the south wall of the series that has been explored as far west as Room 66.

The northeast wall is a cross wall that abuts on the north and southeast ones; it is evidently of the same period as the other walls and is of the same type of masonry. It runs northwest and southeast and most of the plaster with which it was covered is still in evidence.

Three feet, nine inches above the first floor level and 1 foot 2 inches southeast of the north wall, is a pole, 2 inches in diameter, that protrudes 1 foot 2 inches from the wall. One foot one inch southeast of this pole and about 2 inches higher, is a piece of deer antler embedded in the wall, and probably used as a peg.

In the southeast corner, about 1 foot from the floor level and 1½ feet from the southeast wall, the end of a log, about 5 inches in diameter, protrudes about 2 inches from the wall; 8 inches northwest of this and on the same level, is a smaller one that also projects about 1½ inches.

Two stones break the smooth surface in this part of the wall, otherwise it is comparatively even. There is a break in the plaster about 1½ feet from the southeast wall near the ceiling level, and it has brought to light the outlines of what seems to have been an old doorway. At its lower limits there is a beam that shows about 6 inches of its surface, but what office it holds in relation to the old opening, which is now closed with stones, is not evident. This wall is standing to the level of the ceiling beams and is in fairly good condition.

The southeast wall presents the best surface to be seen in the room. It is built of large faced stones and chinked with unusually thin pieces of sandstone. Almost all the plaster below the ceiling level is intact, and the only breaks in the surface are a doorway and a wall pocket, the latter is 1 foot 10 inches above the first floor level and is 6 inches high, 9 inch wide, and 11 inches deep. A large flat stone forms the top while the bottom is formed by parts of two ordinary wall stones. The bottom and sides are covered with a heavy coating of plaster. This pocket is 1 foot 5 inches northeast of the south wall.

One foot one inch above the top of the pocket, is a doorway, almost as wide as high, and with corners rounded with a heavy layer of plaster; the top and base were in bad condition as a great many of the stones had been loosened by the fall of the débris from above. This wall runs northeast by southwest and forms the east wall of Room 60. The ends of small poles still remaining in the side walls of the doorway show that the lintel had been of wood.

The west wall is in good condition and towers fully 10 feet above the level of the ceiling beams.   The masonry is the same as in the other walls, and the only break in the surface is caused by a retangular doorway in the central part, but it has been closed and plastered over.   A little plaster remains in the lower area, but most of it has fallen.   There is a slight difference in the thickness of the wall above the ceiling level, as shown by a narrow ledge which is about 2 inches wide and extends the whole width of the wall.

The northwest corner of the upper part has fallen, but enough remains to show that there has been a corner doorway.   This wall abuts on the north and south walls and is the last wall of this series that runs at right angles to the others.

There were three floor levels in this room, the first is a little below the sill of the doorway in the north wall, the second about 3 inches below this, and the third 9 inches below the second.   All of these floors had hard sand surfaces and the spaces between them were filled with clean yellow sand.

One foot, eleven inches from the joint of the southeast and south walls and 1 foot from the southeast wall, was a stone step which was evidently placed in position after the second floor was made, as there is no break in the lower floor.   This, with the wall pocket, which was probably used as a step, was used to reach the doorway above the stone in the southeast wall.

The thickness of the various walls is as follows: north, 2 feet; south, 2 feet; northeast, 1 foot 8 inches; southeast, 1 foot 7 inches; west, 1 foot 8 inches.

In the northwest corner there was a layer of drift sand about 4 inches thick against the wall, upon this rested eleven pitchers th came from the northwest corner of the room.   (Fig. 131.)   As this sand was stratified, it must have run in after this room had passed into disuse.   Then the pitchers must have been placed upon this sand and more must have washed in, for the pitchers were partly buried and stratified sand was found in them.   Another evidence that they were partly covered when the roof fell is that the part exposed shows the action of fire and smoke, whereas the lower part is unburnt.

Room 100.

Room 100 is situated in the northwestern part of the pueblo and is one of the new rooms of the outer series, at least, the northern part is new, for the southern half is very old.   The north wall forms part of the outer wall of the pueblo and is built of selected smooth-faced stones, chinked with thin layers of sandstone. The wall was not only well built and solidly put together, but the foundation was such that at the time of excavation it stood, almost, if not quite, as perfect as when it was built. The ceiling beams are 11 feet above the floor level and the wall towers 4 feet above the beam level. The wall has no doorways, the only break in its entire surface being the six ceiling beams, whose broken ends extend beyond the face of the wall.

The east wall of the new part extends southward a distance of 8 feet, where it joins the old wall. It is made of the same type of material as the north wall, and is standing at its north end to the height of 15 feet. There is a rectangular doorway in the north end that is 1 foot 10 inches above the floor, 1 foot 9 inches south of the north wall, and 3 inches wider at the bottom than at the top. The sill is composed of flat stones; the lintel is formed by seven poles that average $1\frac{1}{2}$ inches in diameter. There is a peculiar place about midway between the doorway and the south end of the new wall and about on the level of the upper part of the doorway. There had been a slight depression in this part of the wall, probably 1 foot square; this was filled with plaster after the wall was completed and while the plaster was still soft, thin pieces of sandstone had been forced in so that only the edges showed, which gave a very peculiar surface. Some of the pieces were removed and placed with the material from the room.

The old wall that forms part of this room extends southward a distance of 8 feet, thereby making this side of the room 17 feet long. The foundation stones of this wall are over 3 feet above the floor level of the new room. These stones are large flat slabs of sandstone and rest upon a stratified bed of yellow sand. About 1 foot above the floor level of the new room there is a stratum of charcoal about 1 inch thick which extends, on about the same plane, almost the entire length of the exposed sand. The wall itself is of the oldest type found in the ruin, it is composed of large flat uneven stones, that in many cases have sharp edges. These were laid with a thin layer of plaster between them and the space between the ends filled with plaster; the whole face of the wall was then covered with a layer of plaster and thin pieces of sandstone. This facing gave the whole surface of the wall the appearance of being chinked, as the stones protrude from the plaster as though they had been forced in only part of the way. The facing has fallen on the greater part of the wall, but on the lower part and at the south end, it is intact. The wall stands to a height of 11 feet 6 inches above the floor level of the new part, and has a break near the south end that may have been a doorway.

The south wall is built in the same manner and has been faced in the same way as the last one described. The foundation stones are large heavy pieces of sandstone, and extend even below the floor level of the new section.

There is a bench 1 foot 3 inches wide and 3 feet above the floor level on which this wall rests; from this bench to the ceiling beams the facing has fallen save in the east corner near the beams. Three of the beams from the room south of this one protrude from the wall, two of them being over 2 feet long. About 1 foot above these beams are six openings where the roof timbers of the room had entered, these were from 3 inches to 4 inches in diameter, and the wall all about them was blackened from the smoke made by the burning beams. The wall above these beams is the same as the lower part, but the facing was of even smaller stones than that of the lower part, or of the east wall. This wall is standing to a height of about 14 feet. About 3 feet above the ceiling level of this room the ends of five sticks can be seen. These were no doubt the ends of the ceiling beams of the upper room of Room 104. The wall is abutted by the east and west walls and extends westward, forming the south wall of Room 101.

The west wall is solid and forms one of the finest squares of masonry to be found in the pueblo. It is built of selected faced stones, carefully chinked. The only break of any consequence is near the center and just above the ceiling level; here a few stones have been displaced, but not enough to mar the solid appearance of the wall.

The east wall of the new part rests upon a wall that may have been a part of the old building, it projects into the room about 2 feet near the north wall, but seems to have no relation to the present room.

The ceiling of this new room was made with the individual willow strips, such as were used in all the rooms of this outer series. The ceiling over the old part had been almost covered with willows, but the ceiling above was built of slabs to support the adobe.

The measurement of the various walls gave a thickness for each as follows: north, 2 feet 5 inches; south, 1 foot 1 inch, and above the upper ceiling beams, 1 foot 3 inches; east wall of new part, 1 foot 5 inches; east wall of old part, 1 foot; west, 1 foot 6 inches.

This room is just west of and next to the old darkroom and east of Rooms 93 and 101. It is north of Room 104 and its north wall forms the outer one of the pueblo.

Room 101.

Room 101 is situated just southeast of and adjoining Room 93. It is one of the new series of rooms and is bounded on the southeast by Room 107, on the northeast by Room 100, and on the southwest by the angular space between the old and new wall, which was not worked out. The northeast wall is typical of the new form of masonry, and extends from the southeast wall of this room to the outer northwest wall of the ruin, forming the northeast wall of Room 93 in its course. It is built of the same kind of faced stones and chinked in the same manner as the other walls of the series. The surface is devoid of plaster, but is solid and perfect from the floor to the top, which is the same height as in Room 93.

The southwest wall is a small division wall that abuts on both the old and new wall. It is of the new style of masonry and its surface is unbroken. There is a jog at the level of the ceiling beams about 5 inches wide which lessens the width of the upper wall. All the lower part of this wall is blackened but the part above the ceiling beam level is the natural color.

The northwest wall is of the more recent type and is in good condition save at the upper central part where the upper portion of the doorway has fallen.

The doorway is of the rectangular type and although the outlines are discernible, it is in a fallen condition. The only break in the wall, barring the doorway, is an opening near the northeast wall, about 10 inches square, with a flat stone for the top and two of the regular small stones for the bottom. It extended into Room 93 and was either for ventilation or for a communicating doorway between the rooms, probably both.

About 1 foot above the passageway where a beam has entered there is an opening about 10 inches in diameter. Near the southwest end of this wall, which abuts on the northeast one, the ends of about fifteen ceiling beams may be seen.

The southeast wall was the old outer wall of the pueblo. It is made of rough uneven stones and the surface is composed of a facing of thin pieces of sandstone with only the edges showing. It is rounded to some extent, while the northwest wall presents a straight surface. The upper part of this wall fell during the progress of the work, and therefore no record of its surface peculiarities could be obtained. The lower part, however, remained intact and rested upon a foundation of large flat stones.

The work in this room was carried to a depth of several feet below the floor level. The walls showed a comparatively uniform thickness, the measurements being as follows: northwest, 1 foot 7 inches; southeast, 1 foot 5 inches; northeast, 1 foot 6 inches; southwest, 1 foot 6 inches.

Room 102.

Room 102 is a large room of the old outer series in the western part of the pueblo and is bounded on the northwest by Room 94, on the northeast by Room 107, on the southeast by Room 108, and on the southwest by Room 103. The south wall (southeast) has a rectangular doorway in the lower central part; it is 5 feet 4 inches above the floor. The top floor has fallen, but the sides are in good condition. They are well plastered and rounded. This wall is built of rough flat stones with uneven edges. At one time, the surface was evidently covered with a heavy layer of plaster which covered all the irregularities caused by the undressed stones.

At the north end the corner was rounded with stones. There were no other breaks in the wall; all of the other walls were plain and had no doorways or other openings. All the walls were built of the same flat stones and presented quite a contrast when viewed in connection with the uneven walls.

The northeast and southwest walls were quite thin and abutted on the northwest and southeast walls. One of the ceiling beams is in position near the northeast wall and others were found near it, but were broken. The walls showed a thickness as follows: northwest, 1 foot 6 inches (approximate, not dug out); southeast, 1 foot 5 inches; northeast, 1 foot 2 inches; southwest, 10 inches. This room was seemingly filled with refuse stones and débris and in the mass a number of dog skeletons and part of a beam were found.

Room 103.

Room 103 is another room of the old outer series. It is separated from Room 102 by a thin division wall and bounded on the west by Rooms 94–95; on the east, lies Room 109; on the south, it is flanked by an unworked room.

The northern part of this room had been cleared to the floor level by other parties, so that our work consisted in the removal of enough of the remaining débris to make sure that there was nothing in the room.

There was a doorway in the south wall, but its limits could not be de-fined. The other walls had no doorways. They were built of large flat stones and were even more unstable than those in Room 102. ⸜ The plaster had not only washed from the surface, but also from between the stones, leaving practically a dry wall.

The room had evidently been considered unsafe and had been filled with adobe and stones. At all events, these were the materials en-countered, and they were packed in in such a way that there must have been a method in the filling. The floor level was over 15 feet below the surface and the ceiling was 11 feet above the same point. The thickness of the various walls was as follows: north, 10 inches; south, 11 inches; east, 2 feet.

Room 104.

Room 104 is a small room just south of Room 100, the south wall of Room 100 forming the north wall of this room. This wall is one of the old series and is built of large flat stones, as described under Room 100. On this side, however, it is covered with a thick layer of plaster that is rounded at the bottom, thereby making the floor cup-shaped at this end. This wall is 11 inches thick from the floor to a height of 3 feet 3 inches above it; from this point to the top it averages 1 foot 1 inch in thickness, but in some places it projects beyond the lower wall over 6 inches. The plaster on the surface of this wall is in good condition save at the upper and lower part of the west end.

The east end abuts on the east wall, but passes the west wall and forms the north wall of Room 107. The south wall is also roughly built and covered with plaster which conceals the sharp irregular edges of the stones. It abuts on the east wall, but extends westward beyond the west wall. It is 9 inches thick and well preserved for an old wall.

The east wall is also of the old series, built in the same manner as the other two, and 1 foot thick. Its surface is covered with plaster, most of it in good condition. The wall is standing only 2 feet above the floor and bulges near the north wall. At the bottom the plaster is rounded as at the north side; the wall extends from the south end of the new east wall of Room 100 to the south wall of this room; here it joins the thick east wall of Room 111.

The west wall is a division wall and is of the new type of masonry; it abuts on the north and south walls and is composed of very large and thick stones and chinked with uncommonly large pieces of sand stone. It is 2 feet 2 inches thick and has no plaster on its surface. It is one of the thickest walls noted in the ruin.

The floor is heavily plastered with adobe and is rounded or cupped, on the north, east, and south parts. There is a large post in the southeast corner, 7½ inches thick and standing 2 feet 3 inches above the floor. It was probably used as a step in getting out of the room, the doorway probably being in the ceiling. The beams under the overhanging part of the north wall were seemingly placed there to support the upper part for there are no holes in the wall opposite, and everything points to the fact that this ceiling was much higher than this level. These beams are all broken, but they probably extended no further than the edge of the overhanging wall. The two beams in the east end of the wall have fallen out but the angle of the holes in the wall suggests that the beams, had they been long ones, would have reached almost to the floor on the south side of the room; then too there are some willows in place over the beams that seem to indicate that the space between the beams and the wall stones was filled with willows and then plastered. The walls had fallen to such an extent that the ceiling level could not be located.

Room 105.

Room 105 is situated just west of and adjoins Room 25. It is well built and is part of the new section that extends along the western part of the pueblo. It had evidently passed into disuse, for it was used as a rubbish pit.

The north wall, below the ceiling beams, is built of the typical large faced stones, but the chinking is of much larger pieces of sandstone than the new masonry in the northwestern part of the ruin. It abuts on the east and west walls and has a very high rectangular doorway in the lower central part. There are no other openings in the walls and save for a small space about the doorway the wall is in perfect condition. The doorway is filled with sand and rubbish and the lintel is composed of poles. This wall may have been covered with plaster, but none of it now remains. Part of the upper story wall is still standing and in it there is a rectangular doorway, that has eight poles for the lintel. The wall itself is of the same type as the lower part, but most of the stones used for chinking have fallen out. This wall has been exposed to the elements and therefore presents a much warmer surface than the walls of the lower room.

The south wall is really a counterpart of the north wall; it is built in the same manner and of the same kind of material and has a high doorway in the lower central part. This doorway has a double lintel, a space of about 4 inches intervening; this space was filled with mortar. The lintel poles are much smaller than in the north doorway, being only 1½ inches in diameter. The west edge of the doorway was straight and well-squared, but the opposite side was bulged near the bottom, thereby ruining whatever symmetry it may have had. The sides were not plastered and the opening was filled with stones and rubbish. The western part near the ceiling level, was cracked and badly broken, and there was quite a space at the beam level where the stones had fallen out. There was no plaster on this wall and barring the defects mentioned, it is in good condition.

The second story wall is still standing to a height of about 8 feet and, save in a few places where individual stones had fallen out, presents an unbroken surface. It is built of faced stones and, as in the opposite wall, most of the chinking has disappeared. This wall (south) abuts on the east and west walls, and as a partition wall, is very solid.

The east wall is very solid and presents as fine a specimen of alternating layers as can be found in this part of the ruin. Layers of large faced stones are sandwiched between broad layers of well-laid small pieces which give a very pleasing effect and form a good wall, the best work in the upper northern part. There has evidently been a doorway in the lower center of this wall, but all traces of it have been destroyed by the stones being either torn out or having fallen from their places; at all events, at present there is only an opening about 4 feet high by 2 feet wide, that breaks the otherwise perfect surface of the wall.

There is a jog at the north end of this wall that runs in a northwest direction and cuts off a corner of the room. This angular wall originally formed the west wall of Room 25 and part of it still projects into that room. The wall of Room 105 really abuts on this wall, or, in other words, marks the starting point of the east wall of Room 105 and extends southward. As the walls are built into each other and the workmanship is the same, there is therefore no break where they join.

The main wall is not plastered, but the lower part of the angular wall is covered with quite a heavy layer. About 5 feet from the floor and 10 inches from the jutting wall, there is an opening in the angle wall where a stone has fallen out. Through this place a beam fully 5 inches in diameter may be seen; it is placed horizontally in the wall and was evidently put there to strengthen it. The whole east wall, including the angle part, stands to a height of 1 foot above the ceiling beams, six of which protude from the wall.

The west wall is solidly built, but is warped to such an extent that the surface presents a series of waves. There are a few stones that have been detached in various places but otherwise, the wall is intact. There is a rectangular doorway in the central part that is filled with a well-laid wall, its sides are unplastered and the edges are well-squared, but the masonry is so nearly like that of the main wall that it almost seems that it was closed when the wall was made, and that the opening was simply made for some future use. There are eight lintel poles in place that average 3 inches in diameter. The only portion of this wall that is standing above the level of the ceiling beams is at the south end; here a piece about 3 feet wide reaches a height of 6 feet. The surface of this wall is devoid of plaster.

The floor of this room was uneven, but was hard, as is the case in most of the rooms. The walls were uniform in thickness and showed the following measurements: north, 2 feet; south, 1 foot 11 inches; east at north end, 4 feet 3 inches; east at end of main wall, 2 feet 4 inches; east at south end, 2 feet 7 inches; west, 2 feet 3½ inches; center, 2 feet 5 inches; angular wall, 1 foot 7 inches.

Room 106.

Room 106 is situated just east of Room 25; its north wall forms the south wall of that room. Work was commenced in the southeast part and had been carried to a depth of but a few feet when a copper bell was found. (Fig. 132.)

Fig. 132.   Two Copper Bells from Room 106.

What had at first appeared to be one large room soon proved to be two rooms, for a division wall was found as the work progressed. This wall was about 4 feet 2 inches west of the east wall and proved to be only 4 feet high, its foundation being the débris with which the room was filled. It averaged 1 foot 3 inches in thickness and was not a well built wall.

When Room 106b was worked, the division wall had to be removed for safety's sake. When all the débris had been removed, a very aesthetic room was seen, the walls were so even and well laid. The material in the room was simply the waste from the houses, but before the western part was complete, a second copper bell was brought to light. This was found near the floor level and only a few inches from the west wall.

The north wall of this room presents as perfect a surface as one would wish to see; it is made of large smooth-faced stones and chinked with small pieces of sandstone, and although a great portion of the plaster is still in place, the wall would have been an ornament to any room without being covered. There is not a break in the surface: it is one of the most even to be found in the pueblo. This wall abuts on the east wall, but its western end either passes the end of the west wall, or else that wall is built into it, a point that can be determined when the next room is worked.

The south wall is a division wall and abuts on the east and west walls; it is made of large faced stones and is chinked after the manner of the north wall. There is a round piece of sandstone embedded in the lower west central part of the wall, more properly speaking, it is a cylindrical piece with the faced end forming a part of the wall. There are a few loose stones in the central part, but otherwise the surface is unbroken; this wall also retains some of its plaster.

The east wall is built of smaller stones than the north and south walls, and there is an absence of the pronounced chinking. There is a rectangular doorway in the lower central part that is filled with well-laid stones. The stones above the doorway have fallen, thereby loosening the wall above. This has caused a collapse that has greatly damaged the upper central part of the wall. Most of the plaster is still in place and the wall was a very solid as well as artistic one.

The west wall is similar to the east wall in the form of its masonry; the stones are slightly larger, but there is the same absence of chinking. There is a rectangular door in the lower central part that is filled with rubbish; the lower part of the doorway has been filled with stones. From the extent of the sides it seems that it at one time extended below the floor level. A great deal of the plaster is still in place on the lower part.

The position of the ceiling beams could not be ascertained as the walls had fallen below the ceiling level. The floor was rather uneven and there were fireplaces in the east-central and northeast part.

Room 107.

Room 107 is just south of Room 104 and north of Room 102; to the west lies Room 101, and to the east, Room 108. Three walls of this room belong to the old period, but the north wall is new.

The north wall is built of large pieces of sandstone and chinked with quite large pieces of the same material. It is a very strong wall, abutting on the east and west walls and its surface is unbroken. Its purpose was evidently to brace the thin walls at either side of the room. It was evidently built at the same time that the north wall of Room 101 and Room 93 was constructed. Its surface is devoid of plaster and, as there are smoke streaks on the stones, it probably was left unplastered.

The south wall was a thin partition wall of the old type, the rough irregular stones of which it was made being covered with plaster. There was no doorway in this wall and the ends had been built into the east and west walls to strengthen them.

The east wall was built of various sized flat stones, in the southern and upper parts small stones predominated, but the northern part, both above and below this doorway, was made of large slabs. There is a rectangular doorway in the north central part that has a board for a lintel, and the plaster at the sides is rounded.

About 1 foot 6 inches above this doorway, the ends of three ceiling beams protrude from the wall, which extends about 4 feet above them. At one time, this wall had been heavily plastered but most of that on the upper part has fallen. On the lower part almost all of it is in place. The north end of the wall is lost behind the heavy abutting northeast wall; it formed the east wall of Room 104, where it joins the south wall. The plaster is rounded.

The west wall is composed of large flat irregular stones and most of the plaster has been washed from between them. There are no openings in the wall and it is in poor condition for even an old wall.

The floor was still in place and on it were found a number of interesting arrow foreshafts (Fig. 133), also a stone knife with a handle (Fig. 134). This floor when torn up, showed first a layer of adobe, below this was a layer of cedarbark, and then another smoothed adobe surface into which the cedarbark had been partly pressed by the upper adobe stratum. Next was another layer of cedarbark, then a layer of split pine boards, or slabs, that rested upon the finest series of poles noted in the ruins. These poles ran north and south and in turn rested upon a series of logs that extended east and west and almost filled the space, as did the poles; above them were four new timbers which were, on an average, 5 inches in diameter, all but one of which had been broken by the weight of the débris that rested on the floor.

The old series of beams, which were blackened by smoke and soot, were seemingly cottonwood poles of various sizes, shapes, and conditions;

Fig. 133.   Foreshaft of an Arrow from Room 107.

Fig. 134.   Hafted Stone Knife from Room 107.

Fig. 135 (8473).   Decorated Bone Scraper from Room 108.

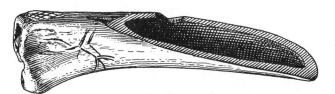

Fig. 136 ab (10717, 9446).   Knife Handles from Rooms 171 and 110.

327

these were decayed and the new timbers probably put in when the general changes were in progress in this part of the pueblo. All of the ceiling poles were saved, also specimens of the new and old timbers, and some of the split slabs.

The lower part of this room was similar to the upper part; the north wall extended to the floor level and its surface was as well made as at its upper part. There were no breaks in its surface as in the upper part. Its surface was devoid of plaster.

The south wall had an unbroken surface and was covered with a thick layer of well-smoothed plaster; it was so smooth that it was particularly noticeable.

The east wall was built on a foundation of large flat stones that formed a bench 2 feet 6 inches high and 1 foot wide; the surface of this bench was made of slabs of sandstone standing on edge; and the upper and northern parts were plastered. There is a doorway just above this ledge and about 2 feet 6 inches from the north wall. It is of the rectangular type; a ring of plaster about 6 inches wide extends around it and forms a rounding surface at the edges of the doorway. This wall was well plastered and in its upper part there were two pegs. The south corner is rounded and the plaster is very thick at this point. The doorway has a lintel composed of poles.

The west wall is made of large flat pieces of sandstone and almost all of the plaster has washed from between them. There is no opening in its surface and its condition is practically the same as the room above.

The floor was of the usual adobe and there were no fireplaces in evidence.

The walls of the upper and lower rooms were practically the same in width and measured as follows: north, 2 feet 2 inches; south, 1 foot 2 inches; east-west, 1 foot 3 inches. The north and south walls were straight but the other two showed quite a curve.

Rooms 108 and 109.

These rooms overlie the underground rooms described in connection with Room 3. Nothing of interest developed in their examination except a few specimens, one of which is shown in Fig. 135.

Room 110.

Room 110 is situated just north of Room 57; on its eastern side lie Rooms 58 and 63; on its north is Room 111, and on the west, Room 108. This room is one of the highest perfect rooms in the pueblo; it is part of the old building and below it are two open rooms. These were described in 1896 in the series of underground rooms. (See p. 39). The one directly beneath Room 110 is the one through which we gained entrance to the series; this was through a hole broken in the wall and not a regular doorway, the lower room was reached through a hole in the northwest corner.

Room 100 is a bin-like affair; the sameness of the plastered walls was relieved by a doorway in the east wall and the end of a large beam in the south wall.

The north wall presents a plain plastered surface, it abuts on the east and west walls and is composed of various sizes of irregularly shaped laminae of sandstone.

The south wall has a well-plastered surface and is unbroken save at a point 1 foot 1¾ inches from the floor and 10 inches from the east wall line, a beam 10½ inches in diameter is to be seen, its smooth end flush with the wall surface. This wall is built of irregularly shaped stones and abuts on the west wall.

The east wall is well plastered and has a doorway near the central part, it is of the rectangular form and has a stone slab for the sill, only part of it remains as the wall has fallen, carrying part of the top away.

Two feet ten inches from the south wall and 4 feet 6 inches from the floor, there is a beam rest in the wall. It is about 3 inches in diameter and about the same in depth. There is a corresponding place in the west wall that is also built of flat irregular stones and abuts on the south wall.

The west wall has, in keeping with the others, a heavy layer of plaster on its surface. This gave the room a finished appearance and besides hiding the rough stones, served to strengthen the wall. There are no openings in its surface, but 8 inches north of the south wall and 4 feet 6½ inches from the floor, there is a sort of pocket; it is an irregular affair and measures 7 inches in width by 5 inches in height and extends into the wall about 6 inches, the top is arched and very little care was shown in making it. The beam support mentioned as being in this wall is 2 feet 11 inches from the south wall and 4 feet 7 inches from the floor. The plaster has fallen from about its edges, but its dimensions are about the same as the one opposite. The walls of this room average 5 feet 6 inches in height, all of them being below the ceiling level, as no evidences of that point are to be seen. The floor is well plastered and in good condition and the thickness of the walls is as follows: north, 1 foot 5 inches; south, 1 foot; east, 1 foot 6 inches; west, 1 foot 3 inches.

There is a wall that forms part of the east wall of Room 97 (92) and runs parallel with the west wall of Room 110 and rests against it, making a thickness of 3 feet.

Room 111.

Room 111 lies just north of Room 110, south of Room 104, east of Room 108, and west of Room 63. The lower part of this room was broken into through the south wall in 1896 and added another to the list of underground rooms. A part of the upper room was exposed and during the winter of 1897–98 Al. Wetherill, Thomasita, a Navajo, and O. H. Buck, dug out of the débris that rested upon the floor, and then after removing the floor beams, continued their work beneath the floor level of the lower room. It was in this place that the large corrugated olla, purchased from Mr. Buck, was found. This room is part of the old series, the walls being composed of irregularly shaped stones and the surface heavily plastered, as in Room 110. There are no openings in the upper walls, and where they have been exposed to the elements a goodly portion of the edges of the stones are showing, the plaster having washed out. No ceiling beams were used, but the poles ran east and west. In the description given in 1896 mention was made of beams that ran north and south under the ceiling poles and parallel with and near the east and west walls, these were supported on posts and served in lieu of beams, such as are usually set into the walls.

The lower room is well plastered and there is a doorway of the rectangular type in the west side but otherwise the walls present unbroken surfaces.

The doorway in the west wall is of the rectangular type and has poles for a lintel. About 4 inches below the poles there is a board and the space between is filled with thin slabs and plaster. The sides have been covered with a heavy layer of plaster that was rounded at the top.

The lower part of the north wall slants northward fully 8 inches from the perpendicular, but the top wall is comparatively straight. The south wall abuts on the east and west walls, the west wall abuts on the north as does also the east. The inner surface of the east wall, if extended, would be almost on a line with the outer surface of the east wall of Room 104, but the east (Room 111) wall is rounded where it joins the north wall.

The thickness of the walls is as follows: north, 9 inches at top but wider at the lower part; south, 1 foot 5 inches; east, 1 foot 9 inches; and west, 1 foot 6 inches.

Rooms 112 and 113.

These rooms adjoin Rooms 103 and 109 and contain nothing of special interest. However, attention may be called to the exposed ceiling of Room 112 (Fig. 137) showing a detail of construction.

Fig. 137.   Detail of Ceiling in Room 112.

Room 114.

Room 114 is one of the outer series of rooms of the western part of the pueblo. It is bounded on the north by Room 96, on the south by Room 115, on the east by an unworked room, and on the west by the outer ruin wall. It is one of the new series of rooms as shown by the faced stones and general appearance of the masonry.

The floor of the room was comparatively level and showed no evidences of fireplaces.

The north wall was a partition wall and abutted on the east and west walls. It is built of large faced stones and chinked with smaller ones. No plaster is in evidence on the surface. There is a well-built doorway in the lower central part; it is broad at the bottom but decreases in width toward the lintel, which is composed of poles; there are eight of them laid so that the sides touch. The first one is visible on the eastern side of the opening and extends 1½ feet into the wall. Some of the chinking has fallen on the western side revealing a withe ½ inch broad that evidently held the poles together while the wall was being built. The sides of the doorway are well-laid, but there is no plaster on them. There are no other openings in this wall.

Fig. 138.   Fig. 139.

Fig. 138.   Jet Ornament with Bird Wing Design Carved on Surface, Room 131.
Fig. 139 (12819).   Wooden Object Painted in Red, Yellow, and Green, Room 169.

The south wall was practically a counterpart of the north, built in the same way, of the same material, abutting on the east and west walls and having the same form of doorway in the lower central part.

The doorway was the same in form as the other, but the lintel poles were not so well preserved; they were about 2 inches in diameter and there were seven of them; the outer one extended on the west side of the doorway. To the west side of the doorway to the west wall, on the opposite side, it was covered with the masonry. This wall was also devoid of plaster.

The east wall presented one long surface of beautiful masonry; there were no doorways nor openings of any kind to break the surface and every stone was in place. It was of the new form of masonry and in a perfect state of preservation. It was the sandwich form of wall, i. e., large faced stones separated by layers of thin pieces of sandstone; this interesting stratum averaging about 2 inches in thickness. This wall was strikingly convexed, the curve being more noticeable from the center to the north wall. A perpendicular section would show a slight bulge, which, however, was so general as to cause no special defect. The wall was straight to a height of about 4 feet from the floor level, the bulge commencing at that point. There was no plaster on the surface, although small pieces, covering some of the chinked parts, showed that there might have been a layer over the entire surface at one time.

The west wall was the same as the others from the masonry standpoint, but the stones were larger, on the average, than in the other three.

Fig. 140.   Fig. 141.

Fig. 140 (10350).   Dipper Handle, showing mending, Room 168.
Fig. 141 (10354).   Bone Ornament, Room 168.

There is a closed doorway in the lower central part and, in filling the space, the same form of stones was used as in the regular wall, and the layers of large and small pieces were faithfully carried out. Some of the stones had fallen or been taken from the top, which revealed a lintel of poles about 1½ inches in diameter; as nearly as could be ascertained, there were nine of these poles that formed the lintel. This doorway was rectangular in form and the corners were well pointed.

Just above and to the north of this doorway there is an opening in the wall about 1 foot in diameter where stones have been removed, the stones forming its edges are in place, and firm, and even the stratum of small stones at the bottom is in place; it is 5 feet 5 inches above the floor and is filled with débris, but the stones were evidently removed during occupancy. Barring these two openings the wall is unbroken and the unplastered surface presents a good specimen of probably the latest style of architecture in the building. There is a slight bulge in the wall beginning at the southern edge of the doorway and extending to the north wall, the area affected extending from the floor to a point 4 feet above it. Where this wall joins the north one there is an interval between them that at one place is 2 inches wide. This begins at the lintel level of the doorway in the north wall and extends to the top. It shows that the outer wall has drawn away from the north one, but were it not for the crack, it would not be noticeable.

The east, west, and south walls of this room are comparatively the same in height, but the north towers fully 4 feet above them at its eastern end. The north wall is 1 foot 6 inches; the east, 1 foot 6 inches; and the west, 2 feet 5 inches.

ROOM 115.

Room 115 is bounded on the north by Room 114, on the south by Room 116, on the west by the outer wall of the ruin, and on the east by an unworked room of the old series. This room is one of the new series that stretches along the western part of the ruin. The masonry is the same as that of Room 114.

The north wall is in perfect condition and presents the same characteristics as on its north side, in Room 114. The doorway is larger at the bottom than at the top and the first lintel pole almost reaches both the east and west wall.

The south wall is built of the same form of stones as the north and chinked in the same way. The eastern part of this wall, from the height of the lintel of a doorway in the lower central part, about half the upper part, has been exposed for years and almost all of the plaster has been washed from between the large stones, thereby loosening the chinking. The doorway in the lower part of the wall is slightly narrower at the top than at the bottom, and has a lintel of poles, only two of which were visible, as the débris was not cleared away. These poles were about $1\frac{1}{2}$ inches in diameter. This wall, like the north wall, abutted on the east and west walls.

The east wall had no doorways nor other openings in its surface. The masonry was the same as that of the east wall of Room 114, of which it is a continuation. The northern and lower part of the wall is in good condition, but the upper southern part has been exposed, as was the adjoining part of the south wall, and the strata of small stones had fallen out in some places, and in others were loosened from the washing out of the plaster. Otherwise, the wall was in good condition.

The west wall is made of larger stones than the others, but as a rule the chinked layers are composed of smaller and thinner pieces than those in the outer walls. There are no doorways nor openings in the surface, but there is a closed doorway in the lower central part of the wall. In closing it the different horizontal strata were carried out, and it has the appearance of having been closed when the wall was made; simply built

Fig. 142.   Pottery Vessel.

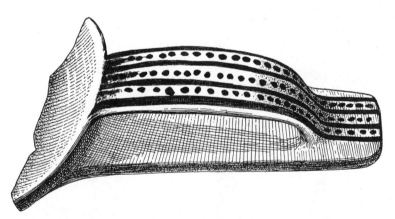

Fig. 143 (9780).   Handle of Pottery Incense Burner showing how Bowl was attached, Room 141.

Fig. 144. Floor of Room 159

Fig. 145. Interior of Kiva showing Ventilator, Room 162.

Fig. 146. Circular Room in Eastern Court, Room 190.

in to be used later if necessary. The wall around this doorway is weakened and some of the stones have fallen out. This wall is more broken in the upper central part than at the ends where it stands to the height of the north and south walls.

Rooms 116 to 190.

Minor excavations were made in a number of rooms ranging from Rooms 116 to 190. Nothing of special interest was developed in these excavations aside from the specimens shown in Figs. 138 to 154.

FIELD NOTES FOR EXCAVATIONS IN BURIAL MOUNDS.

June 1st. Commenced work on a mound situated on the southern side of Chaco Cañon and southwest from Pueblo Chettro Kettle.

The first find was a small pitcher on the north line in Section 1, 4 feet 4 inches from the eastern end of the section. Further digging revealed the skeleton of a child. The body was lying northwest by southeast, the head toward the southern point. The cranium was 2 inches below the surface and from the frontal bone to the eastern stakes was a distance of 3 feet $8\frac{1}{4}$ inches. The distance from the pelvic bone to the top of the cranium was 1 foot 3 inches, and from one elbow joint to the other $11\frac{1}{2}$ inches—the cup rested upon the left elbow. The leg bones could not be found. From the position of the skeleton, the head being the uppermost part, the bones should have been in place, but there is a possibility of their having been washed out.

Skeleton 2 was discovered six inches below the surface in Section 2. The right temporal bone was 1 foot $6\frac{1}{4}$ inches, from the eastern part of the section. The northern line of operations crossed the skeleton 1 inch below the clavicles where they were lying against the vertebrae. The skeleton was lying on its back with the knees bent upward and eastward; it was lying almost directly north and south, the head being at the latter point. The body measured 3 feet 4 inches in length as it lay in the ground. The skeleton was in such a condition that the bones could not be preserved.

Skeleton 3 was found 3 inches beneath the surface in Section 3. The distance from the occiput to the northern trench line was 11 inches and this point was 2 feet 2 inches west of the eastern line post. The skeleton was lying northeast by southwest, the head toward the northeast. The arm bones were lying close to the sides of the body, and the legs had been pressed up against the left side. Resting upon the right shoulder and against the upper jaw, was a bowl (H-49) 9 inches in diameter. It had been broken previous to interment as holes had been drilled in the several pieces in order to mend it—faint decorations on the interior were noticed.

Inside of this bowl was found a square piece of pottery (H-50). Resting against the left shoulder was a pitcher 7 inches high and 3 inches in diameter at the top. It had a handle and was complete,—faint ornamentation on the exterior.

Skeleton 4 was found in Section 4, 10 inches below the surface. The body, that of an adult, was lying on its back with legs drawn up toward the chin. It was lying east and west, the head toward the east. The distance from the eastern section stake to the left parietal bone, was 3 feet 4 inches, the greater part of the body was inside of the section, but the right shoulder and part of the ribs were outside, the head was crushed and the whole skeleton was very brittle. Resting against the left temple was a bowl

5½ inches in diameter, ornamented on the inside and of the usual whiteware (H-52). Almost touching the bowl was a pitcher (H-53), 5 inches high and 2¼ inches in diameter at the top. It has a corrugated handle and is ornamented on the outside. At the western part of the skeleton was a large bowl (H-54), part of the pelvis resting upon the rim. To the east of this bowl is a large stone that was probably placed in position beside the bowl.

Skeleton 5 was discovered 1 foot 1 inch below the surface in Section 4. The body was extended, lying northwest by southeast. At the head was a large bowl and in this, was a smaller bowl and a pitcher; at the feet were large portions of the rim and sides of a large corrugated pot. The body was in an advanced stage of decay, in fact some of the bones had wasted away. The body measured 5 feet as it rested in the ground. The head was 4 feet west of the eastern section post and 5 feet south from the northern line. The large bowl (H-55) at the head measured 10½ inches and had decorations on the interior. The smaller bowl (H-56), was 7 inches in diameter, decorated inside; the pitcher (H-57) was 6 inches high with a 3 inch opening. The corrugated jar (H-58) at the foot of the skeleton measured 8½ inches. The skeleton protruded 1 foot into Section 5 and the feet were 3 feet 6 inches from the northern line.

Skeleton 6 was found in Section 1, 4 feet below the surface. The body was lying on its back with the head resting on its left side, the right arm was folded across the body, and the left lay parallel with it, the femora were lying at right angles to the trunk. Five inches northeast of the upper jaw there stood a corrugated jar (H-59) 5½ inches high and 3½ inches in diameter at the top. Southeast of this jar was a water bottle (H-60) 8 inches high and 7½ inches in diameter in the middle. This bottle was broken, inside of it was a smaller one (H-61), also broken, 4½ inches in diameter at the middle, and 4½ inches high. The body was lying northwest by southeast, the head toward the former point. It was in the southern part of the first section, the head was 1 foot 1½ inches from the southern section line, and 2 feet 6 inches from the western line. The calcaneum and a few of the other bones of the right foot extended into Section 6. The body measured 3 feet 3 inches *in situ*.

Skeleton 7 was found 8 inches below the surface in Section 6. The body was lying upon its back, inclined a little on the right side. The left arm was folded across the breast, and the right was lying parallel with the side. The legs had been doubled up towards the chin˙and when the flesh decayed, fell a little outside of the body, i. e., to the south of it. The body measured 3 feet in length and was in fair condition compared with some of those near it. The body extended outward, to the east of the section, the part inside, the head, being 6 inches in length. From the northern section parts to the left temporal bone was 2 feet 5 inches. The body was lying almost directly east and west. Resting against the left ribs and almost touching the middle section of the left humerus, was a pitcher 6 inches high and 5 inches in diameter at the top. One peculiarity about this pitcher (H-62) is that the lines forming the ornamentation of the exterior are red, something never before observed on the pottery from this region. Resting against this pitcher and running south 10 inches from it was a rounded portion of a broken corrugated jar (H-63).

Skeleton 8 was found in Section 1, 4 inches below the surface, i.e., measuring from the uppermost portion of the cranium, as all such measurements are made. The body was lying northwest by southeast, the head toward the latter point. The skeleton measured 3 feet 4 inches *in situ*, the head projecting outside of the eastern section line 7½ inches. The distance from the southern section part on the eastern side to the left temporal bone, was 2 feet 7 inches. The femora had projected above the surface and were broken off about the middle. The body was greatly decayed, the face being entirely gone, and nothing was found with it.

Skeleton 9 was found in Section 6, 3 inches below the surface. The body was lying upon its back with the legs drawn up across the trunk, it measured 2 feet 10 inches *in situ* and was lying north and south, the head being toward the south. The head was 1 foot west of the eastern section line and 2 feet 7 inches from the northern line. Near the head of the northeastern side was a portion of a jar (H-64), the only pottery found with the body. Resting near the left femur was a bone awl (H-65).

Skeleton 10 was found outside and to the east of Section 6, and 3 feet below the surface. From the eastern section line of Skeleton 6 to the lower jaw was 3 feet 1 inch, and from the northern section line, carried out, 1 foot. The body was lying north and south and was decayed to such an extent that I had trouble in getting even its outlines for a photograph. It was the body of a child and resting against its frontal bone, was a pitcher (H-66) 4 inches high and 2 inches in diameter. At the opening, and just to the north of this was a fragment of a vessel showing part of the rim (H-67).

Skeleton 11 was found in Section 11 with the head 1 foot 2 inches below the surface. The body measured 5 feet 9 inches as it lay in the ground. It was lying on its back with the legs bent upward and the soil was so hard that the bones had preserved their upright position where the flesh had decayed. The arms were stretched at the sides and the body was lying about east and west, the head toward the latter point. The knees were 1 foot below the surface. The left temporal bone was 5 feet 4 inches from the northern section line and 2 feet 8 inches from the western section line was the occiput.

A body was found in a narrow strip between two holes that had been dug by the Wetherill party during the winter of 1895–96. All that was found of the body was the upper portion of the cranium which was mashed almost flat. Near the fragments of the skull were found a broken jar of corrugated ware (H-72) and a fragment of another vessel (H-73). These were preserved, but no measurements were taken defining the position of the remains, as it was that part of the mound that had been dug out by other parties. About 3 feet away from the corrugated jar in the side of one of the holes, where a skeleton had been unearthed, was found a small bone celt (H-75) ornamented with lines running around the implement. Nothing else could be found in the vicinity. During the general digging a shell ornament (H-74) was found in the surface soil.

Our next place of operation was a burial mound near the mouth of the cañon that runs south from Chaco. It was on the right hand side facing south and is in reality in the Chaco limits. Richard Wetherill had done some excavating here. One of the peculiar things found during his digging was a stone grave, one stone of which was still in place. It was about 1 foot below the surface and consisted of two large flat stones placed on edge about 2 feet apart. Between these the body had been placed and the soil filled in upon it, then on the sand were placed a number of flat stones, but these were some inches above the upper edge of the grave stones. I mapped out a line 40 feet long and running about east and west. This was on the southern side of the mound. I divided this line into five parts and then squared each part, thereby giving me five sections, each 8 feet square. These sections were numbered, commencing from the eastern end.

Skeleton 12 was found in Section 4 and was 3 feet 3 inches below the surface. The skeleton was lying west-northwest and east-southeast and measured 3 feet 3 inches *in situ*. From the southern section line to the top of the skull was 4 feet 4 inches and from the lower jaw to the eastern section line was 5 inches. The body was lying upon its back with the head facing east. The body was lying with its head toward the northwest point of the above position. The bones were the softest we had encountered and it was therefore hard to get them uncovered for photographing. About 1 foot 6 inches above the body a mass of stones was found, some of them being 3 feet long by 2 feet wide. They were quite thin but had not been dressed in any way. There were seven or eight, which made quite a layer over the body. About half the body extended into Section 3.

Skeleton 13 was found in Section 7, about 9 inches below the surface. The bones lay about and were greatly disconnected. The head was 2 inches north of the southern section line and 5 inches east from the western section line. The body was lying northwest by southeast, the head toward the northwest. The head, indicated by a single piece, was just northwest of the large bowl (H-77), and probably the bowl rested against it. Three feet from the large bowl was a smaller one (H-78) broken, and about 6 inches south of this was a sandstone gourd (H-79), broken in half, that may have been used. About 8 inches of the skeleton, the femora, etc., projected south into Section 2. The body was 3 feet 10 inches long as it lay in the grave.

Skeleton 14 was found in Section 6 with the head 2 feet below the surface. It was enclosed in a stone grave. The head was lying under a large flat stone and had been flattened by it. From the southern section line to the skull was 8 inches and 10 inches east from the western section line. The large flat slab was facing due northeast and was standing on end inclined toward the north. It was 1 foot 8 inches long and the same in width. It had no doubt originally rested in a horizontal position, but had settled to its present position, either through the natural settling of the sand or from being undermined by rats. The stones as they lay formed a pyramidal space, the base being toward the north. The side along the large slab measured 1 foot 10 inches, the opposite side, which was formed by a stone that had been used to grind axes, measured 1 foot 9 inches and the base was 1 foot 3 inches long. The place worn in the stone where axes had been ground was 9 inches long, 4 inches wide, and about 1½ inches deep in the center. The grave was photographed, before the stones were removed, and a photograph was also taken showing the head as it rested under the large slab.

In Section 5 a rubbing stone (H-80) was found. It was 3 feet below the surface, 4 feet north of the southern section line, and 6 inches west of the eastern line.

A bowl (H-81) was found in the northern part of section 4; it was 1 foot below the surface, 2 feet 4 inches west of the eastern line, and 7 inches south of the northern section lines. It was broken into small pieces, probably from the weight of the earth.

A pendant made from a piece of red pottery (H-83), possibly a handle, that has a hole drilled through the narrow end, was found 6 inches below the surface in the center of Section 8.

A shell ornament (H-84) was found near a piece of a child's skull, 2 feet below the surface in Section 7. It was 1 foot south of the northern section line and 5 feet west of the eastern section line; no other bones were found near it.

Skeleton 15 was that of a small child, measuring 1 foot 10 inches as it lay in the grave. It was found in the northwestern part of Section 6 and projected into Section

Fig. 147. Ceiling and Wall Structure of a Room in the Northern Part of the Ruin.

343

Fig. 148.   Pictograph on Rock in Chaco Cañon.

Fig. 149.   Outer North Wall of Bonito, looking northwest from Within, showing Junction of Old and New Walls.

Fig. 150. A Closed Doorway.

Fig. 151. A Corner Doorway.

345

Fig. 152.   A Partly Closed Doorway.

Fig. 153.   An Open Doorway.

7. It was 1 foot 7 inches below the surface and was in the gravel bottom, whereas all the other skeletons were in the sub-soil. The body was lying northwest by southeast, the head toward the former point. The body was lying upon its back with the arms at the side; the legs were at right angles to the trunk, the right femur being across the pelvis.

Skeleton 16 was found 1 foot below the surface in Section 9. In a caving of the bank the face was brought to view and when the earth fell it carried with it the greater part of two pieces of pottery that had been buried with the skeleton. One piece of the large bowl (H-85) was left in the bank, and the balance with the corrugated jar (H-86), was among the clods of earth below it. The head was uncovered enough to show its position, and the bank, pottery and all, was left just as it was when the bank fell. The head was 1 foot 10 inches from the northern line of Section 9 and 3 feet 7 inches from the western line of the same section. The pottery had rested against the lower jaw, as the piece in the bank shows. The fragments of a red bowl (H-91) were found under the corrugated jar mentioned above.

Skeleton 17 was found in a fragmentary condition just east of Skeleton 15. It was in Section 6 and was lying 8 inches below the surface. The bones looked as though they had been thrown into the hole and no definite direction could be ascertained from the few bones that remained.

Skeleton 18 was found 1 foot 6 inches below the surface in Section 12. Only a few teeth and portions of the ribs were found in position. In the surrounding soil, in rat holes, were found fragments of vertebrae and other bones. The body was probably lying northwest by southeast, the head toward the former position, for at that point some teeth and fragments of the skull were found. Seven inches south of the teeth was a corrugated jar (H-88) 6 inches deep and 4½ inches in diameter at the top. One foot one inch east of this jar was a bowl 4½ inches deep and 8 inches in diameter, ornamented on the interior with a design composed of broad lines (H-89).

The bone awl (H-90) was found 3 feet deep in Section 9; it was 3 feet south of the north section and 1 foot east from the western section line.

A portion of a red bowl (H-91) found under the corrugated jar (H-86) when the pottery was removed from the place where it fell is mentioned under the description of Skeleton 16.

In Section 11 there were some pieces of bone and there had probably been a skeleton there, but as there were no vessels nor any implements near the place, we could not be certain that it had been an entire body.

Skeletons 13, 14, 15 were unproductive and as there was no evidence of other remains, which we ascertained by sounding in various places, I concluded to stop operations in this part of the mound, so mapped out another section having a fronting of 40 feet facing the west. It was on the same side of the hill but further to the north.

The new trench line was mapped out so that it ran directly north and south. We commenced at the foot of the hill, which was toward the east, and worked in a westerly direction.

The first skeleton, 19, was found 1 foot below the surface in Section 1, this being the one at the southern end of the trench.

The body was that of an adult, probably a male, and was lying on its back; the right hand was lying across the abdomen and the left arm was stretched along the side of the body. The femora were standing in a perpendicular position and no tibiae or fibulae could be found, and only fragments of the foot bones. The left side of the superior maxillary was missing and was possibly carried away by rats. The bones of the body were better preserved than any we had found before, but the cranium was in a very bad condition. The body was lying north and south, the head being toward the south. From the northern line of Section 1, to the pelvic bone was 8 inches, and from the western stake line to the same point was 2 feet 5 inches. The body measured 2 feet 10 inches *in situ.*

Fig. 154.   Burial in Mound No. 2, Skeleton 20.

Skeleton 20 was found 1 foot 6 inches below the surface in Section 4. The head was 2 feet south from the north line of the section, and 2 feet 5 inches east of the western line. The body was that of a young person, the skull was lying on its face and was in a very poor condition. Resting a little above and a little to the north of the skull was a bowl (H-92) 6 inches in diameter. It was ornamented on the interior and had a handle on either side. Just below this bowl was a pitcher (H-93) 4½ inches high and 2 inches in diameter at the top. Just below the large bowl was a fragmentary bowl (H-94) which had a peculiar interior ornamentation. About on a level with the skull, and a little to the east of it, was a grooved stone (H-95); it had three grooves on the angular ridge, and in the east would be termed a net-sinker. About ½ foot above the head of the skeleton was a fragment of a bowl (H-96) but only a portion of the rim could be made out. The direction of the skeleton could not be ascertained as rats had scattered the bones in all directions.

Skeleton 21 was found in Section 6. The head was 1 foot 8 inches below the surface, 7 inches south of the northern section line and 3 feet 4 inches west from the eastern line. The body measured 4 feet 2 inches *in situ* and projected about 10 inches into Section 1. The body was lying east and west, the head being toward the latter point. About 3½ inches north of the head was a portion of a red bowl (H-97) 9½ inches in diameter and 4½ inches deep. It was ornamented on the interior. Inside of this redware bowl was a fragment of a white bowl (H-98) and under this was the bowl of a ladle (H-99), having a heavy pattern on the interior. Lying between the femora was a portion of a corrugated jar (H-100), and just east of the body and a few inches below it was another fragment of the same jar (H-101), its uppermost part almost touching the tibia. The body was in a very poor condition.

Skeleton 22 was found 1 foot below the surface in Section 7 and only a few bones were intact to show that there had been a body there. It was lying with the head possibly toward the west, as a bowl was at that point; it was 1 foot 2 inches west of the eastern line of Section 7 and 2 feet 4 inches south of the northern line. About 4 feet west of the nearest bone was a white bowl (H-102) 10½ inches in diameter, ornamented on the interior. The few bones that remained were not in good condition nor were they in their proper relation to each other to give a clew as to the direction or position of the body.

Skeleton 23 was found 10 inches below the surface in Section 8. Skeleton 98 was that of a child and the bones were in a very poor condition. The skull was 1 foot 3 inches west of the eastern section line and 2 feet 5 inches north of the southern line. The body was lying east and west, the head toward the latter point. Leaning against the cranium and to the south of it was a fragment of a large bowl (H-103), and inside of this was a bowl-shaped jar (H-104), with an opening about 1 inch in diameter, and a perforated handle on either side. The body measured 1 foot 5 inches as it lay in the grave.

Skeleton 24 was found 10 inches below the surface in Section 8, the head being on the same level as that of Skeleton 23 and only 6½ inches to the northeast of it. The body was lying on its back, inclined a trifle to the right side, the legs had been drawn up, as is usual in most of the burials. It was lying northwest by southeast, the head toward the latter point. The head was 8 inches west of the eastern section line, and 3 feet 6 inches south from the northern line. It measured 3 feet 4 inches *in situ*. Lying to the northwest of the cranium and 4 inches from it, was a portion of a bowl (H-105), that was part of the bottom of a larger one. Inside of it was a corrugated jar 5½ inches high and ¾ inch in diameter at the top (H-106); between the bowl and its cranium was a bone awl (H-107). The cranium was broken into bits and the whole skeleton was greatly decayed.

Skeleton 25 was found 10 inches below the surface in Section 9. It was that of a young person; the bones were badly decayed and had been scattered about by rats. The body was lying north and south, the head being toward the latter point. The body measured 1 foot 9 inches as it lay in the grave. From the eastern section line to the head was 3 feet 2 inches and 1 foot 3 inches from the northern section line to the same point. About 4 inches south of the head and 2½ inches below it was a red bowl (H-108), measuring 4½ inches in diameter at the top.

The bone awl (H-109) was found 1 foot below the surface in the central part of Section 10, and almost against the eastern section line.

Skeleton 26 was found in the middle of Section 7, all that could be found in a sufficient state of preservation to allow of being uncovered was the upper jaw. This piece was lying 1 foot 6 inches below the surface; it was 3 feet north from the southern section line, and 3 feet 4 inches from the eastern line. A fragment of a bowl (H-110) was lying just below it, about 2 inches, and a little to the eastward of it, a large fragment of a white bowl (H-111), was lying 6 inches west of the jaw, and just below this piece on the southern side, and with the edge lying under the whiteware bowl mentioned above, was a very peculiar bowl (H-112); it was $4\frac{1}{4}$ inches in diameter and $2\frac{1}{2}$ inches deep. It was heavily ornamented on the interior and about $\frac{1}{2}$ inch below the rim were four perforated handles, placed at equal distances from each other. Three inches south of this bowl was a ball-shaped corrugated jar (H-113). It was $2\frac{3}{4}$ inches in diameter at the top and 3 inches deep. Two inches further south, was a large fragment of a corrugated jar (H-114). Four inches west of this corrugated jar was a fragment of a red bowl (H-115). The body had completely wasted away so that the position in the grave could not be ascertained.

Skeleton 27 was found in Section 8, it was 1 foot 3 inches below the surface. The body was greatly decomposed, only a portion of the head, the occiput, remaining. The legs were drawn up and the vertebrae were so soft they crumbled when even a brush was applied. The body was lying north and south, the head being toward the latter point, and measured 3 feet 5 inches *in situ*. From the eastern section line to the head was 3 feet, and from the head to the south section line was 2 feet 10 inches. Five inches northwest from the head was a fragment of a bowl (H-116) and 2 inches north of this was a water jar 6 inches high and $1\frac{1}{2}$ inches in diameter at the mouth. There was a corrugated handle on either side (H-117).

Skeleton 28 was found 10 inches below the surface in Section 10. All that could be measured for photographing were the legs and front of the pelvis, the other bones had entirely wasted away. The leg bones were in a very poor condition, their surfaces being greatly weathered. From the southern section line was 5 inches and from the western line, 2 feet 7 inches, from the point of the bended knees to the end of the pelvic bone, 2 feet $5\frac{1}{2}$ inches. The skeleton probably lay north and south, the head being toward the south and no doubt extended some distance into Section 9, but no bones were found in this section. The bones were very large, the perfect femur was 1 foot $6\frac{1}{2}$ inches long and the outer tibia was 1 foot $2\frac{3}{4}$ inches. No vessels were found with the body.

Skeleton 29 was found 1 foot 1 inch below the surface in Section 10, the head being 11 inches north of the leg bones of Skeleton 28. The body was lying northeast by southwest, the head being toward the latter point. The body was probably that of a woman, and lay on its back, the head being some inches higher than the rest of the body. The skull was crushed and the teeth of the upper jaw were missing from age. Only five teeth remained in the inferior maxillary. The body measured 2 feet 8 inches *in situ*. The legs were drawn up across the body and some of the vertebrae and ribs were missing, probably the result of a rats' burrow. The head was 3 feet north from the south line and 3 feet 10 inches from the west line. A little to the west and slightly above the head was a fragment of a pitcher (H-118).

Skeleton 30 was found 7 inches below the surface, all that was found of the skeleton was the occiput and two femurs, which were crossed. The head was 9 inches east of the western line of Section 10, and 2 feet 10 inches north of the southern section line. The bones were 2 feet northwest of the head, and from the northern line to the point where the bones cross was 2 feet 11 inches. The femora were crossed on the section line, half of them thereby lying in Section 15. Resting against the cranium was a pitcher (H-119), it was 6 inches high and 3 inches in diameter at the top. Resting against the pitcher on the northwestern side was a bowl 5 inches high and 4 inches in diameter at the opening, and heavily ornamented on the exterior.

TABULATED DATA.

A general discussion of Bonito culture will be published later.   In the meantime we present a table showing the dimensions of the rooms excavated and the approximate distribution of artifacts.   These will not only give an idea of the relative number of finds for each type of artifact but show their distribution in the ruin.   The numerals under the various headings in the tables indicate the number of such artifacts recognized by the excavator, but in some cases the number of fragments and other insignificant forms was so large that no exact count was made.   These are designated by an x.   The dimensions of rooms are from inside measurements. The tables were prepared by Mr. B. T. B. Hyde.—EDITOR.

TABLE 1.
DIMENSIONS OF ROOMS.

Room	Height		North		South		East		West		Northeast-Southwest (Diagonal)		Northwest-Southeast (Diagonal)		
	Ft.	In.	Ft.	In.	Ft.	In.	Ft.	In.	Ft.	In.	Ft.	In.	Ft.	In.	
1	6		11	5	11	5	5	1	5	9					
2	6	3	10	3½	10	3½	5	½	5	4½					
3															
4	6	7	11	5	10	11	5	5	5	4					
5	8	2	10	9	10	7	8	3	8	2					
6															
7			14	11	12	7	5	6	3	4					
8			7		7		6	8	7						
9			13	7	14	8	8		7						
10	7		13	2	12	6	7	3	8	4					
11			13	5	15	8	7	9	6	8					
12	14		12	6	12	4	9		8	2					
13			8	6	8	4									
14															
15															
16															
17															
18	5	7	6	2	2	6	4	4	7	2					
19															
20	12		12	6	12	3	10		10	7					
21			10	2	10		10		11						
22			10		10		10		10						
23															
24	16		10	6	12		14	6	12	2					See Room 73
25			9		8	1	16	10	18	10	18	5	21		
26															
27															
28	14		25	7	25		7	10	7	8					
28a	8	6	13		13		7	10	8	2	14	10	15	10	
29															
30															
31															
32															
33			6		6	3	5	10	6	10					
34	6		6	10	6	8	11	10	11	8					
35	6	2	12		11	11	12	3	12	5					

TABLE 1 (*continued*).

DIMENSIONS OF ROOMS.

Room	Height		North		South		East		West		Northeast-Southwest (Diagonal)		Northwest-Southeast (Diagonal)		
	Ft.	In.	Ft.	In.	Ft.	In.	Ft.	In.	Ft.	In.	Ft.	In.	Ft.	In.	
35a	5		6	6	6		10	2	10	6					
36	7		11	9	12	10	12	4	12	1	17	2	17	3	
37	6	6	10	7	11	3	11	11	12	2	15	5	16	2	
38	6		32	2	27	8	10	2	13	9	33	4	30	5	
39			21	1	20	3	9	8½	8	3	22	10	21	10	
39a	5	9	7	8	7	6	8	10	8	5	12		11		
39b	6		7	4	7	6	8	7	8	10	11	7	11	3	
40	6		22	6	22	6	11		11						
	11		22	6	22	6	11		11						
41	5	9	7	9	7	11	13	6	11	4					
42			14				9	5	9	10	14	5	16	10	
43			5		5	8	6	4	7	1	8	3	8	3	
44			13	10	14		5	1	5	2	14	8	14	6	
45			19		17	8	7	5	6	10	19	7	19	2	
46	6	2	5	6	5		7	2	7	2	9	5	9	3	
47	7		6		6				10	9	11	1	12		
48	12		13	5	11		7	11	6	10	15	7	15	7	Lower Room
48	5		8	6	8	2	7	5	7	3	11	2	11	7	Upper Room
49	6		9		9		1	10	2						
50	7		4	3	4	8	7	9	7	8	8	10	8	11	
51			11	6	10	9	9	2	8	4	14	10	13	9	
51a	5	7	7	9	6		8	2	8	2	10	7	10	8	
52			9	3	9	6	5	11	6	4	10	3	12	4	
53			11	6	10	5	14	2	13	5	17	10	17	5	
54			24	7	25	3	10		8	5	27		26	2	
55	6	5	7	2	6	4	8		7	3	10	10	10		
56	5	8	6	7	5	3	16	3	13	10	17	4	16	10	
57	7	10	7	8	6	10	7		7		10		10	6	
58			6		6		5	7	6	2	8	11	8	3	
59			10	10			6	6							Kiva
60			15	5	6	5	13	5	10						
60a			7		5	3	6								
61	6	3	11	1	9	4	11	6	10	4	15	6	14	4	
62	8		19	11	20	9	7	5	10		22	2	22	9	
63	7	7	6	2	5	9	16	1	16	1	17	1	17	1	
64															

TABLE 1 (*Continued*).

DIMENSIONS OF ROOMS.

Room	Height		North		South		East		West		Northeast-Southwest (Diagonal)		Northwest-Southeast (Diagonal)		
	Ft.	In.	Ft.	In.	Ft.	In.	Ft.	In.	Ft.	In.	Ft.	In.	Ft.	In.	
65			11	7	12	7	10	3	11	9	15	4	14	6	
66			11	1	9	9	9	4	9	9	14	2	13	11	
67															Kiva
68			14		13	8	14	2	11	10	18	6	18	6	
68a															
69			18		18	7	10	6	9	10	20		20	6	
70	5		6	1	11	10	6	10	8	5	12	8			
71			18	8	15	11	8	4	10	2	19	3	19	7	
72			5	3	2	8	10	3	20	7					
73			15	11	18		13	6	9	3	20	10	21	2	
73ne					8	9	5	7	6	2	10	3	10	6	
73se			7	6	5	9	9	3	10	6	11	4½	12	1½	
74			9	4½	9	3	11		9	5	13		14	6	
75															Kiva
76	9		16	1	16	1	7	5	7	5					
77			5	8	6	7	10	3	10	3	12	2	11	9	
78			21		18	9	8	2	8	11	21	7	22	8	
79															
80			18	5	18	5	9	11	10	2	21	9	20		
81															
82			11	9	10	9	10		10		15	2	15		
83	6		20	8	18		10	7	11	9	21	8			
84			10	3	9	7	9	7	9	2	13	9	13	9	
85															
86			15		14	6	8	8	9	2	18	10	18	7	
87	10		17	2	17		8	4	8	10	19	8	18	3	
88	9	2	16	10	17	2	8		8	2	19	6	17	11	
89			16	9	16	9	7	11	7	11	19	2	17	9	
90			18	5	18	6	10	1	10	3	21	8	20	8	
91			13		12		14	11	14	10	19	7	19	5	
92			14	6	13	7	5	6	9	9	14	10½	16	9	
93	7	8	19	4	15	8	7	2	5	11	20	2	20		
94			21	5	20	9	5	11	4	8	21	11	21	10	
95			17	4	16	11	6	7	6	8	17	9	18	6	
96			6	3	6	2	19	7	20	2	20	6	21		

TABLE 1 (*continued*).

DIMENSIONS OF ROOMS.

Room	Height	North	South	East	West	Northeast-Southwest (Diagonal)	Northwest-Southeast (Diagonal)	
	Ft. In.	Ft. In.	Ft. In.	Ft. In.	Ft. In.	Ft. In.	Ft. In.	
97		14 6	13 3	6 5	10 2	15	17	
98		17 1	16 11	8 8	8 3	19 3	18 8	
99		14 11	17 2		8 9½	17 7	19 4	
100		4 2	4 6	17	16	17 10	16	
101		14 18	12 4	5 10	2 9	14 11	13	
102		18 6	16 5	8 2	9 6	19 2	18 9	
103	11	16 10	16 5	8 5	8 4	17 9	19	
104		4 2	3 2	5 8	6 9	7 4	7 2	
105		10	12 2	12 5	16 8	21 2½	17 10½	
106		13 7	12 7	16 10	16 9	23	19 1	
106b								
107		10 9	9 2	7 7	6 9	12 3	11 11	
108								
109								
110		5 10	5 7	10	11 4	12 2	11 11	
111		6	5 10	13 6	11 10	14 6	13 3	
112								
113								
114								
115								
116		5 6	5 9	17 3	18 6	18 11	19	
117		9	9	18	19			
118		9	9	18	19			
119		9	9	19	19			
120		10	10 4	16 7	15 4	18 9	19	
121		9	8	16	17			
122		8	8	17	16			
123		7	7	16	16			
124		8	8	9	9			
125		9	9	10	10			
126		12	12	10	10			
127		13	13	10	10			
128		15 6	15 6	10	10			
129		16	16	10	10			
130								Kiva
131		13	13	9	9			

TABLE 1 (*continued*).

DIMENSIONS OF ROOMS.

Room	Height Ft. In.	North Ft. In.	South Ft. In.	East Ft. In.	West Ft. In.	Northeast-Southwest (Diagonal) Ft. In.	Northwest-Southeast (Diagonal) Ft. In.
132		10	10	9	9		
133		11	11	9	9		
134		11	'11	9	9		
135		10	10	9	9		
136		10	10	9	9		
137		15	15	9	9		
138		8	8	8	8		
139		8	8	6	6		
140		11 6	11 6	9	9		
141		13 6	13 6	9	9		
142		19	19	9	9		
143		6	7	16	17		
144		6	6	16	16		
145							
146		7	Kiva	11	20		
147			11		10		
148		24	Kiva	18	13		
149		10 6	K4	22	17		
150		K	9	24	15		
151		9 6	10	6	6		
152		10	12	14	13		
153		7 6	8	7 6	7 6		
154		8 6	8 6	7 6	7 6		
155		11	11	7 6	7 6		
156		9	9	7 6	8 6		
157		10	10	8	10		
158		18 6	18 6	8	8 6		
159		10	5	13	11 6		
160		7	15	11 6	13		
161							
162							
163		10	11	9	9		
164		9 6	10	6 6	6 6		
165		8 9	9	13	13		
166							Passageways
167							

TABLE 1 (*continued*).

DIMENSIONS OF ROOMS.

Room	Height	North	South	East	West	Northeast-Southwest (Diagonal)	Northwest-Southeast (Diagonal)
	Ft. In.	Ft. In.	Ft. In.	Ft. In.	Ft. In.	Ft. In.	Ft. In.
168		18 6	18 6	12	12		
169		18	18	12	12		
170		17	16	19	18		
171		11 6	13	12	11 6		
172		15	16	12	12		
173		21	21 6	13	13		
174		16 6	15	12 6	12 6		
175		12	12	13	13		
176		10	10	13	13		
177		10	10	20	18		
178		9	9	1 8	17		
179		9 6	9 6	17 6	18		
180		9 6	9 6	16 6	16		
181		10	10 4	16 7	15 4	18 9	19
182		10	10	19	19		
183		10	10	15	15		
184		9 6	9 6	13 6	12 6		
185		8	8	17 6	17 6		
186		8	8	19	19		
187		9	8 6	11	11		

TABLE 2.

DISTRIBUTION OF POTTERY.

Room	Cylinder Jars	Corrugated Jars	Plain Bowls	Corrugated Bowls	Pitcher	Effigies	Vessel, Animal Form	Ollas	Special Redware	Pipe	Dipper	Handle	Ornamented Sherds	Plain Sherds, White	Plain Sherds, Black	Plain Sherds, Red	Plain Sherds, Red-and-Black	Plain Sherds, Buff	Corrugated, White	Corrugated, Black	Corrugated, Red	Corrugated, Red-and-Black	Corrugated, Ornamented	Corrugated, Worked
2			3							1				2										
3		1												1										
4		1												1										
6														1										
9				1					1		1													
10		1							12					1										
11									1		1													
12									4															
.13			3										1	1										
19									1															
20		2					1								1							4		
22														1							66			
24					2						1	2		1										1
25				1	4							77					1			1			2	
26												1												1
27																			1					
28	111		39	24	1	1								2										
28a										1	1													1
29				1																			1	
31											1													
32	3		15	10									4											
33														1										
36	2		1	1							1													
38		3	1		2						4			2										
39		2		1							1													
39b	19	1	1							1				2										
40											1													
42								1						1										
44			1																					
45			1					2						1										
48					2									1										
51			1											1										
51a											1	1		1										
52	20																							
53	1		1		2	1		1																

TABLE 2 (*continued*).

DISTRIBUTION OF POTTERY.

Room	Cylinder Jars	Corrugated Jars	Plain Bowls	Corrugated Bowls	Pitcher	Effigies	Vessel, Animal Form	Ollas	Special Redware	Pipe	Dipper	Handle	Ornamented Sherds	Plain Sherds, White	Plain Sherds, Black	Plain Sherds, Red	Plain Sherds, Red-and-Black	Plain Sherds, Buff	Corrugated, White	Corrugated, Black	Corrugated, Red	Corrugated, Red-and-Black	Corrugated, Ornamented	Corrugated, Worked
54								1		1			1	1										
56													1											
58													1											
59			1									1	1											
60		1	1						1			3	3											
62													2	1			1		1					
62	2	18		13									3											
64		1	2					1					1											
65	1					3							1											2
66							1						1											1
67	1		1			8	1			2		1	2	2	1			1		1			1	3
68									1															
69								1												1				
70													1											1
71													1											1
72				1						1			1											
73													1											
74													1											1
75													1										1	1
76	1			1															1	3			2	7
77																					1			
78		2		1	2		1			1	2	2	1										4	22
79													1											
80		1		2							2		5								1			
82		1		1							3		1										1	
83													8							2				
84				1									1											
86		1	3						1				1					2	1					
87				1									1	1	5			1	1			2		1
88								1					1				1	1	1	1				
89							2										1	1	1					
90								1							1	1	2		1	1				
92													2			1			1	3				
93													1											
96					1																			1

TABLE 2 (continued).

DISTRIBUTION OF POTTERY.

Room	Cylinder Jars	Corrugated Jars	Plain Bowls	Corrugated Bowls	Pitcher	Effigies	Vessel, Animal Form	Ollas	Special Redware	Pipe	Dipper	Handle	Ornament Sherds	Plain Sherds, White	Plain Sherds, Black	Plain Sherds, Red	Plain Sherds, Red-and-Black	Plain Sherds, Buff	Corrugated, White	Corrugated, Black	Corrugated, Red	Corrugated, Red-and-Black	Corrugated, Ornamented	Corrugated, Worked
97														4	1									
98														1					1					
99			12		1							2		2		3			1					
101														1	1									
102			1	2	1									1		2			1					2
103														1					1					1
105	1	2	4	5	2			1	4	2	1			2		2			1	1	2			
106		2		1	6	2		1	1	1	1			1	8	1			1	1				1
107														3	1	2		1	2					
108														5					2	4				17
109	1	1	3	1	2	4	2				3	8		3	1	1			5	1	2			28
109			1		2					1	1	3	1	3		3			1	1	2		1	
110				1										1										
111								1																
122														1	1				1					
125									1						17				1					
127			1		1						1			1					1		1			1
129											1								1	1				
130		1			1						1	1		3	1	1			1					2
131											2	1		1	1				1		2			
132		2							1					1								1		6
134					1				1										2	1	3			1
136	1		1		1														5	1	3			1
137									1										1	1				
140		1												1							1			1
141		1												1					1		1			1
142														1	1	1			1		1	2		1
143															1	1			1				1	
144														1	1	1			1					
146														2	1	1			1					
149														1	1				1					
150														1					1		1			
153														1					1		1			
154									1					1					1	1				
158									1					1								1		

TABLE 2 (*continued*).

DISTRIBUTION OF POTTERY.

Room	Cylinder Jars	Corrugated Jars	Plain Bowls	Corrugated Bowls	Pitcher	Effigies	Vessel, Animal Form	Ollas	Special Redware	Pipe	Dipper	Handle	Ornamented Sherds	Plain Sherds, White	Plain Sherds, Black	Plain Sherds, Red	Plain Sherds, Red-and-Black	Plain Sherds, Buff	Corrugated, White	Corrugated, Black	Corrugated, Red	Corrugated, Red-and-Black	Corrugated, Ornamented	Corrugated, Worked
159				1							2		1						1	2	1			
160		1	1		3	1		2			1	2	3	1	1				2					1
161		⁝							1	1			3		7				2	2	2			
162				1																				
163	1	1										1	1	1	1				1	1				7
164															1		1							
165													1		1					1				
168		3					1				1	1	6	1	3					3	1			
169										1	3	6	5		3				2	2				11
170		1								1	2	6	6		1			1		3				1
171		1			3				1			1	2		1					3				2
172												1	1		1					1	4			
173		3			9							2	8		1				5	1			1	4
174													1		1					1				
175					1								1		1					1				
177												1												
181													1		1						1			
188													1								1			
189																			1					

TABLE 3.

DISTRIBUTION OF MOST IMPORTANT STONE OBJECTS.

Room	Axes	Beads	Celts	Cylinders	Disks	Drilled Objects	Grinding Stones	Hammers	Hoes	Jar Covers	Knives	Lapstones	Manos	Mauls	Metates	Miscellaneous	Mortars	Ornaments	Pestles	Pipes	Polishing Stones	Rubbing Stones	Scrapers	Slabs	Smoothing Stones	Vessel
1		1																								
2					1			1		18												2				
3													4									2				
4						1				1												1				
6																		1								
7											1														5	
8																					3					
9											1		5								3	1	1			
10					2			22							1	1			1	1						
12			2			1			1			3						2	2		2					
16		6																								
17																9	1					5				
18												1														
19								3		3			3													
20								3		1		1	15			1	1									
24					4																		1			
25								15		6	3		6				1	1	1			27			2	
26		1						1																		
27																		1	1							
28										75	2															
28a										3			7								1				19	
29								1		1															1	
32								1		8																
33										2																
35								1																		
36										2	1		4			1					1	2			1	
37		1	1							9			2												4	
38								1	2	2			30		1	1	1		4						10	
39			1					54		1			15			14			1						4	
39b								1		28															1	
40				1							1		1			1									1	
41	2										1		9			2										
42								3					142			6	1					1	1			
44																1										
45								5					12						1						2	
48	1												7			33									1	
51						1										4										
52										1															1	
53										1																

TABLE 3 (*continued*).

DISTRIBUTION OF MOST IMPORTANT STONE OBJECTS.

Room	Axes	Beads	Celts	Cylinders	Disks	Drilled Objects	Grinding Stones	Hammers	Hoes	Jar Covers	Knives	Lapstones	Manos	Mauls	Metates	Miscellaneous	Mortars	Ornaments	Pestles	Pipes	Polishing Stones	Rubbing Stones	Scrapers	Slabs	Smoothing Stones	Vessel
54								39	1	8	2		57			11					1	1		8	3	
55								1																		
56							1			1																
57								2		2			3													
58								3																		
59								6																	3	
60				1				6		1			7											2		
61	1									1						1								2		
62	1						1	4		4	1		7		2									2		
64	1						1	20					4											2		
65	1							8		5	2				4	1					1			1		
66								6		5			8		1									2		
67							1	20		4						1					1	1		1		
68								27		1			38			1			1	1				3		
70			1					7		2	1													2	1	
71							1	21					20								1			1		
72								4		2			32											1		
73								1		1			1													
75								6		1														2	1	
76								23		1			6											1		
77											2		2											1		
78	1			1			1	56			4		10						1					4		
79													2													
80								65					33				1							1		
81								16		1			6		3										2	
82								3													1	8				
83							1	12		1	1		5		4				1					9	1	
84													5											3		
85		2					1	12		9			1		2	2	1		1		1	2		7	1	
86								2			1		2				2							3	2	
87								9			1		1													
89										1	1		1									1				
90							2			1												36		1		
92			1							1												2	1	2		
96										1												1				
97													1									8				
98																								1		
99							1			1			2											1		1
100																										1

TABLE 3 (*continued*).

DISTRIBUTION OF MOST IMPORTANT STONE OBJECTS.

Room	Axes	Beads	Celts	Cylinders	Disks	Drilled Objects	Grinding Stones	Hammers	Hoes	Jar Covers	Knives	Lapstones	Manos	Mauls	Metates	Miscellaneous	Mortars	Ornaments	Pestles	Pipes	Polishing Stones	Rubbing Stones	Scrapers	Slabs	Smoothing Stones	Vessel
102								1		1		2	1									12				
103																						2				
105							3	12		4			8				3							40		
106			1	4				1					2	1								50		17	2	
107									11															11		
108								2		1			1											7		
109							2	24		16	2		22			2		1			3			10		2
110								2		2														3		
121																		1								
122																								3		
127							2	5		2	1					4								1		
129								1																		
130							1	8					3											2		
131							2	16		1	1		19										4	2		
132										1														1		
134								13		3			1			1								1		
136								3		2	1		1											3		
137													1													
141							3	1		1			1											3		
142								10		2			2								1		1	6	1	
144							1	4					1													
151													1													
153								2					1													
154													1													
156								2																		
159								1		2			3			1										
160						1		15		2	1		10													
161		1						1		2	3		2			2								2		
165								4												1						
168							1	18					3									1				
169								16					1									1				
170							2	14		2			4			1		1				2		8		
171							3	7			1		3													
172													2											8		
173		2		1				13					9										1	7		
174																								1		
175								2																		
180											1															

TABLE 4.
DISTRIBUTION OF WORKED BONE.

Room	Awls	Bodkins	Scrapers	Implements	Beads	Dice	Knife	Worked Pieces	Totals
2	1			1					2
3				1					1
8							1		1
9				1					1
10	1								1
11	2			1					3
12	3								3
19	2								2
20	5			1			1	11	18
24	12		1	1	4	1			19
25	14		2	4	9		2	2	33
26	15				1				16
28	2			1					3
29	3								3
30								1	1
31	1								1
32								1	1
33								1	1
35	3								3
36	3								3
37	3								3
38	3								3
39	5		1		1	1		1	9
39b								1	1
41	2								2
42	8		1	1					10
45	3		1	1					5
51a	2								2
51	1								1
52	1								1
54	5		1						6
55	1								1
58	1								1
59	1								1
60	1		1	1				1	4
61	1							1	2
62	3		1		1				5
64	7			1	1			2	11
65	9		1					1	11
66	6							6	12

TABLE 4 (*continued*).

DISTRIBUTION OF WORKED BONE.

Room	Awls	Bodkins	Scrapers	Implements	Beads	Dice	Knife	Worked Pieces	Totals
67	31		6	7	1			1	46
69								7	7
70				1					1
71	1								1
72	7		1						8
73	2			1					3
74	3								3
75	10			1				1	12
76	12		1					2	15
77	2								2
78	13		2		12				27
80	7			1				3	11
82	6							2	8
83	2		1	1		1		1	6
84								1	1
85	5			1					6
86	3								3
87	1								1
89	3		2	1					6
90	6				1				7
92	2								2
96	3					1			4
97	4				1			1	6
99	4		2		1				7
102			1						1
103	1								1
105	24		1		2		1	6	34
106	13			3	1			2	19
107	3			1	1			1	6
108	2			2	1				5
109	9	13	3	2	3	1		7	38
110	3	5				1			9
122					1				1
127		1		2					3
130	1			1					2
131	3	1	1	1	2			1	9
132	2	1						2	5
134			1						1
136	1		1		1				3
140	2			1					3

TABLE 4 (*continued*).

DISTRIBUTION OF WORKED BONE.

Room	Awls	Bodkins	Scrapers	Implements	Beads	Dice	Knife	Worked Pieces	Totals
142	3	5							8
144	1							1	2
151		2							2
153		2							2
156	1								1
160	6	5		2				1	14
161	26	22		2	1				51
162	2								2
163	6	5	1	4				1	17
165					1				1
168	3	1			1				5
169	7	2		2				1	12
170	1	1		3				4	9
171	6	7	1	1	6			1	22
173	3	9	2	2	3	1			20

Total　708

TABLE 5.

WOODEN OBJECTS.

Room	Arrows	Parts of Arrows	Tool Handles	Boards	Sticks	Worked Pieces	Special Objects
1	3				4		
2	10					194	1 walnut, 3 reeds, 2 arrow points, game sticks
4					3	5	5 pointed sticks
6				7	2		10 torches
6a						17	1 wooden dish, 1 fire stick
8	2						
10						7	1 ball, 2 painted sticks, 1 wound stick
11						3	3 drilled sticks
12						2	
14						1	1 ceremonial stick
18						3	2 ceremonial sticks, 1 implement
24		1	1		3		1 knife, 1 fire stick, painted game stick
25		11	2		11	3	2 walnut drilled, 1 reed drilled, 3 arrow points 1 reed bead, 1 cylinder
28					1	1	
32	37	5			2	403	1 painted slab, 1 flute, 2 slabs, ceremonial sticks, prayer sticks
33	2	2				51	8 flutes, 43 ceremonial sticks
35					2		ceremonial sticks
36						1	pointed stick
38					4		
44						1	nut inlaid
52						1	
53						3	2 cradle boards
54			2				
55						2	2 ceremonial sticks
60					x		
61					2	1	
62				1	x	5	2 broken knives, 1 cylinder
64						1	
66					1		
67						1	
70						7	game, ceremonial, and kicking sticks
83						2	implements
85		1	1			13	1 knife, 3 slabs, 1 ceremonial stick, 2 flutes, implements
92					1	4	ceremonial stick
95	1					1	
97	1					12	8 sticks. 1 slab

TABLE 5 (*continued*).

WOODEN OBJECTS.

Room	Arrows	Parts of Arrows	Tool Handles	Boards	Sticks	Worked Pieces	Special Objects
99						4	1 painted slab, painted sticks
100						3	
105	1				17	11	willows,—drilled walnut, fire sticks
106	1					2	walnut, game stick
107	2	9		2	10	4	
108						7	
109						9	walnut, slabs, sticks
110				1		7	
112						1	carved bird
159						5	
160						8	
161						2	
164						1	
168						3	
170	1				3	14	torch, disk
171	2		1			7	walnut
172						2	fire sticks
173						5	board, ornament
176						1	carved animal

TABLE 6.

DISTRIBUTION OF SHELL.

Room	Shells	Crinoid	Fossil	Trumpet	Beads	Bracelets	Rings	Disks	Pendant	Miscellaneous
4				1						
6	x	5	137							
6a			1							
10	10		60							
12	2	4	555	1	1					
13	1									
14					1					
16					164					
17				5						
25					2					
28					5	2				
33	13				831	98	x	4	104	2
35	x									
40	x				x					
67	4									
72						1				
74						x				
85	x				64	1	1		1	
86	x									
105						x				
107	1					x			2	
131						2				
161						5				
163	x					9				
164						1				
169						1				
N. of 63					x	8			2	

TABLE 7.

DISTRIBUTION OF TEXTILES AND FEATHER-WORK.

Room	Baskets	Mats	Sandals	Cloth	Cord-String	Fiber—Yucca	Feathers—Quills
1				1	8		23
2	2	2	6				5
25	3	1	2	6	8	3	3
32	1						
35							2
62	4	2	5		2		2
85	1	1	4		4		
86					8	1	
92					13		2
97			1		2		2
98	2				1		
99	1						
110	1		2				1
168		2	1		2		
170		1					
171		1			1		
173		1					

TABLE 8.

DISTRIBUTION OF COPPER OBJECTS.

The copper objects found were as follows: Room 83, bell; Room 28, a fragment; Room 89, a fragment; Room 106, bell; Rooms 127 and 150, 2 fragments; Room 168, bell; and Room 179, fragment.

TABLE 9.

DISTRIBUTION OF ARTIFACT MATERIALS.

Materials	Rooms
Azurite	12, 65, 68, 73, 85, 108, 109, 110, 163, 164, 170, 175
Calcite	110
Chalk	76, 83, 105, 106, 161,
Coal	54
Copper	68
Crystal	6a, 12, 28
Ferris Oxide	67
Galena	6a, 29, 32, 37, 45, 85, 107, 159
Garnets	10
Gypsum	10, 12, 24, 38, 78, 83, 90, 106, 107, 109, 110, 130, 131, 132, 136, 140, 144, 159, 160, 161, 165, 168, 170, 172, 173
Hematite	12, 25, 64, 67, 85, 106, 107, 109, 127, 131, 171
fron concretion	107
Jet	13, 33, 38, 78, 85, 105, 106, 110
Kaolno	67
Lignite	67, 86, 90, 92
Limonite	109, 130, 131, 134, 142, 159
Malachite	24, 76, 83, 85, 106, 108, 109, 122, 131, 164, 168, 170
Mica	28, 68, 90
Obsidian	9, 10, 20, 24, 29, 67, 76, 83, 89, 90, 92, 98, 99, 105, 106, 109, 110, 129, 131, 132, 134, 136, 140, 142, 144, 146, 160, 163, 165 168, 169, 170, 171, 173
Ocher	83, 85, 86, 88, 97
Ore	28, 106
Paint (blue)	38
Petrified wood	10, 12, 61, 105, 106, 129, 131, 134, 140, 141, 142, 144, 160, 168, 170
Pink stone	13, 20, 161, 173
Pumice	37, 170
Pyrites	12, 65
Stag black	108
Turquoise	6a, 10, 12, 13, 26, 28, 35, 37, 39b, 40, 42, 51, 53, 57, 68, 72, 78, 85, 86, 99, 102, 109, 110, 127, 142, 164, 170, 173

CONCLUSION.

Architecturally, the large prehistoric dwellings of our great Southwest present a fascinating study. From evidence at hand it would seem that the selection of material for house construction was governed almost entirely by geological environment. In the Chaco Cañon the cretaceous sandstones presented an admirable building material, readily acquired and easily worked. To this fact may be attributed the high degree of cultural development so strongly emphasized in the walls of the more recent parts of Pueblo Bonito.

The older walls are of undressed stones and are purely utilitarian. The later ones, especially those in the northern part of the pueblo, are of carefully shaped blocks with faced surfaces and laid in varying combinations, some with alternating layers of thinner pieces, the evident intent being aesthetic.

The various types of doorways, many of which were changed from time to time, either from choice or necessity, present a rich field of research for future investigators.

The ceilings of the rooms show as marked an evolution as do the walls: those of the earlier type are of undressed branches and twigs, placed in sufficient numbers to form a firm foundation for the adobe floors, whereas the later ones demonstrate the efforts of the architects to construct a ceiling in keeping with the more ornate walls.

The investigations in this prehistoric pueblo show conclusively that it was occupied for many years—perhaps centuries. The interlacing of walls under the rooms of the first story and the superimposing of estufas over the walls of others that had served their purpose and passed into disuse, are stepping-stones that may lead to a solution of the history of this old walled-in town. A methodical survey of this ruin, an exhaustive study of the architectural refinements, and a general study of the underlying strata were planned as a part of the extension of the work, but, owing to circumstances beyond the control of those in charge, this most desirable phase of the investigations was impossible.

As in most pueblos of this type the majority of the rooms were angular. Ceremonial rooms, in the form of circular estufas, were represented by many examples and some of the smaller of these showed unusual outlines. Judging by the ceremonial paraphernalia found in the angular living rooms, many of these were employed for ceremonial clan rooms or for clan ceremonies. The most striking example of this kind was Room 38, where were found the remains of macaws and a platform

375

on which rested encrusted objects and other ceremonial pieces that had no doubt been used by members of a macaw clan, a clan now represented among the Zuñi and known as the Mulakwe. The great number of skeletons of the macaw that were found in the eastern end of the room and the finding of the remains of macaws beneath the floor are mute evidences of the reverence in which these birds were held. When we consider the distance that separated these birds from their natural habitat, in connection with the fact that very few bones of this bird were found in the other rooms of the pueblo, it is safe to assume that the macaw clan must have been in existence at this early period in the history of the Southwestern pueblos.

The use of certain rooms for burial purposes seems to have been secondary, although intramural burial was not confined to this particular group as other bodies were found beneath the floors of some of the angular rooms at the sides of estufas. The inconsequential number of bodies found in Pueblo Bonito naturally prompts the question as to the general cemetery wherein were buried the hundreds who must have died there. From the character of the deposits in the series of burial rooms, of which Rooms 32 and 33 were a part, and from the accompaniments with the bodies, it is evident that these were members of the priesthood or, at least, people of great importance in the life of the pueblo. Buried with such great stores of treasure, it is but natural to suppose that they were placed in a position secure from the possibility of defilement or of theft.

When the first general survey of the pueblo and the adjacent land was made, the writer was impressed with the possibility of finding the cemeteries in the mounds on the opposite side of the cañon, but later investigations showed that these small places of interment were those belonging to the house groups that were found near them. Owing to the fact that the major part of the investigations was confined to the pueblo itself, no adequate tests were made in the area to the east and west of the building. As the present surface is covered with a deposit of silt and sand and, in view of the fact that the refuse heaps south of the ruin were not used for burial purposes, it is possible that the quest for the great cemetery may end at the places mentioned. An extensive cemetery has been found west of and near Pueblo Pintado, the easternmost pueblo of this group. Similar conditions should obtain in the case of Bonito and the other large pueblos of the Chaco Cañon.

The artifacts from this pueblo cover the greater part of the activities that one would expect to find among a sedentary people who had reached the high plane of development that is shown by the architecture. The preservation of perishable objects is remarkable, especially when compared with the results of investigations of cañon or mesa ruins that are known to be of a later period. Many of the ceremonial sticks were as firm as when they were deposited in the rooms and the preservation of a large bundle of arrows with reed shafts, wooden foreshafts, the sinew wrapping that binds the stone point to the foreshaft, in place, and even vestiges of the feathering, shows that in many of the sand-filled rooms the elements had but little effect in the way of decay and disintegration. These, with sandals, both woven and plaited, fragments of cloth, marked pieces of buckskin, fiber cords, and many other semi-perishable objects present for the student much tangible data that are lacking in most pueblos of this period.

The aesthetic attainment of the old Bonito people is shown most forcibly by the designs in color on the wooden tablets and especially in the elaborately decorated stone mortar. Their mosaic and encrusted ceremonial pieces, as shown by the mosaic basket, the inlaid scrapers, the hematite bird, the lignite frog, and by many other objects, is indicative of the skill of their artisans and the advance of the arts as applied to objects of a ceremonial nature. Nowhere in the Southwest have there been found such masses of turquoise beads, pendants, and inlays as were uncovered in Room 33. Living but a short distance from Los Cerillos, where most of the turquoise was no doubt obtained, the supply was unlimited and love of this particular stone prompted the dwellers at Bonito to carry on extensive quarry work in this particular formation.

The pottery of the pueblo shows a wide range of forms, but relatively few types that were of a definite ceremonial form. The majority of the vessels found in the rooms were of the usual corrugated type of cooking jars and the grayware with geometric designs in black such as are found throughout the Chaco region and in many parts of New Mexico and Arizona. Fragments of vessels of human form show that this rather advanced form of the potters' art was in evidence in the pueblo, but the motive was no doubt received from the south and had not been developed to any great extent. The finding of cylindrical jars in Room 28 added a new type to the ceramics of the Southwest. Deposited in one of the group of ceremonial rooms and next to the one containing the ceremonial sticks, these jars were undoubtedly used in certain ceremonial observances and may have been made for the express purpose of holding the ceremonial sticks as part of altar paraphernalia.

The stone and bone implements, although representing a wide range of form and uses, present no series worthy of special note other than the descriptions as given in the notes relating to the rooms in which they were found. Objects of a ceremonial nature, fashioned from both of these materials, were found, including the decorated stone mortar, a large metate with a scroll design pecked about the surface surrounding the grinding trough, and with the trough itself covered with red paint, and other smaller metates that, judging from their form, must have been used for the grinding of pigments for ceremonial purposes. The ceremonial use of pulverized white sandstone had reached such proportions that a special room for the preparation of such material became a necessity and this room presented one of the few large stone mortars and the only one that was found in place. Belonging to the same series of rooms was the one containing the compound metates in situ in which, no doubt, meal for ceremonies was ground. Opposed to this was the long row of mealing bins in one of the northern rooms. In the arrangement of the bins and the slope of the supports for the individual metates this utilitarian type practically duplicates similar milling places in some of our modern pueblos. Owing to the fact that these bins were found in one of the later portions of the pueblo and in view of the lack of such rows of bins in the older rooms, it is possible that this type of multiple mealing places was a development of the last few years of occupancy.

Of the bone objects, the most elaborate were the inlaid scrapers found in Room 38. Many other scrapers of similar form, but with no attempt at decoration save an occasional figure scratched near the handle end, were found in varying parts of the pueblo. There was no evidence of human bones having been employed in the preparation of ornaments or implements. The finding of cracked and calcined human bones in some of the rooms brings up the question of the eating of human flesh by the people of this pueblo. There was no evidence of human bodies having been buried in rooms above the first floor and only portions of skeletons were in evidence in Rooms 61 and 80 which contained broken and charred bones. During the period of our work in Pueblo Bonito some of our Navajo workmen cleaned out a number of rooms in Penasco Blanco and in one of these a great many human bones were found. Some of these, including portions of the skull, were charred, and the majority of the long bones had been cracked open and presented the same appearance as do the animal bones that have been treated in a similar way for the extraction of the marrow. It would therefore seem that these Pueblo Indians, either through stress of hunger or for religious reasons, had occasionally resorted to the eating of human flesh.

The utilization of shell for ornaments and for other purposes is shown by the fragments of shell mosaics, entire abalone shells used as receptacles for turquoise and shell ornaments, shell bracelets, pendants, and beads and shell trumpets made of the entire shell of a univalve.

Their basketry was represented by many examples, but this particular group suffered more through decay than any of the other groups mentioned. Various sizes of the bowl type were found and a general deposit of large and small baskets accompanied the pottery vessels in the bins that were found under the floors in Room 62. These bins, with stone sides and bottoms, filled with pottery and baskets, and partly covered with large tray-shaped baskets, remind one of similar deposits found in the Basket Maker region of southern Utah and northern Arizona. As the southern range of this seemingly restricted people is not known, it is impossible to state how near to the Chaco their southernmost boundaries extended, but it is possible that groups or individuals of this interesting tribe may have joined the people who occupied Pueblo Bonito and that their former practices are reflected in this series of deposits.

An exhaustive comparative study of the artifacts from this ruin must be left for the future student but it is the hope of the writer that the recording of these unembellished field notes may be of some assistance to others who may elect to carry on investigations in the Chaco Cañon and especially in Pueblo Bonito.

NOTES ON PUEBLO BONITO.

By N. C. Nelson.

NOTES ON PUEBLO BONITO.

At the suggestion of the Editor, I have attempted below to summarize the results of some preliminary observations made under the auspices of the American Museum in July, 1916, when I spent two weeks at Pueblo Bonito. During the preceding fall I accidentally traversed the Chaco Cañon, and naturally took rough notes, plots, and photographs covering the principal ruins. My interest was immediately excited by the refuse heaps at Peñasco Blanco, Bonito, Chettro Kettle, and Alto, with the result that permission was sought to test them out. This permit was granted but was later restricted to Pueblo Bonito, to which I accordingly limited my attention. The actual work done may be dealt with under four separate heads: the test sections of the refuse heaps, pottery samples from the Chaco ruins, observations on the architectural development of Pueblo Bonito, and, finally, some notes on the rather remarkable piece of engineering work connected with the detached cliff block back of the ruin.

THE REFUSE SECTIONS.

In spite of the comparatively uniform character of the broken pottery scattered about all but one of the ruins of the Chaco region, it seemed a *priori* impossible that stylistic changes should not have taken place during the long interval of occupation suggested by the size of the refuse heaps. It was with some confidence, therefore, that small trial sections were made of each of the two somewhat distinct heaps lying in front of Pueblo Bonito. These sections measured 2 by 4 feet on the horizontal and reached a depth of 11 feet 6 inches in the eastern heap and slightly over 16 feet in the western. The broken sherds found were segregated for each 6-inch level and totaled 1040 and 1083 for the respective sections. Mr. Earl H. Morris assisted with the work, which occupied about five days. The results were thoroughly disappointing —so disappointing that I have not hitherto considered it worth while to publish the data until I could section the mounds on a larger scale. The fact seems to be that, as was also discovered long ago by Mr. Pepper, the mounds are not made up exclusively of household refuse, but include a good deal of broken rock as well as adobe mortar. In other words, the mounds have accumulated at a more rapid rate than has ordinarily been the case. In my sections this rock and adobe material was especially excessive in the middle third and probably has intimate connection with changes or restorations that took place in the great communal house.

At the present time, when it seems likely that investigation of the Chaco ruins is to be carried forward by other institutions, and when consequently my chances of following up the subject any further come to an end, it seems proper that I should submit such results as I have. Perhaps they may encourage others to carry the study to completion. The pottery fragments have accordingly been tabulated and the results, while unsatisfactory, are not so absolutely useless as at first appeared. In effecting the tabulations the sherds were segregated into major groups, as follows: corrugated, black-on-white, red, and shiny black wares. Each group was further subdivided according to the type of decorative element or combination of elements exhibited. This subdivision, in the case of the black-on-white ware alone, yielded more than twenty variations. No account has been taken of the nature of the vessels represented, only of the general type of the ware and its particular style of decoration.

By comparing the two tables consistent agreement is found on the following points:—

1. Corrugated ware is present from top to bottom, constituting in one section a fourth and in the other section something less than a third of the whole.

2. Red ware occurs very sparingly and, what is more to the point, is either exceedingly scarce or altogether absent in the lower half and grows numerically stronger toward the top.

3. Shiny black ware, of the type at home in the Tularosa Valley region, is somewhat more plentiful, but this also is either very scarce or totally absent at the bottom, though well represented in the upper levels.

4. The most typical varieties of the black-on-white ware, such as those with hachured ornamentation, combined solid and hachured, plain solid pattern, solid figures (or lines) edged with dots, widely spaced parallel thin lines, checker patterns, and interlocking curvilineal elements, occur either steadily or sporadically from top to bottom. The first-mentioned, i. e., the hachured variety, is throughout the sections numerically about as strong as all the other varieties combined. This is one of the surprises, for I had expected that type of decoration to have been most popular in late times and the ware having the solid figures (or lines) with dotted or escalloped margins to have been comparatively common in early times.

5. The fine, smooth-surfaced variety of black-on-white ware that is most easily recognized as typical Mesa Verde appears first toward the

middle of the sections and shows distinct signs of weakening again toward the top.

6. All groups and varieties of wares tend to be numerically strong in the upper third, weak in the middle third, strong again at the top of the lower third, and, finally, weak again near the bottom of both sections. The explanation of this lies no doubt largely in the presence or absence of the rock-and-adobe débris before mentioned.

7. Judged by the relative positions in the two sections at which corresponding changes in the ceramics and the rock-and-adobe features take place, it would seem probable that the eastern mound was started at a somewhat later date than the western.

It is not my purpose to discuss further the significance of the preceding inductions, tempting though it is in connection with points 2, 3, and 5. The sporadic gaps in the tables for several varieties of decoration that actually range from top to bottom of the refuse clearly show that my sections were too small and that therefore any conclusions based on the available results would have to be regarded as purely tentative. The undertaking was designedly preliminary and as such, I should say, is sufficiently promising to warrant investigation on a larger scale.

POTTERY OF THE CHACO REGION.

Having thus failed to obtain decisive results about the time distribution of the different pottery styles represented in the Bonito refuse sections, there still remains the possibility of gaining some light on the subject from the broken sherds gathered on the surface about the various ruins of the locality.

The data available for such study consist of sherds collected by myself in 1915, together with some additions obtained by Dr. Hrdlička and by the Hyde Expedition in former years. The sites represented by these collections include all the larger and many of the smaller ruins ranging from Pueblo Pintado on the east to Peñasco Blanco and Kinbenaiola on the west and thence south as far as Crown Point. Other ruins characterized by the Chaco types of pottery exist in distant parts, east, south, and west—not to mention intermixture on the north—but of these more at some future time.

The data unfortunately are not of a character to yield reliable quantitative results, such as could be reduced to a percentage basis after the manner employed by Professor Kroeber and Dr. Spier. My own material was gathered with no statistical objects in view. At the time, the aim was simply to obtain as full a record as possible of the presence or absence of the various styles of decoration. In consequence of this, duplicates of any given style were not picked up in unlimited numbers; and, besides, in the preliminary grouping of the sherds—done on the spot—the more imperfect examples were left behind. Nevertheless, the amounts gathered vary directly with the richness of the sites and the samples thus procured range from 25 pieces at Pueblo del Arroyo to 191 at Pueblo Pintado. In the case of the small-house ruins, the samples taken were proportionately smaller, and wherever these small ruins occurred in groups the pottery samples taken were lumped together. I take pains to state all these conditions so that the future student who attempts to apply statistical methods may profit by the neglects and errors here noted. But while the resulting analysis of the material at hand will thus have doubtful quantitative value, the qualitative character remains unimpaired—in fact is heightened—and should serve as an ultimate check on the findings in the refuse sections.

The table devised covers nineteen lots of sherds, tabulating some 1250 pieces. The same method of classification was followed as in the case of the section material dealt with above. The results, it may be stated at once, are in all their broader aspects remarkably like those observed in the refuse heaps and would therefore seem to confirm the essential validity of those findings. That is to say, while there is much irregularity in the occurrence of many of the less conspicuous types of ware, those wares most typical of the Chaco are present almost everywhere. The few points perhaps worthy of note are the following:—

1. Corrugated wares with decorative designs, punched or incised, appear to be absent in the small-house ruins.

2. A certain style of black-on-white ware, the decoration on which consists of straight lines each crossed by a zigzagging line, resulting in two opposed series of small alternating triangles, is confined almost entirely to the small-house ruins.

3. True Mesa Verde ware occurs at only seven sites, and ware resembling that of the Mesa Verde is found at five additional places. The absences are noticeably confined to the small-house sites and to the distant ruins at Crown Point.

4. Pueblo Wejegi alone yielded no straight-line hachured decoration, while, on the other hand, decorative elements with dotted margins are well represented. This condition is so singular and unexpected that for the present I hesitate to accept it as anything but an accident. Wejegi, because of its comparatively excellent state of preservation, I

have been inclined to regard as of late date. Moreover, I have thought it a pueblo which was never brought to completion. At any rate, it certainly was not inhabited for any length of time because, for one thing, pottery fragments are scarce in its vicinity, only thirty-six pieces being picked up.

5. The shiny black ware of Tularosa origin is completely absent except for a single piece, found at Pueblo Pintado. This remarkable consistency shows with what caution statistical results based upon limited data must be regarded; for while this Tularosa ware is doubtless scarce in the Chaco region, and while not a single fragment was found among the 242 picked up on the surface about Pueblo Bonito, yet in the Bonito refuse this ware ranged as high as eighteen percent in the upper levels of the sections.

There are other points of more or less significance, but as it is obvious that our data, if not exactly inadequate, at least require extended treatment, we may as well stop at once. Summing up, as far as we have gone, therefore, it may be stated that the Chaco ceramics underwent no such complete revolutionary changes as have taken place in the Rio Grande region and elsewhere. At the same time it is safe to affirm that several minor changes—the disappearance of certain design elements and the appearance of others—did take place during the long course of occupation. There remains but to add that these minor changes dealt with on a strictly quantitative basis would undoubtedly yield chronological results such as should enable us to arrange the Chaco ruins in their approximate relative order of antiquity. This work could probably best be done on the ground and in view of the facts presented by point 5 would have to be tolerably exhaustive.

ARCHITECTURAL FEATURES OF THE BONITO RUIN.

Never having seen a satisfactory plot or groundplan of Bonito, I took occasion for my own satisfaction to make one, devoting some three days to the task. My only means were a table, a compass, a steel tape, and some stakes; but I venture to hope that the general outline of the ruin as a whole, and also the really visible details of it along the southern and eastern sides, may be found to be tolerably correct. For although not made with this publication in mind, the plot has served, at least in part, as the basis for the appended groundplan, Mr. B. T. B. Hyde having, I believe, made some slight modifications as well as some additions based upon Mr. Pepper's photographs, in that way making the groundplan exhibit features that are not now exposed to view. However.

as the appended groundplan differs in several minor particulars from mine, e.g., in the vicinity of Room 76, I do not wish to be held entirely responsible for notable errors that may be discovered.

In connection with this plotting, the various types of masonry, as well as the independent systems of walls to be seen in different parts of the ruin, forced themselves upon my attention. Doubtless the author of the paper has already treated the subject at length, he having had opportunity to see much more of the evidence during the process of excavation than is now visible, and I need not trespass on his territory beyond merely indicating the general nature of my observations and the conclusions drawn from them.

Briefly stated, then, and in words written on the spot, one cannot view the remains of Pueblo Bonito for long without becoming aware that the place has had an exceptionally long and interesting history. Nothing short of the complete clearance of the ruin will enable us to tell the details of that history, but some of the facts are obvious at the present moment. Bonito was not originally conceived as a complete unit structure, as was the case probably with some of the other ruins in the Chaco, its present size and shape having been the result rather of many alterations and additions. The evidence for this is twofold. First, the excavations have revealed in several places ancient substructures that form no part of the later pueblo. The deeply buried walls are not sufficiently massive and besides do not conform to the final groundplan. Second, the superstructure itself, or the finally completed Pueblo Bonito as we see it above the ground level, is made up of two, perhaps four or five, distinctly different types of masonry, presumably not all of the same date.

The most ornate, if not the most substantial of the masonry, viz., that made of surfaced blocks laid in fairly regular horizontal courses and spaced both horizontally and sometimes vertically by two or more courses of fine chinking, would seem to be of comparatively ancient date. Of later date, undoubtedly, is the unchinked masonry, laid up with little or no mortar and for the most part composed of small and thin rough-surfaced slabs, but also often interspersed with more or less regular courses of fair-sized blocks. Finally, there is a degenerated form of the last-mentioned type of masonry, the courses of which are laid rather irregularly, often of sharp-edged slabs, spaced with a good deal of mortar. This masonry, which I venture to guess to be the latest of all, is especially noticeable in the northwest portion of the ruin, though it is not at all abundant. My reason for believing the chinked masonry to be the oldest is that it is characteristic of the central portion of the ruin, in particular

of the back wall, beginning off Room 15 and running southwest beyond
Room 116, where it swings into the interior of the structure and is lost
track of finally in the vicinity of Rooms 23 and 25. In the opposite
direction another trace of this masonry appears in the interior, as, for
example, in Room 60. What the groundplan of the Bonito just preceding
the present one was like is uncertain, perhaps will always remain so;
but I should not be surprised to learn that it had been oval, or essentially
of the same nature as that of Peñasco Blanco. In any case, it is hardly
to be disputed that the southwest corner, and also nearly the whole
eastern wing, were comparatively late additions.

The manner of joining the chinked and unchinked masonry in the
rear wall off Room 15 forms an interesting study, particularly with
respect to the slant of the joint and the introduction of nearly regularly
spaced binding timbers. From the slant of the joint I was at first dis-
posed to conclude that the unchinked masonry must be of late date, and
was greatly puzzled until Mrs. Nelson called my attention to the unchinked masonry forming the top story a little to the west, above the
Wetherill cabin. One point especially worthy of notice is that the old
outer wall of chinked masonry contains several doorways, a fact not
generally observed in the other types of masonry. But here again I
am simply stating my impressions for what they may be worth, hoping
that some one else may find them useful as a starting point for exhaustive
study. It would not seem too much to expect that further investigation
of the masonry in all the Chaco ruins might lead to valuable conclusions
in regard to their relative dates of occupation.

Other points of interest suitable for consideration are the apparent
eastward extension of the front wall, the many evidences that Bonito
was in part destroyed by fire, and so on; but these matters may better
be left for the future excavator.

The Shored-Up Cliff Block.

The vertical cañon wall directly behind Pueblo Bonito has suffered
a number of fractures, with the result that several great blocks have
been detached from the main cliff. These blocks still stand erect, but
have settled more or less into the alluvium of the cañon floor. One of
them has been considerably broken up, the fallen sharp-edged bowlders
having rolled away from the cliff base almost across the ninety-foot
interval to the wall of the pueblo. Whether this collapse happened
during the occupation of the village is an interesting problem; but at
any rate it is certain that the inhabitants were fully aware of the damaging possibilities of these blocks and took precautions accordingly.

The easternmost, and probably also the largest of these detached blocks, has a visible height of about 100 feet, is 150 feet long, and averages perhaps 20 feet in thickness (I have lost some of my measurements). In other words, the block is an immense thing, weighing not less than twenty thousand tons. As a result of erosion and the falling away of the lower front portion, up to a particular cleavage plane some 26 feet above the cañon floor, this block has assumed a wedge-like shape, and unsupported would be in imminent danger of toppling over. If this had happened, it would have meant certain destruction to the adjacent portion of the pueblo and doubtless considerable loss of life. It is most interesting, therefore, to see how the "ancient engineers" met this emergency.

What they did was to support the block with a series of heavy timber props, which they further reinforced by an extensive terraced masonry pier. Precisely how much labor was expended on the undertaking is uncertain, because only excavation can reveal how much of a cavity was eroded in the front base of the block and likewise how deep the supporting masonry may extend into the alluvium of the cañon floor. Superficial indications are that they built a foundation pier of solid masonry more than 12 feet high and from 18 to 26 feet or more broad, along the whole extent of the 150-foot block. At this 12-foot level they left a terrace, or, in other words, drew in the width of the pier to a line lying just outside the plane of the upper front face of the cliff block. The face of this secondary pier slopes gently toward the block, and at a height of 14 feet doubtless met the front and top of the overhang, i.e., the cleavage plane before mentioned, which marks the upper limit of erosion in the block. Embodied in this upper masonry pier are the nearly upright timber supports above referred to. The half dozen props still visible are placed from 6 to 15 feet apart and are logs of spruce or pine 10 to 12 inches in diameter. Neither the masonry nor the props reaches the shoulder of the cliff block at present, and there is even some doubt that the upper part of the masonry in question ever was a solid mass, filling out the cavities in the cliff block; possibly it was a wall with a number of rooms behind it.

Whatever the case, there is no evidence that the great cliff block has settled subsequent to the construction of the pier, for had it so much as begun to lean on the wooden props the weight would undoubtedly have split them. Nevertheless, though the threatening danger may not really have been imminent during the lifetime of Pueblo Bonito, it seems probable that the sensible procedure of the great builders of the Chaco will save the cliff block indefinitely, simply by preventing further erosion at its base.